How the West Grew Rich

HOW THE WEST GREW RICH

The Economic Transformation
of the Industrial World

Nathan Rosenberg

&

L. E. Birdzell, Jr.

Basic Books, Inc., Publishers   *New York*

Library of Congress Cataloging in Publication Data

Rosenberg, Nathan, 1927–
  How the West grew rich.

  Includes index.
    1. Europe—Economic conditions.   2. United States—
Economic conditions.   3. Capitalism—History.
4. Economic history.   I. Birdzell, L. E. (Luther Earle)
II. Title.
HC240.R67   1985   330.9172′2   85–47551
ISBN   0–465–03108–0   (cloth)
ISBN   0–465–03109–9   (paper)

Contents

Preface

It is by now relatively easy to write a history of the development of capitalist institutions, because everyone knows what those institutions are: free markets, private property, money, deposit banking, insurance, bills of exchange, freedom to organize economic enterprises, and so on. It is more difficult to write a history of the development of the wealth of Western economies, because there is little agreement on how it happened. Perhaps we need to take a hint from the experience of biologists, who, in the last century-and-a-half, have learned that evolutionary processes in nature can generate systems, ranging from protein molecules to the ecology of a swamp, whose subtle and even devious complexities overtax human powers of understanding. There is an analogous absence of overall human design, as well as an analogous presence of accident, experiment, and survival standards, in the evolution of the West's system for generating economic growth. In any case, the West's achievement of wealth is historically unique, and the least the biological analogy can do is to warn us against the expectation that the explanation lies ready at hand.

Before we turn to the history of Western economic growth and the search for its causes, we want to raise some preliminary points. The first is the part played by noneconomic factors in the West's escape from poverty, including the part played by nineteenth-century governments. The second is the importance of organization to economic activity and a caution against the assumption that hierarchies are the only way to organize. The third is the propriety of applying the term *capitalism*, or any other term with the ideological connotations of a word form ending in *-ism*, to describe the experimental, often pragmatic, economic approach employed in the modern West. This approach has often led to policies and practices quite different from the textbook view of capitalism.

Noneconomic Sources and Consequences of Economic Growth

It is appropriate, in an essay on economic history, to acknowledge that the economic development of the West from poverty to wealth had formidable noneconomic consequences and sources. Certainly the demographic effect—a rise in population resulting jointly from an increase in the number of human beings and an extension of the average life-span of individuals—was the most important consequence of Western wealth, as measured by the value the West has come to place on human life. Another important consequence was the urbanization of Western society—the change from the predominantly rural society of the Middle Ages to the almost wholly urban society of the modern West. In a world where people do not live by bread alone, so drastic a reconstruction could not have been accomplished had not the noneconomic sectors of society accommodated themselves remarkably well to radical change.

It is also appropriate to recognize the part played by the political institutions of Western Europe in its rise to wealth. A prominent and crucial feature of nineteenth-century and early-twentieth-century Western economies was the existence of a manufacturing and trading sphere largely autonomous from political or religious action or restriction, at least as compared to restrictions of, say, the 1300s. Yet the practice of laissez faire was only occasionally characteristic of Western economies. On the contrary, both nineteenth-century and earlier Western governments were very active in trying to facilitate manufacturing and trade. Governments supplied courts of law to enforce trading agreements and to protect credit by making loans collectible; they vigorously defined and protected property rights, which are essential to investment and trade; they supplied legal modes of organization responsive to the needs of enterprises; they subsidized railways, canals, and turnpikes; rightly or wrongly, they protected domestic enterprise with tariffs and quotas against competition from foreign imports; and they supplied a currency that, in many countries, provided a stable measure of value. Some of the government contributions, such as free compulsory education and transport systems, were monumental. Government assistance to ocean transport—for example, mainte-nance of aids to navigation, docks, breakwaters, dredging, safety inspection, life-saving stations, training seamen, marine hospitals—is of interest because it has gone on for centuries without disturbing anyone's principles. Government grants of monopolies to encourage the formation of new industries are even older; and the grant of patents for new inventions, specifically authorized in the United States constitution, was common practice by the end of the eighteenth century.

In a more general sense, though relations between the political and economic spheres were marked by a high degree of autonomy of the economic sphere, they included a range of other elements. The monopoly of the social uses of violence, which is the most fundamental characteristic of the political sphere, implied the creation of a system of courts of law for the nonviolent settlement of disputes in the economic sphere; it implied also the definition and protection of property rights, including limitations on political expropriation and taxation. The provision of a money medium of exchange for trade was an ancient political prerogative, always exercised in the West. The notion that economic growth is a form of change reminds us that change is never limited to the economic sphere of life; it extends also to the social and political.

But while it was de rigueur for the political authorities to facilitate manufacturing and trade during the main period of Western growth, in the nineteenth century it was comparatively out of fashion to regulate trade, tax it appreciably, control prices or wages, or seek to iron out the spectacular differences in individual incomes. The working assumption was that industry and commerce served the general welfare, so that it was the business of government to support and encourage them.

The emphasis on the freedom of the economic sphere from political influence is appropriate to an essay in economic history, but it tells only half the story. The relative freedom of the political sphere from responsi-bility for the economic sphere enabled political leaders to concentrate on other aspects of government, leading to political advances in the nineteenth and early twentieth centuries that were as historically unprecedented as were the economic advances. The nation-states were consolidated; the electoral franchise was extended; republican and democratic governments superseded absolute monarchies; lawyers focused on judicial reform, to good effect in many places; penal systems were overhauled; free public schools were introduced; international relations were so improved that general wars in Europe were avoided from 1815 to 1914; life and property became more secure as voluntary obedience to law became more general and the suppression of crime more effective. These advances were accomplished with the help of taxes that seem, in retrospect, unbelievably low. Efficient government was of value for its own sake, and it unquestionably contributed to the security of life and to advances in material welfare.

Organization

Most political discourse has dealt with problems of economic organization as questions of which activities should be organized and which should be left unorganized, as matters of individual choice. This approach assumes that the only form of organization is the directive type used in military, political, and some religious bodies, and built around hierarchical relations of leaders and subordinates. Economics uses a different concept of organization, broad enough to embrace practically all economic activity and posing questions of how, rather than whether, any specified activity should be organized. A preliminary explanation of the difference may be helpful to those who find it strange to think of organization except in terms of hierarchy.

In economics, it has become orthodox to hold that all economic activity is organized. Thus people who buy and sell in markets are collectively choosing goals, dividing the work of attaining them among large numbers of people and rewarding those who help. Even an apparently simple economic task like supplying eggs to the consumer's breakfast table involves a network of thousands of individuals scattered through many countries, not linked by any common hierarchy, yet each regularly performing a small role in close synchronism with the others. The task could not be performed as reliably as it is in capitalist economies were not markets a powerful organizing force, capable of inducing large numbers of people to form shared goals, dividing the work of achieving the goals among many specialists, and supplying the rewards and incentives needed to get the work done.

There are two aspects to the choice between market and hierarchy as modes of organization. As to the firm, which is ordinarily taken as the basic unit of economic organization, we find some organized hierarchically, others not. The second aspect of choice involves the economy as a whole: above the level of the firm, economies may be organized by market relations or by hierarchical relations, exclusively or in combination. Since firms come in many sizes and forms, the number of possibilities of different combinations of hierarchical and market modes is virtually unlimited.

Preface

Those who stress the effectiveness of economic organization by markets are not saying merely that less organization is sometimes better than more. What they assert is that, under some circumstances, cooperation among numerous people organized by market relations will be more efficient than cooperation organized by command, as measured by the conformity of output to the desires of the participants and the magnitude of output achieved from economic resources employed in its production. Also, a reason commonly advanced for the superiority of market organization is that its rewards and penalties are both greater and more certain than the rewards and penalties administered in hierarchies, so that those organized by markets feel greater pressure to do their best. The difference between hierarchical and market organization is thus not a question of more or less organization, for by some tests the market mode is the more efficient and intensive form of organization.

Hierarchical and market forms of organization are not the only ways of inducing people to cooperate in the pursuit of shared goals. The manorial system was a third mode of economic organization. It was used to organize the economic aspects of rural life around the political and military realms of the feudal system. Like Western economies of today, it had both hierarchical and nonhierarchical elements. In chapter 8, when we turn from the economic sphere of social life to the sphere of science, we find an efficient and enormously productive mode of organization in which scientists relate to one another in ways that cannot be described in terms of either hierarchies or markets.

If human societies were composed of Robinson Crusoes, each individual isolated from the rest and producing solely for his or her own needs, it is safe to say that the economic outputs would be only a tiny fraction of these societies' actual magnitude. Since almost all output thus depends on cooperation, differences in the way cooperation is achieved in different societies are one of the more promising sources of explanations for differences in economic output and growth. In order to investigate the differences, we need first to understand that organization is not all of one kind—hence these preliminary comments.

Are Western Economic Systems Capitalist?

The view that a primary characteristic of Western economies has been openness to technological and organizational experiment and diversity of organizational form poses the question of what to call such economies.

Twentieth-century practice has been to refer to the economic systems of the Western countries as capitalism. This term has the sanction of usage. But the dominant fact about the economic institutions that emerged in Europe with the decline of feudalism is their wholly pragmatic character and their lack of ideological commitment to any economic principle other than economic effectiveness and survivability. The system that generated Western economic growth evolved before it was recognized as a system or advocated as an ideology. There was plenty of ideological commitment to relevant economic ideas and institutions—private property, freedom from arbitrary confiscation or taxation, and the like—but the ideology was not based on the role these institutions served in any recognized system of economic life. It was 1776 before Adam Smith first produced the systematic rationale that furnished the basis of a laissez-faire ideology, and by then the basic Western economic institutions were in place and economic growth was well under way. Indeed, if the West can be credited with an economic ideology during the first century or two of its economic growth, that ideology would be mercantilism, which Smith passionately and eloquently controverted. Neither the *Communist Manifesto* nor *Capital* (volume 1) employed the term *capitalism*, though Marx did use it in 1877 in correspondence. The *Oxford English Dictionary* lists its first use, apparently in the sense of the condition of possessing capital, by Thackeray in 1854; its first use in the sense of an economic system was in *Better Times*, a book by Douai in 1884. Marx's followers developed the use of *capitalism* in late-nineteenth-century Marxist literature as a term of opprobrium for the economic system they wished to overthrow. As conceived by its inventors, the concept was not designed for rational defense; nevertheless, defenders of Western economies found that the convenience of the word outweighed the rhetorical principle that one should never adopt one's opponents' terms.

The term *mixed economy* would be more apt, for Western economies have always been mixed. But in current usage *mixed economy* assumes that an age of purer capitalism occurred earlier. So, albeit reluctantly, we shall follow the tradition and use the term *capitalism* as others have used it: not as defining an ideology properly termed an *-ism*, but as a convenient term for any of the changing sets of economic institutions that arose in Western European countries during the West's centuries of economic growth.

Acknowledgments

We are deeply indebted to Stanley Engerman, who read the complete manuscript, for his many helpful comments and suggestions. It is a pleasure also to acknowledge the great help we received from the comments, criticisms, and suggestions of Thomas Moore and Robert Hessen on earlier drafts of the manuscript. Needless to say, they have no responsibility for the instances in which we persisted in error. We are indebted also to Jeffery Oxley, whose researches aided almost every aspect of the work.

How the West Grew Rich

1 / Introduction

Poverty as a Norm

If we take the long view of human history and judge the economic lives of our ancestors by modern standards, it is a story of almost unrelieved wretchedness. The typical human society has given only a small number of people a humane existence, while the great majority have lived in abysmal squalor. We are led to forget the dominating misery of other times in part by the grace of literature, poetry, romance, and legend, which celebrate those who lived well and forget those who lived in the silence of poverty. The eras of misery have been mythologized and may even be remembered as golden ages of pastoral simplicity. They were not.

Only during the last two hundred years has there come to Western Europe, the United States, Canada, Australia, Japan, and a few other places one of history's infrequent periods when progress and prosperity have touched the lives of somewhat more than the upper tenth of the population. For brevity, albeit at the sacrifice of geographical accuracy, we will call these places, collectively, the West. In England, the United States, and parts of Western Europe, it became evident early in the nineteenth century (and later in other countries of the West) that an unusually high proportion of people were becoming better fed, healthier, and more secure than in the ancient Middle Eastern, Indian, Chinese, Greek, Roman, and Islamic civilizations—that is, than at any other time in human history.

The move from poverty to wealth is, in a social sense, an advance in material well-being. It is not adequately captured in statistics of gross national product, national income, or real wages. Death has always been the ultimate threat, and the move from poverty to wealth is first of all a move away from death. Its first indicators are statistics on life expectancy, death rates, and infant mortality. Famine and hunger are next on the list; again, the move from poverty to wealth is a move from famine and hunger, as indicated statistically by a declining incidence of malnutrition and its related diseases. Plague is the next of the ancient afflictions, and it may be taken as symbolic of all fatal or disabling diseases; the move away from them is another move from poverty to wealth. Poverty tends to be associated with illiteracy, superstition, ignorance, and life lived within an extremely narrow setting. The move from poverty to wealth is a move toward literacy, education, and variety of experience. A life of poverty is a life in which survival is the first and almost the only order of business, in which housing is so crowded as to make privacy unknown, and in which choices are narrowly restricted. The move to wealth is a move toward greater possibilities of privacy and individual choice.

There are several reasons why simple statistics cannot capture the transition from poverty to wealth. To apply generally to the myriad products and services produced in even a simple economy, statistics have to be stated in units of money. Money is the common measure of economic quantities, no matter what the differences in the products or services being measured may be. Hence statistics would be the same if economic growth consisted in producing more and more of the same goods and services as they would if economic growth consisted—as it does—of changing the whole life-style of a society and drastically altering the goods and services it produces and consumes.

Even at the beginning of economic expansion, there are changes in what people consume, in the work they perform, and in their overall manner of living. In the West, the initial changes were pathetically small— the addition of a few vegetables and a little meat to the average diet and the shift from wooden shoes to leather—and overall numbers could give a fair idea of what was happening. But as Western expansion continued, the lives of human beings were completely changed. Early years spent at work became early years spent at school; a life of work on the manor or farm became a life of work in an urban trade, a factory, or a profession. Home changed from a rural hut to a row house or apartment in a town. No general statistics can depict the effect of the shift from a rural to an urban economy, or the revolution in living patterns resulting from the introduction of railroads in the nineteenth century and automobiles in the twentieth. It may be true of individuals that the rich differ from the poor only in having more money, but in the case of societies, the rare examples we have of rich societies differ from the poor not simply in having a higher per-capita gross national product, but in creating an entirely different life for their members.

A more extreme statistical problem arises from the fact that household work was never transformed into dollars except as it resulted in a product sold (like farm products). So, as women moved from household work to paid employment, twentieth-century statistics counted their gross pay as a rise in gross national product (GNP), even though some may argue that it may be a retrogression in quality of life. There is yet another difficulty with overall statistics: some economic goods and services are converted into dollars at prices set in market transactions, but others are converted into dollars as a consequence of taxation or regulation. There is no reason to expect the two conversions to produce equivalent measures of what the two types of transactions contribute to material welfare.

It is still worth considering, at least in passing, the relative magnitude of the contributions of growth and inheritance to Western economies. In a December of a typical year, perhaps 95 percent of the output of a typical Western economy will be attributable to the portion of the economy that was in place and functioning at the beginning of the year and 5 percent or less will be attributable to the year's growth. But in the longer range, the relative importance of the current economy and the growth economy are nearly reversed. In the United States, after adjusting for price changes, more than 85 percent of the per-capita output in 1985 represented growth since 1885.

These numbers are, of course, imperfect indicators of the changes in the material welfare of the country's citizens. But the 1985 life-style is clearly preferable, and, except perhaps for the very rich, the qualitative gain is as impressive as the numerical indicators would suggest.

It is, of course, possible for a society to move from poverty to wealth without producing a people serenely satisfied with itself; in fact, it may be doubted that self-satisfied people could move from poverty to wealth in the first place. It is even possible that the psychological restlessness of a people in good physical health will, as a rule, be more intractable than that of a people numbed by hunger. But even though a nation that achieves wealth must expect to support a busy mental-health industry and put up with the social dissonance which goes with an extension of individual choice, there continues to be widespread interest in how such a move is accomplished. It is, after all, in the nature of social change to supply societies with a new set of problems in exchange for an old set, and people are hardly to be blamed for preferring the problems of wealth to those of poverty.

The story of the move from poverty to wealth offers enough mysteries, surprises, exposés, triumphs, and tragedies to make it worth the retelling for its own sake. Moreover, a better understanding of how economic

5

growth came about in the West should be helpful to those Westerners who are concerned with public policy, the comparative significance of the West's many economic institutions, the future of the Western economies themselves, and most of all to those who feel some responsibility for passing along to the next generation an opportunity to better their own conditions at least as much as has the current generation.

Gradualness of the Growth of Western Wealth

As we turn to the problem of explaining Western economic growth, we must begin with its most puzzling aspect: its gradualism.

The advanced Western countries completed their escape from poverty to relative wealth during the nineteenth and twentieth centuries. There was no sudden change in their economic output, but only a continuation of year-to-year growth at a rate that somewhat exceeded the rate of growth of population—a growth of the same kind that had begun earlier in England and Holland. Even Japan, whose success in assimilating Western industry after 1868 has become legendary, attained that success in small annual increments. In all these countries, both population and per-capita output have multiplied, but over a long period.

Over a year, or even over a decade, the economic gains, after allowing for the rise in population, were so little noticeable that it was widely believed that the gains were experienced only by the rich, and not by the poor. Only as the West's compounded growth continued through the twentieth century did its breadth become clear. It became obvious that Western working classes were increasingly well off and that the Western middle classes were prospering and growing as a proportion of the whole population. Not that poverty disappeared. The West's achievement was not the abolition of poverty but the reduction of its incidence from 90 percent of the population to 30 percent, 20 percent, or less, depending on the country and one's definition of poverty—a concept that seems to keep growing in content with economic growth itself. The continued expansion of Western economies through the twentieth century created an enormous gap between their wealth and the poverty from which they had escaped, but in which most of the world's people still live.

It is possible to identify many monumental innovations—technological, economic, and political—that contributed to this growth. But the statistical record of gradualism is conclusive despite the monuments. Gradualness is due partly to the fact that even when great innovations were notably clustered together in place and time, as in the Industrial Revolution, they directly affected only part of the economy and took decades to work out their effects. It is due also to the fact that a multitude of small additions to knowledge had a cumulative effect on economic growth, and the law of large numbers tended to spread this cumulative effect more or less evenly in time. There was never a day, nor even a generation, when a television anchor or a newspaper editor, however astute, could have led off with news of an economic or technological development which "rescued the West from poverty." There were many economic and technological developments that turned out to be important, but none was memorialized by an immediate and conspicuous increase in the rate of growth that could set it off from the short-term peaks and valleys attributable to wars, crop failures, financial follies, and the business cycle.

The explanation of gradual growth, so long continued, has to reside in an institutional mechanism, built deep into the structure of Western economies and continuously seeking out and adopting growth-inducing changes. *Deep* is the key word, for the mechanism is so far buried that it has seemed impossible to many observers that the future could hold anything but stagnation or decline after so long an expansion of production and growth in numbers of people. The rate of growth of output in the last century or so is commonly stated at around 3 percent a year, and in most branches of human experience, this kind of geometric progression, in which each term is 1.03 times the preceding term, tends to run into insurmountable barriers and taper off in considerably fewer than two hundred successive terms. As early as the end of the eighteenth century, Thomas Robert Malthus argued that an exponential growth in population would very quickly meet an insurmountable barrier in the form of limited supplies of food.[1] A century later, the population of Malthus's native Britain had quadrupled, and it was living at a much higher standard than in his day. If Malthus, writing almost two centuries ago, could not foresee continued growth in the branch of the economy which supplies food, it is easy to see why contemporary neo-Malthusian movements, based on the substitution of other resources for food in the Malthusian argument, should find it impossible to conceive that Western growth can continue for much longer.

Again, after World War I, Oswald Spengler made his widely read prediction of *The Decline of the West*.[2] No reasonable prophet, writing in Spengler's day, could have foreseen that in the next half-century the population of the United States would nearly double and gross national product (GNP) per capita (in constant dollars) would increase more than two-and-a-half times. It is not just that Spengler mistimed his forecast of an inevitable exhaustion of a geometric progression. The more serious point is that Spengler, a thinker of talent and insight, both misconceived and underestimated the forces behind Western progress and just as clearly misconceived and overestimated the forces corrupting and eroding it. He was far from alone.

We will find that the West has created a powerful system for economic growth, of a sort which could keep generating growth and even substantive advances in material welfare for decades after the spirit had burned out of it. The very inertia of such systems makes them deceptive. The people who work within them and who make them work may continue doing what they have always done long after all the incentives for creative work have vanished, leaving the system driven only by habit and the lack of anything better for its people to do. Such a system could run down so slowly, in response to causes separated by so many years from their effect, that by the time its degeneration became apparent, it might be irreversible. Indeed, social systems can continue to expand long after the events that made their collapse inevitable. The stock lesson from history is still supplied by the political empire of Rome rather than by the economic empire of the West: it continued to expand for more than a century after events which all but guaranteed its eventual disintegration.

It is important to keep this long and uncertain time gap between cause and effect in mind when we attempt to evaluate possible explanations of Western growth. Many Western institutions that might help explain the dynamics of Western economies have been substantially changed by the political and social currents of the latter part of the twentieth century. Despite the changes, Western economic growth has continued, and it is even arguable that there has been no long-term deterioration in the rate of growth. This is ground for caution in relying on these changed institutions as explanations of Western growth, but it is not a sufficient reason for ruling them out altogether. The effects of comparatively recent institutional changes may not yet be obvious, or growth might have occurred at a higher rate without the changes. Unhappily for certainty in economic history, there are no conclusive experiments to guide inquiry through the puzzles created by multiple causation, the capacity of human beings and their institutions to adapt to change in ways that obscure its effects, the possibility—even likelihood—that Western growth had different causes at different periods, and the propensity of effects to surface decades after their causes have been forgotten.

Some Previous Explanations

The causes of the West's rise from poverty to wealth have been extensively explored for a century-and-a-half. The more widely credited explanations are worth a brief preliminary review, both of their truths and their weaknesses.

1. Science and Invention

The most popular explanations of Western prosperity are focused on science and invention. But why, if science and invention are a sufficient cause of national wealth, were not China and the Islamic nations, which were the leaders in science and invention when the West turned from feudalism and entered into the modern era, the countries that escaped from poverty to riches? Another difficulty with these explanations is that science and invention are forms of knowledge which, one would think, are easily transferable from one society to another by lectures and the printed page. But the difficulty of transferring the keys to economic growth from the West to the Third World has proved far greater than the difficulty of teaching science. We are far from denying that technology was important, but it is evidently not the sole explanation of Western growth.

2. Natural Resources

Another common explanation of the wealth of nations is that it is a consequence of their natural resources or of their access to natural resources on favorable terms. Karl Marx, for example, attributed some of the new wealth of the West to its imperialist conquests and its commercial acquisitions of raw materials from overseas, beginning in the sixteenth century. The late nineteenth-century imperialists of England, France, Germany, Italy, Belgium, and Holland similarly argued the importance of owning natural resources. And much of the writing on the limits of growth in our own day combines a more sophisticated concept of natural resources with a belief in a simple link between ownership of natural resources and economic growth.

But the prosperity of the Low Countries and Switzerland has long plagued these explanations. More recently, the phenomenal growth and prosperity of Japan have hopelessly undermined them. After World War II, other Western countries with limited natural resources, and now without colonies, have persisted in growing richer while some Third World countries with extensive natural resources have lingered in poverty. In short, natural resource explanations do not fit the facts.

Finally, explanations based on natural resources are subject to the difficulty that a society's economic resources are not its natural resources as such, but a relation, internal to the society, between its natural resources and its organizational and technological skills in extracting or otherwise acquiring and utilizing those natural resources for advancing its people's material welfare. Resources that contribute to economic wealth are not simply material; they are a subtle combination of materials present in nature with the human knowledge and social organization required to use those materials (and, by extension, the efforts of human beings) to satisfy human needs. To the American Plains Indian, for example, the oil, coal, iron ore, forests, and farmlands of North America were not economic resources, but the buffalo herds were resources of the utmost importance. The West's *economic* resources *are* its wealth; the problem is how the West generated the organizational and technological skills required to produce and exploit that wealth.

3. Psychological Explanations

Marx also, and more emphatically, attributed Western economic growth to the driving force of a competitive economy that pressed capitalists to a frenzied pursuit of ever larger sales and ever larger profits, creating what was, even in his day, a formidable "capitalist engine." He regarded Western technology not as a separate source of growth, but as derived from this driven pursuit of personal riches. But to Marx, the behavior of capitalists was not so much an independent psychological phenomenon as it was a response to the peculiar pressures of capitalist institutions. Capitalist economic growth was not for Marx merely a concession that he was prepared to make for purposes of argument, but a central point of his theory of inevitable revolution. To him, capitalist growth in economic output, by creating the possibility of a better life for workers, made it inevitable that workers would take advantage of the possibility by revolutionary seizure of the means of production. If the theory seems implausible today, it is because seizure of the means of production has not proved to be a necessary precondition to widespread worker participation in the benefits of economic growth. The essential point for Marx was his belief that capitalism was incapable of translating its great growth potential into higher standards of material well-being for the workers.

Economic growth is unlikely to occur unless the economy is so organized that those who can bring about growth have incentives for doing so, and Marx was no doubt right in stressing the importance of the profit-and-loss incentives supplied by contemporary capitalism. But a century after his death, when we can observe the Third World's efforts to achieve growth, it has become evident that more than incentives are needed. Incentives cannot enable a community to do what it does not know how to do. Knowledge, and an institutional structure which gives knowledge room to grow and incentives room to operate, are at least as important.

The great difficulty of identifying the sources of Western economic growth has led to some psychological explanations which are little short of desperate. One that has gained fairly wide acceptance is that the decline of feudalism was somehow linked to a psychological mutation, creating market institutions out of some new capitalist spirit or out of the intensification of acquisitive impulses above and beyond those that existed in China, India, or Islam. This has been argued by Werner Sombart and others.[3] But it is not so much the urge to advance one's own interests which has varied conspicuously through human experience, as the possibilities of gratification and the way these possibilities have been pursued. Max Weber questioned the central importance of what he called "the economic impulse":

> The notion that our rationalistic and capitalistic age is characterized by a stronger economic interest than other periods is childish; the moving spirits of modern capitalism are not possessed of a stronger economic impulse than, for example, an oriental trader. The unchaining of the economic interest merely as such has produced only irrational results; such men as Cortez and Pizarro, who were perhaps its strongest embodiment, were far from having an idea of a rationalistic economic life. If the economic impulse in itself is universal, it is an interesting question as to the relations under which it becomes rationalized and rationally tempered in such fashion as to produce rational institutions of the character of capitalistic enterpise.[4]

4. Luck

We will find that the history of Western economies includes at least three, and perhaps four, groups of events that might fairly be called revolutions. Beginning in the fifteenth century, there was an expansion of trade and commerce that can be viewed as a mercantile revolution. Three centuries later, in the eighteenth century, there occurred the Industrial Revolution. At the end of the nineteenth century and the beginning of the twentieth, the introduction of electric power and the internal combustion engine amounted to a second industrial revolution. In our own day, developments in electronic storage and switching networks, embodied in communications systems and computers, seem likely to lead to an information revolution, if they have not already done so.

One could explain the West's rise to wealth as the consequence of the extraordinary luck of having experienced these four beneficent revolutions in five centuries, just as one might explain the collapse of the antecedent feudal society by the bad luck of having experienced too many plagues, wars, and famines in the fourteenth century. But when lightning has struck four times in one place, it seems appropriate to inquire what it is about the topography of the place that attracts it so persistently.

In another sense, luck is the true explanation, for the origins of Western economic institutions cannot be traced to the wisdom of any identifiable human beings. They are a product of history, unintended consequences of action taken for entirely different reasons. They were well advanced by the time Adam Smith began the modern work of understanding their structure. To this day, that work is nowhere near completion. What produced the wealth of the West was luck in the sense that the results of biological evolution are luck, but still those processes, their results, and their interrelations are abundantly worthy of study.

5. Misconduct

A different group of explanations of Western wealth has been widely advanced in political discourse. Western wealth has been attributed to various forms of misconduct, some of it highly reprehensible by modern standards, if not by the standards prevailing at the time of its occurrence. The forms of misconduct most commonly charged to Western economies are increased inequalities of income and wealth, exploitation of workers, colonialism and imperialism, and slavery. As devices for encouraging charitable giving, national and international, supporting social legislation, and for checking Western hubris, these explanations have been very useful. There is less to be said for their adequacy as explanations of Western economic growth.

6. Inequalities of Income and Wealth

Of the explanations of Western wealth which center on misconduct, the most fundamental maintains that inequalities of income and wealth are unjust, but necessary to Western economic systems. Some critics of inequality contend that income and wealth are social products which a society ought to divide equally among its members, so that the inequalities resulting from the operation of capitalist markets are ipso facto unjust. Others allow inequalities to be justified by differences in the economic or social contribution of different individuals or families, but hold that the actual inequalities prevailing in Western countries are not so justified. Either way, it is safe to say that inequalities are not a sufficient explanation of economic growth. Income and wealth inequalities have occurred in earlier Western societies and in a great many non-Western societies without setting off advances in economic welfare comparable to those experienced by the West in the last five centuries. Indeed, many Third World countries today have far greater inequalities than the United States.

Although it is clear that inequality of income and wealth is not a sufficient condition for economic growth, there is some reason to think that it may be a necessary condition. The reason is simple. Wealth may be a social product which originates in a social inheritance, but individuals and nations make very uneven marginal contributions to its production, over and above the original social inheritance. It is those marginal contributions which can be stimulated or repressed by rewards or penalties. A society which wishes to use rewards and penalties to encourage the production of wealth must somehow treat those individuals who make marginal contributions more favorably than it treats those who contribute only their share of the social inheritance. The only reason for stopping short of the conclusion that the resulting inequalities, in some uncertain degree, are an absolutely necessary condition of economic growth is the possibility that there may be ways of inducing people to engage in wealth-producing activity without such large rewards and penalties. To date, the possibility is conjectural, for no advanced society has managed without rewards and penalties, though many have stressed penalties more and rewards less than the West.

Whether inequalities arising from the operation of capitalist markets are unjust, and, if so, to what extent they can be remedied without creating further injustices, are questions with many ramifications, some highly controversial. The difficulties are due only in part to the inherent complexities traceable to the fact that extremely high income and wealth, like extreme poverty, have numerous causes, and their suppression would require a variety of political measures, some less acceptable than others.

A more objective difficulty is that the occupations essential to the orderly functioning of a modern society require widely different talents and skills and vary greatly in working conditions, social and cultural status, risk of unemployment and other forms of loss, and the sense of doing something interesting, valuable, or uplifting. Capitalist markets use variations in money income to match the number of people attracted to each occupation (the labor supply) to the number of jobs available in that occupation (the labor demand). A wage rate that matches supply and demand does not tell anyone what he or she is worth, but only how much can be earned by entering a given job or occupation. It supplies one datum relevant to the individual's choice to enter or leave. In the absence of variation in wage rates, it would be necessary to use some form of compulsory labor to avoid an oversupply of workers in the more attractive occupations and a shortage in the less attractive. Inequalities are thus a socially workable alternative to a system of compulsory labor.

Despite their limitations, capitalist markets developed historically as an advance on medieval markets where prices were set with a view to doing justice, at least as justice was perceived by those who set the prices. The substitution of a system of pricing to match supply and demand for the systematic injustices of legally fixed prices may or may not have made for a more just society, but it certainly made for a freer and wealthier society. The new markets were more efficient economically, and their growth was intertwined with the expansion of trade and output. They exemplified a recurring ethical dilemma in conflicts between justice and economic efficiency, for though they priced for economic efficiency without attempting to assess the relative worth of human beings, their economic efficiency contributed markedly to the reduction of poverty, the most pervasive injustice of all.

7. Exploitation

In its dictionary use, *exploitation* is part of all economic activity, if only in the sense of exploiting the actor's economic capabilities. In Marxist terms, the word is used invidiously, to describe the process by which the capitalist class is said to appropriate part of the product of labor, its "surplus value," particularly in industrial modes of production. The question is whether exploitation, even in this special sense, adequately explains Western growth. Its explanatory power seems limited to the growth of Western capital and capitalists' income. It is not helpful in explaining the growth of labor's income, which comprises most of the growth in question.

Even as to capital, exploitation explains accumulation better than it explains the opening up of opportunities for capital investment. Economic growth requires both capital and opportunities to use it profitably, and after the experience of the 1930s, few Western economists believe that the opportunities follow automatically from capital accumulation. Marx argued that capital accumulations supplied capitalists with an incentive to form new industries and develop overseas markets in order to employ the accumulated capital, but the existence of an incentive does not guarantee accomplishment. More recent appreciation of the importance of technological and social change and the expansion of trade in the creation of investment opportunities suggests that causation may have run in the other direction—that is, that the existence of investment opportunities may have been the incentive for the accumulation of capital. This was especially so in the first stages of the Industrial Revolution, when the builders of the early factories responded to perceived needs for improvements in textile production, with no indication that a desire to utilize whatever surplus capital accumulations may have existed in prefactory England played a part in their efforts. If capital accumulation had been their purpose, the early factories would have been failures, for they required relatively small amounts of capital by comparison to the agriculture, shipping, or mercantile trade of their times.

A type of investment opportunity particularly relevant to exploitation consists in the opportunity to establish a factory where labor can be hired at lower costs than those prevailing among existing competitors. Opportunities of this type have been important in the economic development of Third World countries, but there are many older examples. Employment of factory workers at wages below those of guild artisans was a basic source of complaint in the England of the Industrial Revolution, and wages below those of New England were an important cause of the development of the textile and shoe industries in the American South. Marx would presumably have regarded these opportunities as exploitive, and workers who were being paid the former prevailing wages tended to agree. On the other hand, to countries or regions whose principal economic resource is an abundance of unemployed labor, employment of that labor on the best terms available is likely to seem not only a reasonable path of economic development, but morally imperative.

Whether driving down wages is a systemic or a merely opportunistic characteristic of capitalism is another question. Low wages encourage labor-intensive, rather than capital-intensive, methods of production and so tend to lessen the need for capital accumulation. For this reason, the corporation which replaces an old plant in Chicago with a new one in Korea may actually reduce its need for capital. In practice, however, the main thrust of capitalist development has been toward capital-intensive production. Had low wages been inherent in capitalist systems, one might have expected capitalists to stay with labor-intensive production and apply the money so saved to personal or other uses. Moreover, an international perspective is essential here. Opening a new plant in Korea will tend to *raise* wages in Korea.

As it is, real wage rates in the West have been rising for more than a century. Exploitation can hardly explain that rise. One might even observe that a long-continued rise in wages can make the question of exploitation irrelevant, for not even Marx contended that the expansion of output (which made the rise possible) was solely attributable to the proletariat.

8. Colonialism and Imperialism

Several explanations turn on the relations between Western countries and other, economically less developed, countries. Marxists describe these relations as imperialism, though the meaning of the term is clouded by differences in its treatment by Marx, Lenin, post-World War II theoreticians, and upward of a hundred years of variation in the economic history and development of both capitalist and precapitalist countries. There is considerable disagreement as to whether capitalism is a progressive force for development in precapitalist societies or an obstacle to it.

Colonialism is a slightly more neutral term for the relations between capitalist and precapitalist countries. In the sense of permanent colonization by residents of a mother country, colonialism is a very ancient practice, more often benign in its effects than colonialism in the later sense of imposing foreign rule on a large native population, after the manner of the British in India or the gradual extension of the Great Russians' domination over their many subject peoples. A mix of the two, in which colonists from a mother country become a significant minority, dominating a culturally different majority descended from earlier inhabitants and not readily admitted to the colonists' economy, is politically explosive, generating the violent modern histories of Algeria, Kenya, and Rhodesia and the contemporary political passions in South Africa. One might even add Ireland to the list.

Westerners began to colonize the American continents, in the first sense of colonialism, in the sixteenth century. Colonization was not entirely a matter of occupying nearly empty real estate, for the casualties included the highly developed Aztec and Inca cultures of Mexico and Peru. In the second sense of colonialism, the West asserted political hegemony over many densely populated and politically organized regions of India, Africa, Southeast Asia, and the East Indies—a process so far advanced by the closing decades of the nineteenth century that the newly formed German Empire complained of the lack of remaining opportunities for colonial enterprise.

If only because colonialism has become synonymous with infamy, it is worth recalling that from the Greek colonization of the Mediterranean to the colonial ventures of the West, some colonies were immensely successful from the viewpoints of both the colony and of its country of origin. Colonialism planted the seeds for the early development of today's North and South American economies—an awesome accomplishment. But the Spanish, Portuguese, English, French, and Dutch colonial experiences and their consequences were various, even in the Americas. Spain and Portugal became major colonial powers without ever becoming advanced capitalist economies, either at home or in their colonies. Their most valuable colonies were in Latin America, and the home countries lost these to independence movements while they themselves were in a precapitalist stage of development.

By far the most striking accomplishment of British colonialism was that it seeded several advanced Western economies, to the substantial benefit of the colonies: the United States, Canada, Australia, New Zealand, Hong Kong, and Singapore. These colonies' economic accomplishments also benefited Britain, for controlled and exploitive trade with an economically backward colony is much less beneficial to an advanced country than its trade with other advanced countries. France built and lost a large colonial empire, remembered for the violent collapse of its Indo-Chinese rule and the almost equally violent end of its rule over what was probably its most economically successful colony, Algeria. In retrospect, there is little reason to think that its colonial ventures contributed positively to France's economic growth.

Sometimes, the claim that Western economic advances arose from imperialism is based on the fact that colonies provided part of the market for the goods produced in the more advanced countries. This line of thought cannot be pressed much beyond the benefits to the individual firms engaged in colonial trade. First, poor and undeveloped countries do not as a rule provide markets large in relation to the output of advanced economies, so that the possibilities of exploitation are relatively small for the advanced economy as a whole. Markets large enough to encourage a major expansion of production in advanced countries are, almost by definition, markets in countries that are themselves economically advanced, though not necessarily industrialized. Second, the more solid benefits of trade with nonindustrialized countries came from trade that was not subject to effective imperialist political control. This trade arose from the development of overseas sources of food in both colonial and politically independent areas of North and South America, Australia, and Africa. It has been of immense economic benefit to the growing populations of Western Europe in the last century and a half, not because of exploitation, but because increased production kept world food prices from becoming a severe burden on European economies.

But the primary reason for doubting that an adequate explanation for Western growth is to be found in imperialism is the absence of any general correlation between the magnitude and timing of Western countries' economic growth and the magnitude and timing of their participation in imperialism. Imperialist Spain and Portugal did not achieve long-term growth; Switzerland and the Scandinavian countries, which did grow, were not imperialist countries; Germany and the United States, which achieved long-term growth, were latecomers to imperialism. Imperialist Britain and Holland grew, but they were already strong before they became imperial powers and they continued to grow after they gave up their empires. The eighteenth- and nineteenth-century history of most imperialist countries makes their economic growth seem more a cause of imperialism, stimulating overseas political adventures in the irresponsible exercise of new-found economic power, than its result. Of course, it is no comfort to non-Western countries injured by Western imperialism to suggest that the injury was gratuitous.

9. Slavery

Another explanation of Western economic growth stresses slavery. Slavery was rarely, if ever, used in Western industry. The reason was probably not moral, since slavery was an ancient and widespread institution—accepted, at the time of the Industrial Revolution, in English colonies though not in England itself. In the United States, if we wish to believe pre-Civil War Southern slaveholders and modern economic historians, slavery was not found in industry because free labor was available at less cost.

Since slavery was not used in industry, whatever contribution slavery made to Western development depended on the profits realized from the slave trade or on the use of slave labor in producing raw materials for Western factories. Profits from the slave trade were small by comparison to other sources of capital in the Western countries that engaged in it. The principal example of the use of slaves in the production of raw materials for factories is that of the British textile industry and its Southern suppliers. In the decades before the Civil War, England met much of its rapidly growing need for raw cotton by imports from the Southern states, where slave labor was widely used in cotton production. The growth in cotton imports was clearly a consequence, rather than a cause, of Britain's industrial revolution. How much slavery, as an institution, contributed economically to the growth of the cotton textile industry depends on how much the British saved by importing slave-grown cotton rather than cotton grown by free labor in the South, or in Egypt or India. Assuming cotton produced by free labor would have been more expensive, the higher cost would tend to increase the price, and reduce the volume of sales, of cotton and cotton textiles; encourage production of cotton in Egypt, India, and Brazil; reduce the value of Southern cotton plantations; and modestly alter the economic incentives for technological developments in British textile production. The sum of these tendencies is that if the British had not imported slave-grown cotton, there is a reasonable possibility that the rate of growth of the British textile industry might have been a little slower in the years up to 1861.

An earlier use of slavery, notoriously in the West Indies, was in the production of sugar. But sugar was produced for consumption, not as a raw material for European factories.

To Western Europeans, slavery was an institution that arose almost entirely from colonization. The European countries which developed growth economies without colonialism also eschewed slavery. In contrast, Spain and Portugal were early leading colonizers, and both used slavery widely in their colonies. Yet both lagged in the development of modern growth economies. As in the case of imperialism, slavery, as an explanation for Western economic growth, suffers from a mismatch between the practice of slavery and the occurrence of economic growth.

It is worth stressing again that we are concerned with the question of whether colonialism and slavery explain Western economic growth. Whether some of the West's former colonies would have grown more rapidly had they not been colonized is a different question, again with answers that vary from one former colony to another.

What passes for an acceptable explanation often depends in part on the reason one wants an explanation. For some purposes, if one asks how James J. Hill built the Great Northern Railroad, the answer, "By stealing," suffices. But such an explanation would be of no assistance to someone who is contemplating the financing and construction of a railroad. Similarly, for some purposes, a sufficient explanation of how the West grew rich would be, "By the sweat of the poor and the plunder and enslavement of the weak." But if a non-Westerner wants to understand Western economic growth with a view to furthering the economic growth of his or her own country, or if a Westerner wants to understand it in order to safeguard existing growth, further explanation is needed. After all, exploitation has been pervasive outside the West, as well as in the ancient and medieval West itself, without duplicating the modern Western achievement.

An Explanation from History: A Western Growth System

Where, then, can we find an explanation?

The immediate sources of Western growth were innovations in trade, technology, and organization, in combination with accumulation of more and more capital, labor, and applied natural resources. Innovation emerged as a significant factor in Western growth as early as the mid-fifteenth century, and from the mid-eighteenth century on it has been pervasive and dominant. Innovation occurred in trading, production, products, services, institutions, and organization. The main characteristics of innovation—uncertainty, search, exploration, financial risk, experiment, and discovery—have so permeated the West's expansion of trade and the West's development of natural resources as to make it virtually an additional factor of production.

Ours is not the first period of Western European economic advance, though it much exceeds the earlier periods in magnitude. The era of the Roman empire, when England, France, and Spain were Roman colonies, came first. After the fifth century, when the Roman empire collapsed into the Dark Ages, the West suffered economic retrogression, rather than progress, for approximately five centuries. The West then experienced a second period of economic progress, beginning no later than the tenth century: a period of advance from the Dark Ages characterized by an increase in population, a steady extension of agricultural settlement into what had been wilderness, a growth in the number of towns, and appreciable advances in the technologies of war, architecture, transportation, and agriculture. The growth of Northern Europe from the tenth to the fourteenth century was primarily accumulative, as a growing population brought more land under cultivation. Expansion without innovation, however, eventually encounters serious limits to the continued growth of output per capita.

Growth resulting from innovation and growth resulting from the accumulation of capital and labor are not always easy to distinguish. Innovation frequently requires a concomitant growth of capital and labor, and, over a long enough time, some innovation can almost always be detected in even the most conservative expanding economy. The distinction rests partly on which type of growth predominates. It is also partly a question of whether the line of causation runs from innovation, providing opportunities for profitable investment, to the accumulation of capital and other resources, or from the accumulation of capital to the development of opportunities for investment.

Either way, the West has increasingly placed its primary reliance on innovation. As the Western economies expanded, so did their stocks of capital, their expenditures on education, the accumulation of skills by their work forces, and their populations. But the growth of these conventional factors of production was often a response to innovation, the deliberate fulfillment of a precondition to carrying through innovation. The line of causation was not all one way, but investment opportunities traceable to innovation became, predominantly, more the cause than the consequence of the accumulation of capital. Even the rise in population, which was not as rapid as the rate of economic growth, was made possible by innovations in agricultural techniques and the numerous types of innovation, including those in public health, required for urbanization.

After more than two centuries of Western economic growth linked to innovation, Western economies have been so dissected, scrutinized, and analyzed that there is little likelihood that the features of Western systems responsible for that innovation have completely escaped observation. More likely, some of the same elements of Western economic systems that are regularly used to explain current prices, output, and distribution are also parts of the growth system, perhaps less obviously because their effects occur in small increments, lost in the flow of current economic events and spread over periods of time so long that the causal connections become tenuous and controversial. For example, both firms and markets played important parts in innovation, and so did competition. Let us begin with firms.

By the mid-nineteenth century, Western societies had given their enterprises certain rights which can be viewed either as a grant of authority to make a number of decisions which had been made by political or religious authorities in most other societies, or as a grant of freedom from many common types of political or religious control. Four of these rights set the stage for economic growth based on innovation. First, individuals were authorized to form enterprises, with less and less political restriction. The formation of enterprises was extensively restricted by lack of money, lack of talent, or both, but not by lack of license from the political authorities nor by lack of ecclesiastical blessing. Second, enterprises were authorized to acquire goods and hold them for resale at a profit or loss, again with little or no restriction. Third, enterprises were authorized to add activities and to switch from one line of activity to another that seemed more promising, again with little restriction. Political or religious restriction arose only at the outer bounds of the numerous economic choices open to the enterprise: that is, the products or services it would make, how it would make them, the extent to which it would make them or buy them from other enterprises, how it would sell them, and the prices it would charge. Finally, while the assets of the enterprise and such profits as it accumulated from its activities might be taxed at predetermined rates, its property came to be regarded as immune from arbitrary seizure or expropriation by the political authorities.

In sum, the economic enterprise had become a unit for making a wide range of economic decisions, and its gains and losses from the decisions were expected to accrue to the enterprise or, less abstractly, to its owners. Virtually without thought or discussion, the West delegated to enterprises the making of a decision basic in the innovation process: which ideas should be tested and which should be allowed to die. For economic innovation requires not only an idea, but an experimental test of the idea in laboratory, factory, and market. Such tests are costly; they require resources and competence in engineering, manufacturing, and marketing, especially if the innovator is to capture the financial rewards of the innovation. These resources existed in the ordinary firm described in economics textbooks, and they made the firm a readily available unit for organizing innovation.

An essential aspect of the diffusion of authority over economic decisions generally, and innovational decisions in particular, was the emergence of markets. Likewise comparatively free of political and religious controls, markets became institutions for the resolution of the conflicts of interest among enterprises, consumers, and employees. As firms assumed a role in innovation in addition to their more familiar role as producers, markets assumed a role in innovation in addition to their role in determining prices and allocating resources. Markets determined who won the rewards of innovation and the quantum of the reward. The response of the market was *the* test of success or failure of an innovation. Governments could be asked to fund innovations that failed or seemed unlikely to succeed in markets, but the appeals were seldom successful except for military hardware, other products primarily of interest to governments, and research into the public health or food supply.

Competition also became involved in innovation. The market rewards of innovation depended largely on the innovator's ability to charge a high price for a unique product or service until such time as it could be imitated or superseded by others. The rewards depended, in other words, on the innovator's margin of priority in time over imitators and successors. This was true even of patents, which go to the first inventor, and whose economic life is measured by the time it takes to find a better alternative. Given the multiplicity of Western enterprises, the possibility of forming new ones, and the possibility that old ones could shift to new activities, the process of gaining the rewards of innovative ideas takes on the characteristics of a race, informal but still competitive. The competitive nature of the process was intensified by the Western practice of leaving the losers to bear their own losses, which were often substantial. This use of a competitive spur to stimulate change was a marked departure from tradition, for societies and their rulers have almost always strongly resisted change unless it enhanced the ruler's own power and well-being.

In the first centuries of Western growth, Western artisan inventors and their enterprises originated most of their own technology. Western science developed almost independently of Western industry until after 1800. Its contributions to industrial technology, still rare at the beginning of the nineteenth century, became more numerous as the century wore on. The introduction of the industrial research laboratory, toward the end of the nineteenth century and the beginning of the twentieth, systematized the links between science and industry and made it much easier for the West to nourish economic growth by drawing on a growing body of scientific knowledge.

HOW THE WEST GREW RICH

The West's system of growth required a social class with the capacity to effect innovations, with incentives or motives for innovation, with a source of ideas for innovation, and with immunity from interference by the formidable social forces opposed to change, growth, and innovation. Since innovation works against the status quo, the innovating class had to act collectively as though it had more interest in change than in the status quo. Whatever diversity of interest existed among its individual members had to be regularly resolved in favor of the members interested in change.

We have emphasized the part played by innovation in Western growth. The decentralization of authority to make decisions about innovations, together with the resources to effectuate such decisions and to absorb the gains or losses resulting from them, merits similar emphasis as an explanation of Western innovation. This diffusion of authority was interwoven with the development of an essentially autonomous economic sector; with the widespread use of experiment to answer questions of technology, marketing, and organization for which answers could be found in no other way; and with the emergence of great diversity in the West's modes of organizing economic activity.

It is not difficult to trace the outlines of the development, in the West, of these aspects of what amounted to a growth system.

1. The Emergence of an Autonomous Economic Sphere and a Merchant Class

The West's sustained economic growth began with the emergence of an economic sphere with a high degree of autonomy from political and religious control. The change from the coherent, fully integrated feudal society of the late Middle Ages to the plural society of eighteenth-century Europe implied a relaxation of political and ecclesiastical control of all spheres of life, including not only the economy, but also science, art, literature, music, and education.

This relaxation of political control over the economic sphere took several forms. There was an increase in the volume of trade at unregulated prices, as distinguished from trade at prices determined by political authority. This trade, and its profits, helped produce a merchant class who lived by buying and selling, as distinguished from one selling products they had made with their own hands. There was likewise a weakening of guild and government control over starting new businesses. In England, particularly, where the guilds' charters gave them authority over entry into particular lines of trade or manufacture within a town or borough, aggressive individuals could and did evade guild authority by establishing enterprises

24

in the countryside or in other towns or boroughs. There was no sudden repeal of price controls or general deregulation movement; rather, in a development traceable from small beginnings in twelfth-century Northern Italy, enterprising merchants and artisans searched out more and more opportunities for relatively unregulated trade and manufacture until, by the end of the eighteenth century, the older forms of trade by "regulated companies" of merchants or artisans had become moribund. As Adam Smith sardonically observed in 1776, "To be merely useless, indeed, is perhaps the highest eulogy which can ever justly be bestowed on a regulated company."[5]

2. Innovation by Extension of Trade and Discovery of New Resources

As merchants succeeded more and more in escaping political control, they ventured into trade in more commodities and between more places. The early long-distance trading voyages, which brought exotic products back to European ports from the mysterious East, were enormously profitable when they were successful—scandalously so, to some observers. But for purposes of understanding the elements of Western growth, nothing could be more revealing than the early merchants' discovery of the enormous rewards to be reaped from introducing a new product that was popular with buyers and had no immediate competitors. They may have scandalized their late-medieval colleagues by skimming off consumers' money for exotic foreign goods instead of for the sober products of the local guilds, and they may have outraged their fellow burghers by drawing promising youngsters from honest trades into the hazards of voyages to unknown and often pagan places. But in modern terms, what they did is called innovation and competition by innovation. It would not be easy to ov᠎ ˑstate their importance to Western economic growth.

One characteristic of an economic system that is closely related to growth is the degree to which the economy employs trade and exchange, both domestic and foreign. This is partly a statistical artifact, since most statistics on economic growth measure the volume of some aspect of trade, but it has a deeper significance also. Exchange does not normally occur unless each party sees some advantage in it: usually, giving something it can produce (or otherwise acquire) more easily than it can produce (or otherwise acquire) what it accepts from the other party in exchange. Many communities have tried to supply most of their own needs by local production, like the manors of medieval Europe or the village economies of the Third World. When such communities begin to meet their needs through trade and exchange with other communities and with foreigners—as happened in England during the decline of the manorial system—the change implies specialized production and a new pattern of trade-based cooperation among the communities. It thus leads to increased wealth.

The Western search for trade was, at least in the beginning, not just for novel or exotic products from the East, but also for more familiar natural resources that could be netted, trapped, mined, felled, or plowed to yield something that could be sold in European markets. Fishermen preceded trappers to North America, and trappers preceded farmers, lumberjacks, and miners. The development of overseas exploration, overseas and domestic trade, and the finding and use of new natural resources were closely linked in an innovational process.

3. Innovation by Lowering the Cost of Production

The merchants gained wealth by being first with a novel import. When, a little later, enterprising artisans began to circumvent guild restrictions by setting up relatively large shops, or manufactories, outside guild jurisdiction, they extended the merchants' formula of being first, this time to being first with a lower-cost method of production. Late in the eighteenth century, during the Industrial Revolution, this same formula of competing with the status quo by new, lower-cost methods of production was used, this time by introducing more power and powered machinery to production processes.

4. Innovation by Introducing New Products

Innovation by devising and manufacturing new products was not a high road to great wealth so long as the individual inventor produced on a small scale. There were new products before the factory system—many of them, from improved wagons and carriages to improved clocks and watches. But what the inventive watchmaker or other artisan could collect in premium prices, however superior the product might be, did not add up to a great fortune, simply because the total quantity each sold was small. That changed with the introduction of the factory system of production, and in the nineteenth century, the introduction of new products became highly rewarded (sometimes).

In most societies, new products have tended to be of more interest to the rich than to the poor. It is an oddity of Western economic growth that, while it made some individuals extremely rich, it benefited the life-style of the very rich much less than it benefited the life-style of the less well-off. The reason is to be found in the nature of the innovations that the West most conspicuously rewarded. Innovations that reduced the cost of producing goods did not appreciably change the life-style of people who were abundantly able to pay pre-innovation prices, and the most lucrative new products were those with a market among the many, rather than among the few. Thus the first textile factories produced fabrics of inferior quality, which the rich did not want, and, a century later, the great automobile fortune was Henry Ford's, not Henry Royce's. The very rich were as well-housed, clothed, and adorned in 1885 as in 1985. Improvements in the transportation and preservation of food have benefited both rich and poor, but the main difference in the eating habits of the rich stems from the modern idea that obesity is medically inadvisable. A measured condescension toward innovations in mass entertainment, such as professional sports, movies, television, and rock music, is today almost an indicium of upper-class status, along with education outside the new system of public schools and colleges. It is much easier to think of innovations which benefited only the less well-off than it is to think of innovations which have benefited only the rich, and, in fact, the innovations of positive value to the rich are relatively few: advances in medical care, air conditioning, and improvements in transportation and preservation of food. It is a nice question to what extent modern electric gadgetry compensated the rich for the loss of their servants. The real point, not often recognized but essential to understanding why the benefits of Western growth were so widely diffused, is that the West's system of economic growth offered its largest financial rewards to innovators who improved the life-style not of the wealthy few, but of the less-wealthy many.

We noted earlier that statistics on national output in widely separated periods do not adequately reflect the consequences of differences in products. The existence of a bias in Western systems toward the development of products and services for mass markets suggests that the differences in products have probably tended to favor the many rather than the few. Near the top of the wealth pyramid, it hardly matters, but a little further down—where one may expect to find people whose self-image of superior cultural and social status is not supported by a correspondingly superior life-style—the resulting exasperation may find expression in the characterization of advanced Western societies as lowbrow, tawdry, vulgar, cheap—or even consumerist.

5. The Development of Sources of Innovative Ideas

The development of an economic sphere within which individuals were allowed to engage in new ventures, to launch new business enterprises, to change the activities of existing enterprises, and to charge whatever prices seemed likely to yield the highest profits, all without asking official permission, offered immense possibilities of wealth to those who could furnish goods that were too new to the market to have any competitors, and that were highly valued by buyers. But it is one thing to know that both individual and social wealth flow generously from introducing lower-cost methods of producing old products, or from introducing new products, and it is quite another thing to know how to go about generating the required advances in method and product. For this, the Western growth system needed a source of invention. The development of this source followed two roughly parallel paths.

In the seventeenth century, the West developed a mode of scientific procedure conventionally associated with the names of Galileo and Bacon. It was based upon observation, reason, and experiment. By insisting upon the experimental verification of scientific explanations, Galileo and his successors established a general test of scientific truth which enabled scientists specialized in widely different disciplines to accept and use each other's results. The shared method created an organized scientific community, with a division of labor among scientists in numerous specialized fields, all contributing to the accumulation of a coherent body of knowledge. By the close of the seventeenth century, the scale of the West's scientific effort was already overwhelmingly greater than in any contemporary or earlier culture, and so was the West's progress in understanding natural phenomena. Even so, it was little more than the seed of what it was to become.

The advances of the seventeenth century established the method, organization, secular viewpoint, and the early beginnings of the basic knowledge upon which modern Western science has been built. Yet in industrial technology, parallel advances of more direct economic importance originated mostly in hands-on invention and experiment by artisan inventors until late in the nineteenth century. The influence of scientific discovery was indirect, although some chemists formed early links between scientific explanation and industrial practice. The progress of Western industrial technology during the eighteenth and nineteenth centuries was, nevertheless, no less striking than that of Western science.

Today, we recognize a rough division between pure science, which develops explanations for natural phenomena, and industrial science, which develops commercial products and production processes. Late in the nineteenth century, the paths of pure science and industrial technology converged in the fields of chemistry, electricity, and biology. The earlier artisan inventors of industry gave way to professional scientists, simply because industry was now working with phenomena which could be understood only in terms of the explanations devised by pure science, and these explanations were accessible only to specially trained professionals. It was not so much that the possibilities of artisan invention were exhausted as that the expansion of science had opened a new world of professional invention. It thus took approximately two hundred fifty years for Galilean science to reach the point of dominating the West's industrial invention.

6. Uncertainty and Experiment

Uncertainty runs throughout the process of innovation. The outcome of invention is, by definition of invention, unpredictable. The cost of development is initially unknown, and so are the benefits, dependent as they are on the advantages and cost of the final product and the opportunities for exploiting it commercially before imitators compete down the margin of profit. Human experience, judgment, and planning can reduce the uncertainty, but they can never come close to eliminating it.

The only known device for resolving the uncertainties surrounding any given innovation proposal is experiment, up to and including the manufacture and marketing of a product. Such experiments are costly; on the other hand, the failure to undertake them precludes the possibility of innovation. And the consequences of successful experiments are economic growth. The West has threaded its way between the horns of this dilemma by what amounts to a form of insurance. Authority to undertake an innovation is diffused among a comparatively large number of firms and individuals who can bring together the required money and talent, thus reducing the risk that a desirable proposal may be rejected because of a viewpoint peculiar to a single decision maker. Along with the authority goes the responsibility: the innovator bears the losses of failed experiments and gains such of the benefits of the successful ones as the innovator can capture.

This system of diffusion of authority, experiment, and responsibility presupposes an ownership relation between the holders of authority to innovate and the required funds, laboratories, factories, and distribution systems. For a socialist system to replicate the Western system for inno-

29

vation, it would be necessary to give the managers of socialist enterprises roughly the same authority—to determine the uses to be made of the enterprise's assets, what products the enterprise might produce and by what methods, and what prices it should charge—that the owner of a capitalist enterprise possesses. It might not be necessary to give the managers the owners' right to all the profits and all the responsibility for the losses; after all, many Western innovations originated under the direction of managers compensated by salaries and bonuses. On the other hand, the relationship between private owners and a salaried manager is not identical with the relationship between the state and a salaried public employee, and some Western innovations have originated in owner-managed enterprises. It is doubtful that a socialist society could be as innovative as the West without using the main substantive features of private ownership of the means of production and without curtailing central authority over the uses of the means of production so greatly as to make the feasibility of planning dubious. Put the other way around, the West's system of innovation is interwoven, probably beyond separation, with its system of private property rights.

7. Overcoming Resistance to Innovation

The diffusion of authority to initiate innovations served also as the West's way of guarding against a chronic menace to innovative change—the interest of the status quo in suppressing innovation. An innovation will seldom be authorized or financed by government or corporate officials whose careers would be adversely affected by the success of the proposal. Sometimes the success of an innovation means the end of an entire industry, entailing large capital losses as well as the loss to its employees of their human capital of training and experience. The opposition to innovation can be, and has been, very powerful.

The West's methods of overcoming the obstructionism of the status quo included a system of decentralized decision making in capital investment. Not all capital investments fund innovations; a decision is sometimes made, though not often, to spend funds to replace old equipment or rebuild old facilities without modernizing them at all. But a diffusion of the authority to make investment decisions generally is so closely related to the diffusion of authority to select innovations as to make the two practically inseparable.

The comparative impotence of the forces opposed to innovation may have rested ultimately on the general Western belief that innovation is a good thing, but there is little record of its having been debated in those terms. Like the rest of the Western growth system, it originated in a much more devious and far less rational way. During the Middle Ages, guilds and corporations that wished to obtain power to exclude others from their trade got it by purchase of a charter from the Crown. The issuance of such charters was a substantial source of royal revenues. When English judges were presented with the question whether an individual who wished to enter a lawful occupation was liable for the consequent injury to those already there, an eye to the royal revenues made the answer predictable: no charter, no liability. By the seventeenth century, English merchants were strongly resisting the continued issuance of such charters. In this backhanded way, the right of individuals to use their personal efforts and property in trade and manufacturing without having to answer to their competitors became embedded in English law. By the late eighteenth century, when the introduction of the factory system seriously disrupted some types of earlier handicraft production, there was rarely any way to prevent innovation except by force. Force was sometimes employed, but it was illegitimate force, indignantly suppressed by political authorities acting against riots, arson, and sabotage.

8. Innovation in Organization: Diversity

We have stressed innovation in technology as a major element in the West's growth system. But innovation in organization also played a part worth emphasizing; indeed, it can be reasonably argued that the West's success in technological innovation is attributable to its success in organizational innovation.

From the fifteenth century on, changes in the internal economic organization of Western societies proliferated. The relationship between the political and economic spheres began to change. European governments and merchants joined in the invention of new forms of enterprise, sometimes successfully and sometimes with scandalous or disastrous results. Later, the Industrial Revolution of the late eighteenth century made it necessary to devise new modes of organization for new kinds of economic enterprise. The problem was not simply one of legal forms— corporate, partnership, or proprietorship. There were also the more novel problems of devising ways to organize groups of workers much larger in number than those employed in artisan shops and specialized to many more skills, of finding ways to minimize the risks of investing great blocks of capital in one enterprise, of deciding what different lines of business should be combined in one enterprise, and of protecting the interests of owners in enterprises increasingly managed by hired professionals. By continuing experiment, the West found solutions to these problems. The solutions were often transient, but the experimental process by which they were found proved basic to Western economic advance.

As the economies of Western countries have grown, and as they have changed both their methods of production and their products, they have constantly modified the size and structure of their enterprise organizations. The size of enterprises and their form of organization (partnership, proprietorship, or corporation) had to be adapted to the new environment of factory, railroads, and the apparatus of urbanization: transport, gas, and electricity. In addition, the competitive element within Western economies, particularly rivalry for the rewards of being first with innovations, led enterprises to try to differentiate themselves from other enterprises in ways that carried a competitive advantage. An attempt to be first with a new product or a lower-cost way of producing an old product is an attempt at differentiation. This combination of necessary adaptation to a changing environment and competitive attempts at self-differentiation has produced a striking diversity in the size, economic functions, and organization of enterprises.

This diversity is worth emphasizing by way of balancing two quite different schools of thought which underemphasize the diversity of Western enterprises. In orthodox economic analysis, the firm is viewed as an organizational black box, sometimes called a production function, but in any case a basic unit of analysis not further differentiated. The resulting simplification works well in explaining existing production and distribution, but it does not explain economic change and growth, perhaps because it neglects the process of enterprise self-differentiation in which change and growth originate. It also produces a peculiarly peaceful distillation of the concept of competition, free of the stresses and pressing rivalries usually associated with the term, again because it neglects the deliberate self-differentiation which is, in competitive rivalry, the nearly universal strategy for winning. The other school of thought emphasizes the role of very large industrial enterprises in Western economies, giving inadequate recognition to the part played by smaller enterprises both in economic activity generally and in bringing about change and innovation. Here, too, the price of simplification is the loss of the capacity to explain either Western economic growth or the competitive stresses which are notoriously characteristic of Western economies.

Conclusion

Our general conclusion is that the underlying source of the West's ability to attract the lightning of economic revolutions was a unique use of experiment in technology and organization to harness resources to the satisfaction of human wants. The key elements of the system were the wide diffusion of the authority and resources necessary to experiment; an absence of more than rudimentary political and religious restrictions on experiment; and incentives which combined ample rewards for success, defined as the widespread economic use of the results of experiment, with a risk of severe penalties for failing to experiment.

The experiments embraced not simply the abstract creation of a new product or service or a new organizational device, but also the testing of the product or service by actually offering it for public use, and of the organizational device by using it in active enterprises. This type of experiment required an economic sector with autonomy from political intervention, in which experiment could be tried and results used with little outside interference. Experimental adaptation to the inherent diversity of both human wants and the resources available for satisfying them involved self-reinforcing, two-way causation, for experiment created both additional human wants and additional resources, thereby inviting additional diversity in the system for satisfying them. This causal loop generated great diversity of sizes and types of both enterprises and markets. This diversity in the forms of economic life, like the diversity in biosystems, is important not for its own sake but because it is an earmark of successful adaptation and full utilization of the resources available. The thematic terms are thus *autonomy, experiment,* and *diversity.*

This system of commercial experiment owed its accomplishments in part to the immense achievements in another department of Western life—the scientific sphere. But it was not entirely a matter of dependency on science. In the three-cornered relations of technology, the experimental economy, and growth of material welfare, the experimental economy served as a more efficient link between science and growth than any other society had achieved, and the economy was itself the source of much of its own technology.

The system involved, and indeed required, a division of labor among the political, religious, scientific, and economic spheres of social life, which allowed each the degree of autonomy needed to enable it to concentrate on its own affairs with much less interference from the others than has been common in other societies. The result was not just an improvement in the conduct of economic affairs, but also in the conduct of political, religious, and scientific affairs.

It is worth dwelling on the special importance of experiment to organization. The organizational innovator is typically dealing with well-informed and highly intelligent people who react vigorously, ingeniously, adversely, and even vengefully to organizational changes not in their interests—and to a good many changes which are in their interests, at least as perceived by the innovator. It is thus inherent in organizational innovation that the outcome can never be predicted more than tentatively, nor known without experiment. By comparison, physicists, geologists, and biologists work with materials that are sometimes almost perversely resistant to understanding, but such materials only appear to have minds of their own. It is the organizational innovator who is open to counterinvention by those in the organization who are opposed to the change, and the uncertainty of the outcome is implied by the definition of *invention*. Of all the fields of human endeavor, none is more unsuited to ideology than organizational innovation, and nowhere else does ideology rise so far above experiment in pressing its claims.

Initially, the West's achievement of autonomy stemmed from a relaxation, or a weakening, of political and religious controls, giving other departments of social life the opportunity to experiment with change. Growth is, of course, a form of change, and growth is impossible when change is not permitted. And *successful* change requires a large measure of freedom to experiment. A grant of that kind of freedom costs a society's rulers their feeling of control, as if they were conceding to others the power to determine the society's future. The great majority of societies, past and present, have not allowed it. Nor have they escaped from poverty.

Guide to Following Chapters

The explanation we have summarized for the West's rise to wealth developed from a review of the history of the emergence of the West's economic institutions. This history is the principal subject matter of the succeeding chapters.

Introduction

In the main, the West's journey to wealth began in the Western European economies of the High Middle Ages, though it is easy to trace some of its origins even farther. In chapter 2, we describe this point of departure. The West had made progress, perhaps slow and irregular but still substantial, for five hundred years. Yet it was, by modern standards, poverty-stricken. A series of disasters, beginning in the fourteenth century, made it clear that the European countries were not capable of maintaining sustained growth. Their institutions are worth describing and remembering as a contrast to the subsequent institutions which fostered Western growth, and perhaps also as a reminder of how easy it is for the reform of capitalist institutions to take an atavistic turn.

Western wealth began with the growth of European trade and commerce, which started in the twelfth century in Italy and accelerated after the mid-fifteenth century. In chapter 3, we carry the account to 1750. During this period in Europe, there developed a relatively autonomous class of professional merchants who, in one way or another, largely escaped the political and religious controls characteristic of the earlier feudal regime. Europe was still predominantly agricultural, but during this same period agriculture moved away from feudalism and toward the modern money agriculture. Guild control over production was simultaneously weakened by the spread of shops outside guild jurisdiction. In short, it was a period of development of a plural society, in which the economic sphere (as well as the scientific, religious, literary, artistic, and other spheres) gained appreciable autonomy from political control. A whole set of institutions required for the efficient functioning of an autonomous economic sphere was introduced. In chapter 4, we summarize the development of a number of these institutions.

In chapter 5 we discuss the period from the Industrial Revolution to 1880, the time of the development of the industrial segment of Western economies. This was the most striking period of economic expansion thus far, but its institutional foundation changed only modestly after 1750. From the earlier period of the development of trade, the West inherited the moral system, property rights, modes of organization, banks, insurance, credit instruments, and similar institutions needed for the much higher level of industrial development reached by 1880.

After 1880, Western industry turned increasingly from older modes of enterprise organization to the corporation. In chapter 6, we recount the background of the development of the numerous forms of corporations, particularly the business corporation. In chapter 7, we discuss the period from 1880 to 1914, especially in the United States, a period of continued rapid growth that included what is sometimes called a second industrial revolution and during which an important part of U.S. industry was recast into the mold of the large industrial corporation.

Since about 1880, what we now call pure science has played a larger and larger part in Western industrial technology and, by implication, in Western economic growth. Up to then, industrial technology had been mostly the product of artisan inventors with only modest connections to formal science. In chapter 8, we explore the connection between science—both pure science and industrial technology—and Western wealth.

In chapter 9, the diversity in the size and function of Western economic enterprises is discussed, particularly in Western economies conceived as growth systems. We offer some reasons for thinking that the growth of Western economies has *not* rested on their use of conspicuously large industrial enterprises, but rather on their use of enterprises of whatever size and type seem best adapted to the circumstances and strategy of the enterprise.

Chapter 10 is a discussion and comparison of policy, beginning with some observations about the growing role of the political sphere in economic matters and ending with a discussion of policy choices open to the Third World for achieving growth.

NOTES

1. Thomas Robert Malthus, *An Essay on Population*, 2 vols (London: H. M. Dent and Co., 1914). First published in 1798.

2. Oswald Spengler, *The Decline of the West*, 2 vols (New York: Knopf, 1926–28).

3. Werner Sombart, *Der moderne Kapitalismus*, 2nd ed. (München: Duncker and Humblot, 1916).

4. Max Weber, *General Economic History* (New York: First Collier Books Ed., 1961), p. 261.

5. Adam Smith, *An Inquiry into the Nature and Causes of the Wealth of Nations*, vol. 2 (New York: Oxford University Press, 1976), bk. 5, p. 735.

2 / The Starting Point: The Middle Ages

To trace the West's rise to wealth, we need to begin with a period when the West was at least as poor as its contemporary economies. The Middle Ages will serve as such a starting point. The West was not only poor, it had little of the apparatus of technology, mass production, mass transportation, mass communication, and finance which we associate with the wealth of the modern West. It was a period when, in the view of most scholars who have made the comparison, Chinese and perhaps Islamic technology were more advanced than the West's. Likewise, it was a period before banking had been invented, when merchants had but a small role to play in the economy, and when factories were almost unknown.

To give this starting point a date, the latest period in which we can view the institutions of medieval Western society as functioning in an approximately normal way is the thirteenth century, and even that may be too late a date for Italy. The fourteenth century, especially its last half, was a time of disaster in European society: an apocalypse of wars, plagues, and famine resulted in a major reduction in population and a contraction in the land area inhabited and under cultivation.

The fifteenth century was a period of recovery, but recovery did not take the form of a return to medieval institutions. Both politically and economically, the West of the 1400s was unmistakably replacing medieval with modern institutions. Politically, central monarchies were established in France, Spain, Portugal, and England; they eventually became the modern nation-states. Economically, there were very important advances in the art of shipbuilding during the latter half of the century. By lowering transportation costs, these advances led to an expansion of interregional and international trade and commerce and, with it, the growth of a merchant class functioning on terms more modern than medieval. European mariners took advantage of these same advances to begin the momentous explorations which included the discovery of America.

To visualize medieval society as it was, and to see how different it was from contemporary Western society, it is helpful to have three points in mind from the beginning.

First, the medieval economy was overwhelmingly agricultural. For this reason, we begin with a review of the agricultural economy and then go on to the economic life of the towns.

Second, we shall find that in both agricultural and urban areas, political and economic authority were combined in the same institutions—the manor in the country and the guilds in the towns. An autonomous economic sector still lay in the future.

Third, the medieval way of determining the terms of exchange was by custom, usage, and law, not by negotiation between traders. The division of labor was well developed by the Middle Ages, and there was a corollary exchange of products and services among specialized workers. But the use of custom and law to set the terms of trade was as fundamental to the medieval economy as the unity of its political and economic institutions.

Exchange was also usually compulsory, in that the great majority of artisans and agricultural workers were obligated to supply their products and services on terms dictated by custom or law. Agricultural workers were bound to the land in a system of serfdom, a hereditary status assumed at birth, and they had no right to select a more attractive occupation. Townspeople were not given much more choice of occupation, for having a trade (as distinguished from being a vagrant) depended on an apprenticeship, usually arranged by one's father and often in the father's guild. A member of the guild had to work and sell on the guild terms; there was no right to decline business at the fixed rates.

The ideology of the system was epitomized in the phrases "just price" and "just wage." Prices and wages expressed a moral judgment of worth. Supply and demand were morally irrelevant. The modern concept of prices and wages as pragmatic devices for clearing markets and allocating resources, implying no moral judgment, came much later. The medieval world experimented with the economic utility of prices that equate supply and demand on the worst possible occasions; it was mainly in times of famine or siege that prices forced their way into that role. And these episodic and very steep rises in the price of food were considered a moral outrage perpetrated by the sellers who charged them.

The medieval period has been more determinedly romanticized than any other in Western history. The romanticization was not entirely the work of literary imagination; R. H. Tawney has left us the words of a sixteenth-century surveyor, one Humberstone, who sighed "for the social harmonies of a vanished age, which 'knyt suche a knott of collaterall amytie betwene the Lordes and the tenaunts that the Lorde tendered his tenaunt as a childe, and the tenaunts again loved and obeyed the Lorde as naturellye as the child the father.' "[1] The reality was utterly different: the essence of the feudal system was, in Tawney's words, "exploitation in its most naked and shameless form."[2]

Agriculture: The Dominance of the Rural Economy

The medieval economy was overwhelmingly rural and agricultural. This point easily escapes those of us whose knowledge of medieval society is based on political history, historical novels, medieval literature, or visits to medieval monuments. For most people, life in the Middle Ages was not lived in castles, towns, cathedrals, or inns, but in the peasant's hut and in the fields. Medieval society was preoccupied with the elementary task of providing food. This condition was not specifically medieval: Braudel estimates that 80 to 90 percent of the world's population was engaged in raising food between the fifteenth and eighteenth centuries.[3] The same condition characterized all of human history and prehistory, and it obtains in much of the Third World today.

These percentages must be read with one qualification. While 80 percent to 90 percent of the medieval population did agricultural work, those who did agricultural work also had to devote considerable time to other kinds of work. Peasants transported their produce to market themselves and sold it themselves. Their wives not only helped out in the fields, but also did the spinning, weaving, sewing, and cooking. When local roads were built or repaired, the villeins of the manor did the building or repairing. In short, agricultural specialization was not carried nearly so far as in modern times. Thus, statistics which show that 80 percent to 90 percent

39

of the population was engaged in agriculture need to be discounted somewhat to make them comparable to modern statistics, which show 5 percent similarly engaged. However, no such adjustment need be applied to make the medieval and modern figures comparable as measures of the distribution of population between towns and the countryside. The modern world is irretrievably urban, and the medieval world was just as unmistakably rural.

That producing the food supply preoccupied so large a part of the population is an indication of the precariousness of that supply,[4] which was a fundamental source of the insecurity of life in medieval society. Sometimes a poor crop was local, owing to drought, pest infestation, or the passage of armies, and its effect could be contained by buying and transporting food from nearby. But the very limited capacity of medieval commerce and transportation to supply food is illustrated by the small size of the cities they could sustain. Cologne supported only twenty thousand inhabitants by the fifteenth century,[5] though it was located at the meeting point of two branches of the Rhine and was thus far more favorably situated for the transportation of food than most medieval towns. In much of medieval society, a poor crop, even locally, meant hunger, malnutrition, and greater vulnerability to disease, and crop failure meant starvation.

Agriculture: The Manorial System

Rural life in medieval society was organized around the manor; indeed, the economic life of the Middle Ages is reasonably encapsulated in the term *manorialism*. In some ways, manorialism accentuated rural isolation and inhibited social experiment. In other ways, its very burdens impelled revolt and escape to the towns, to the Crusades, and to the marauding armies.

The manors were production enterprises of considerable size and complexity. They not only grew their own crops, usually several, and raised animals for food and farm work, but they milled their own grain, baked their own bread, spun thread and wove cloth, made their own plows, and did almost all their own metalwork in the manor smithy.

As a form of economic organization, the manors had three major features worth special emphasis, because they reflected ancient and nearly uniform human practice, and so contain at least a suggestion of why the West's eventual break with them made its later experience unique:

1 The unity of the political and economic spheres of human activity.
2 The widespread use of servile labor.
3 A high degree of self-sufficiency.

These features were mutually reinforcing. The last two buttressed the force of custom, usage, and law in determining the terms of exchange of labor for the necessities of subsistence, while the fact that the economic administrators of the manor also had the physical, coercive power to hold labor in servile subjection was a necessary, and quite possibly a sufficient, condition for the maintenance of a servile labor force.

1. Unity of Political and Economic Spheres

The manorial system was part of a larger feudal society. *Feudalism*, by definition, is a system in which occupants of land hold it as tenants of the sovereign in exchange for military service. In other words, it is an arrangement in which a hierarchy of land-tenure relationships parallels the hierarchy of military relationships. Given the military and political origins of the authority of the lord of the manor, it is scarcely surprising that his authority was as much political as economic. The manorial system did not supply the serfs with a political chief to whom they owed political allegiance and an employer or landlord to whom they had economic obligations. The two roles were simply not distinguished, but were instead consolidated in the person of the seigneur. This consolidation of authority thoroughly intertwined the political and economic spheres of manorial society. There was no way that distinctions between political and economic rights and privileges could arise, and such distinctions were simply unknown. It was the essence of the manorial system that the lord of the manor performed governmental functions: "It is only when rights of government (not merely political influence) are attached to lordship and fiefs that we can speak of fully developed feudalism in Western Europe."[6] Moreover, it was taken for granted that the lord would exercise his political authority in ways which would be materially beneficial to him— a profitable power qualified by the fact that if the lord of the manor did not furnish the public services necessary to its operation (defense, roads, bridges, a court), no one would, and so the lord's revenues might be expected to decline.[7]

In short, the manor was a complete system of political and economic relationships; it was not merely a system of economic relationships in a predominantly agrarian society. Although we may separately identify and analyze the economic aspects of the manorial system, the participants were involved in a network of additional relationships—legal and political relationships which constituted the larger structure of medieval life. The great French historian Marc Bloch summed up the manorial relationship as follows:

> [T]he lord did not merely draw from his peasants valuable revenues and an equally valuable labour force. Not only was he *rentier* of the soil and a beneficiary of the services; he was also a judge, often—if he did his duty—a protector, and always a chief, whom, apart from any more binding and more personal tie, those who "held" their land from him or lived on his land were bound, by a very general but real obligation, to help and to obey. Thus the *seigneurie* was not simply an economic enterprise by which profits accumulated in a strong man's hand. It was also a unit of authority, in the widest sense of the word; for the powers of the chief were not confined, as in principle they are in capitalist enterprises, to work done on his "business premises," but affected a man's whole life and acted concurrently with, or even in place of, the power of the state and the family. Like all highly organized social cells the *seigneurie* had its own law, as a rule customary, which determined the relations of the subject with the lord and defined precisely the limits of the little group on which these traditional rules were binding.[8]

The religious life of the manor came closer than the political or economic to autonomy. The medieval church was not manor-centered, and this qualifies the view that the manor was a closed social system. The lord of the manor was not a priest; and even where the lord had the power to nominate the parish priest and contributed heavily to the financial support of the parish, the priest remained part of a hierarchy outside legitimate manorial authority. The daily routine of religious service may have been thoroughly localized, and yet it had aspects which drew the inhabitants of the manor to a world outside it. Of these, the most significant in stimulating change turned out to be the Church's armed pilgrimages, the Crusades. There is, however, no indication that the Church set itself up in opposition to the manorial system or to the interests of the seigneurs.

A second qualification of the view that the manor was a closed social system arises from the fact that the lord was himself ordinarily a subordinate member of a feudal hierarchy, owing allegiance directly or indirectly to a king or independent prince. The later history of the decline of the manor and the rise of the nation-state is, in part, a history of the decay of the lord's role as a political intermediary between the rank and file and the sovereign. There came to be substituted direct rights and obligations between the kings and the inhabitants of the manors—a conversion to national citizenship from manorial citizenship and an expansion of the right of access to the king's courts.

In merging economic and political controls, manorialism was not introducing a new evil into the organization of large enterprises, but rather following the human race's earliest precedents. The first precedents in large-scale agriculture were the "hydraulic empires" based on the irrigation systems of the valleys of early civilization—Mesopotamia, the Nile, the Indus, the Hwang-Ho.[9] The organization necessary to irrigation agriculture was supplied by religious and political institutions. Irrigation works, so undertaken, helped unify the political, religious, and economic life of early cultures. Speaking of the Sumerians, William McNeill describes how "priests regularly served as managers, planners, and co-ordinators of the massed human effort without which Sumerian civilization could not have come into existence or long survived."[10] Whether or not the unifying effect of irrigation works deserves the emphasis given them by rechristening their cultural habitats "hydraulic societies,"[11] there is little doubt that the organization required to maintain the irrigation systems, upon which the first river-valley civilizations depended, made no more distinction between political and economic authority than did the medieval manors. The distinction was a later invention.

In short, the lord of the manor was a father figure, reminiscent not only of the ancient kings and priest-kings of the hydraulic societies, but also of the even more primitive forms of family, clan, and tribal leadership to which the priest-kings no doubt owed their origins. In weaving the political, economic, religious, and social threads of community life into the pattern of a single fabric, under the leadership of a father figure, the Middle Ages reiterated the most ancient forms of community organization.

2. Servile Labor

Compulsory labor was a fundamental characteristic of the manorial system. Essentially, the villeins received the right to cultivate some of the lord's land for their own benefit in exchange for their labor in cultivating the rest of it (the lord's demesne) for his benefit. In addition, under the manorial version of the social contract, the villeins agreed to pay the lord a whole network of other dues, in money or kind, also in exchange for the use of his land, so that a considerable part of what they produced for themselves ended up in the lord's hands.

As the system worked under the conventional open-field arrangement, the manor was divided into several fields, and each field into narrow strips. Each villein held several strips, scattered through the fields. Originally the lord's demesne included strips similarly distributed through the fields. Later, the demesnes tended to be consolidated. The work of plowing, sowing, cultivating, and harvesting the fields was done by the villagers, working partly together and partly individually.

There was nothing voluntary about the arrangement from the viewpoint of either the villeins or their lord. The lord inherited his villagers, and the villagers inherited their lord and their obligations to him. All were born to their status. But the status to which the villeins were born compelled their labor. In form, it differed from slavery in that the lord had no right to sell his villeins except as an incident of the sale of the manor, and there were customary limits on the amount of labor the villeins owed the lord. But the runaway villein was as much liable to recapture by his master as the runaway slave.

Thus the villein cultivated the fields on which his own sustenance and that of his family depended and his life was also extensively preempted by the obligation to work the lord's demesne. Servile labor was a basic form of social control: the inherited burdens of compulsory labor went far to assure that one born a villein did not have the time or opportunity to become an artisan or trader. The later mercantile economy developed entirely outside the manor because it required full-time merchant traders, acting at their own risk and in their own self-interest, who simply could not have functioned within the framework of manorial subordination or in the time left the inhabitants of the manor once they had performed their obligations to the seigneur. The oppressive meanness of the manorial farmer's condition has been well summed up by Marc Bloch:

> To this lord, as they called him, the cultivators of the soil owed, first, a more or less important part of their time; days of agricultural labor devoted to the cultivation of the fields, meadows, or vineyards of his demesne; carting and carrying services; and sometimes services as builders or craftsmen. Further, they were obliged to divert to his use a considerable part of their own harvests, sometimes in the form of rents and sometimes by means of taxes in money, and preliminary exchange of produce for money being in this case their affair. The very fields that they cultivated were not held to be theirs in full ownership, nor was their community—at least in most cases—the full owner of those lands over which common rights were exercised. Both were said to be "held" of the lord, which means that as landowner he had a superior right over them, recognized

by dues owed to him, and capable in certain circumstances of overriding the concurrent rights of the individual cultivators and of the community.[12]

It was one of the implications of the unity of the political and economic spheres that the incentives for the performance of labor were not simply contractual and monetary, but also political and punitive. The duty of the cultivator to his economic superior was inseparable from the duty of the villein to his lord. The obligation of the worker rested not on wages, but on a complex of political and social status, loyalty, and duty, reinforced by coercion. Both in theory and in practice, the whole system was deeply oppressive, not merely by modern standards, but as measured in its own day by the desperation of peasant uprisings, repeated over and over no matter how bloodily repressed. Tawney spoke of them as revealing "a state of social exasperation which has been surpassed in bitterness by few subsequent movements."[13]

Most participants in the manorial system were spared the responsibilities of deciding what occupation to follow, what trading enterprises to attempt, what crops or animals were likely to command the highest price in the fall. Under the three-field system, the fields were rotated. The fields lay fallow, or were planted in spring or fall. Even decisions about what crops would be planted, when, and where, belonged not to the peasant, but to the manor. With status fixed by birth, upward mobility implied flight from the system by some such device as escape to a town or joining a military unit. The system was not limited simply to villeins: a miller or a smith was a miller or a smith for life, and quite likely by hereditary right. Like the peasant's dues to his lord, the fees charged by the miller or smith were customary, and changes were a major event, affecting the whole network of manorial obligations.

The history of servile labor on the manor illustrates an ancient problem inherent in the exchange of labor for goods or money. The first requisite of a well-drawn contract is that a violation by either party should be easy for the other party to detect and prove. This requisite is well fulfilled by specific agreements to pay money or to deliver specified goods. It is least fulfilled by contracts to provide labor, since it is, as a rule, very difficult to tell when workers are or are not performing with reasonable diligence. We are so accustomed to thinking of workers as having less bargaining power than employers that the underlying contractual balance seems paradoxical: the employer's obligation to pay wages is far clearer, and more readily enforceable, than the employee's obligation to deliver an honest day's work.

This contractual problem has never been solved satisfactorily. For nonfactory work (and there were no factories on manors), there are two common modern solutions, both with serious disadvantages. One is the solution of artisan manufacture and small-holder agriculture: pay the workers by exchanging their output for money rather than by exchanging their time and effort for money. The other is to make the contract "at will" or for a very short term, with either worker or employer free to terminate it if dissatisfied with the performance of the other. The first solution was widely used in the towns of the Middle Ages, but not on the manors. The second solution made no headway in the custom-bound context of medieval society and is still unpopular, because it implies an ever-present sense of insecurity of employment.

So, resting as it did on an elaborate contract of exchange of labor and numerous other obligations for the right to occupy land and receive protection, the manorial system followed ancient practice in resorting to servile, compulsory labor, to reconcile—however awkwardly and even brutally—the employer's interest in suppressing the workers' shirking with the workers' interest in the security of their employment. The ability of European peasants to evade their obligations to their landlords has become legendary; but, apart from legend, we have little historical evidence of whether the ancient solution produced an industrious and productive peasantry. We can make something, but not too much, of the etymological observation that the meaning of *villein* changed from *peasant* to *scoundrel* (the spelling changed to *villain*)—a transition made easy because, by the fourteenth century, the word had come to mean not only one of base status, but also of base character. Individuals left powerless by oppression have few ways to fight back except by a combination of servility, hypocrisy, and deviousness, and it would not be surprising if life on the manor cultivated these responses in a way akin to a modern prison. We may also make something of the fact that the substitution of small agricultural holdings for manors was accompanied by increases in production, but the increases may have been due as much to the concurrent introduction of better methods of agriculture as to increased effort of the peasants. The conservatism of the manors toward new methods was, in itself, an aspect of the contractual problem: almost all changes in method implied a change in contract, and almost no changes in method were worth the trouble and risk of renegotiating the contract.

3. Manorial Self-Sufficiency and Payment in Money

Another key feature of the medieval manor was the relatively modest use of exchange mediated by money. Obligations payable in money were subordinate to hereditary dues payable in labor or kind. The manor itself was oriented inward. Its economic rhythms were shaped by custom and by authority relationships within its own boundaries, not by the pressures or inducements of prices in markets either nearby or distant.

Like the manor itself, the markets of the Middle Ages had a specific location. Some markets were temporary institutions, perhaps a local town market for the sale of agricultural products on a specific day of the week. But the more famous and important fairs, such as those at Sturbridge (wool), St. Denis (wine), or at Champagne or Lyons, which might convene for several weeks or several months of the year, belonged to the towns rather than to the countryside, and it was the towns and, eventually, the cities which were to become the nodes of capitalism, not the manors.

Within the manor, the fundamental exchange was the trade of labor for the use of land. While this basic exchange was not mediated by money, money was in use within the manor for a number of transactions. For one thing, the serf was subject to a system—sometimes an extensive system—of fees and fines which had to be paid in money and which therefore presupposed some opportunities for the sale of agricultural products, whether to the miller, smith, the lord's men-at-arms, or neighboring townspeople. Payment in money was often required for the use of facilities which were supplied only by the lord of the manor: a mill to grind grain, an oven to bake bread, a wine press, a sawmill, and so forth. Fees were likely also to be charged for the loss of potential labor to the manor when, for example, a daughter married or a son left to serve an apprenticeship. Manorial courts imposed fines for the failure to perform certain customary duties or for other infractions of the rules of the manor. Thus at no point did money totally disappear from use.[14]

There was also trade between the manor and the world outside it. Had some of the products of the manors not been sold outside, "this would have meant that their masters had gone without arms or jewels, had never drunk wine (unless their estates produced it), and for clothes had been content with crude materials woven by the wives of tenants."[15] Somehow, also, when crops failed, money was found or borrowed to buy food from districts better off.

Yet, if we keep in mind that the principal product of the manor was food, and that only some 10 to 20 percent of the consumers of food lived outside the manor, it is evident that only a minor fraction of what the manorial system produced was likely to have been consumed outside it. And, as we have just seen, the fundamental exchange within the manor was not mediated by money.

In almost all the buying and selling which did take place, the sellers were selling the product of their own work and the buyers were buying for their own use. Well-developed market relationships bring into being specialized traders, those who buy the handiwork of others and sell it to someone else. In the Middle Ages, such traders were rare, and only a very small part of the produce of the manors passed through their hands: "The society of this age was certainly not unacquainted with either buying or selling. But it did not, like our own, live by buying or selling."[16]

When examining the sources of the economic growth that followed the Middle Ages, it is hardly possible to overstress the fact that the complexities of the peasants' inherited barter obligations "knyt such a bond" between lord and tenant as to make farming methods extraordinarily conservative. Methods varied from place to place, but very little from year to year, and sometimes not even very much from century to century. They were not responsive to changes in prospective prices, and indeed they were so bound by custom that they responded only very slowly to the discovery of improvements in agricultural methods. The Gordian web of manorial obligations could not be renegotiated to accommodate every passing change in the relative scarcity of land and labor or to allow the introduction of every improvement in agricultural technique. Even so formidable a disaster as the great decline in population in the 1340s and after did not significantly change agricultural methods. The poorer fields were dropped from cultivation for lack of people to work them, but the remainder were cultivated by methods little different from those used when labor was more readily available.

This conservatism precluded the manorial system from adapting to changes in its economic and political environment and eventually proved its undoing. When the pressure for change became irresistible, the change was fundamental: a new agricultural system based on the exchange of money for the use of land superseded the manorial system of exchange of labor for the use of land. In Holland and, later, in England, the rise of the towns increased the demand for food and at the same time offered alternative employment to agricultural labor. The combination of a rise in the potential profits from agriculture with a rise in the difficulty of keeping workers on the land increased the bargaining power of the workers and led landowners and workers to a mutually profitable revolution, beginning with the decline of serfdom.[17] The decline of serfdom meant a decline in servile labor. The lords' demesnes came to be worked for money and the villeins' strips gave way to individual holdings, either rented for money or bought outright. Only when the money agriculture of individual holdings displaced the open-field agriculture of the manorial collective was it possible, first in the Holland of the sixteenth century and then in the France and England of the seventeenth and eighteenth,[18] to introduce changes in agricultural methods which led to an appreciable increase in the food supply, a general improvement in diet, and a rise in the proportion of the population that could live in towns.

The change to a money agriculture solved manorialism's basic problem of lack of adaptability. If a change in agricultural method implied some renegotiation of a rent or wage, renegotiation was feasible, for it concerned primarily a single money term. There was no question of having to renegotiate the whole social contract which governed manorial life, nor of having to share the benefits of the change among an entire manorial community. But as a rule, no renegotiation was required. A change in method which promised to improve productivity simply redounded to the direct and immediate benefit of the landholder who had the authority to make the change, whether the land was the lord's demesne, a tenancy, or a small farm owned by the farmer. It is much easier to understand the immense moral significance of the change from servile to free agricultural labor than to realize that the economic effects of the change to a money agriculture arose, not solely or even principally from an economic superiority of hired labor over servile labor, but from greater flexibility of the terms of agricultural land tenure and from the creation of a class of owner-workers and tenant-workers who were paid by what they produced and undertook responsibility for entrepreneurial decisions and risks. The new system of agriculture was essential to Western growth, for it is hard to believe that the static network of manorial political and social relationships could ever have produced the advances in agriculture which were essential to Western urbanization and economic expansion.

The Towns: Urban Centers

Urban life always existed within medieval society. Even during the Dark Ages following the fall of Rome and before the full flowering of medieval culture, towns survived, even if they are scarcely remembered except as prey for raiding Vikings. Some urban communities existed in response to needs not narrowly economic, serving as administrative centers or for military or ecclesiastical purposes. But whatever their purpose, they were far less self-sufficient than the manor, and of necessity they became centers of trade. If townspeople were to be fed, they had to import food from the countryside and export their own products and services to the countryside. The raw materials of the town's industry—wood, leather, wool, iron—came from the countryside. So did the wood, coal, or peat for fuel. Inevitably, relations based on exchange with the world outside it became far more important to the town than to the manor. As towns grew in the late Middle Ages, so, unavoidably, did trade and, with towns and trade, new economic relationships. Very little of this trade was conducted by barter; it was almost entirely conducted by exchange of money.

The towns were not only centers of trade with the outside world, a trade mediated by money, but trade was overwhelmingly more important to a town household than to a villein's household. As a rule, the town household acquired most of all three of the basic necessities of subsistence from trade: food, clothing, and the house itself. The town household consumed a smaller portion of its own output, and sold a larger portion, than the country household. Since trade presupposes ownership by the traders of whatever they are trading, and since trades based on future delivery or payment are a central subject of contracts, urban life almost inevitably gives much the same central place to property and contract that they occupy among capitalist institutions. It seems quite plain that, as A. P. Usher has pointed out, property and contract are a "response to urban life," not "to capitalist production upon a mechanized basis with segregation of ownership or control of capitalized producer goods in the hands of an employing class."[19] The common etymology of *burgher* and *bourgeois* suggests the intimate association between urbanization and a later emergent capitalism. In short, capitalism, with its peculiar legal and institutional requirements and social relationships, is hardly conceivable without urbanization.

Even in the Middle Ages, urban dwellers possessed some kinds of special privileges and some powers of self-government which were totally different from anything enjoyed on the manor and which were an accompaniment of the totally distinct conditions of urban life. An example of the urban dwellers' nonfeudal privileges is the property interest of the town merchant or artisan in a combined dwelling and shop. That interest was much more akin to the property interest of the lord of the manor than to the temporary holding of the peasant. In fact, given the likelihood that the lord held his manor by enfeoffment of a feudal superior, the interest of the holder of property in town, being outside the feudal system, was even closer to modern concepts of private property than the interest of the lord in his manor. A further example is supplied by the household of the merchant or artisan, considered as an economic unit. It had an autonomy which, like the property interest in the building, was much more like that of the manor than that of the peasant household.

Still, the towns were a part of medieval society, and the fact that they were towns did not make them totally different in spirit from their age. The manor, with its familial, paternalistic, rule-bound structure, was the prototypical feudal economic institution because familial, paternalistic, rule-bound organization of the human community was the feudal ideal, urban as well as rural, religious as well as political. Within the towns, most lines of industry and trade were the exclusive monopolies of the guilds. The church's notions of a "just price" and a "just wage" gave moral sanction to guild regulations covering prices, wages of apprentices and journeymen, standards of product quality and workmanship, admission to the trade, and a duty to ply one's trade at the established prices and wages. The guilds had the political authority to make binding rules and to judge, fine, and punish violations of their rules. They frequently provided benefits for their members in sickness, old age, and at death of the kind we now include under the term "social security." Sometimes they furnished the companies of the town militia. The holding of markets and fairs was permissible only under license, and their conduct was as rigidly regulated as the trade of the guilds themselves.

Despite the consolidation of economic and political roles in the guilds of the towns, the government of the guilds offered nothing like the possibilities for exploitation inherent in the status of the seigneurs in the manorial system. The guilds were undemocratic in that membership was far from open to all aspirants, but guild leaders had no such power to exploit guild members for the leaders' personal benefit as the seigneurs possessed over their villeins. The path of escape was from manor to town, not from town to manor. *Stadluft macht frei,* as the German proverb went.

Also, however closely bound the typical medieval town may have been to the ethos of its times, exceptions existed, and they were important seeds of the future. These were the few towns that were centers of market economies in something approaching the modern sense. They developed principally in Italy, the Low Countries, and Northern Germany, out of exceptional combinations of trading volume and political power. They were the first segment of Western European society to escape the feudal system. We will return to them later in the chapter, when we discuss the medieval city-states.

Security, Risk, Markets, and Calculation in Medieval Life

For all its network of custom, usage, and law, medieval society was far from free of risk, insecurity, and uncertainty. The greatest uncertainty was the success of the year's agricultural efforts; the risks ranged from deficient nutrition to famine. Even the customary feudal dues were a source of insecurity, for while some of the dues were predictable and calculable, others occurred very erratically. The obligation to ransom a feudal lord who was captured in battle is illustrative. The cost could be enormous, and the burden was wholly unpredictable. Obligations incident to the conduct of warfare by the lord or by his feudal superior were similarly uncertain. There was the risk of outright expropriation, either systematic or casual: the rents, dues, and other contributions to which feudal kings and lords were entitled from their vassals and tenants were specified, but the suzerains sometimes had the military power to expropriate or pillage other people's tenants, if not their own. The introduction of governments with the power to levy regular and predictable taxes to meet their financial requirements had to await the emergence of the central monarchies and the subsequent bourgeois revolutions.

But the acceptance of these uncertainties did not prepare the way for the acceptance of the uncertainties of a wholly different kind introduced by market trading. The market's uncertainties involve responses of buyers and competitors, how much the peasant or artisan will be able to realize from the finished work, the prices the merchant can get in the future for stock bought today, and all the consequences of unanticipated changes in supply and demand. The merchant with funds to use in buying and selling faces choices: what to buy, when to buy, when to sell, whether instead to lend some money to others at interest or for a share in someone else's voyage or other enterprise. Which of such choices will result in the most gain or the least loss is, perhaps, the greatest uncertainty of all. In a medieval society where economic roles were inherited, regulated, and priced by custom and law, such choices were alien to the system. The calculation of the most favorable choice verged on the immoral.

We can never quite succeed in attempts to place ourselves inside the minds of the people of other cultures or even of the ancestors of our own culture. Thus we can hardly grasp the degree to which it was alien, in the Middle Ages, for anyone to guide present economic activity by the deliberate calculation of future consequences. In both country and town, what one did for a living was what one had done for years past and expected to continue to do, in the same way and on the same terms, until death ended the round of sowing and reaping. Rules as old as the Old Testament made it prudent to lay aside the surpluses of a good year for the deficits of the lean years, and deliberate accumulation of wealth through industry and thrift was an aim as much of the peasant as of the town artisan. But thrift was itself an ancient rule of prudence—a matter of coping with risk by rote rather than by intelligent calculation.

The very idea of varying and changing what one did in response to calculations of future consequences and present conditions of supply and demand lay outside the normal pattern of medieval economic life. *Calculation* is the crucial word here. The possibility of calculation, of assessing prospective magnitudes of cost and revenue and the probability of alternative outcomes in a novel enterprise, of profiting from judicious buying and selling (how could it be done if both prices were "just"?) rather than from diligent service to one's lord or from industriously plying one's trade, was wholly alien to the customary order of feudal society. To the naked eye, the merchant looked like an idler who did no useful work, spinning not, nor sowing either, but profiting hugely from the sober industry of others. The feudal courts functioned to enforce feudal dues and feudal rules. Merchants' trading contracts were beyond the pale of feudal society and outside the feudal conception of justice. They were unenforceable by the medieval legal procedures used in the English royal courts; indeed, in England, the king's courts did not fully come to terms with the enforcement of merchants' contracts until the time of Lord Mansfield, in the eighteenth century. The amassing of wealth through skill and luck in the calculation of future consequences, through the discovery of new customers and new sources of goods, and through the artful sharing and hedging of risks transcended medieval understanding and had no legitimate place in the medieval system.

It was not simply the method of dealing with future contingencies by the application of calculation to the business of merchants which was beyond medieval understanding. There was a similar lack of understanding of the usefulness of calculation in dealing with contingencies when they occurred. The application of calculation to such matters as varying methods of cultivation or artisan production to accommodate changes in the available supply of labor—changes which became drastic beginning in the middle of the fourteenth century—simply escaped medieval economics. No matter what, people tried to go on doing the same old things in the same old ways. In some degree, what we now regard as inexorable economic laws eventually compelled custom and law to adjust themselves to the resources available, though in just what degree is currently a subject of scholarly controversy. It is clear that the first reaction of medieval lawmakers to a shortage of labor, which drove up wages, was to enact new laws that more stringently controlled wages and that prohibited laborers from leaving their masters or their trades. Thus in 1350, three years after the first of the major fourteenth-century outbreaks of the plague, the English Parliament enacted the Statute of Labourers,[20] which required servants and laborers to be "content" with what they had received five years earlier. It seems never to have occurred to anyone that the system might have been more productive had it assigned new priorities for the use of a reduced supply of labor, cultivating more land less intensively perhaps, or that the plague could in any way have been made less disastrous than it was.

Ironically, in seeking security through a life wholly regulated by custom, usage, and law, in preference to the insecurity of unregulated trade, medieval society appreciably *reduced* the security of its people. Much of what trading occurred at negotiated prices was born of crisis—famine and war, in particular. Poorly adapted as the political and economic institutions of medieval society were to any kind of unregulated trading, they were even worse adapted to unregulated trading in a crisis. These trades were not a balanced exchange of goods for goods, mediated by money and with the cost of imports regularly paid by receipts from exports. The importing took place out of a short-term need that could not be denied, at times of financial stress due to bad crops, no crops, or war. Buying thus implied borrowing. But the feudal economy did not encourage the development of credit. The normal operations of the relatively self-sufficient manors and towns did not create large foreign-trade balances, whether in the form of debts owed to the manor or town by outsiders or in the form of a store of gold or silver. There was no prospect that a loan to buy grain in a lean year could readily be repaid out of balances likely to arise in a good year; in a good year, there would be very little trade to create balances. The church's strictures on the taking of interest no doubt reduced both the number of people willing to lend money and the likelihood of their being repaid if they did so, thus further constricting the supply of credit. It is no wonder that trade was not always the consequence of a failed crop; often the consequence was famine.[21] Efforts to avoid injuring the stability of the network of feudal relationships increased the hardships wrought by the disasters which inevitably occurred, with the ultimate result that the feudal system, like the proverbial oak that would not bend with the wind, met its end in part through its own rigidity.

The Starting Point: The Middle Ages

Of course, no one who lives in the late twentieth century can afford to be understood as ridiculing medieval efforts to cope with the inherent insecurities of economic life through law, custom, political control, and invocations of social justice. Famines still occur, almost always in consequence of failure to improve sufficiently on the medieval mechanisms for acquiring, transporting, and distributing food for the famine-stricken areas. The real embarrassment is deeper. The medieval viewpoint shielded people from the painful psychological consequences that attend a belief that personal disasters may very well be attributable to one's own miscalculations, and it gave a clanking chivalry and a luxurious religious hierarchy the comfort of thinking that their oppressions served the cause of justice instead of being, as they were, outrageously crude banditry. The embarrassment stems from the realization that later societies have sometimes been drawn to ideologies that, like the medieval, free the many of responsibility and the leaders of guilt.

The Towns and Political Rights

Typically, medieval towns obtained a measure of political autonomy by the purchase of charters from their suzerains. The charters were negotiated, not always without violence, and they conferred varying degrees of self-government, sometimes to the point of virtual freedom from feudal allegiance. These lines of development were possible only in the countries which failed to establish strong central monarchies. In France, England, and Spain, the towns tended to ally themselves with the rising monarchies in the struggles between the monarch and the feudal nobles, with the political result of reducing the towns' feudal obligations to the losers. But the establishment of central monarchies substituted an even more formidable political authority over the towns for the authority of the feudal lords. It did not liberate the townsmen. That required, in seventeenth-century England and eighteenth-century France, successful resort to arms against the monarchy.

The issues in the multiple struggles between the towns and their feudal superiors varied with place and time. The towns had a financial interest in gaining control of their own powers of taxation and arranging the remission of feudal dues into fixed payments. They had an interest also in gaining control of the town's trading monopolies: the guilds, internally, and the power to trade with other towns and to hold market fairs. They sought their own courts, in substitution for the lord's justice. Often, however, struggles between towns and their feudal superiors were not simply matters of financial interest. In Germany and the Low Countries, from the sixteenth century on, the Protestant Reformation furnished the high passions for much bloodletting between towns and their sovereigns, and in Italy, local factional struggles for town and regional control were overlaid by competing alliances with outside interveners from Spain, France, and Austria.

What is missing is any indication of a conscious desire on the part of the towns to end the rigid political control of trade that was characteristic of the feudal system. The merchants and guilds wanted control of taxation and trade to be in their own hands: they did not want an end to taxation or the control of trade. Economic organization independent of political control was conceptually as alien to the towns of the Middle Ages as to the manors. In England, the House of Commons was elected by townsmen (women were not allowed to vote) and small landowners, and its control of the power to tax was a substantial issue in the civil wars of the seventeenth century. In England also, the power to grant monopolies over trade was a bone of contention between Crown and Parliament—not as to the propriety of its existence, but as to which power holders should exercise it. In France, history took a different turn. The kings gained the power to tax without the consent of the Estates General by the expedient of exempting the feudal nobility and the clergy from the taxes, and they shattered the French national market into some thirty or more regional markets by internal tariffs and endless grants of local monopolies to towns and guilds—interventions in economic affairs in which the French bourgeoisie were willing partners. In the end, the French economy they created was the stage set for the fall of the monarchy in the French Revolution, but by then the Middle Ages were long past.

Medieval Technology

Much of the discontinuity of technology resulting from the barbarian invasions and the fall of Rome seems to have arisen from a simple loss of markets for luxurious products in troubled times. The element of continuity was stronger in the Eastern Roman Empire, which survived in slowly diminishing vigor until 1453, than in the West. But in the Mediterranean, the contacts between the West and the Eastern Roman Empire were never broken, and there Roman technology continued to be available.

There was not much loss of demand for the products of the iron industry, which had been a Northern European specialty even in Roman times. If anything, brigandage and wars made the products of the iron-masters more essential after the fall of Rome than before. One common product of the smith, the horseshoe, was a Roman invention which never went out of use. From the eighth to the thirteenth centuries, there was a gradual expansion of iron production in Styria, Carinthia, Franconia, Westphalia, Swabia, Hungary, the Basque provinces, many parts of France, and the Forest of Dean, in England. In the fourteenth century, water-driven bellows for the smelters' furnaces were introduced.

As early as the eighth century, foundries began casting bronze church bells. Five or six centuries later, Western experience in casting church bells supplied the skills needed for casting cannon, both in bronze and iron. The waterwheel was applied, once again, to the hammers used in forging the blooms.

Medieval chemistry is remembered for the alchemists' goal of transmuting base metals into gold. But in its less ambitious moments it also produced soaps, paints, varnishes, dyes, sulphur, and saltpeter. With one exception, drugs were almost entirely an Islamic monopoly, and the less said of medieval medicine, the better. The exception was alcohol. Discovered by distillation in Italy around 1100, it became the basis of distilled liquors so rapidly that in the next century the first regulations relating to drunkenness and other aspects of alcoholic consumption were enacted.

In the making of ceramics and glass, the Roman methods were carried forward into medieval times and improved to the point of a technology foɪ making stained glass in the high-medieval cathedrals that still escapes duplication. In the making of textiles, especially in Italy, there were appreciable advances on the Roman heritage. In architecture, which became primarily religious, the transition from Roman to Romanesque to Gothic is well known.

In agriculture, by far the largest industry of all, the basic tools seem not to have lost ground through the Dark Ages, but the organization of agriculture was completely revamped by the introduction of the manorial system. Even in Roman times, the Northern Europeans had developed a heavy, iron-shod plow suited to turning over the sod common in Northern Europe, and it was adequate for cultivating areas across Europe from the tenth century, or earlier. The introduction of the padded horse collar in the twelfth century is looked upon as a major advance, because it led, over four hundred years, to the substitution of horses for oxen in plowing, mainly because of their greater speed.

By most standards, the most formidable technological achievement of the high Middle Ages was the invention of the clock in the late thirteenth century. The clock, with its gear train and escapement, is important technologically because, in the pursuit of ever more accurate timekeepers, the clockmakers' shops became the research universities of Western knowledge of the mechanical arts, of friction, of precision metalwork, and of the varying behavior of metals and other materials at different temperatures and under different loads. It also had a more subtle social importance, cultivating the sense of time crucial to the organized collaboration of large numbers of people.

It is possible that an even more fundamental development was the emergence of Western interest in optics, for two optical instruments—the telescope and the microscope—contributed mightily to the Western scientific revolution of the seventeenth century. Medieval interest in optics was marked by the invention of spectacles in Italy. A sermon preached in 1306 fixes the date at 1286 or a little later (the friar's phrase was "not yet twenty years since"), but Friar Giordano did not tell us who invented spectacles, or where. Optics had Greek origins and was developed by Islamic writers of the eleventh century whose works became available in Latin translations in the twelfth century. But the pace of optical development was slow. The first spectacles were convex lenses and corrected the farsightedness of the aged, presbyopia. It took more than a century and a half for concave lenses to be used to correct myopia and another century again to combine a concave lens with a convex lens to make a telescope, and then a microscope. By that time, it was the seventeenth century, and their maker was the optician Galileo.

Over a period of a thousand years, from the fall of Rome in the fifth century to the beginnings of the modern age in the fifteenth, one might have expected appreciable changes in Western technology, and some occurred. Toward the end, these changes, especially those spurred by the urgencies of life and death in battle, accelerated. We can trace their development in armor, from the chain mail of the thirteenth century, to chain mail reinforced by breastplates and helmets in the fourteenth, to the elaborate suits of plate armor introduced in the fifteenth century, just in time to succumb to the introduction of firearms.

It is never easy to make an overall assessment of anything so diverse as medieval technology. Advances in technology were made by artisan invention, for there was no medieval equivalent of the modern scientific community or the industrial research laboratory. Over centuries, ways of cultivating the land, logging, mining, smelting, spinning, weaving, building, and making pots, bricks, and glass changed, but so slowly that, as with the hands of a clock, one could hardly notice the movement. The pace quickened from the thirteenth century on, during the centuries when feudalism began to lose its grip on Western life to towns with institutions developing outside the feudal system.

No doubt the Westerners of the First Crusade, in 1095, were impressed with the relative luxury of the Byzantine court and the life-style of some of their Saracen adversaries, as were the Spaniards who, nearly four hundred years later, finally succeeded in expelling the Moors from Spain. But how does one compare the technology of the Alhambra to a Gothic cathedral, or a Damascene blade to one from Milan? Islam was surely in advance of the West in having a decimal number system, and the Islamic pharmacopeia was sought by Westerners unfortunate enough to need medication. But even the Islamic remedies were folk medicine; there was little inkling of modern theories of the causes and cures of disease. What the West's feudal system had within itself, in its very diffusion of power and its capacity to create towns and cities outside itself and different in their fundamental framework from feudal institutions, was a capacity for development into a successor society which accelerated technological change to a rate which eventually left other societies far behind, including the West's own feudal antecedents.

The European City-States

There were, here and there, towns which became major centers of trade and which escaped the restrictions of feudal society well before their neighbors. These were the politically autonomous city-states, such as Venice, Genoa, Florence, the Hansa towns of the North Sea and the Baltic, and the Dutch cities.[22] The extent of self-government which eventually emerged and persisted for long periods of time in these European cities and city-states was without an exact parallel in other cultures. The closest precedents were European, the Greek city-states which flourished from the sixth to the fourth century B.C. Nothing very similar can be found in the great civilizations of Asia or the Muslim world. As Max Weber pointed out, there have not been "cities in the sense of a unitary community" outside the West.[23] And one of Britain's most distinguished economists, Sir John Hicks, explains the city-state as a uniquely Occidental phenomenon, a "gift of the Mediterranean," which was at once an artery of trade and the locus of numerous "readily defensible" city sites.[24]

The city-states of Holland and the Hanseatic League would no doubt quarrel with a reading of history which makes them a gift of the Mediterranean, and it may not be literally true that the city-state is uniquely European. But there is no doubt that the European city-states were major centers of the growing mercantile trade in Europe from the thirteenth century until the full emergence of the centralized monarchies in the sixteenth century, and they continued to be important for some time after that.

There is little evidence that their political or economic principles favored freedom to trade without political interference. Politically, they tended to be dominated by merchant families to whom trading rights and monopolies were the natural rewards of political power. But these trading monopolies were opposed by rival merchants who were intended to be excluded from the trade and who were supported in many cases by the influence and power of their own rival city-states. Unlike China and the ancient empires, the Europe of the late medieval city-states and the early monarchies came to the age of discovery without a central authority strong enough to check the determination of its merchants to gain access to profitable trading opportunities, even though some satrap or other had forbidden such access or claimed it as a private preserve. The central authorities which eventually emerged did not take the form of a single monolithic empire, but of a group of nation-states which continued, among themselves, the early city-state competition for trade.

A Qualification: The Pluralist Aspects of Feudalism

Whatever their shortcomings, Western European and probably Japanese feudalism seem to have contained the seeds of social arrangements suited to sustained economic growth. The medieval development of towns and a small class of professional merchants and traders is one of the threads which can be traced from the Dark Ages to the present. But there is another aspect of feudalism which may be even more fundamental to economic development—a sense of pluralism.

In essence, feudalism was the parallel structuring of military authority and land tenure. That is, land was conceived as belonging to the sovereign, who parceled it out to his military chieftains to maintain and support them in exchange for their military services; they in turn allotted some or all of their holdings to their subordinates in the same kind of exchange of land for military service. In the East, this method of supporting the military structure was usually carried only to the point of giving the soldiers a life interest in land. Their tenure did not pass to their heirs; upon each soldier's death his land was redistributed among his military successors. In the West and in Japan, however, the chieftain's tenure of the land, along with the obligation to perform military service, stayed in the family.[25]

The most striking political effect of Western and Japanese feudalism was to create a plurality of power centers, each combining major or minor military strength with the economic base necessary to its support. Braudel is probably right in thinking that the right of inheritance was essential to this process.[26] The reason is that if a chieftain had only a life interest in his land holdings, as he grew older the more ambitious and perceptive of his immediate subordinates would tend to attach their long-term loyalties not to him, but to the higher authority that would redistribute his holdings upon his death. The effect would have been to lessen the growth of loyalties to feudal vassals and strengthen loyalties to the sovereign. Like capitalism, feudalism evidently belongs to the class of societies with plural hereditary power centers, and it is tempting to believe that capitalism first arose in such societies in Europe and Japan because hereditary property and a substantial measure of personal autonomy (albeit only among those in the top strata of society) were already established institutions.

As a matter of general political philosophy, the most comprehensive concept of sovereignty treats the personal sovereign or the state as absolute owner of all her, his, or its subjects and of all the property in the realm. Just such a concept was effectively applied in Islam, China, India, the more ancient empires, and in nineteenth-century German philosophy. To believers in this most comprehensive concept of sovereignty, feudalism was no more than anarchy. The kings and princes who functioned at the apex of a feudal pyramid—and in Europe there were many independent feudal hierarchies—were not so much true sovereigns as they were individuals who, by contract with other individuals, their vassals, had established certain rights and obligations. There remained a dream of a Holy Roman Emperor at the apex, but it was little more than a dream. Worse still, the obligations were mutual, in that the king or other lord had obligations to the vassal, such as the obligation to aid in case of attack and the obligations to protect the vassal's holdings during the minority of an heir and to transfer the holdings to the heir when he attained his majority. The feudal concept of a two-way contractual relationship between sovereign and vassals is, again, analogous in a general way to the later concept, characteristic of capitalist societies, of government as a contract between the state and the governed and dependent for its legitimacy on the consent of the governed.

To catch the full force of this contractual system of obligation as it applied in the Middle Ages, the term *feudalism* has been extended to include the manorial system of holding land in exchange for servile, nonmilitary services. In this sense, the manorial system extended the sphere of contractual obligation beyond military feudalism, so that it reached serfs and villeins who held land in exchange for nonmilitary services and dues. The early towns also had feudal suzerains to whom they owed various obligations and dues.

In a society which followed Eastern precedent in conceiving of all its people and property as belonging to the sovereign, feudalism might well have taken the form of a transfer to the military vassals of the sovereign's absolute and unlimited powers over the land and its inhabitants. In Western Europe, however, the inhabitants carved out, by custom, usage, and charter, definitions of their own obligations to their overlords and statements of their own rights and privileges, akin to the charters which defined their immediate lords' own relationships to their feudal superiors.

There is thus a political perspective from which feudalism can be seen as an antecedent of capitalism, logically as well as temporally, in that feudalism preceded capitalism in rejecting the notion of an absolute state in favor of the notion of a state with powers and limits determined by agreement with its inhabitants and with other autonomous social institutions. The military power needed to maintain this rejection may very well have depended on the institution of inheritance of the estates of the intermediate military chieftains. In the interest of understanding Western sources of wealth, it is worth adding that life tenure, of the sort more common in the military feudalisms of the East, has the economically adverse effect of giving the life tenant every incentive for short-term overexploitation and no incentive for reinvesting income in long-term improvements. This appears to be one more instance of institutional arrangements which served to diffuse political power and authority and also turned out to be economically more efficient than the probable alternative.

The Starting Point: The Middle Ages

The Decline of Feudalism

Feudal institutions were directed to security and stability rather than to change and growth. As Western society moved from stability to growth, its institutions and classes changed their relationships with each other. Some old institutions and classes rose in both absolute and relative importance, others declined, and new institutions were introduced. This process as a whole will be easier to follow after we have explored the expansion of trade and the rise of the merchant class in the next chapter. What is worth noting here is that the stability-oriented society of the feudal period owed its decline directly to innovation of a sort that could not be merely repressed, for it was an innovation in the art of war. Feudalism was at heart a military compact between king and vassal, and the immediate cause of its demise was a line of military development which destroyed the military basis of the compact. In the latter part of the fifteenth century, the military capability of the feudal chivalry entered a period of rapid decline, and the feudal castle became obsolete as a military stronghold. Of these two developments, the most direct factor in the decline of military feudalism was the first: a loss of military capacity on the part of the armored cavalry fielded by the feudal lords.

The backbone of military strength changed from the feudal chivalry to professional armies that combined infantry (pikemen, crossbowmen, musketeers) with siege artillery and cavalry. In its Italian origins, the change was not a simple question of the introduction of gunpowder. It was a matter, first, of the effectiveness of an infantry formed by town militias, reinforced by crossbowmen using a new weapon whose production created an armaments industry in Italy. Then, as the coordination of crossbowmen, pikemen, and cavalry came to exceed the skill of part-time soldiers, there was a shift to professional armies.[27]

If the immediate cause of the decline of feudalism was a change in methods of warfare, few would accept as mere coincidence the fact that the successful development of the answer to feudal military power took place in Italy, which led Europe in the rise of the towns, the development of commerce, the urgency of its need for protection of its commercial wealth from the feudal chivalry, and its ability to pay for a new military technology. Here and there, an occasional earlier battle had foreshadowed the end of the military domination of the feudal militias. Swiss pikemen had defeated a force of German knights at Sempach in 1387, and English longbowmen had established their superiority over French knights at Crecy (1346) and Agincourt (1415), during the Hundred Years' War. But it was in Italy, in the late fourteenth century, that cities engaged the professional armies which supplied the model for a new military system.

Further north, in France, the change took place late in the Hundred Years War between France and England. In the fourteenth century, at the beginning of the Hundred Years' War, the military power of the French kings rested in great part on the feudal militia, serving pursuant to feudal obligations. The subtle change in the balance of military power from an armored chivalry to coordinated operations by several types of infantry and cavalry took place during that war and included the technological change to guns, large and small. By the end of the fifteenth century, France and the other nation-states were regularly drawing their armies from paid professional soldiers rather than from the feudal levies.[28] The military services of the feudal lords and knights, in exchange for which they held their manors, were no longer crucial to military power.

Besides the shift from a feudal to a professional army, there was another important aspect of the feudal lords' loss of military power and the substitution of central governments with a practically effective monopoly of coercive force. Before the introduction of siege cannon, the lords' castles had supplied them with fortified bases from which they could defy their feudal superiors almost with impunity, for it was seldom worth the trouble to assert superior authority if its assertion meant besieging the vassal's castle. Hence, in its political effect, the medieval castle was a powerful force for the diffusion of authority. Richard Bean puts the importance of castles this way:

> The existence of numerous castles made it possible for quite small regions successfully to resist much larger opponents. Nominal feudal superiors and foreign invaders faced the same handicaps: Very often it simply cost more to conquer a region than the region was worth. Castles had to be starved out one by one, and the besieging army had to be fairly large ... But a large besieging army was difficult to sustain for months at a time in one place because foragers from the invading army quickly stripped bare the area around the besieged castle. The result was that the besiegers often starved faster than the besieged and the siege failed.[29]

The introduction of siege cannon ended the military usefulness of the castle at about the same time that the introduction of professional armies ended the dominance of the feudal cavalry in field operations. By the early part of the sixteenth century, ways had been found to build fortresses resistant to cannon fire. But just as it had become beyond the financial resources of feudal barons to hire companies of cannoneers, so the construction of the new fortresses was beyond the means of most nobles. Also, by the sixteenth century, the royal authorities in France and England, at least, were strong enough to see to it that members of the nobility did not build themselves modern fortresses.

The changes had all sorts of consequences—economic, political, and social. For example, the new central armies presented a new version of an old question: How were they to be financed? Under the feudal system, kings were expected to support themselves from the revenues of the royal manors and from the feudal dues owed by their vassals. Taxes over and above the customary feudal dues were looked upon as a breach of the basic social contract, not to be allowed without the consent of the vassals. As a result, in late fifteenth-century France, and a little later in England, the additional revenues required to support the new central armies had to be raised outside the feudal system—that is, from the merchant class and from the guilds of artisans.[30]

The French kings achieved the power to levy a *taille* (a direct tax), *aides* (a form of sales tax), and the *gabelle* (from the salt monopoly) by the expedient of granting exemption to the nobility and clergy. The English kings, being unsuccessful in establishing their own power to tax without the consent of Parliament, had even stronger incentives to rely on revenues from monopolies. Thus in both England and France, not only did the basic feudal obligation to provide military service lose its military value, but the succeeding military system was financed from outside the feudal system, leaving the remaining feudal dues of only secondary political importance.

Important though these changes in methods of warfare were, they were not the only factor in the erosion of the feudal system. Of equal importance was the decay of the barter economy of the manors and the substitution of a money agriculture for feudal villeinage based on the barter of labor for land. The manorial system of servile labor gave way slowly. The villeins first developed an inheritable property interest in the manor, in the form of an expectation that their tenure would be renewed from year to year and would pass to their heirs—upon the payment of an entry fee, perhaps, but still the expectation was that it would pass. At first peasants could not sell their interest; hence, leaving the manor meant abandoning a small holding that might have been in the family for several generations and for which the present tenant had probably paid a substantial entry fee. This element of forfeiture made it harder for the tenants on the manor to resort to exit as a protest against the lord's exactions. Whenever they could, the peasants bought themselves free of their feudal obligations to their seigneurs, sometimes by lump-sum payments and sometimes by substituting a periodic money rent. This liquidation of feudal dues and duties, in combination with the acquisition by the peasants of a saleable interest in the land they cultivated—a long process, rather than an event, that occurred earlier in Holland, England, and France than elsewhere—marked the end of manorialism and the substitution of a money agriculture, with a large small-holder sector coexisting with the surviving estate agriculture. The change amounted to a revolution (albeit a slow one) in the economic organization of agriculture, opening the way, as we have seen, to the adoption of improved agricultural methods, an increase in the food supply, and the eventual shift from a rural to a predominantly urban society.

One must also take account of the fact that the latter half of the fourteenth century was an age of disasters which in themselves would have disrupted any social equilibrium: plague, wars, crop failure, and above all an unprecedented drop in population. These disasters can be interpreted as grim solutions to population pressures built up by the completion of a process of land settlement that had been going forward in Europe for four hundred years or longer. The feudal system, its prices and obligations bound in a network of perpetual contracts, was not well suited either to give warning of, or to adapt to, fundamental changes in the relative scarcity of labor and land.

Western Europe accommodated to all these events by changing the system. Having changed military technology in ways that transformed the political role of its landed aristocracy from that of semi-independent feudal baron to that of politician and courtier, Western Europe changed the mode of landholding to one that substituted money agriculture for servile agriculture and, more than incidentally, started a steady decline in the proportion of the population required for agriculture and a steady rise in the proportion of the population that dwelt in towns and cities.

As we shall see in chapter 3, the period after the mid-fourteenth century was an age in which the tides of change were running so strong that they could hardly have missed washing away the armored chivalry and their castles, along with the society to which they gave political and economic form and structure. This age of disasters was at the same time an age of growth of trade—of autonomous enterprises dealing across the boundaries of local authority, local religion, and local custom; of a merchant class conscious of its own interests and at once fearful, envious, and contemptuous of the aristocracies of the sword and the cloth. It was an age of new knowledge and technology learned on trading voyages and on the Crusades, or carried by refugees from the Islamic conquest of the Eastern Mediterranean. It was, in short, too much of an age of change for a social system based on stability.

Conclusion

The Europe which embarked on the road to wealth in the fifteenth century left behind a society that possessed many features deeply embedded in human history. It was a society that lived, worked, and traded by custom and rule, not by strategy or calculation. Its political and economic order, whether in manor or guild, had its roots in the father figure, the family, the tribe, and the household. Political and economic leadership was one and the same. The authority and obligations of king and seigneur were those of the shepherd over his flock, the father over his household. It was an age easy to romanticize, for its institutions reflected the ancient human yearning for the kind of security offered by the fundamental human social organization, the family itself.

Yet it nourished within itself the beginnings of a new order. The society of the Middle Ages gave high status to adventure, whether the travels of a Marco Polo, the pilgrimage or Crusade to the Holy Land, or the myths of knight errantry. Its political pluralism, arising from the failure of Charlemagne's successors to establish a consolidated political power in Western Europe and the eventual disintegration of real political authority into the hands of a multitude of local barons, provided opportunities for experimenting with new modes of trade and warfare. It also opened the door to the development of towns and cities, some few of which were chartered as virtually independent entities outside the feudal system.

From the tenth century on, the history of Europe included a gradual increase in urbanization, with its associated growth of trade and development of a merchant class. The advances in architecture, art, music, literature, crafts, and warfare that we know as the high medieval period came during this same period of development of towns and trade. Beginning with the great plague of 1347, this long period of progress gave way to a century of disasters—disasters epitomized in a sharp decline in population. By the time the decline in population was reversed and Europe began a recovery from this time of troubles, changes in the technology of warfare had effectively transferred political power from the feudal barons to the central monarchies, and feudalism had lost most of its political meaning. Then, in a process spread over some two centuries (more in some places and less in Holland and England), the feudal organization of agriculture, based on barter of labor for land, gave way to an agriculture based on money and small holdings. By 1600, when the population of Europe had again reached the level of 1347, feudalism had yielded to a new economic order characterized by money trade rather than by barter, with prices negotiated between buyer and seller rather than fixed by custom or law. But that is the subject of chapter 3.

NOTES

1. R. H. Tawney, *Religion and the Rise of Capitalism* (New York: Harcourt, Brace & Company, 1926 [1937]), p. 57, n. 104, p. 302.

2. Ibid.

3. "Now the world between the fifteenth and eighteenth centuries consisted of one vast peasantry, where between 80% and 90% of people lived from the land and from nothing else." Fernand Braudel, *The Structure of Everyday Life*, trans. Sian Reynolds (New York: Harper & Row, 1981), p. 49.

4.

> If one wants to study and understand human society in the past one must realize that until about a hundred years ago it was predominantly agricultural. Such a large proportion of human effort went into farming that other economic possibilities were considerably restricted. A still greater handicap was the concentration on cereals and consequent dependence on the varying yield of one particular crop, reminiscent of the monocultures of tropical and sub-tropical lands. The foundations of European society rested on a narrow and dangerously unstable basis which men have contrived to broaden and strengthen in the course of centuries.

B. H. Slicher Van Bath, *The Agrarian History of Western Europe*, trans. Olive Ordish (London: Edward Arnold, 1966), pp. 3–4.

5. Braudel, *Structure of Everyday Life*, pp. 51–52.

6. Joseph R. Strayer, "Feudalism in Western Europe," in Rushton Coulborn, ed., *Feudalism in History* (Princeton: Princeton University Press, 1966), p. 16.

7. In Strayer's words:

> Public authority had become a private possession. Everyone expects the possessor of a court to make a profit out of it, and everyone knows that the eldest son of the court-holder will inherit this profitable right, whatever his qualifications for the work. On the other hand, any important accumulation of private property almost inevitably becomes burdened with public duties. The possessor of a great estate must defend it, police it, maintain roads and bridges and hold a court for his tenants. Thus lordship has both economic and political aspects; it is less than sovereignty, but more than private property.

Ibid., p. 17.

8. Marc Bloch, "The Rise of Dependent Cultivation and Seignorial Institutions," in M. M. Postan, ed., *The Cambridge Economic History of Europe*, vol. 1, *The Agrarian Life of the Middle Ages* (Cambridge: Cambridge University Press), chap. 6, pp. 235–36.

9. For an account of the early technology, see M. S. Drower, "Water-Supply, Irrigation, and Agriculture," in Charles Singer, E. J. Holmyard, and A. R. Hall (eds.), *A History of Technology* (New York: Oxford University Press, 1954), vol. 1, chap. 19, pp. 520–57.

10. William H. McNeill, *The Rise of the West* (Chicago: University of Chicago Press, 1963), pp. 33–34.

11. Wittfogel attributed special importance to the integrative effect of work on irrigation projects in the formation of his "hydraulic societies," which included most ancient civilizations except the Greek and Roman. See K. Wittfogel, *Oriental Despotism: A Comparative Study of Total Power* (New Haven: Yale University Press, 1957). Cf. R. McAdams, *The Evolution of Urban Society, Early Mesopotamia and Prehistoric Mexico* (Chicago: University of Chicago Press, 1966). He maintains that irrigation was not a necessary condition to the emergence of these early despotisms. For a summary of descriptions of ancient civilizations as instances of state socialism, see Igor Shafavarevich, *The Socialist Phenomenon* (New York: Harper & Row, 1980), pp. 132–92.

12. Bloch, "Rise of Dependent Cultivation," pp. 235–36.

13. Tawney, *Religion and the Rise of Capitalism*, p. 58.

14. See M. M. Postan, "The Rise of a Money Economy," *Economic History Review* 14 (1944), as reprinted in E. M. Carus-Wilson, *Essays in Economic History* (London: Edward Arnold, 1954), pp. 1–12. According to Postan, "from the point of view of English history, and even from that of medieval and Anglo-Saxon history, the rise of a money economy in the sense of its first appearance has no historical meaning. Money was in use when documented history begins, and its rise cannot be adduced as an explanation of any later phenomenon." (P. 5.)

15. Marc Bloch, *Feudal Society*, vol. 1 (London: Routledge, 1961), p. 67.

16. Ibid.

17. See R. H. Hilton, *The Decline of Serfdom in Medieval England* (London: Macmillan, 1970).

18. See Douglass C. North and Robert Paul Thomas, *The Rise of the Western World: A New Economic History* (Cambridge: Cambridge University Press, 1973), pp. 143, 151.

19. A. P. Usher, *A History of Mechanical Inventions* (Cambridge: Harvard University Press, 1954), p. 32.

20. 25 Edw. III, st. 2 (1350).

21. See Braudel, *Structure of Everyday Life*, p. 74:

... France, by any standards a privileged country, is reckoned to have experienced 10 *general* famines during the tenth century; 26 in the eleventh; 2 in the twelfth; 4 in the fourteenth; 7 in the fifteenth; 13 in the sixteenth; 11 in the seventeenth and 16 in the eighteenth. While one cannot guarantee the accuracy of this eighteenth-century calculation, the only risk it runs is of over-optimism, because it omits the hundreds and hundreds of *local* famines (in Maine, in 1739, 1752, 1770 and 1785 for example), and in the south-west in 1628, 1631, 1643, 1662, 1694, 1698, 1709 and 1713. They did not always coincide with the more widespread disasters.

22. See J. R. Hicks, *A Theory of Economic History* (New York: Oxford University Press, 1969). Hicks develops an interesting "economic theory of the city state" in chap. 4 of this little volume. Cf. Max Weber, *General Economic History* (New York: First Collier Books Ed., 1961), p. 260. See also the discussion of cities and their relationships to the nation-states of the sixteenth century in Fernand Braudel, *The Mediterranean*, vol. 1 (New York: Harper & Row, 1972), pp. 312–52.

23. "[O]utside the occident there have not been cities in the sense of a unitary community. In the middle ages, the distinguishing characteristic was the possession of its own law and court and an autonomous administration of whatever extent." Weber, *General Economic History*, p. 261.

24.

The fact that European civilization has passed through a city-state phase is the principal key to the divergence between the history of Europe and the history of Asia. The reason why it has done so is mainly geographical. The city state of Europe is a gift of the Mediterranean. In the technical conditions that have obtained through the greater part of recorded history, the Mediterranean has been outstanding as a highway of contact, between countries of widely different productive capacities; further, it is rich in pockets and crannies, islands, promontories, and valleys, which in the same conditions have been readily defensible. Asia has little to offer that is at all comparable.

Hicks, *A Theory of Economic History*, p. 235.

25. Fernand Braudel, *The Wheels of Commerce*, trans. Sian Reynolds (New York: Harper & Row, 1982), pp. 595–96. Braudel finds the seeds of capitalism more specifically in the economic entities which grew autonomous amid the quasi-independent political entities of feudalism: "In Japan ... the seeds of capitalism had been sown by the Ashikaga period (1368–1573) with the coming into being of economic and social forces independent of the state (whether the guilds, long-distance trade, free towns, merchant groups who were often answerable to no one)." (P. 589.)

26. Ibid. Braudel attributes the importance of inheritability in the origins of capitalism to the need for accumulation (p. 599) and to the need for a target pool of wealth which the rising merchant class could take over from the declining feudal nobility (pp. 594–95). In the American experience, the part played by accumulation was less impressive than it may have been in France; and the displacement of a feudal nobility by a rising merchant class was a nonevent.

27. William H. McNeill, *The Pursuit of Power* (Chicago: University of Chicago Press, 1982), pp. 73–77. Richard Bean, in "War and the Birth of the Nation State," *Journal of Economic History* 33, no. 1 (March 1973): 203–21, put the same point as follows: "In 1400 A.D. no prince could prevail against any substantive portion of his feudal barons unless he enjoyed the active support of a similar number of the barons. In 1600 A.D. most princes could be confident that their standing army would suppress all but the most widespread rebellions." (P. 203.)

28. McNeill, *Pursuit of Power*, p. 81: "When the Hundred Years War (1337–1453) began, the French king still relied primarily on the infeudated chivalry of his kingdom to meet and repel the English invaders." And:

[B]y the time the French monarchy began to recover from the squalid demoralization induced by the initial English victories and widespread disaffection among the nobility, an expanded tax base allowed the king to collect enough hard cash to support an increasingly formidable armed force. This is the army which expelled the English from France by 1453 after a series of successful campaigns ... The kingdom of France thus emerged on the map of Europe between 1450 and 1478, centralized as never before and capable of maintaining a standing professional army of about 25,000 men year in and year out. (Pp. 82–83.)

29. Bean, "War and the Birth of the Nation State": 203–21. P. 207.

30. North and Thomas point out that Spanish revenues from the Low Countries, with their highly developed commerce, were ten times or more their revenues from the Indies during some times in the sixteenth century. See North and Thomas, *Rise of the Western World*, p. 129.

3 / The Growth of Trade
to 1750

The period between the middle of the fifteenth century and the middle of the eighteenth was an era of growth in trade and of the invention and growth of institutions suited to a trading world. It ended just before the introduction of the factory system of production, which occurred in the latter half of the eighteenth century. By then the West had already contained, and begun to push back, the Islamic civilization that had pressed hard against European frontiers from the eighth century to the siege of Vienna in 1683. The West had also established a foothold in India, destroyed the Aztec and Inca civilizations of America, and colonized both North and South America. In short, the West was already well on the road to technological, political, and economic dominance well before the introduction of the factory system, and it had achieved economic advances on a scale that had even then divided the world into the "have" and the "have not" nations. The point is nowhere better illustrated than by the visits of the Russian Tsar Peter the Great to Holland in the seventeenth century to learn Western shipbuilding and other industrial arts, and by his efforts to modernize Russia.

If the growth in trade that marked this era had a technological source, it was the introduction of the three-masted trading vessel in the latter fifteenth century, with its workaday possibilities of lower costs of transportation and trading over greater distances and the almost fantastic possibility of carrying Westerners to the farthest corners of America and Asia that it offered. It is true that from the early seventeenth century on, the West virtually established the foundations of modern science, beginning with the work of Galileo. This was the period in which Isaac Newton published his *Principia Mathematica*, which laid down the basic outlines of physics that were followed for nearly two hundred years; of the introduction of the telescope; and of the invention of the microscope and the discovery of microscopic forms of life. Important as these developments eventually became to the history of Western technology, for the most part they were not directly linked to the contemporaneous growth in trade. There were exceptions, such as the link between astronomy and the practical arts of navigation. But Western mercantile capitalism had its origins elsewhere.

The growth in trade that occurred after the fifteenth century was both a quantitative change, reflecting a rise in volume of trading, and a qualitative change, reflecting a shift from medieval exchange on terms set by custom and usage to market pricing based on negotiation between traders. The qualitative change, more than the quantitative, required institutional invention—a point developed in chapter 4.

The quantitative expansion of markets was important because it made possible greater specialization within the network of economic relationships. Greater specialization of economic activity required markets sufficiently large to provide for an intensive utilization of specialized agents. In Adam Smith's time-honored dictum, "the division of labor is limited by the extent of the market."[1] We will see in chapter 5 that the growth of markets ultimately stimulated, and in its turn was further stimulated by, the rise of the factory system. But events outlined in the first part of this chapter were increasing the volume of European trade for several centuries before the introduction of factories.

The qualitative change was, in a way, a complete reversal of past practice and belief. In our account of trading in the Middle Ages in chapter 2, we left market pricing in the position of an institution incompatible with medieval values, allowed in only a few cities that had already left feudalism behind and in the lawless cracks between the jurisdictions of medieval polities. How, then, did this disreputable exception to the normal practice and values of Western society achieve its preeminence in the economies of the West? The second part of this chapter suggests some of the reasons.

In the last part of the chapter, we examine the effect of the rise of a merchant class on the old feudal landholders and on other classes of postfeudal society as well as its relationship to the theory that history is a story of the displacement of one dominant class by a subsequent one that follows on its heels.

The Expansion of Markets: The Voyages of Discovery

What generated the growth of markets?

The answer that most commonly springs to mind is that markets were generated by the expansion of Europe's overseas trade, which followed swiftly upon the great feats of European exploration—Vasco da Gama's remarkable rounding of the Cape of Good Hope and the opening of an all-water route to the Far East, the discovery of the New World, and so forth. These overseas markets provided great profit-making opportunities and thus offered powerful incentives for capitalist development.

Just as important, they supplied a political opening for that same capitalist development. By the beginning of the sixteenth century, feudalism and manorialism were no longer regnant, but their successor had not yet emerged. There were no political institutions sufficiently developed to preempt the new opportunities overseas from the reach of the merchant class. The central monarchies were only beginning to emerge. Besides, overseas markets were not subject to the control of a single sovereign, and the papacy's attempts to allocate overseas markets only added fuel to the Protestant Reformation. There was, in short, a vacuum of authority, and the rising merchant class energetically took advantage of it to carry through a capitalist development of overseas markets. It may even be claimed that this injection of a vigorously acquisitive merchant class into the dying feudalism of Europe was the last and fatal shock to the old order.

This explanation is precisely the one offered by Marx and Engels in the *Communist Manifesto* of 1848. They viewed the overseas markets of America, the East Indies, and China as creating growing wants the guilds could not satisfy, with the result that the "manufacturing" system took its place, only to be in its turn replaced by the "steam and machinery" of the "giant, Modern Industry." Their account has been widely influential, and it is worth quoting:

> The discovery of America, the rounding of the Cape, opened up fresh ground for the rising bourgeoisie. The East-Indian and Chinese markets, the colonization of America, trade with the colonies, the increase in the means of exchange and in commodities generally, gave to commerce, to navigation, to industry, an impulse never before known, and thereby, to the revolutionary element in the tottering feudal society, a rapid development.
>
> The feudal system of industry, under which industrial production was monopolised by closed guilds, now no longer sufficed for the growing wants of the new markets. The manufacturing system took its place. The guild-masters

were pushed on one side by the manufacturing middle class; division of labour between the different corporate guilds vanished in the face of division of labour in each single workshop.

Meanwhile the markets kept ever growing, the demand ever rising. Even manufacture no longer sufficed. Thereupon, steam and machinery revolutionized industrial production. The place of manufacture was taken by the giant, Modern Industry, the place of the industrial middle class, by industrial millionaires, the leaders of whole industrial armies, the modern bourgeoisie.

Modern industry has established the world-market, for which the discovery of America paved the way. This market has given an immense development to commerce, to navigation, to communication by land. This development has, in its turn, reacted on the extension of industry; and in proportion as industry, commerce, navigation, railways extended, in the same proportion the bourgeoisie developed, increased its capital, and pushed into the background every class handed down from the Middle Ages.[2]

The growth of opportunities for overseas trade, emphasized by Marx and Engels and many others, is without question an essential part of the story of the expanding markets that gave rise to capitalism. But there is a temptation to exaggerate the economic importance of overseas trade, arising in part from the exotic aura of voyages to strange and distant lands and in part from its special interest to the finances of the new nation-states. The newly developed overseas trade, by its very novelty, was wide open to royal exploitation through taxation and the grant of trading monopolies, while domestic trade was much more likely to be covered by existing charters or simply to generate more serious political opposition to new imposts. Inevitably, rival royal governments competed for the prizes in overseas trade, not merely commercially but also militarily. But despite the high drama of overseas trade and its importance to royal exchequers and international politics, it may be legitimately observed that there were other, much less dramatic, sources of market growth that have been unduly neglected: rise in population, growth in interurban trade, growth of cities, and improvements in transportation.

Population Growth and the Expansion of Domestic Markets

A most important factor in the development of trade was a growth in the total population of Western Europe. The growth in population had a powerful and pervasive effect on all aspects of economic activity. European population, according to the most conscientious estimates, had been rising throughout the later Middle Ages—from the eleventh century on. By the beginning of the fourteenth century it had risen to more than seventy million.[3] This growing population expanded into new, unsettled regions, enlarged the amount of arable land in older regions, and increased the intensity of cultivation generally. There is reason to think that the rate of growth started to fall early in the fourteenth century.[4] In 1347 an outbreak of the plague, combined shortly with several years of disastrous crop failures and the Hundred Years' War, brought about a traumatic reversal of population growth.

The growth in population resumed in France early in the fifteenth century and in England late in the same century.[5] Shortly after 1600, the population of Europe had again reached the 1347 level. The upturn took place earlier in some parts of Europe than in others; but in any case the population of Europe more than doubled, to about 170 million, between 1600 and 1800.[6] It may be inferred, from this growth in population, that the size of European domestic markets was increasing concurrently with the expansion of overseas trade and exploration.

The full significance of the resulting intra-European trade has been obscured by the great emphasis usually conferred upon the growth of overseas trade. In fact, even before the voyages of discovery, Europe had already developed a very extensive trade in bulky commodities. This trade was based upon differences in climate, natural resources, and population densities within the continent. The Baltic region had long served as a source of timber (an immensely important raw material in pre-industrial societies) and other forest products and, later, of cereals. The Iberian Peninsula exported wool, vegetable oils, dyestuffs, iron ore, and some fruits. Even in the late Middle Ages, much of this trade flowed north and south "from forest, corn land, territories rich in copper, lead or iron, and seas in fish, to vineyard, olive grove, sheep pasture, salt lagoon, textile workshop, smithy and shipyard, meeting, crossing and restarting in the great junction of the Netherlands, and, at different points, feeding or being fed by subsidiary streams."[7]

There were many other examples of the substantial interregional trade carried on in Europe in the late Middle Ages. In the absence of refrigeration and modern preservatives, spices of Asiatic origin were more than luxuries, perhaps necessities, throughout Europe, and the spice trade supplied much of the incentive for the early voyages of exploration. In Eastern Europe, the demand for meat and the self-portability of cattle created a fairly long-distance trade between grazing areas and the towns. The discovery that meat could be preserved by salting, made about the fifteenth century, created an important trade in salt. And there was a trade in munitions. Milan was a preferred center of the production of armor in the Middle Ages. With the invention of gunpowder, Liege became a preferred source of firearms. The invention of cannon made the trade needed to buy or rent them a condition of military survival in regions that lacked cannon foundries.[8]

The details of the growth of trade in Northern Europe, in the Mediterranean littoral, and between Northern and Southern Europe have been well explored by others and need not be further developed here.[9] Two points regarding the development of interurban trade are, however, worth passing mention because of their later consequences.

First, England, which later shared with Holland the leadership in developing the institutions of capitalism, was, throughout most of the Middle Ages, essentially an economic colony of Western Europe. Its role was that of a supplier of primary products to the specialized manufacturing communities of Europe—minerals and food products but, above all, wool, which was essential to the cloth-producing economies of Italy and the Low Countries. Thus, foreign trade was more important to England than to most European countries from a very early date. Its colonial status changed only with the rapid and remarkable growth of the English cloth industry in the second half of the fourteenth century.

Second, the role played by Northern Italy in the growth of capitalist institutions was crucial. Indeed, many apparent innovations in commercial organization in Northern and Western Europe were, in fact, the diffusion, sometimes long delayed, of practices that had been developed in Northern Italy.[10] This diffusion is recalled by Lombard Street in London, whose name memorializes Italian traders and bankers who must have felt, at the time, very far from home.

Whatever the details, it is commonly agreed by economic historians that a marked growth in European trade occurred during the late Middle Ages and continued after the collapse of feudalism. Our present concern is not with the details of that growth, but with the historical connection between the growth of trade in general, on the one hand, and the associated growth of cities and capitalist institutions, on the other.

The Growth of Trade to 1750

The Rise of a Merchant Class

A first consequence of the late-medieval growth in the volume of European trade was the development of specialized traders—that is, a merchant class. We have already mentioned how small a part full-time traders played in medieval commerce. So long as trade was on a sufficiently small scale, it could be undertaken part-time, as a second activity of people who were primarily peasants, fishermen, landlords, nuns, or monks. For them, trade was merely a way to convert their primary output into money; it was not their primary occupation.

There were other conditions requisite to the development of a specialized merchant class than a simple growth in the volume of trade. For part-time traders, an urban location was not always necessary. But for full-time specialists who subsisted by trade, the constraints of a rural location were intolerable. To make a living from trade, one must have freedom to decide when and at what price to buy and when and at what price to sell. Essential though these freedoms were to the merchant trader's livelihood, they were incompatible with the innumerable restrictions of feudal society, including its principle that trade should occur only at a just price.

Postan makes this point, that a class of specialized traders presupposed the elimination of a whole array of feudal restrictions on personal freedom and property:

> In order to be professional and to conduct trade all the year round merchants and artisans had to be exempt from the ties and liabilities which restricted the liberty of movement and freedom of contract of the lower orders of feudal society. Their houses and tenements with their shops had to be free from the obligations which burdened the rural tenures; their transactions had to be judged by a law better suited to dealings between merchant and merchant than were the feudal custumals and common law. Hence the essential function of the medieval towns, as non-feudal islands in feudal seas; and hence their appearance in large numbers in the eleventh century—the time when trade grew and the feudal order matured. Hence also the crucial part which the charters or privilege (which were nothing less than guaranteed exemptions from the feudal order) played in the origin and development of towns. Charters of this kind created boroughs out of villages, and cities out of castle suburbs; and charters of this kind punctuated the subsequent progress of urban communities on their way to full urban status.[11]

In short, traders could not function if they were also villeins, living on a manor and subject to the obligations of a villein to a seigneur. They had to live in towns, outside the manorial system.

HOW THE WEST GREW RICH

It is true that the medieval world always had some full-time professional merchants. Trade and a professional merchant class have never wholly disappeared from Mediterranean and European life since the time of the Phoenicians. All through the Middle Ages, Venice, the cities of Lombardy, the towns of the Hanseatic League, the inhabitants of the island-studded Frisian coast from Holland to Denmark, and even the Vikings engaged in long-distance trade by ship, pack train, and caravan, in ways that required full-time merchants. The typical seigneur or artisan preferred to be paid at once for goods that were to be carried on distant trading voyages, and the distant foreigners who supplied a return cargo had even more reason to exact payment on the spot. Anyone who had the time and skill to carry a cargo to a distant port, sell it, buy a return cargo chosen for its marketability at home, and bring it back to the home market was a merchant by definition. Even in trades that were routine, like the trade in wool between England and the Low Countries, the use of merchant intermediaries was well established in the Middle Ages. There were, in addition, the peddlers who have always been part of rural life. Thus it would be a mistake to suppose that a rise in trade in the late Middle Ages led to the reinvention of an occupation forgotten since the fall of Rome. Rather, from the eleventh to the fourteenth centuries, the activities of merchants increased in parallel with the flowering of a feudal system that utilized their services without providing them with a legitimate niche in the feudal scheme of things. The merchants were consigned to the towns, and the towns themselves were nonfeudal islands in a feudal world.

Urbanization

The growth of markets and commercial relationships was intensified by the expansion of urban centers and by greater manufacturing specialization in specific places such as the Low Countries and Northern Italy. The impetus for their growth came not only from the rise in population, but from a rise in the towns' and cities' share of the population. Urbanization and industrial specialization both require and create an extensive network of market relations.[12] Through trading networks, urban industry draws raw materials from a multitude of geographically dispersed mines, forests, farms, and grazing lands, and it gets its products to increasingly distant users through other trading networks. The agricultural sector turns from production almost entirely for its own needs to production much in excess of its own needs. Its surpluses are processed, transported, and distributed to the towns through still other trading networks, and a considerable part of the resulting agricultural revenues are spent on products of the towns through yet other trading networks. Sometimes the growth of towns and industries furnishes the impetus for expansion of raw material and food production, sometimes the discovery of new natural resources or the opening of new trade routes supplies the impetus for expansion of town and industry, and most often of all the direction of causation is indeterminate, as all these types of growth move concurrently and incrementally. Cities live on the difference between what they have to pay for raw materials for their shops and factories and what they can obtain for the finished products, plus what they can net from outsiders by selling such specialized services as banking, insurance, warehousing, commodity trading, medicine, law, government, and religion. Agricultural life requires less trading than urban life because the farm (let alone the manor) is more self-sufficient than the city apartment: a movement from farm to city is inevitably a movement toward more trading.

Thus, in addition to the spectacular growth in overseas trade beginning in the sixteenth century, Western Europe, from the twelfth century on, had experienced a gradual penetration of its economic structure by the commercial institutions and relationships that accompanied the emergence of urban populations, urban institutions, and urban producers whose economic roles were vitally dependent upon commerce.

There is another way to look at the causal relationship between urbanization and the growth of trade. A reasonable model for the development of a town must assume the discovery of some initial basis, in comparative advantage, for trade between the town and its supporting *countryside,* an open-ended term which, in the later age of intercontinental trade, came to mean the whole world. The dimensions of the comparative advantage set the limits within which the town could maintain a viable balance betweens its sales and its purchases—between, that is, what it drew from its countryside and what it gave back in exchange. It is no wonder that urbanization presupposed and created extensive trading relationships, for potential trading relationships were the DNA of urban development.

In a developed, living city, it is hopeless to try to separate growth in trade and growth in population and identify one as the cause of the other. The towns whose trade prospered increased in population, and towns whose trade did not prosper must then, as now, have faced the problems of decline. Wealth flowing from successful trading no doubt made some towns attractive to immigrants from the countryside or elsewhere, and so made trade—or, rather success in trade—a cause pro tanto of a rise in population. It is not easy to find places in Europe where a high density of population so distinctly preceded growth in trade that one might reasonably view it as a cause of growth in trade. The Low Countries and Lombardy were the most densely populated parts of Europe in the late Middle Ages, but even there growth in trade and growth in population seem to have gone on together, rather than sequentially.

Population became a stimulus to trade later on, after the Industrial Revolution, when a local pool of employable workers (which is not quite the same thing as population in the large) became a significant factor in the choice of factory locations. But in the late Middle Ages and the early postfeudal period, the almost wholly anonymous discoverers of opportunities for trade deserved a measure of credit both for the rise of towns and cities and for the growth of their population.

Improvements in Transportation and the Growth in Trade

Having observed that growth of trade and growth of cities were so intertwined, so dependent upon each other, that it becomes hard to tell which was cause and which effect, we need not be surprised to find a similar symbiosis in the relationship between the growth of trade and cities and improvements in transportation. It is easier to examine the relationship as if it were simply one between trade and transportation, provided we keep in mind the qualification that cities do not grow and flourish without the transportation needed to feed their industries, nourish their populations, and distribute their products. In this context, the word *trade* is a proxy, not just for the merchants' profit-seeking bargaining, but for the lifestream of cities, and *growth in trade* and *urbanization* are nearly equivalent expressions.

That substantial improvements in maritime transportation occurred during the fifteenth century is easily demonstrated. The causal links between these improvements in transportation and the economic advance of the West are much less easily identified.

The most important improvement in transportation was the emergence of the full-rigged ship, which served as the main carrier of Western maritime commerce until the latter part of the nineteenth century. At the beginning of the fifteenth century, the typical Atlantic merchantman was a cog, itself a relatively recent advance on the ships in which William the Conqueror invaded England, as recorded on the Bayeux Tapestry. The cog was a "round" ship—so-called because its length was only about three times its beam—fitted with a single mast and a single square sail.[13] As early as the thirteenth century, a foremast and foresail were sometimes added. Since such a rig was unbalanced, a beam wind tended to blow the bow to leeward, making the ship difficult to steer and placing an excessive strain on the rudder. To balance the foresail, a mizzenmast had to be, and about the middle of the fifteenth century was, added aft of the mainmast. We do not know the name, nor even the nationality, of the inventor. The first clear representation of a three-masted ship was on a French medal of 1466, and we know that French shipbuilders of Bayonna, near the Spanish frontier, were much admired by their contemporaries, but it is only a guess that the admiration may have had something to do with building the first three-masters.

The mizzen was usually lateen-rigged. The lateen rig used a triangular sail set on a spar carried at a sharp angle to the mast, in contrast to the more familiar rectangular sails set on spars carried square to the mast. This rig, common in the Mediterranean, was valued for its ability to drive a ship to windward. In the Atlantic ships of the late fifteenth century, most of the driving power in a following wind still came from the single large sail on the mainmast, but the addition of foremast and mizzen made for faster and much handier ships with the wind from any direction but dead aft.

The new type was known as a carrack. The Portuguese developed a slightly different rig, using lateen sails on all three masts. These lateen-rigged ships were given the name caravel and seemed preferable for coastwise sailing, perhaps because of the lateen rig's greater ability to sail to windward and so avoid being driven on to a lee shore in a storm—an acute hazard of coastwise sailing. For ocean sailing, the carrack seems to have had the advantage, if we may judge from the fact that Columbus's smallest ship, *Nina*, began his 1492 voyage as a caravel, but was rerigged as a carrack at Grand Canary.

To sailors, much of the importance of the change to a three-masted rig resided in its improvement of the ability of merchant ships to sail close to the wind. A sailing vessel cannot sail directly against the wind, but it can sail at an angle to the wind. For a modern sailing yacht, the conventional practicable angle is about 45°, but full-rigged ships were lucky to make good a course at any angle less than 60° to the wind. The wind is a sailing vessel's uncertain master, and the greater the range of wind directions over which a vessel can sail well, the quicker it will complete its voyages. Yet, from Roman times, merchant ships had been designed, in hull and rig, to sail nearly dead downwind. Sterns were rounded to accept a following sea, and the bows were not designed to drive into head seas. The single large sail was ideal for downwind sailing, but much less well adapted for sailing with the wind abeam or forward of the beam. Hence the traditional merchant ships spent much time in port awaiting favorable winds. The full-rigged ships used from the fifteenth century on also sometimes had to wait out headwinds—but not nearly so often. On all trade routes, the new rig made for faster and more dependable voyages. Beyond that, some of what later became the world's major trade routes were distinguished by winds that blew steadily from one direction for months at a time, and regular round-trip trading voyages would have been nearly impossible without the new rigs.

Modern knowledge of Northern European merchant vessels of the late Middle Ages is too sketchy to give us a complete picture of the other improvements in seagoing vessels accomplished in the fifteenth century. The pre-fifteenth-century wooden ships have not survived, except for a few fragmentary remnants. They were not built to plans, so we have no plans. Some Viking ships that were buried with their owners in earlier periods have been found, but they are no guide to the later merchantmen. Maritime historians are reduced to drawing inferences from medieval artists' pictures, which often seem more symbolic than literal. They do show, unmistakably, the substitution of three masts for one. We also know that, during the fifteenth century, northern shipbuilders changed their hull construction from clinker planking (overlapping planking of the general type used in the Viking ships), to carvel planking (edge-to-edge), which had been used by the Romans and had persisted in the Mediterranean. Whatever the exact character of the fifteenth-century improvements may have been, Columbus's detailed description of surviving a cyclonic storm on the return voyage in *Nina*, the smallest of his ships, is witness to a remarkable overall advance in seaworthiness over the cogs of a hundred years before.

Merchant vessels also increased in size, at least on average, during the fifteenth century. It is not clear that there was any close relationship between increases in the size of merchant vessels and such improvements as the three-masted rig and carvel planking. The improvements were used on small vessels (such as *Nina*) as well as on large vessels, the technology for building ships as large as any of the eighteenth century was known to the Romans, and European shipbuilders may have built some relatively large cogs before the fifteenth century. On the other hand, many everyday maneuvers of sailing vessels in anchorages and docking must have been very difficult to accomplish with the single sail of the cog rig. Later ways of anchoring, docking, and sailing off in varying conditions of wind and tide often depended on having sails available at both ends of the vessel, because they could be used to point the vessel in the desired direction when it was moving too slowly for the rudder to afford effective steering. Hence, the greater maneuverability of ships with the three-masted rig would have made larger vessels much more acceptable to the sailors who had to maneuver them in harbors. It is a fair guess that clumsiness in maneuvering was a practical pre-fifteenth-century objection to larger cogs—not necessarily a fatal objection, but still one that would have kept the number of relatively large vessels smaller in a world of cogs than in a world of carracks, all other things being equal.

A major advantage of larger vessels is that they are faster than small vessels, since it is a rule of naval architecture that, ceteris paribus, the maximum practical speed of a ship is proportional to the square root of its waterline length. There is also an economy of scale, since the cargo-carrying capacities of ships of different lengths are approximately proportional to the cubes of their waterline lengths, while the costs of building depend on the weight of the hulls, which are more nearly proportional to the square of the waterline lengths. There were further scale economies of manning. The larger vessel required proportionally fewer hands to work its sails, and such other members of the ship's company as captain, watch officers, carpenter, and cook numbered the same whether the vessel was small or large. Size also made for seaworthiness. The bigger ships were more appropriate for the storage of the fresh water (beer, on the early voyages), provisions, and spare parts required for longer voyages. The larger ships also afforded greater protection against pirates.[14]

The one great disadvantage of larger vessels is that they draw more water, and their use is restricted to ports that have deep harbors. The long-standing preference of the Dutch for smaller vessels and the use of small caravels by the Portuguese in their African voyages can be explained in part by the need to navigate shallow coastal waters and rivers, where a channel deep enough for a large ship might be narrow or nonexistent, and sandbars and reefs hard to avoid. The persistent popularity of small vessels in some Mediterranean trades has a similar explanation.

Whatever the navigational advantages and disadvantages of a ship's size, the economical size for a merchant ship is subject to a ceiling fixed by the size of the cargoes that can be dependably obtained for it, for the advantages of the larger vessels turn into liabilities when available cargoes are small and irregular. Thus, the successful introduction of the larger ships of the fifteenth century was a reliable sign that, even before the voyages of discovery, intra-European trade had created a rising and dependable demand for cargo space. And while growth of trade increased the demand for cargo space and so made larger ships profitable, the ships themselves, by lowering transportation costs and affording greater security, were in turn a powerful stimulus to the growth of trade.

There is an interesting parallelism between the turning point from improvements in *coastal* navigation, up to about 1500, to improvements in *ocean* navigation, after that date, on the one hand, and the turning point, about that year (or should we specify 1492?), from growth in *domestic* trade to growth in *overseas* exploration and trade. The compass, for example, was used in Europe as early as the fourteenth century. But in the sixteenth century, what took center stage was the study of local magnetic variation, which varied from place to place across the world and mattered most on the long voyages of the ocean mariner. The quadrant, cross-staff, and astrolabe, for taking elevations, were familiar before 1500, but were used to measure height, and, by triangulation, distance off the familiar landmarks of the coastwise pilot. After 1500, they became tools of celestial navigation, measuring the angular height of the sun and the North Star above the horizon. It was not until after 1600 that the Mercator chart, the first one reasonably suited to ocean sailing, came into popular use.[15]

The two-way relationship between the growth of trade and improvements in maritime transportation was not necessarily limited to growth in the size of vessels. So long as we keep in mind that the origins of the three-masted rig are unknown, we can allow ourselves to claim that the growth of trade increased the probabilities of such improvements as the three-masted rig by making the limitations of the single-masted cog less bearable and setting more and more mariners to thinking of new rigs which would allow their ships to sail faster with the wind abeam or even forward of the beam. Once they were introduced, the carracks and caravels of the fifteenth century, both large and small, undoubtedly helped in the further expansion of the trade that had inspired them. It was these full-rigged ships of recent development which were employed on the voyages of discovery in the second half of the fifteenth and on into the sixteenth century. And it should be noted that these ships were almost all small, even for their time, from Columbus's three ships, through Magellan's, to Drake's *Golden Hind.* It is also to be emphasized that the ships of the voyages of exploration were not specially designed for the purpose. For the most part, they were everyday merchantmen, acquired secondhand for the expedition and sometimes (like Magellan's) already much past their prime. It is worth noting also that the resources devoted to the exploratory voyages and to early overseas trade were pitifully small, even by Spain, which had struck gold.

Of course, the exploratory voyages did not require the same cargo-carrying capacity as voyages in an established trade. Indeed, history is full of dramatic explorations and ocean crossings in small open boats, rafts, and outrigger canoes, made sometimes of reeds, skins, or hollowed-out logs. We do not mean to denigrate the accomplishments of St. Brendan, Eric the Red, Leif Ericsson, the Micronesians, Captain Bligh, or the hundreds of other voyagers whose seamanship overcame the limitations of their vessels, but the development of extensive trade in bulky merchandise required ships they did not have.

Since the fundamental improvements in ocean transport preceded the voyages of overseas exploration, they cannot be considered responses to the development of European overseas trade. The overseas voyages began in attempts to find all-water routes in which the new carracks and caravels could be substituted for the difficult and costly overland trade routes with the Far East. They were thus attempts to exploit commercially a new shipbuilding technology by Western countries which had already learned, from trading with each other, the value of maritime trade and which had, again in trading with each other, already developed ships adequate to carrying substantial cargoes on long ocean voyages. Thus, to the extent that the carracks and caravels originated in social and economic needs rather than in the general ebullience of the Renaissance, they were the effect of the earlier sizable growth of intra-European trade, which was, in turn, a trade that grew with the growth of population, urbanization, and specialization.

Thus, what happened in the fifteenth century was an interlinked growth of trade and maritime technology, each feeding the other. Both were essentially urban, rather than rural, activities, the product of life in port cities that lived and grew in wealth and population by trading and especially by finding ways to push trade beyond its old patterns. European overseas trade was a late consequence of expansionist trading impulses that can readily be traced to twelfth- and thirteenth-century Italy, and which had spread to Spain, Portugal, the Low Countries, France, England, and Germany during the fourteenth and fifteenth centuries—trading impulses that were nourished on local, regional, and international trade within Europe and by which Europeans developed the institutional and technological means to trade beyond Europe and the Mediterranean basin. Once the ships developed for local trade became adequate for overseas voyages, the extension of the European trading system along the African and American shores of the Atlantic was as much a consequence of the dynamics of the system as its earlier extension north and west from Italy. Like its earlier growth within Europe, expansion overseas reinforced merchant capitalism and nourished its further growth. But overseas trade was a branch on an older tree, not part of its roots.

Technology and Early Growth in the Size of Markets

Between the fifteenth and the eighteenth centuries, the growth of markets was gradual and steady rather than revolutionary. It was accompanied by growth in science and technology, especially during and after the seventeenth century. Many economic historians believe that the growth of markets was the cause of the concurrent Western technological advances. By this view, technological progress was not an independent force in Western growth, but a series of dependent responses to economic needs as the needs developed, made by artisans who usually drew their inventions from nothing more original than craft knowledge and varying degrees of patience, experiment, and personal ingenuity. Both markets and technology expanded gradually, almost always in small increments, from the fifteenth to the eighteenth centuries, and there is little doubt that there were many instances of technological progress that came almost automatically when the economic need arose. On the other hand, the full-rigged ship is an example of a technological improvement that furthered the expansion of commerce, setting up a reverse causation from technology to market growth. Since it satisfied economic needs that had existed for two thousand years with technologies that had also existed for many centuries, its invention came hundreds of years too late to fit a simple causal pattern from economic need to technological response. In this instance, causal forces additional to economic forces are needed for a satisfactory explanation.

One of the stronger supports for market-to-technology causation takes the form of an argument that the Chinese had an equivalent and perhaps superior technology around the fourteenth century, but they came to a dead end in a culture more aptly characterized as mandarin than mercantile. The monumental researches of Joseph Needham have richly documented China's extensive achievements in both science and technology. Needham has presented a formidable mass of evidence to support his belief that "between the first century B.C. and the fifteenth century A.D., Chinese civilization was much *more* efficient than occidental in applying human natural knowledge to practical human needs."[16]

Needham argued, moreover, that the social and economic systems of medieval China were, in many respects, more rational than their counterparts in medieval Europe. Whereas Europe was dominated by a ruling class entrenched by hereditary succession, China was ruled by mandarins, a class of civil servants with no prospect whatever of hereditary succession. Thus, Chinese civilization was more rational in the very specific sense that people were admitted to positions of leadership on the basis of ability and not of birth. The imperial examination determined entry into the bureaucracy and thus assured the continuation of a nonhereditary elite, drawing into itself the best brains of each generation.

But despite these advantages, Needham's conclusion is that the social and cultural values of Asian "bureaucratic feudalism" were simply incompatible with capitalism and, for that matter, with modern science. He leaves us with the disturbing thought that holders of political power will, if they can, check the development of economic power centers capable of achieving economic growth:

I believe that it will be possible to show in some considerable detail why the Asian "bureaucratic feudalism" at first favored the growth of natural knowledge and its application to technology for human benefit, while later on it inhibited the rise of modern capitalism and of modern science in contrast with the other form of feudalism in Europe which favored it—by decaying and generating the new mercantile order of society. A predominantly mercantile order of society could never arise in Chinese civilization because the basic conception of the mandarinate was opposed not only to the principles of hereditary aristocratic feudalism but also to the value-systems of the wealthy merchants. Capital accumulation in Chinese society there could indeed be, but the application of it in permanently productive industrial enterprises was constantly inhibited by the scholar-bureaucrats, as indeed was any other social action which might threaten their supremacy. Thus, the merchant guilds in China never achieved anything approaching the status and power of the merchant guilds of the city-states of European civilization.[17]

What Needham called an "agrarian bureaucratic civilization" never arranged for its men of trade and crafts to bring the knowledge of its men of mathematics and natural science to bear on the problems of satisfying the material needs of everyday life. As he put it, "Interest in nature was not enough, controlled experiment was not enough, eclipse-prediction and calendar-calculation were not enough—all these the Chinese had. . . . Apparently the mercantile culture alone was able to do what agrarian bureaucratic civilization could not—bring to fusion point the formerly separated disciplines of mathematics and nature-knowledge."[18] To this, one may add that the Chinese mastery of navigation, with seaworthy vessels fully capable of long voyages, was also not enough.

A conclusive answer to Needham's problem in comparative social dynamics obviously cannot be attempted here—or perhaps anywhere, for that matter, in view of the very modest accomplishments of the social sciences thus far in accounting for the causes of social change. There was surely cultural and economic variety among the regions of the Chinese empire, but perhaps its dominant rice-growing areas had less to gain from interregional trade than the more fragmented European states. What can be said is that the Chinese social system inculcated values that were not only hostile to hereditary aristocracies, such as those that dominated Western feudalism, but also to bourgeois values generally. A class of scholar-bureaucrats held classical learning in high esteem and, at the same time, cultivated a contempt for material goals or acquisitiveness. (Not that these values dictated an ascetic life-style to the mandarins themselves.) The son of a successful merchant aspired, not to expand or even necessarily to perpetuate the family business, but to prepare for the imperial examinations and to enter and eventually rise in the mandarinate. These values underplayed the importance of bettering the material conditions of everyday life; in fact, they came to produce a collective self-satisfaction which might not unfairly be called smugness.

China is of special interest because it was contemporary with the rise of Western capitalism. But it was not unique. Earlier civilizations, including the Greek and Roman, never achieved anything like the interaction between natural science and commerce that has characterized the West in the last four centuries.

In the passage from *The Communist Manifesto* quoted earlier, Marx and Engels also argued that the social transformation that gave rise to capitalism was not primarily technological in nature. Marx and Engels viewed capitalism as arising in the sixteenth century, some two hundred years before the dramatic changes in technology associated with the Industrial Revolution of the late eighteenth and early nineteenth centuries. They were by no means technological determinists. Causality was, in fact, the other way around. Technological changes occur as a *response* to economic forces; the rise of capitalism, in particular, is not directly associated with changes in the methods of production—in technology. For Marx and Engels, the growth of the market was the prime mover that generated a new institutional order which, in turn, was responsible for massive technological changes.[19]

Writing from the vantage point of 1848, Marx and Engels attributed the great technological accomplishments of the Industrial Revolution not to science, nor to human ingenuity, nor to a Protestant ethic, but to a specific institutional system—capitalism, and to the bourgeoisie:

> The bourgeoisie, during its rule of scarce one hundred years, has created more massive and more colossal productive forces than have all preceding generations together. Subjection of Nature's forces to man, machinery, application of chemistry to industry and agriculture, steam-navigation, railways, electric telegraphs, clearing of whole continents for cultivation, canalisation of rivers, whole populations conjured out of the ground—what earlier century had even a presentiment that such productive forces slumbered in the lap of social labour?[20]

They attributed to the bourgeoisie a unique propensity to sponsor industrial, and hence social, change. As they put it, "The bourgeoisie cannot exist without constantly revolutionising the instruments of production, and thereby the relations of production, and with them the whole relations of society. Conservation of the old modes of production in unaltered form, was, on the contrary, the first condition of existence for all earlier industrial classes."[21] Competitive pressures, in their view, lead to the necessity of extracting the largest possible "surplus value" from the labor force. However, competitive pressures were also seen as compelling the capitalists to plow their profits into the expansion of the system. Thus, capitalism became a social system which was inherently dynamic technologically and which generated explosive growth in society's productive capacity by combining rapid technological innovation with rapid capital accumulation.

One word of caution seems in order. To one primarily interested in the study of institutions, it is the influence of institutions on the direction of science, invention, and technology that tends to be the subject in hand and to seem worthy of emphasis. But in chapter 5, when we turn from the development of trade to the development of industry, we will find grounds for inferring that the technology of the Industrial Revolution ignited a nineteenth-century growth of markets which dwarfed the earlier expansion we are considering in this chapter. Of course, the relationship between technology and the growth in the size of markets was not necessarily the same in the fifteenth to eighteenth centuries as in the nineteenth and twentieth and, as in all instances of reciprocal causation, the selection of a point for beginning an account of causation can be made to seem arbitrary. Since the direction and form of the causal links between technology and economic growth need not have been identical in all historical periods and in all instances of invention, whether economic growth causes technological change or is caused by it becomes a question that has to be investigated repeatedly for different circumstances. In chapter 8 we will still be wrestling with the relative parts played by technology and other factors in Western growth.

The Expansion of Market Pricing: Interregional Trade

We now turn from the quantitative growth of markets and take up the change to determination of prices and other terms of exchange by negotiation among those trading in the market.

By the time of the voyages of discovery, the limitations of the technology of transportation were not in themselves a major obstacle to the expansion of trade. The potentialities for trade, in the sense of the mutual advantages that could be derived by European communities from the exchange of regional specialties, had always been great. The first requisite for the release of these potentialities was the expansion of the sphere within which trade could be conducted with some degree of freedom from the arbitrary exercise of external authority. This involved, above all, freedom from intrusion by political authorities, whether feudal or, increasingly after the fourteenth century, national. In view of the often compelling fiscal needs of the state, especially for military adventures, this was exceedingly difficult to attain. Indeed, its degree of attainment varied considerably from country to country and from one period to another, and much of early-modern European history is a story of a continual tug-of-war between a nascent business class and the established political structure. Nevertheless, it may be said that the emergence of a reasonably autonomous business class occurred much more readily in Western Europe than east of the Elbe,[22] and that within Western Europe it happened earlier and more decisively in England and Holland than in France, Spain, or Germany.

The capacity of sovereigns or manorial lords to control prices and other terms of trade was always bounded by their own territorial jurisdiction.

Even more clearly, the capacity of a sovereign to require people to trade on terms fixed by law and usage was limited to subjects of the sovereign. This point, that exchange was compulsory and involuntary, is important. Today, the duty to enter into exchange transactions is limited almost entirely to public utilities and to landlords subject to rent controls. But in the Middle Ages, both on the manor and in the towns, peasant, smith, miller, and artisan alike labored under the obligation to furnish their services to those who offered to pay. So it was that when trade took place between subjects of different sovereigns or lords, or between sovereigns, it was not merely the customary price that was inapplicable. The customary obligation to deal was also inapplicable. Either party could refrain from trading, or trade elsewhere, if the terms of trade were unacceptable.

This is not to say that trade between jurisdictions always conformed to later notions of a free market: far from it. Until the nineteenth century, sovereigns commonly did what they could to exploit their import and export trade by making its various branches the exclusive privileges of state or private monopolies, established on terms aimed at maximizing the revenues of the state. But if a sovereign wanted to trade with another sovereign or another sovereign's subjects, the terms of trade had to be agreeable to both, not just to one. In a world of minutely fragmented sovereignties, this jurisdictional crack in medieval authority offered opportunities for the development of voluntary trade on negotiated terms.

Economically, if not politically, the opportunities for mutually beneficial trade were extensive. We have already noted that Europe of the late Middle Ages was divided by climate and custom into hundreds of small regions with local specialties crying out to be developed by trade with other regions with specialties of their own and that there were many well-developed interregional trading patterns. At the extreme, the periodic recurrence of poor crops or crop failure made interregional trade in grain a life-or-death imperative.

This need for trade in grain was political as well as economic. European agriculture was based on wheat; bread, mostly made from wheat flour, accounted for most of the calories in the European diet. Bread must also have accounted for a major portion of the average European's consumption expenditures. Thus, the price of bread was a political issue of the utmost importance. The usual way the political authorities resolved the issue was to fix the price per loaf, but, to accommodate the fact that there was often not enough grain to supply the market for bread at the fixed price, the size of the loaf was allowed to vary.[23] Still, the very stability of governments depended on finding enough grain to keep the size of the loaf within reason. Under the circumstances, especially in regions along the seacoasts and waterways, interregional trade in grain sometimes became a pressing political necessity, despite the inability of the political authorities to maintain their usual control over prices when they bought from foreign sellers.

Freebooting and the Rise of Free Markets

As we have seen, the fifteenth and sixteenth centuries were periods of important technological advances in shipbuilding and navigation—advances to which we owe the discovery and colonization of America. The new ability to navigate the seven seas had several consequences.

First, policing the oceans proved largely impracticable until the nineteenth century, when rival maritime powers shifted their attention from fighting each other to the suppression of piracy and the slave trade. Until then, merchant ships had to be armed for their own security, and the fact that privately owned vessels were regularly armed made for a considerable degree of insecurity for other vessels.

Second, piracy tended to be a successful enterprise so long as the pirates had secure bases from which to operate and places in which to sell their loot. These bases were regularly provided by nations interested in discouraging the maritime commerce of other nations, from the England of Sir Francis Drake to the North African Moslem ports against which the American navy operated in the early 1800s. In addition, both American and Asiatic coasts included large areas which had not been settled and brought under control of any government: islands in the Caribbean, the Mississippi delta, the Carolina coasts, the Malay peninsula all supplied bases for pirate activity.

Third, the attempts of European governments to establish exclusive control of maritime trade for the benefit of their own selected nationals generated resistance from two sources: first, from the nationals of other governments; second, from their own nationals who had not been selected for participation in the government's grant of a trading monopoly. Resistance took two forms: piracy and smuggling.

Smuggling was of particular importance in Britain's American colonies. Beginning in 1660, Britain adopted Navigation Acts which restricted British coastwise and colonial trade to vessels owned and manned by British subjects. Until after the Seven Years' War with the French ended in 1763, the general British policy was not to tax its American colonies, but to obtain revenue from them by maintaining an exclusive trade in "enumerated commodities." In addition, Britain discouraged the development of manufacturing in the colonies. The enforcement of the Navigation Acts had been lax up until 1763, and a prosperous American merchant marine had developed, much of it illegally. After 1763, the British began a search for revenues to pay off the debts of the Seven Years' War and to support a continuing garrison in the American colonies. They began with attempts to enforce the Navigation Acts. As early as 1764, Rhode Islanders responded by burning a revenue sloop. The British went on to impose direct taxes on the colonies under the Molasses Act and the Stamp Act. Adam Smith had a good deal to say both for and against British policies,[24] but whatever their merits, the political consequences were disastrous. The whole history of American trade outside British law had served to create an American merchant class with a view of their colonial obligations to Britain that was consistent with a ready acceptance of the idea of political independence.

Smuggling was also prevalent in England. Direct participation may not have acquired the social acceptability among leading citizens that it acquired in the American colonies, but there were English coastal communities where smuggling was so widely practiced as to support the conclusion that it enjoyed general community acceptance. In addition, there is little indication of middle-class or upper-class repugnance to wearing, drinking, and eating smuggled goods. Since Adam Smith was a conservative Scot, his views are especially worth quoting as pallid indications of what the average merchant or seaman must have thought of the laws they regularly violated:

> Thirdly, the hope of evading such taxes by smuggling gives frequent occasion to forfeitures and other penalties, which entirely ruin the smuggler; a person who, though no doubt highly blameable for violating the laws of his country, is frequently incapable of violating those of natural justice, and would have been, in every respect, an excellent citizen, had not the laws of his country made that a crime which nature never meant to be so. In those corrupted governments where there is at least a general suspicion of much unnecessary expence, and great misapplication of the public revenue, the laws which guard it are little respected. Not many people are scrupulous about smuggling, when, without perjury, they can find any easy and safe opportunity of doing so. To pretend to have any scruple about buying smuggled goods, though a manifest encouragement to the violation of the revenue laws, and to the perjury which almost always attends it, would in most countries be regarded as one of these pedantic pieces of hypocrisy which, instead of gaining credit with any body, serves only to expose the person who affects to practise them, to the suspicion of being a

greater knave than most of his neighbours. By this indulgence of the public, the smuggler is often encouraged to continue a trade which he is thus taught to consider as in some measure innocent; and when the severity of the revenue laws is ready to fall upon him, he is frequently disposed to defend with violence, what he has been accustomed to regard as his just property. From being at first, perhaps, rather imprudent than criminal, he at last too often becomes one of the hardiest and most determined violators of the laws of society. By the ruin of the smuggler, his capital, which had before been employed in maintaining productive labour, is absorbed either in the revenue of the state or in that of the revenue-officer, and is employed in maintaining unproductive, to the diminution of the general capital of the society, and of the useful industry which it might otherwise have maintained.[25]

The history of commerce in the Mediterranean, both during and after the Middle Ages, is to a considerable degree a history of trading combined with raiding and freebooting. Differences of religion between Moslem and Christian furnished a pretext for mutual depredations. Warfare was chronic. It legitimized the pirates by renaming them privateers, preempted naval forces otherwise available for the suppression of piracy, and weakened governmental authority over areas like Crete, whose ports and trading centers were essential to the profitable practice of piracy and smuggling.

The line between pirates and privateers was often transparently thin. Francis Drake was a pirate to the Spaniards, but when he returned to England from his successful voyage of 1577–1580, Queen Elizabeth knighted him on the quarterdeck of his flagship. And well she might: he returned a profit of 4700 percent to the holders of shares in the joint stock company that financed his voyage, who included Elizabeth and some of her principal ministers. Neville Williams estimates Elizabeth's profit at not less than three hundred thousand pounds, including both the return on her shares and an independent bounty.[26] It is little wonder that the pleas of the Spanish ambassador for the return of the loot went unheeded.

Maritime trade has always been a source of sedition. It has consisted not simply in trade, but in conquest and intercultural and interpersonal contacts that expose those who participate in it to the customs, beliefs, and interests of strange communities and strange peoples. The resulting influences never run wholly in one direction. By the nature of their occupation, sailors were a class removed from the constraints of the community's family, church, and political authority and its apparatus for controlling and directing human drives. The very perils of their occupation separated them from the conventions of home and bred a contempt for the authority of the stay-at-homes who made laws regulating maritime trade without having ventured themselves against its dangers. Yet sailors were not entirely an underclass; the leaders of these maverick seafaring adventurers included merchants and captains of considerable wealth and influence. Some, like Drake, were national heroes.

Maritime lawlessness was not, however, simply the unruly behavior of a few adventurous misfits who went to sea to escape domestic social constraints. From 1500 to 1800, some unknown but surely considerable part of the world's maritime commerce violated the laws of some sovereign state or other. Yet freebooting and smuggling in oceangoing vessels required, then as now, a highly developed land base. Vessels had to be built and equipped, manned and provisioned. Their sailcloth had to be woven, their sails cut, and their cordage twisted in mills that taxed the limits of technology of their times. Cannon could not be cast in island hideouts, nor could small arms be homemade. Captured or smuggled cargoes had to be sold at wholesale in such a way that they could be introduced into legitimate channels of retail trade. Overall, these activities could not conceivably have been carried on in isolation from normal maritime industry. Directly and indirectly, knowledge of lawlessness, contributions to its conduct, and profits from its success must have been widely shared. No doubt the merchants, shipwrights, and chandlers reflected but little on the political and economic philosophy of what they were doing. Had they done so, they might have realized that they had made the shift from the feudal conception of the good society as an ordered, hierarchical, and patriarchal family to the eighteenth-century conception of a society as an association of individuals each endowed with inalienable rights and liberties, not to be abridged, to use Smith's words once again, by laws which made "that a crime which nature never meant to be so."

So it was that during the sixteenth, seventeenth, and eighteenth centuries, maritime trade was at once a major field of economic growth and a field intractably resistant to medieval principles of political control. The efforts of Spain, Portugal, the papacy, and the emerging nation-states to control maritime commerce lacked the universal recognition necessary to confer legitimacy; they were, on the contrary, competing, contradictory, and mutually self-defeating. There were important trading routes, like those of the East India Company and the Portuguese routes to the Far East, in which partial political monopolies could be maintained through military control of the ports at either end of the voyage. But by the late eighteenth century, when Adam Smith supplied an intellectual basis for market pricing as a national policy, market pricing already prevailed over much of maritime commerce by main force of irrepressible lawlessness. Smith's *Wealth of Nations* appeared in 1776, and it was not a coincidence that, in the same year, American merchants and smugglers idealized their occupational objections to British navigation laws in the form of claims to personal freedom and political independence which the old regimes could no longer contain.

Neither the original nor the surviving records furnish a basis for a quantitative estimate of the role of maritime lawlessness in the shift from medieval to modern economic practices. But the medieval synthesis itself, carried forward in the ideology of the early central monarchies, guaranteed lawlessness an important role in effecting that change. The medieval system had few or no mechanisms for adopting new lines of division between politics and trade. Its political structure, well buttressed by the eternal verities of religion and the leadership loyalties of a landowning military aristocracy to their feudal superiors, had no room for admitting error or the possibility of improvement and self-correction. Modern political devices for proposing, discussing, experimenting, and adopting change were unknown. There was no systematic intellectual method of evaluating change by understanding the possibilities and uses of change; the only terms in which it could be discussed were the terms of heresy, immorality, and treason. Change could occur only to the extent that the political authorities overlooked it, ignored it, connived in it, or lacked the power to check it. It was the very completeness and rigidity of the feudal system that made heresy and rebellion necessary ingredients of change, and maritime trade was surely a prolific source of both ingredients.

It was the last quarter of the eighteenth century before Adam Smith advanced his discovery that "natural justice" lay on the side of the smugglers, not on the side of those who were carrying on the medieval tradition of strict control of maritime commerce. It was a discovery made long before by seafarers whose actions, from the fifteenth century on, challenged the medieval tradition more forcefully, if less eloquently, than Smith.

In the next chapter, when we examine the development of modern systems of taxation at fixed rates as a substitute for medieval systems of arbitrary expropriation to meet sovereign needs for wars and other more or less chronic emergencies, we will find that once again lawlessness, to the point of armed revolt, played a major part in the development of modern institutions.

In the next three sections, we will take up some questions concerning the transition from feudalism to capitalism that occurred between 1350 and 1750. First, we want to consider the effect of the rise of capitalism on the antecedent feudal aristocracy.

The Effect of Capitalism on the Feudal Aristocracy

The military power of the feudal aristocracy shifted to the royal governments in the late fifteenth and early sixteenth centuries. The resulting transfer of political power had an easily described effect on the feudal nobility. Initially, as individuals, the changes in the military arts cost the feudal lords the almost complete loss of their individual military and political power. But the effect of the changes on the power of the feudal lords collectively was quite different from its effect on them individually. Their social relationships gave them access to public office, both civil and military, with the result that the feudal families supplied much of the civil and military leadership of the new central governments, reorganizing, as it were, their forms of participation in politics to meet the new circumstances without relinquishing power itself. They were least successful in this process of adaptation in the Low Countries and most successful in Prussia, where the collective power of the Junkers in governmental affairs remained impressive until World War I and even later.

The change in the nature of political power required the seigneurs to move from the country to the urban centers of the royal courts. They became urbanized, spending at least part of the year at the royal court in Paris, London, or Vienna. Well before 1750, the urbanized aristocracy and their literary allies had reduced the rural magnate who never came up to the city to a laughingstock. The royal capitals were, of course, centers of an urban economy based on money transactions, not on trade in kind. In the palaces they built at the royal capitals, the postfeudal landholders found money essential. This need for money was an incentive to increase their manors' surplus production, over and above the needs of the manor itself, because it was this surplus which yielded money when it was sold outside the manor. Increasing surplus production required changes in production methods or reduced consumption on the manor—both hard to achieve within the rigid framework of manorial law and custom. As it became evident to landholders that they could increase their money revenues most readily by replacing the traditional feudal dues with money rents and the proceeds of sale of the products of hired labor, they accepted the sacrifice of feudal traditions and loyalties and converted their manors to a money agriculture. The change could be, and sometimes was, mismanaged by improvident landholders. But the landholders negotiated the change from a position of political and economic advantage, and there is as least as much indication of highly efficient oppression, to the seigneurs' gain, as of improvidence.

A change in seigneurial economic power is very much harder to pin down. The difficulty lies in the ambiguity of the connotations of *economic power*. In its simplest sense, the phrase means the power to satisfy one's economic wants. But it often seems to carry, implicitly if not explicitly, a more invidious connotation of power to prevent other people from satisfying their own economic wants by preempting or monopolizing a society's economic resources. To take the simpler sense first, when a predominantly agricultural economy expands into commerce and industry, the power of the agricultural sector to satisfy its economic wants does not necessarily decline. It is, on the contrary, very likely to be enhanced. Nothing is shifted, nothing is transferred, and nothing more substantial than some comparative statistics (like the ratio of agricultural production to GNP) declines. An expanding economy is an economy that is increasing its total economic power, and every major sector of the economy may well be increasing its own economic power at the same time.

The invidious sense of economic power reflects an unstated assumption that economic resources and economic output are fixed: in a familiar metaphor, a national pie to be divided among the family. The invidious sense tends to drop out of use during periods when economies are expanding and the demeaning incongruity of the notion that people are competing for a share in a fixed pie, like so many pigs at a trough, becomes obvious. In times of expansion, people can see stability or improvement in their own welfare, though perhaps less striking than the improvement in some other people's welfare, and there is less of a feeling that the success of others restricts one's own economic opportunities.

To put the same point another way, a major expansion of the role of merchants in Western European countries would have been inconceivable had not the principal holders of wealth in those countries perceived it to be in their own interests to buy from, and sell to, merchants. For a long time, these principal holders of wealth were, in England and France if not in Holland and Italy, the landholding feudal magnates. By selling their crops, wool, and the products of their forests and mines to merchants and by buying the products merchants brought from places far and near, the seigneurs may have contributed to the creation of an urban economy that eventually outgrew the agricultural sector, but in all likelihood they added greatly to their own material welfare in the process.

For agriculture accounted for more than half of European economic output long after feudalism had become a memory, and large agricultural estates survived widely in Europe well into the twentieth century. Some members of the landed aristocracy, whose estates had valuable mineral deposits or timberlands, profited handsomely from industrial expansion and the later Industrial Revolution; others owned real estate of immense value in London, Paris, and other rising cities. It thus seems altogether likely that the wealth of the seigneurial aristocracy increased, rather than declined, during the centuries of economic growth associated with the decline of feudalism.

Thus the notion of a transfer or decline of the economic power of the agricultural sector, as represented by the landholding class, in consequence of the growth of a mercantile sector, ends as a singularly poor description of what actually occurred. The role of the merchant is to intermediate, through money, the underlying local and distant exchanges of goods for goods. The merchants' products are place, time, liquidity, and risk. They buy here and sell there, buy now and sell later. Normally, these intermediary services are of substantial value both to those who sell to merchants and to those who buy from them. The notion that landowners somehow declined by taking advantage of merchants' services reverses the realities.

In any event, as an incident of urbanization, the Western world shifted to a money economy and concurrently undertook an immense expansion in local and interregional trade of goods for goods, mediated by money. The change no doubt worked to the detriment of some who proved incapable of adapting to it, but it worked also to the great benefit of wealth holders as a class and of the merchants, whose sphere of intermediation simply ballooned.

At the same time, nothing insulated the holders of wealth, whether of the seigneurial class or the merchant class, from the normal hazards of bad luck, war, improvidence, epidemic, and political mistakes in an age when the game was played for heads. By the nineteenth century, only a very few landholding families could trace their titles from the feudal period; but for much the same reasons, neither could many merchant or banking families trace their business origins back very far. The seigneurial class had never been uniformly prosperous. Impoverished members of the aristocracy had found employment in the crusades of the twelfth and thirteenth centuries, in the mercenary companies of the Hundred Years' War and the Italian city-states, and in the royal armies from the fifteenth century on. Some mismanaged their manors and spent themselves into financial ruin when feudalism was at its zenith. That some of them did likewise as feudalism faded into the capitalist age is hardly evidence of a melodramatic conflict between landholders and the rising merchant class.[27]

Considered by itself, the end of manorialism and the substitution of market relationships for feudal relationships in matters of land tenure might or might not have furthered the seigneurial interest. But it did not occur by itself. It occurred in a Europe expanding economically and with a rising population—both factors that almost guarantee a rise in the real value of land. Above all, it occurred in an urbanizing Europe in which an upper class out of touch with urban life and urban political, economic, intellectual, and artistic activity was simply a contradiction in terms.

The documentation of the effect of the expansion of commerce on the families of the seigneurial class is scattered through parish and county records, local histories, and family archives, leaving the historian tempted to generalize from a relatively few, particular cases. A broader basis for empirical judgment of the situation in England is supplied by the research of Lawrence and Jeanne Stone,[28] who traced the history of substantially all the houses used as seats by the large landholders of three English counties[29] from 1540 to 1880. These houses, the semipublic centers of the personal political, social, and economic power of their owners, were costly to build and costly to maintain. They were funded by the rents and other revenues from the agricultural enterprises whose headquarters they were, and the Stones leave no doubt that these enterprises remained prosperous for most of the period. Among the Stones' three counties, Northumberland, which developed a coal mining industry on the great estates, most strongly illustrates "the conflation of landed and monied interests."[30] They found only seven instances in the three counties, during those 340 years, in which the sale of a seat by an inheritor was caused only by financial ruin, and only forty-two in which financial difficulties played a part.[31] Sales of the largest estates, those with over three thousand acres, were rare.[32] As late as 1880, nine-tenths of the richest landowners in England were magnates whose wealth antedated the Industrial Revolution.[33]

Near the beginning of the period, the size of the landholding class was sharply increased by the distribution of Church and Crown lands to courtiers and public officials. After that, the Stones found the class of large landholders to be far more stable than conventional opinion would have it. Transfers because of financial insolvency being extremely rare, a much more common cause of sale was transfer by marriage or inheritance to someone who already had a seat, and who would use the proceeds of the sale to buy other land closer to home. The most likely purchasers were individuals born in the landholding class who were either adding to their holdings or investing fortunes made in public office, the law, the army, the navy, or in the India Company. Merchants and bankers were less often the buyers, and even when they did buy, their heirs were likely to sell, for life as an agricultural magnate was expensive and not necessarily attractive to those bred to mercantile and other pursuits with traditions of their own. Merchants were much more likely to build country houses for leisure and recreation, without investing in the supporting agricultural enterprises which gave the magnates' seats their economic significance, and without the participation in local political affairs which made them political centers.

The rural magnates developed their seats as centers of political power in a system of local government and parliamentary representation in which the franchise was narrowly restricted, voting was open rather than secret, and towns were underrepresented in Parliament. With the political reforms of the nineteenth century, the magnates lost control of the electoral process. This loss of control may well have been due less to the growth of an urban electorate than to the grant of the secret ballot to an enlarged rural electorate more directly affronted by the inherited wealth and power of the great landowners. Still, the change was no doubt linked to economic growth and to the accompanying expansion of the number of individuals who perceived themselves as qualified to vote by education and economic position. On the other hand, the magnates had followed policies generally favorable to the growth of commerce and had invested and participated in commercial growth. Thus, while political differences between the magnates and the new capitalists do not seem to have played a controlling part in the changes, economic growth was a force for democratization and eventually produced a society unmanageable by the old landed elite and their political devices.

No study similar to the Stones' has been made in France or other Continental countries, and it is possible that the landed classes on the Continent may have been affected differently from the landed classes in England. The Stones suspect that the differences have been exaggerated.[34] In any event, England shared with Holland leadership in the growth of commerce and industry, and if one is considering the hypothesis that the development of a merchant and industrial bourgeoisie was a cause of a decline in the wealth and power of the seigneury, it would not help the hypothesis to find that the effect was greater where the cause was weaker.

So we may assume that many members of the feudal aristocracy prospered from the emergence of capitalism and achieved places in the royal governments, in the new worlds of commerce, manufacture, and mining, and often in the new cultural world of the classic revival, religious pluralism, and the art, music, literature, and philosophy which came into its own between the sixteenth and eighteenth centuries. But they were old actors in a new play, and no longer in all the starring roles. For a long time after feudalism had ceased to be significant in Western society, the new upper class may very well have derived most of its wealth and power by inheritance from the old. But their wealth and power were now matched by new wealth and power of a merchant class. The economics of wealth seeking and the politics of power seeking had changed markedly, and there were new paths to membership in the upper classes of European societies. The humor sometimes perceived in the alleged propensity of the rising bourgeoisie to imitate the aristocratic life-style misplaces both the joke and the emphasis. In truth, the aristocracy that survived did so by adopting postfeudal roles, postfeudal culture, and a postfeudal (and therefore bourgeois?) life-style.

It makes a more interesting account of the West's transition from feudalism to capitalism to tell the story as a melodrama in which an ancient aristocracy was gobbled up alive by the upstart wolves of trade. Dramatic though they are, such accounts do not accurately reflect the general experience of either landowners or merchants. For the great landowners especially, the hypothesis that they were somehow less well off in 1700 than in 1300, their lives having somehow declined in the meantime, ought not to have survived even the most casual comparison of surviving examples of fourteenth- and eighteenth-century landowners' housing, let alone comparisons of education (this must be the only historical shift from illiteracy to literacy that is often portrayed as a decline), clothing, transportation, diet, and access to art, music, peer groups, and a wider variety of experience.

The Marxist Problem of Timing the Transition

Marx argued that the course of history consists in a sequence of social systems within which political, religious, and economic institutions are united in the service of a dominant class. The systems displace one another in well-defined, discontinuous steps which can be approximately dated as occurring when one dominant class loses power to its successor. This viewpoint has more than historiographic interest if, like Marx, one sees, in the shift of power from the feudal nobility, as a class, to capitalists, as a class, a historical mechanism that supports the expectation of a further shift in power from the capitalist class to the working class.

The view that one class displaces its predecessor in any active, revolutionary sense becomes hard to sustain if it turns out that the beginnings of the predecessor's decline appreciably antedated the beginnings of the rise of its successor. There is, to say the least, a loss of revolutionary vision in a view of the successor class as born and nourished in a vacuum left by the earlier demise of its predecessor, and periods of transition measured in centuries are hardly more inspiring. So it becomes of some importance to Marxist thought to date the feudal aristocracy's loss of dominance and the capitalist bourgeoisie's achievement of it. As recently as 1946, the publication of Maurice Dobb's *Studies in the Development of Capitalism*[35] gave rise to a debate among Marxists in which the exact timing of the transition from feudalism to capitalism became a central issue.[36]

It is well established that feudal institutions in Western Europe experienced a crisis as early as the fourteenth century—a crisis from which feudalism never fully recovered. On the other hand, it has been common practice to date the capitalist era as beginning in the sixteenth century—indeed the late-sixteenth century of Queen Elizabeth.[37] Dobb, for example, argues that if we think of capitalism in terms of a new mode of production, in which capital was used extensively in the productive process, "either in the form of a fairly matured relationship between capitalist and hired wage-earners or in the less developed form of the subordination of domestic handicraftsmen, working in their own homes, to a capitalist on the so-called 'putting-out system,' "[38] then such a system can be identified only in the late-sixteenth century.[39] If we take the introduction of central armies in the fifteenth century as the end of feudalism, the decline of feudalism is complete a century before the beginnings of capitalism. Thus we encounter a hiatus of two hundred years between the onset of the decline of feudalism (or more than one hundred years from the end of the feudal age) and even the beginnings of the rise of the capitalist mode of production. Dobb speaks of this as a period of "transition."[40]

Clearly, this transition period was, as Sweezy subsequently argued, "not a simple mixture of feudalism and capitalism: the predominant elements were neither feudal nor capitalist."[41] Such an assertion raises awkward questions within the Marxian framework, such as the implication that an institutional system might not have just one ruling class but several or none. Thus, in response to Dobb's position that the ruling class that prevailed during this transition period was still feudal, Sweezy replied:

> Let me . . . put my comment in the form of a query. Why isn't there another possibility which Dobb does not mention, namely, that in the period in question there was not one ruling class but several, based on different forms of property and engaged in more or less continuous struggle for preferment and ultimate supremacy?[42]

HOW THE WEST GREW RICH

It is interesting to recall that the inevitability of contention among different kinds of property holders was precisely what leading advocates of the American Constitution had in mind in urging its ratification by the separate states. In their view, not only was there a basic cleavage between the propertied and the propertyless; in addition there was also a deep cleavage among owners of different forms of property:

> [T]he most common and durable source of factions has been the various and unequal distribution of property. Those who hold and those who are without property have ever formed distinct interests in society. Those who are creditors, and those who are debtors, fall under a like discrimination. A landed interest, a manufacturing interest, a mercantile interest, a moneyed interest, with many lesser interests, grow up of necessity in civilized nations, and divide them into different classes, actuated by different sentiments and views. The regulation of these various and interfering interests forms the principal task of modern legislation, and involves the spirit of party and faction in the necessary and ordinary operations of the government.[43]

A mixed early postfeudal society surely existed, but then all societies are mixtures containing many elements of their pasts together with the seeds of their futures. Thus there was much in the Middle Ages which may fairly be called capitalist, and with equal certainty it may be said that there was never a time in the subsequent history of European civilization when the social institutions of the Middle Ages were completely displaced. It is worth recalling the eloquent reminder of the distinguished English social historian, G. E. Trevelyan, that modern societies preserve many of the institutions and "ways of thinking" of the Middle Ages, including the "idea that people and corporations have rights and liberties which the State ought in some degree to respect"[44]—an idea that capitalism could not do without. But the fact that any two ages are linked by the continuity of some institutions, as ours is to Rome by Roman law and the Catholic Church, does not make the time between a period of transition, save in the sense that all history is a period of transition.

While Marxists have been especially concerned with the problem of timing, there is also a problem of place in the concept of a displacement of a feudal aristocracy by a merchant class. The feudal aristocracy held sway in the countryside and the merchant and artisan class in the towns. Thus the question of *where* capitalism superseded feudalism is hardly less provocative than the question of when.

From an economic viewpoint, feudalism and manorialism were primarily arrangements for the political and economic organization of agriculture. Agriculture was the predominant economic activity, and the shift that took place in the countryside from manorial agriculture to an agriculture of small landowners and tenants was of more importance to more people than anything that was happening in the towns.

But the countryside is not usually looked upon by Marxists as the locus of capitalism. With some exceptions, agricultural production involves neither the employer-worker relationship found in manufacturing nor participation as a holder of circulating capital in extensive trading relationships. If we take these two characteristics to be essential to capitalism, we have to look for its antecedents in the towns and for its predecessor in the economic and political systems of the towns.

And once a town had bought itself free of its feudal obligations, its ruling class became its guild masters and merchants. It was a ruling class outside the feudal hierarchy, not chosen for military prowess, and thoroughly bourgeois. Bourgeois-ruled towns became commonplace in Europe at least two hundred years before the downfall of military feudalism. Thus, in the towns, where capitalism developed, its rise occasioned no change in the ruling class. Similarly, the downfall of feudalism in the countryside brought no new ruling class to the towns—nor to the countryside either, for that matter.

Reading history as an account of successive transfers of political power from one class to another is consistent with the possibilities, because political power rests on an exclusive authority over the military and the police. And because this authority is exclusive, two independent governments can not permanently share a single geographical jurisdiction. For this reason, a transfer of political power from one social class to another implies a conflict whose resolution is both an enhancement of the political power of the newly dominant class and a deterioration of the political power of the displaced class.

Economic power lacks this element of natural monopoly with a transferable franchise, for it is possible for numerous large and powerful economic interests to coexist and prosper in the same economic territory. Indeed, as we saw earlier in the chapter, the relationship between the rising merchant class and the landholding class was in many respects symbiotic. From about 1500 to 1700, the political and cultural situation of the landholding aristocracy had made a degree of urbanization a matter of importance to them, and their entry into a money economy thus also became important to them. The development of a merchant class was essential to the realization of the old aristocracy's goals. It is little more than a matter of choice of misplaced metaphors whether one characterizes the merchant class which facilitated the urbanization of the aristocracy as their servants or as their masters. Nor, in a world of open-ended coexistence of multiple economic interests, does it clarify the problem of the transfer of power to insist that political power is derived from economic power. So it may be, but from which economic power?

There is thus a fundamentally flawed analogy between political power and economic power when one interprets the economic rise of the merchant class as if it were a transfer of economic power from the feudal nobility, akin to the transfer of political power from the feudal nobility to the central monarchies. For if one thing is clearer than another, it is that the merchant class did not get its economic power from the feudal nobility, or by displacing or superseding the feudal nobility in agricultural or other economic activities. The merchant class gained economic power by expanding the trading activities in which it had always engaged. It is no wonder that the seizure-and-displacement story is hard to square with the facts and their order of occurrence, for it is a tale of events that did not occur.

All this is not to question that, as trade and the merchant class that conducted it became more and more important to the economic interests of European countries, prudent governments took more account of the interests of the merchant class than they had in the past. Venice and the Italian city-states were very nearly merchant polities. Elsewhere, as important sources of the funds required for central armies and the other apparatus of fifteenth-to-eighteenth-century government, merchants acquired access to the holders of political power and a degree of political influence—great in the Low Countries, not quite so great in England (where the squirearchy never stopped contesting the power of commercial and industrial interests), modest in France, uneven in Germany, and slight in Spain. Most important, after roughly 1500 the merchant class, its services having become indispensable to the operation of a money economy which fewer and fewer were any longer willing to do without, was more and more successful in asserting its autonomy from political and religious interference in its ever-widening sphere of activity.

The Transition from an Integrated to a Plural Society

At its zenith, around 1300, feudalism dominated the political and economic life of the Western countries. The Catholic Church intertwined with the feudal hierarchy by ritual, moral code, and direct participation. The secular poetry, art, and music of the times exalted the ethics and manners, the cult of courtly love and knight errantry of the feudal nobility who were its patrons. The economy was organized around the concept that status determined one's obligation to work and the fees or prices to which one was entitled for work. This is not to say that the dominance of the feudal nobility, viewed as a class, and of the essentially feudal idea that one's place in the world was determined by status, was beyond dispute. It was challenged by the city-states and the ambitions of the kings, and the feudal nobility itself was so fragmented by internal feuds and disputes as to raise a very real doubt that it regularly functioned politically or economically as an organized group. And the power of the Church was immense. But if, despite the internal divisions among the nobility and the separateness of the Church and the nonfeudal towns or cities, we view the Western European societies of the High Middle Ages as, on the whole, integrated societies, it was an integration that rested not merely on the force of shared ideas, but on the force of a combination of political and economic power in the hands of one social class.

The Western economies of the era of economic growth have been predominantly plural, divided into political, economic, scientific, religious, and other comparatively autonomous departments, with no class so clearly dominant over the others as the feudal aristocracy was in its heyday. One might expect, therefore, to find a less troubled perception of the transition from feudalism to capitalism by viewing it as a change from an integrated to a plural society, rather than as a transfer of all-encompassing power from a landed aristocracy to capitalists. Yet, during the Victorian period, beginning after 1850, the institutions of capitalism may fairly be said to have come to exercise, for a time, a dominance not only of economic but also of political, religious, and cultural life, a dominance akin to the dominance of the feudal aristocracy. Like the feudal synthesis, this dominance was not entirely unchallenged, and it can hardly be said to have survived the First World War, let alone the Second. But some slight measure of the solidity of the capitalist synthesis is suggested by the fact that when, near the turn of the century, Charles Eliot, president of Harvard, put together a "five-foot shelf" of books designed to contain all that an educated man need read, the name "Marx" did not appear in the index.

If it is to be argued that Western capitalism retained its pluralism during the period of its Victorian zenith, the argument must be based on the claim that the several sectors of Victorian society retained their autonomy, even though their interests were, for the time, largely reconciled in a mutually acceptable body of opinion that pervaded all respectable spheres of the Victorian world. So there may have been less disagreement than usual between the Victorian political classes and the Victorian economic classes, but concurrence and consensus are not the same thing as the consolidation of economic and political power characteristic of the feudal age.

In retrospect, we can appreciate that so long as the two modes of power remained separate, the period of consensus was unlikely to last. Our own post-Victorian experience has by now familiarized us with the fact that the political, economic, religious, and social institutions of a society need not be mutually reinforcing—something Marx could hardly have observed in his lifetime. It is, on the contrary, possible for them to be contentious, incompatible, and mutually destructive; or they may rock along in a state of indifferent toleration, where people render unto Caesar that which is Caesar's and unto God that which is God's. Whether a synthesis of society's institutions is desirable is a long-standing subject of controversy among utopians, who almost universally favor it, and libertarians, who view institutional synthesis as totalitarian and dismiss the utopian vision of pastoral contentment within the framework of a universal consensus as bovine.

Conclusion

Our investigation of the way the West got rich began with the economy of the Middle Ages. It was an economy with a familiar sound to those acquainted with modern ideologies. Wages and prices were set by political authority and by custom under a religious standard of justice. Those people who lived within the system (as we shall see later on, there were many who didn't) inherited their occupation, their social and economic status, their duties, and their rewards. Trade mediated by money arose only in the jurisdictional cracks between political authorities. It was a society which dealt with the risks of life by legislating rigidity. Economic growth is inherently a byproduct of change, and the political and religious ideology of the Middle Ages guarded against the heresies of change in every way it could.

Economically, the long move away from the Middle Ages can be traced through some seven centuries of expansion in trade and commerce. The first four centuries of this period of mercantile expansion coincided with the period of greatest growth and development of feudal society—an apparent anomaly made possible by the peculiarly feudal and pluralistic device of chartering, outside feudal jurisdiction, towns where trade could prosper. In the simplest sense, the expansion was a response to the pressures of what modern economists can recognize as comparative advantage, the advantage of regional specialization inside and outside Europe. Especially after the collapse of military feudalism and the emergence of the centralized monarchies, the response to comparative advantage was untidy—compounded of piracy, smuggling, and political corruption as well as of industry, diligence, and thrift. It interacted with technological development, each fueling the other. In this period of expansion, Western Europe created an active merchant class and marked out an arena where it could trade with enough freedom to leave it a world of opportunities ready to hand. It created also a network of markets, commercial and financial relationships, and economic institutions which needed only to be scaled upward in order to process a much larger volume of trade; no substantial generic modifications were necessary for them to exploit the technology of the Industrial Revolution.

By 1750, it could be said that the growth of trade had in itself appreciably improved economic welfare both through greater specialization and through the gains to welfare implicit in the fact that exchange presumptively benefits both parties. Likewise, there had been improvement in methods of production of both agriculture and handicrafts. In England, France, and the Low Countries, the change from manorial agriculture to an agriculture of individual peasant holdings had materially improved the food supply. In the most fundamental sense, capitalism built a new society by grafting an urban world onto a rural world, and this process was well under way before the Industrial Revolution. By the middle of the eighteenth century, the factory system was still to come, but by most tests Europe had developed, in mercantile capitalism, a full-blown economic system that was the successor to feudalism. Improved agricultural methods had created a body of landless farm laborers who were not merely ready for, but in need of, alternative employment. Finally, the West had already fulfilled its aspirations to wealth to the point where it had surpassed or equaled contemporaneous and earlier societies.

NOTES

1. "The Division of Labor is Limited by the Extent of the Market" is the title of chap. 3, bk. 1, *Wealth of Nations*.

2. Karl Marx and Frederick Engels, *The Communist Manifesto*, in *Selected Works*, vol. 1 (Moscow: Foreign Language Publishing House, 1962), p. 35. Note that Marx and Engels use the term *manufacture* to describe a production system which succeeded that of the

medieval guild. New patterns of worker specialization emerged but products were still produced by hand—that is, with no more than simple tools. Marx and Engels are here contrasting the manufacturing system with the later machine technology of an industrial age, which they identify by the term *Modern Industry*. "Modern" is, of course, relative to the state of industrial development in 1848.

3. The estimate of seventy million is from M. K. Bennett, *The World's Food* (New York: Harper &. Co., 1954). Colin Clark, in *Population Growth and Land Use* (New York: Macmillan, 1977), estimated the population of Europe in 1340 at 84.5 million, and in 1600 at 83.4 million (p. 64, table III.i).

4. See the discussion in David Grigg, *Population Growth and Agrarian Change: An Historical Perspective* (Cambridge: Cambridge University Press, 1980), p. 53.

5. Ibid., fig. 8, p. 52.

6. Clark, *Population Growth and Land Use*, p. 64, table III.i.

7. R. H. Tawney, *Business and Politics under James I* (Cambridge: Cambridge University Press, 1958), pp. 21–22.

8. William H. McNeill, *The Pursuit of Power* (Chicago: University of Chicago Press, 1982), p. 113, refers to the Liege gunmakers' skills as "the best and cheapest of Europe and the world" and observes: "Only when the artisans and capitalists of Liege and other arms centers did not have to part with their goods at prices decreed by Spanish or any other political authority, could rulers get what they wanted in the quantities to which they had become accustomed."

9. The best accounts are M. M. Postan, "The Trade of Medieval Europe: The North," and Robert S. Lopez, "The Trade of Medieval Europe: The South," chaps. 4 and 5, respectively, in *The Cambridge Economic History of Europe*, M. M. Postan and H. J. Habakkuk, eds., vol. 2, *Trade and Industry in the Middle Ages* (Cambridge: Cambridge University Press, 1952).

10. For a careful look at evidence concerning the development of commercial institutions in Southern Europe during the Middle Ages, see the extensive materials in *Medieval Trade in the Mediterranean World*, Robert Lopez and Irving Raymond, eds. (New York: Columbia University Press, 1955).

11. Postan, "Trade of Medieval Europe," p. 172.

12. The extent of relationships will, of course, depend upon the pattern of industrial development. The putting-out system, where labor remained in a rural nexus, involved less-extensive trading of food, whereas raw materials were typically secured through some kind of intermediary.

13. Singer et al., *A History of Technology*, vol. 3 (New York: Oxford University Press, 1957), pp. 474–77. See also T. K. Derry and Trevor I. Williams, *A Short History of Technology* (Oxford: Clarendon Press, 1960), chap. 6.

14. One must be careful, however, as to what constitutes an improvement. North and Thomas cite it as an advantage of smaller Dutch ships developed early in the sixteenth century that: "The presence of French, English and Dutch pirates also made it advantageous to divide a merchant's cargoes between several ships, thus reducing the risk of total loss." Douglass C. North and Robert Paul Thomas, *The Rise of the Western World: A New Economic History* (Cambridge: Cambridge University Press, 1973), p. 137.

15. See E. G. R. Taylor, "Navigation Instruments," in Singer et al., *A History of Technology*, pp. 523–29, and "Navigation," ibid., pp. 544–53, for a short account of developments in navigation during the fifteenth and sixteenth centuries.

16. Joseph Needham, "Science and Society in East and West," in Joseph Needham, *The Grand Titration* (London: George Allen &. Unwin, 1969), p. 190. See also E. L. Jones, *The European Miracle: Environments, Economies, and Geopolitics in the History of Europe and Asia* (Cambridge: Cambridge University Press, 1981).

17. Needham, "Science and Society, East and West," p. 197.

18. Joseph Needham, "Mathematics and Science in China and the West," *Science and Society* (Fall 1956): 343. See also Mark Elvin, *The Pattern of the Chinese Path* (Stanford: Stanford University Press, 1973).

19. For a further discussion of Marx's views on the role of technological change, see Nathan Rosenberg, "Marx as a Student of Technology," chap. 2 in Nathan Rosenberg, *Inside the Black Box* (Cambridge: Cambridge University Press, 1982).

20. Marx and Engels, *Communist Manifesto*, pp. 38–39. For further development of

Marx's views on large-scale industry and its consequences, see chap. 15 of *Capital*, vol. 1 (London: Lawrence & Wishart, 1974).

21. Ibid., p. 37.

22. As Landes has observed:

Anywhere east of the Elbe, for example—Prussia, Poland, Russia—the local lord enjoyed so much authority over the population that abusive treatment even of those residents who were nominally free, let alone the unfree serfs, was widespread and unrestrainable. In these areas of seigneurial autonomy, moreover, conditions actually grew worse from the sixteenth to the eighteenth centuries, as the spread of commercial agric 'ture enhanced the incentive to exploit the weak.

David Landes, *The Unbound Prometheus* (Cambridge: Cambridge University Press, 1969), pp. 17–18.

23. Fernand Braudel, *The Structure of Everyday Life*, trans. Sian Reynolds (New York: Harper & Row, 1981), p. 145.

24. Adam Smith, writing at the time of the American Revolution, seemed to think that the Navigation Acts and the restrictions on enumerated commodities did the colonists little harm and helped pay the cost of furnishing military protection from the French. Still, he did remark: "To prohibit a great people, however, from making all that they can of every part of their own produce, or from employing their stock and industry in the way that they judge most advantageous to themselves, is a manifest violation of the most sacred rights of mankind." *An Inquiry into the Nature and Causes of the Wealth of Nations* (New York: Oxford University Press, 1976), p. 582. For the "enumerated commodities," see p. 577. See also pp. 594–641 for a discussion of the shortcomings of trade monopolies, the need to tax the colonies directly, and the possibility of having the colonies represented in the British Parliament.

25. Ibid., p. 898.

26. Neville Williams, *The Sea Dogs: Privateers, Plunder and Piracy in the Elizabethan Age* (New York: Macmillan Publishing Co., 1975), pp. 118, 145.

27. Braudel, in *The Wheels of Commerce* (New York: Harper & Row, 1982), makes the point that merchants used their new-found wealth to purchase land from the older aristocracy, sometimes in settlement of improvident borrowing by a "wasteful, ostentatious and economically vulnerable" nobility. (P. 594.) And he writes: "The same process occurred in Japan, where the merchant of Osaka took advantage of the misfortunes and wastefulness of the *daimyo* ... The dominant class would sooner or later provide a meal for those on its heels." (P. 595.) But this seems to rewrite, in terms of class struggle, the old story of turnover among the wealthy—a story by no means limited to the old nobility and no more than incidentally associated with more fundamental political or economic changes. Taking a few centuries either side of 1350 in either France or England, if one were to make up lists of the most powerful families of 950, 1150, 1350, 1550, 1750, and 1950, how much overlap between any two lists should one expect to find? Not even the royal houses remain the same.

28. Lawrence Stone and Jeanne C. Fawtier Stone, *An Open Elite? England 1540–1880* (Oxford: Oxford University Press, 1984).

29. The counties were Hertfordshire, Northamptonshire, and Northumberland, "selected so as to offer the greatest possible diversity of social experiences." Ibid., p. 41. Hertfordshire was near London, Northumberland as far from London as possible, on the Scottish border, and Northamptonshire in between. The sample included 2,262 owners of 362 houses over 340 years. (P. 53.)

30. Ibid., p. 285.

31. Ibid., p. 157.

32. Ibid., p. 171.

33. Ibid., p. 220. The Stones refer to the period between 1740 and 1860 as "times of unparalleled prosperity for the landed classes." (P. 385.)

34. Ibid., p. 280. Still, the Stones note the argument that no Continental landed elite owned so large a part of its nation's territory in the nineteenth century as the English. (P. 416.)

HOW THE WEST GREW RICH

35. Maurice Dobb, *Studies in the Development of Capitalism* (London: G. Routledge & Sons, 1946), especially chaps. 1–4.

36. Paul Sweezy et al., *The Transition from Feudalism to Capitalism*, 2d printing (New York: Science and Society, 1963).

37. According to Karl Marx: "Although we come across the first beginnings of capitalist production as early as the 14th or 15th century, sporadically, in certain towns of the Mediterranean, the capitalist era dates from the 16th century. Wherever it appears, the abolition of serfdom has been long effected, and the highest development of the middle ages, the existence of sovereign towns has long been on the wane." Karl Marx, *Capital* (London: Lawrence & Wishart Ed.), p. 669.

38. Dobb, *Studies in the Development of Capitalism*, p. 18. North and Thomas, *Rise of Western World*, 144–45, date the putting-out system in the Low Countries as arising in the sixteenth century.

39. Ibid.

40.

It is ... true, and of outstanding importance for any proper understanding of this transition, that the disintegration of the feudal mode of production had already reached an advanced stage *before* the capitalist mode of production developed, and that this disintegration did not proceed in any close association with the growth of the new mode of production within the womb of the old. The two hundred-odd years which separated Edward III and Elizabeth were certainly transitional in character.

Ibid., p. 20.

41. Sweezy, *Transition from Feudalism to Capitalism*, p. 15.

42. Ibid., p. 64.

43. James Madison, "The Federalist Number Ten," in Benjamin F. Wright, ed., *The Federalist* (Cambridge: The Belknap Press, 1961), p. 131.

44.

It is indeed useless to look for any date, or even any period, when the Middle Ages "ended" in England. All that one can say is that, in the Thirteenth Century, English thought and society were mediaeval, and in the Nineteenth Century they were not. Yet even now we retain the mediaeval institutions of the Monarchy, the Peerage, the Commons in Parliament assembled, the English Common Law, the Courts of Justice interpreting the rule of law, the hierarchy of the established Church, the parish system, the Universities, the Public Schools and Grammar Schools. And unless we become a Totalitarian State and forget all our Englishry, there will always be something mediaeval in our ways of thinking, especially in our idea that people and corporations have rights and liberties which the State ought in some degree to respect, in spite of the legal omnipotence of Parliament. Conservatism and Liberalism, in the broadest sense, are both mediaeval in origin, and so are trade unions. The men who established our civic liberties in the Seventeenth Century, appealed to mediaeval precedents against the "modernizing" monarchy of the Stuarts. The pattern of history is indeed a tangled web. No simple diagram will explain its infinite complication.

G. E. Trevelyan, *English Social History* (London: Longman's, Green, 1947), pp. 95–96.

4 / The Evolution of Institutions Favorable to Commerce

The growth of European trade from the fifteenth century on was dominated by private traders in shifting and complex relations with their national political authorities. More was needed for the expansion of trade than a simple abandonment of the medieval objection to trading at negotiated prices. Medieval society was not well adapted to even the most essential trade between regions, and the expansion of trade which occurred in the fifteenth and sixteenth centuries required the invention or adoption of new institutional arrangements to supplement or replace the old medieval institutions.

Some of the institutional innovations reduced the risks of trade, either political or commercial. Among them were a legal system designed to give predictable, rather than discretionary, decisions; the introduction of bills of exchange, which facilitated the transfer of money and provided the credit needed for commercial transactions; the rise of an insurance market; and the change of governmental revenue systems from discretionary expropriation to systematic taxation—a change closely linked to the development of the institution of private property.

Large-scale trade outgrew the family firm whose internal loyalties were based on kinship. What was required was a concept of a firm as an entity distinct from its proprietor and from the family—an entity with a continuity of association among those whose working lives were organized around it and with a capacity similar to that of the family enterprise to create feelings of loyalty and duty. Such an entity required a degree of separation of the individual's property and transactions from the property and transactions of the enterprise unknown in the earlier family firms. The invention of double entry bookkeeping supplied the required separation; perhaps even more important, double entry bookkeeping supplied a financial history and financial picture of the enterprise which enabled other traders to deal with it as an entity and with some understanding of its capacity to meet its commitments.

The need for a form of enterprise which could command trust and loyalty on some basis other than kinship was only one facet of a broader need: the rising world of trade needed a moral system. It needed a morality to support reliance on its complex apparatus of representation and promise: credit, representations as to quality, promises to deliver goods, or to buy goods in the future, and agreements to share in the proceeds of voyages. A moral system was also needed, as we have just seen, to supply the personal loyalties necessary to the development of firms outside the family, as well as to justify reliance on the discretion of agents, ranging from ships' captains to the managers of remote trading posts and including merchants' own partners. The ethical system of feudal society had been built around the same military hierarchy as the rest of feudalism, and it did not meet the needs of the merchants. It was out of the turbulence of the Protestant Reformation that there developed a morality and patterns of religious belief compatible with the needs and values of capitalism. The part thus played by religion in the rise of capitalism is one of the more controversial topics of economic history.

Finally, two political factors affected the growth of trade significantly. The first was the mercantilist partnership between the royal authorities and the merchants. As compared to a system of free trade, this alliance of politicians and traders no doubt lessened rather than increased trade. But by comparison to the antecedent restrictions, it was an alliance that did much to expand commerce. The other factor was that military power was consolidated in several royal governments, rather than in one comprehensive empire. From the sixteenth century on, political power passed from the diffusion of the Middle Ages, to the oligopoly of a relatively few governments. But no government succeeded in achieving monopoly, and competition among governments for the patronage of the merchants was important—even essential—to the formation of an autonomous economic sphere.

It is difficult, because of the close relationship between the rise of trade and the rise of the towns, to distinguish between institutions invented to meet the needs of trade and those invented to meet the needs of urbanization. Even so basic a capitalist institution as private property grew as much from the needs of urban life as from the needs of trading.

We can consider each of these many developments only briefly: (1) legal enforcement of contracts and property claims; (2) bills of exchange and banking; (3) insurance; (4) the substitution of taxation for confiscation and the recognition of property rights; (5) economic association without kinship; (6) double entry bookkeeping; (7) the development of a religious and moral system suitable to the commercial community; (8) the mercantilist partnership; and (9) the divided European political structure and the part it played in allowing the growth of an autonomous merchant class.

The Changing Legal Structure

Large-scale commerce ordinarily involves transactions that take place over a considerable period of time. Unlike the everyday cash sale of goods, the medieval trading voyage, even within the Mediterranean, often lasted six months or more, and trading ventures to the East took years. Thus, the merchant who bought timber, wool, wheat, leather, salt, spices, or other commodities in large quantities was engaged in transactions that took time, and that could not be consummated without unreasonable risk in the absence of dependable commitments at the outset from sellers, shipowners, buyers, and lenders. It was not absolutely essential that these commitments be legally enforceable; reliance could be, and was, placed upon the character and reputation of the other parties to the transaction. But the lack of enforceability added to the risks and thereby raised the cost of trade and limited its volume.

The development of a commercial law and commercial courts was in part a response to the expansion of commerce. A comprehensive and reliable commercial law required judges experienced in adjudicating commercial disputes and the development of a body of precedents for deciding them. Medieval courts could not develop a body of commercial law until the volume of commerce was large enough to generate a regular flow of commercial disputes, and courts were not likely to be presented with commercial disputes so long as their decisions were made unpredictable by lack of precedent, by medieval concepts of discretionary justice, and by possible bias against foreigners. The impasse was broken here and there, in the courts of trading cities, by the late Middle Ages. But it was not until the latter part of the eighteenth century that the royal courts in London had accumulated enough experience in deciding disputes over insurance, bills of exchange, ships' charters, sales contracts, partnership agreements, patents, arbitrations, and other commercial transactions to make English courts and law seem a factor contributing positively to the development of English commerce. The English courts allowed suits by foreign merchants and acquired a reputation for treating foreign litigants with scrupulous fairness. Mercantile transactions, insurance policies, and credit instruments subject to English law seemed more secure, more calculable in their consequences, less subject to the vagaries of sovereigns and changes of heart by one party or the other—advantages reflected in the growth of the British insurance industry, of London as a world financial center, and of British trade generally, as well as in low interest rates. Other Western countries sought to emulate these advantages by adopting commercial codes and establishing commercial courts.

Max Weber emphasized another aspect of European law. The West inherited from Roman law a formal, logical mode of juristic reasoning, ostensibly free from discretionary, ritualistic, religious, or magical considerations. Modern legal thought tends to emphasize and even justify the informal and discretionary aspects of judicial decision, but there remains a striking contrast between a system of law which seeks to make the legal consequences of human action coherent and predictable and the many systems which either have no such objective or allow it to become lost among competing objectives. The Western system lends itself to calculability; the others do not. As Weber put it:

> In China it may happen that a man who has sold a house to another may later come to him and ask to be taken in because in the meantime he has been impoverished. If the purchaser refuses to heed the ancient Chinese command to help a brother, the spirits will be disturbed; hence the impoverished seller comes into the house as a renter who pays no rent. Capitalism cannot operate on the basis of a law so constituted. What it requires is law which can be counted upon, like a machine; ritualistic-religious and magical considerations must be excluded.[1]

The Evolution of Institutions Favorable to Commerce

Thus, systematic law added to the ability to predict the behavior of others, including people of all social ranks, in a wide variety of possible contexts. It thereby reduced the risks of trading and investing with them. This substitution of comparatively dependable rules for the discretionary justice of the manorial courts or the royal father figures, however Solomonic they might be, was an important element in the development of capitalist institutions.[2]

Bills of Exchange

Merchants in Italy began using drafts drawn on their accounts with each other as a substitute for payment in coin during the thirteenth century. The use of bills of exchange permitted merchants to transfer the amounts they owed each other in the same way that we now transfer bank balances—by drawing a check, which is itself a bill of exchange drawn on a bank. In Antwerp, and later in Amsterdam, markets developed for the buying and selling of bills of exchange. In effect, these markets supplied, at low cost, the short-term credit needed to finance a growing commerce.

Deposit banking developed in a somewhat circuitous way, concurrently with the market for bills of exchange. Trading in bills of exchange circumvented the Church's prohibition of the payment of interest, since the purchase of a bill at a discount from its face value was treated as reflecting the risk that the bill might not be honored when it was presented, rather than as a payment of interest. As bills of exchange came into wide use, lesser-known merchants began to deposit funds with more widely known merchants, in order to place themselves in a position to pay by bills of exchange drawn on the more widely known merchants. It did not take long for the merchants who accumulated these deposits to discover that only a small portion of the deposits needed to be kept on hand to cover withdrawals, and that the balance could safely be used to buy bills of exchange at a discount—that is, for lending money at interest despite the prohibition of usury. They thus introduced deposit banking as a profitable and growing business in a society which prohibited the payment of interest.

Insurance

The earliest form of marine insurance was a loan, repayable with a high premium if the voyage succeeded, but not repayable at all if the vessel was lost. Known as a "bottomry and respondentia bond," this form of insurance loan was used by the ancient Greeks. The separation of insurance from financing took place in Italy, perhaps as early as the latter part of the twelfth century, when insurers began to guarantee against loss of the vessel in return for a stated premium. There is, however, only a scant record of the use of marine insurance before the sixteenth century. A Florentine statute of 1523 contained a form of policy which differed but little from the form adopted by Lloyd's in 1779. Lloyd's itself dates from the late seventeenth century. Merchants who were prepared to accept an insurance risk would meet with shippers and shipowners at Lloyd's coffee house, in London, and negotiate the premium. The insurers were individuals who either did not have enough capital to pay for the loss of an entire vessel or who felt it imprudent to accept the whole risk. So, once a rate had been agreed upon, a number of insurers would sign on, each for a portion of the risk.

The development of marine insurance markets in Italy, Amsterdam, and London separated commercial risks from the risks posed by the perils of the sea and made it possible for merchants to venture increasingly large amounts of capital on the commercial outcome of a voyage without subjecting themselves to the less calculable uncertainties of the sea. The commercial risk was that the cargo might not bring prices as high as had been hoped for, so that the voyage might not be as profitable as expected, or might even result in a loss. But only rarely was there a commercial risk that the cargo might prove wholly worthless and produce a loss of the entire capital invested—a risk decidedly present from storms, pirates, and the other hazards of the sea.

The division of risk between the perils of the sea and the perils of the market, with specialized insurers undertaking the former and merchants and shipowners the latter, converted an intrinsically hazardous business into one capable of drawing capital from relatively cautious and conservative merchants. Some such division of risk was essential to the development of maritime commerce. It is possible to think of other ways the risks might have been divided, such as marketing shares in the voyages themselves at Lloyd's instead of shares in the risk of loss from perils of the sea. But this would have required the underwriters at Lloyd's to familiarize themselves

The Evolution of Institutions Favorable to Commerce

not simply with the risks of the sea, but also with the commercial risks involved in every line of trade conducted by sea. The division between specialists in maritime risks and specialists in market risks greatly facilitated the growth of maritime trade.

Substitution of Taxation for Confiscation

Familiar as we are with constitutional systems that deny governments the power to seize the property of their citizens without compensation, most of us find it difficult to visualize societies in which governments had and commonly exercised exactly that power. Feudal sovereigns might have protected individuals' property against the depredations of other individuals, or even of other sovereigns, as a shepherd protects his sheep from shearing by others. But against their own sovereign lord, individuals of all social classes had to protect their accumulated capital and savings as best they could. Arbitrary assessments were always possible, and even some of the established feudal dues were unpredictable in timing and amount. The chronic threat of such assessments made it prudent for any considerable accumulation of assets of the subject to be held in mobile and concealable form.

Mobility and concealment were not, however, devices available to the barons whose accumulated wealth was in land, stored crops, farm animals, farm buildings and dwellings. The alternative was resort to force, and it was with force that the English barons confronted King John at Runnymede in 1215, long before their military power had been lost to professional armies. The result of the confrontation was Magna Carta, the great charter accepted conventionally as establishing the right of subjects to the enjoyment of their property without arbitrary expropriation by the Crown. Although it was a feudal document, sometimes deprecated as overstressing the rights of the great landowners who exacted it of the king, it contained a number of provisions guaranteeing rights to merchants (including foreign merchants), and merchants benefited from the property rights it established as part of English law and political tradition. The establishment of the right to hold property free of the risk of arbitrary seizure was important to the expansion of commerce, and Magna Carta gave the English a considerable lead on their neighbors.

HOW THE WEST GREW RICH

In the fifteenth century, as professional armies, paid and supplied by money, replaced the self-sustaining feudal militias that fought in exchange for land tenure, the new central monarchies required regular and dependable sources of money. The traditional emergency levies might do once in a while, but as regular sources of revenue they could not be depended upon, partly because of cumulative public resistance and partly because of their disruptive effect, likewise cumulative, on economic activity. The upshot was that rulers were encouraged to give up the power to deal with the property of their subjects in an arbitrary way in exchange for the substitution of the power to levy regular taxes at stipulated rates.

This change had an effect whose significance can be appreciated only by contrast to the Asian and Islamic empires, which never adopted it. Arbitrary levies on the property of a subject were a ready means of political reprisal and social control, preventing successful merchants from accumulating wealth on a scale judged inappropriate to mere subjects. The abandonment of arbitrary levies was thus a major step toward allowing those in the economic sphere to develop their own ways of creating and accumulating wealth. Landes describes the change in this way:

> ... the ruler learned that it was easier and in the long run more profitable to expropriate with indemnification rather than confiscate, to take by law or judicial proceedings rather than by seizure. Above all, he came to rely on regular taxes at stipulated rates rather than on emergency exactions of indefinite amount. The revenue raised by the older method was almost surely less than that yielded by the new; over time, therefore, it constituted a smaller burden on the subject. But the effect of this uncertainty was to encourage concealment of wealth (hence discourage spending and promote hoarding) and to divert investment into those activities which lent themselves to this concealment. This seems to have been a particularly serious handicap to the economies of the great Asian empires and the Muslim states of the Middle East, where fines and extortions were not only a source of quick revenues but a means of social control—a device for curbing the pretensions of *nouveaux riches* and foreigners and blunting their challenge to the established power structure.[3]

The result was not entirely a substitution of concealment of assets from the tax collector for concealment of assets from the sovereign's bailiffs. So long as taxes were levied at known rates at known times, a merchant could calculate the prospective profits from investment in goods or real estate too visible and immobile to escape taxation, deduct the prospective taxes, and at least occasionally make a decision in favor of investment in taxable wealth.

120

The Evolution of Institutions Favorable to Commerce

The distinction between confiscation and taxation made the greatest difference in England and Holland, where the royal governments lost the power to impose arbitrary levies without gaining the power to impose arbitrary taxes. In both countries, the power to impose taxes resided in parliaments in which the merchant class was strongly represented, and the two countries were the leaders in the accumulation of visible forms of mercantile wealth.

In retrospect, it is difficult to see how even modest amounts of trade could have been carried on except where merchants had a measure of immunity from arbitrary seizure. Substantial commerce required a tangible apparatus scarcely less visible than real estate, though for the most part much more mobile: ships, stocks of goods, and warehouses in quantities roughly proportional to the volume of trade. Both commerce and its tangible apparatus were bound to grow more rapidly where the apparatus enjoyed security from arbitrary expropriation—that is, in England, Holland, and the trading cities that had gained similar immunities through feudal charters.

Feudal and early modern monarchs incurred the political risks of expropriation and extortion because they badly needed the money, mainly to finance chronic wars with each other. At the time of Runnymede, King John had inherited the resentment left by the exactions of his predecessor Richard the Lion Heart, whose highly romanticized crusade, ransom from captivity in Austria, and recurring wars with Philip Augustus of France had been military failures of negligible benefit to the subjects who had been forced to pay for them. John himself was financially pressed by the cost of resisting the French king's conquest of Normandy. Both English and French monarchs also resorted to the sale of monopolies, a mode of extortion whose long-term burdens could exceed the burden of intermittent expropriations, and in France almost certainly did so. There, the monopolies were local, and in combination with internal tariffs they precluded the development of a French national market until after the Revolution of 1789.

The practical exercise of political power over the merchant class was circumscribed by physical limits to the ability of officials to suppress smuggling and piracy and by the possibility that sufficiently disgruntled capitalists might move their enterprises and capital to another country. Amsterdam seems to have benefited greatly from such movements. Also, the invention of bills of exchange had made it easy for merchants to keep their liquid capital, if not their tangible assets, beyond the reach of the royal fiscal agents. "Dozens of . . . refuges for entrepreneurs were scattered across the face of Europe, thanks to its peculiarly fragmented political geography."[4] In an age of concern about Swiss bank accounts and Caribbean tax refuges, it is useful to remember that it was not until the nineteenth century that merchants developed enough confidence in governments to invest in large, immobile factories rather than in bills of exchange, ships, and movable stocks of goods.

In some instances, of course, the conflict between the fiscal requirements of the state and the insistence on autonomy by a vigorously expanding capitalist class could be resolved only by a resort to arms, as in seventeenth-century England and sixteenth- and seventeenth-century Holland, which spent decades fighting itself free of the financial exactions of its Spanish overlords. In England, the conflict was not simply a question of Cromwell's period of Puritan rule or the Glorious Revolution of 1688. It was a question once again of irrepressible lawlessness. As Nef described it:

> During the reigns of James I and Charles I, from 1603 to 1642, the policies of industrial regulation and direct taxation of property practically broke down because of the resistance of leading English merchants and industrialists. They used their growing influence as justices of the peace, as municipal officials, and as members of the House of Commons to defeat policies which seemed unfavorable to their interests. The inability of the Stuart kings and their privy councils to enforce unwelcome proclamations, orders, and other regulations which were issued without the support of Parliament, gave the English merchants and industrialists advantages over the French in developing heavy industry. A weakening of effective administrative control over economic life facilitated the early English "industrial revolution."[5]

The elimination of arbitrary exactions and the substitution of regular taxation belong in the category of government policies that tended to assure that the benefits of trade and accumulation would accrue to those who did the trading and accumulating—what North and Thomas have characterized as definitions of property rights in which private benefits and costs parallel social benefits and costs. Although such policies are important to trade and accumulation, before the nineteenth century instances where governments adopted such policies as a matter of deliberate choice, as distinguished from having the policies thrust upon them by armed revolt of the burghers, are rare. Almost always, government measures that altered property rights were adopted for the primary purpose of increasing revenues. When such measures had a favorable effect on property rights, it was a lucky accident, not a result of a belief held by anyone in authority that the measure might further long-term economic growth. Inevitably, measures favorable to property rights were offset by opportunistic measures of the opposite character.[6]

The Evolution of Institutions Favorable to Commerce

As exceptions to the general tendency of governments to put immediate fiscal interest ahead of the rational development of property rights, North and Thomas mention the administration of the Low Countries by the Burgundian dukes and the early Hapsburg rulers, whose enlightenment eventually faded as their need of money for wars grew more acute.[7]

In order to judge whether increased security of property in fact contributed to the growth of trade, one has to ask whether there really was greater security of property in 1750 than in, say, 1300. The struggle of merchants to secure their possessions from arbitrary seizure by their own sovereigns took place through centuries of chronic warfare, and the gain in security of property was at least partly offset by the looting and requisitions of invading armies. However, until after the French Revolution, European wars tended to be fought on a small scale, with comparatively little pillaging of the merchants. There were conspicuous exceptions, such as the Hundred Years' War in France. But after that ended, in the mid-fifteenth century, France remained substantially free of invaders until 1814. A second exception was the devastating Thirty Years' War fought in Germany from 1618 to 1648. Still, it is a fair conclusion that the wars of the times fell short of offsetting the gains in security of property interests vis-à-vis the merchants' own sovereigns. This was especially clear in England and only a little less so in France and, after the sixteenth century, in Holland. We may conclude that there was, in fact, a net increase in the overall security of property during the period of growth of Western trade.

Economic Association without Kinship

The family is no doubt the most ancient of social institutions, and in all likelihood it is also the most ancient of economic organizations. We take for granted the economic role played in agriculture by every member of the extended family except the very youngest. In the Middle Ages, the business enterprise, like the family farm, tended to be a family affair, built on a family fortune, and with key managerial and technical skills bound to it by family and kinship ties. Even in so advanced a mercantile community as Venice, commerce was organized around family partnerships and ad hoc joint ventures. The need for long-term investment in shipping

123

and shipbuilding on a scale too large for family enterprise was supplied by the state.[8]

Apart from the family, the Middle Ages offered no satisfactory models for mercantile enterprises. The two great hierarchies were the feudal system itself and the Church, and both embodied the obligations of subordinate to hierarchical superior in elaborate ritual and oath. Solemn though they were, neither produced, in the practice of the later Middle Ages, the practical relationships of trust and confidence needed for long-term economic association.

Yet, where the required scale of trading exceeded the capacity of family firms and of ad hoc joint ventures, private firms could conduct trade and investment only if there existed some basis, beyond kinship, for mutual trust. The expansion of nongovernmental, secular trade and investment after the sixteenth century would simply not have been possible without the creation of a purely economic form of organization, capable of producing the necessary equivalent of family ties. Without it, some solution like the Venetian oligarchy, with the state financing projects too large for families and joint ventures, would have been unavoidable.

How these loyalties were created, what psychological sources were tapped to bring into being new forms of fidelity to institutions wholly alien to the moral and religious structure of the age then passing, we cannot know for sure. Even today, every Western country has its share of individuals who feel themselves incapable of forming attachments to economic enterprises grubbing for sales and profits, and what we have left of such feelings is only a small residuum of the attitudes that must have prevailed in the immediate aftermath of feudalism. Creating the seventeenth-century version of the organization man was no small achievement. Later on, commercial enterprises became common, and the requisite organizational loyalties become explicable by the personal associations formed in long years of apprenticeship and subordinate service. But in their origins, nonfamily enterprises must have borrowed from other sources.

The notion of loyalty to an enterprise also presupposes an enterprise. Sombart claims that capitalist enterprise involves:

> ... the emergence of a separate economic organism, above and beyond the individuals who are engaged in economic activity: all business transactions that formerly occurred in a more or less separate way—side by side or one after the other, in various ventures—are now included in one conceptual unit, namely, the enterprise. This unit is a going concern, continuing beyond the lives of the participating individuals and appearing as the "carrier" of the economic actions.

The Evolution of Institutions Favorable to Commerce

It is true that in earlier times supra-individual organizations had occurred, particularly in the economic sphere, but they were organisms binding together natural groups of human beings in all aspects of their life. The continuity of such communities or total associations was the consequence of the natural sequence of generations. Tribe, clan, family, even village community and guild, were examples of this kind of supra-individual organism, and economic actions were a part of their existence, viewed in relation to them.[9]

Group loyalty, mutual trust, and mutual reliance were sentiments cultivated out of necessity among those who shared the dangers of military life or life at sea, and it may not be coincidence that many English and Dutch merchants of the turbulent sixteenth and seventeenth centuries had been warriors or mariners. It is easy to imagine business enterprises formed among companions who learned to trust each other at war or at sea, for it happens often enough in our own times. (The generation which fought the American Civil War in their twenties, for example, invented that epitome of enterprises not based on kinship, the modern industrial corporation, in their forties.) But there were other conceivable sources of such ties. The groups of merchants of the English and Dutch towns and cities were relatively small, often organized in guilds, and united by a passionate interest in the political outcome of the Dutch struggle against the Spanish or the British merchants against the Stuart monarchs. Their personal status among their peers depended largely on their record of fulfilling their commitments and standing behind their representations— habits which, carried over into organized enterprises, would go far to meet the requirements of our organization man.

In the early corporations, the trust and confidence required had to bridge a more remote and distant relationship. It was not a matter of relying on close business associates, but of the reliance of a large number of investors on the integrity and skill of the directors and managers of a corporation. Somehow, appreciable numbers of people with money (those who invested in corporations) must have come to believe that others (those who directed and managed corporations) were honest, diligent, and could be trusted. Such trust presupposes a widely shared sense of business morality, and that sense of business morality could hardly have been borrowed from the teachings of the Catholic Church or from the older aristocracy. Its sources have to be sought, in part, in the associations of merchants within a trading community, perhaps reinforced in England and Holland, the leading trading countries, by the appeal of the Reformation and its concomitant morality—a subject considered at greater length later in this chapter. The very contempt in which the clergy and the older aristocracy held the rising merchant classes could only have encouraged the merchants to develop a code of honor pivoting on scrupulous care in timely payment of debts and on loyalty to superiors—both points of striking weakness in the aristocratic code.

Perhaps the historians who wonder at the emergence of organizational ties not based on kinship thereby betray an aspect of their own feudal inheritance: an aristocratic disdain of bourgeois moral values. It is certainly more usual to stress the aggressiveness and acquisitiveness of post-feudal merchants than to stress their moral creativity, but the inescapable fact is that the merchant class evolved a moral system suited to life in highly organized enterprises. In no other way could the enterprises that went beyond family and organized such ventures as colonization, foreign trade, and canal building (and, later, railway building) have found the institutional loyalties essential to carrying out their economic functions—and find them they plainly did.

Double Entry Bookkeeping

In order to create an economic enterprise distinct from the family, it was necessary first to conceive of an enterprise distinct from the family, and second to establish some way of distinguishing the affairs of the enterprise from the family and household affairs of its principals. This was not easy to do in an age when the members of the family and the members of the enterprise were one and the same, when the enterprise and its owners dwelt in the same premises,[10] and when all the members of the family traded for the joint account of the family.

In a world of family enterprises, the need for a distinction between family and individual assets must have arisen from the desire of individual members of the family to trade for their own account or to distinguish between their own assets and the assets of the family, at least sometimes. It was necessary to do more than simply list the assets of the enterprise separately from the assets of the individual owners. The record of the enterprise's transactions had to be separated from the record of individual transactions, and it had to be related to the assets of the enterprise rather than of the individual. The successes of the enterprise had to be recorded as enhancing its assets, the failures as diminishing them.

The Evolution of Institutions Favorable to Commerce

The most obvious reason for merchants to adopt double entry book-keeping was that it provided a check on the clerical accuracy of the entries for each transaction. The general principle behind the complex rules of the system was that one member of each pair of entries recorded a change in assets (or income) and the other an equal change in liabilities (or expenses). Entries of the two types could be separately totaled, and if the totals did not match, an error must have occurred. Neither the principle nor the merchants' interest in clerical accuracy carried any hint that double entry bookkeeping might be the source of the idea of the continuing enterprise as an entity separate from its owners, except for one point: for liabilities to equal assets, the liability accounts had to include both liabilities to third persons and the liability of the enterprise to its owners—its net worth.

Thus a bookkeeping system whose practical appeal lay in its ability to detect errors compelled the merchants and bookkeepers who used it to acquire the habit of thinking of the enterprise, either as a debtor to its owners or as itself the owner of its own net worth. Either way, it was an abstraction created by its own books of account. Sombart went so far as to say that "One cannot imagine what capitalism would be without double-entry bookkeeping."[11] For double entry bookkeeping is an actualization of the profit-seeking firm as a truly autonomous (indeed, one might add, as did Sombart, an abstract) unit, the property of which is no longer mixed up with that of the family, the seigneury, or other social units.

There was another reason for developing a formal record of the assets and transactions of the enterprise, going much beyond the need to distinguish the enterprise from its individual owners. It was indispensable to the growing use of credit to find an objective, quantitative method for evaluating the financial status and prospects of the firm. The needed method eventually emerged from double entry bookkeeping as a set of rules for expressing all economic transactions in numerical terms. It grew into an agreed-upon procedure for recording all economic events in a measurable and therefore calculable way. In a very real sense, economic reality became that which could be expressed in numerical terms in the books: *Quod non est in libris, non est in mundo.*

It was not, in other words, so much the initial advance represented by double entry over single entry bookkeeping that made the great difference in the development of Western capitalist institutions, as it was the impetus which that advance gave to the development of financial accounting and the practice of evaluating the credit of the enterprise by viewing its status in terms of its balance sheet and its activities in terms of its statement of profit and loss.

HOW THE WEST GREW RICH

The Development of a Moral System Suitable to Commerce

There is another facet to the emergence of an autonomous business sphere that, historically, was of immense importance. The growth of commerce created a world in which individuals were free to enter into contractual relations on terms that reflected current supply and demand conditions and the risks of the transaction. The morality needed for forms of economic association outside the manor, guild, and family was only a beginning. The whole complex of the promissory and agency apparatus of commercial capitalism needed a morality epitomized in such terms as "honest dealing," "promise keeping," and "punctuality," and (in the case of employees) "industry," "diligence," "honesty," and "fidelity." At least in the sixteenth and seventeenth centuries, the source of this morality had to be in religion.

The social teachings of the Catholic Church came from the Middle Ages. During the Middle Ages, the custom of the manor rigidly prescribed the terms of manorial economic relationships, and in the towns the rules of the guilds were nearly as comprehensive. A morality inherited from a medieval economy based on faithful compliance with customary relationships could not have been expected to fit a commercial economy in which individual choice and bargaining had superseded custom as the basis of exchange, and which was eventually to displace most of the earlier customary relationships. The prohibition of the charging of interest is the most often cited example of Church doctrine running head-on into the needs of a rising merchant class. But something more important was missing: a moral outlook that would facilitate, encourage, and legitimize the rising world of market relationships.

What was required for the growth of Western economies did *not* include a high degree of moral concern for the welfare of the least well-off members of society, nor did it contain a suggestion that unusual economic success was not evidence of personal merit, was evidence of defects of character, or might be an obstacle to one's eternal salvation. There is little indication of any widespread belief that greater equality of distribution of income might be morally desirable. Many modern moralists put these matters near the center of political and economic morality, concerned as it thus becomes primarily with questions of distribution. But almost no one thinks of them as relevant to economic growth or to the development of Western economic institutions—matters which turn chiefly on questions of productivity and supply. The perception of poverty as morally intolerable in a rich society had to await the emergence of a rich society, considerably later than the period with which we are now concerned.

The moral outlook required for mercantile capitalism was supplied in the sixteenth century by the Protestant Reformation. The specific connection between the historic rise of capitalism in Europe and the Protestant Reformation, beginning early in the sixteenth century, has been hotly debated. The debate has raged, without letup, ever since the publication of Max Weber's *The Protestant Ethic and the Spirit of Capitalism.*[12] Weber, while he was careful to state that he was not attempting to present a monocausal explanation of the rise of capitalism, argued that Protestantism had served to promote it. As Landes explained, Weber:

> . . . never argued that Protestantism alone made capitalism; indeed he specifically adduced other factors to complete his explanation of the development of a modern industrial economy: the rise of the modern nation-state resting on a professional bureaucracy; the advances in science; the triumph of the rationalist spirit. But he came to the problem of capitalism with a worldwide perspective. He wanted to know why industrial capitalism appeared in the West, specifically in northwestern Europe, and not for example in China, which only a few hundred years before had been far richer and more advanced politically, economically, and technologically. And he found that Protestantism was one of the salient differentiating characteristics.[13]

Weber had in mind particularly the Calvinist branch of Protestantism. Calvin placed great emphasis on the notion of the "elect" who are predestined for salvation. In Weber's view, Protestantism cultivated an intense devotion to one's work or "calling," in order to assure oneself that one had in fact been selected for salvation.

Weber may have missed the point, though not in a way that mattered very much to his argument. In the context of his quarrel with the Roman Catholic Church, Calvin was concerned both to deny that the Church hierarchy had the power to dispense salvation and that the priesthood had moral responsibilities or other powers which set them apart from laymen. The doctrine of predestination contradicted the idea of a church with the power to supply salvation.[14] To those naturally curious about whether they were predestined for salvation or destruction, Calvin offered assurances based on the evidence of their calling, faith, and flight from sin, along with contrary and calamitous assurances to those who did not hear the call, lacked faith, or persisted in sin.

It is easier to recognize a directly influential factor in the economic success of Protestant communities in another doctrine also related to Calvin's rejection of special powers of the priesthood, that is, the doctrine that the work of all members of the Christian community, and not just those engaged in specifically church work, is a form of service to God. He drew the inference for everyday work, that "we shall not rush forward to seize in wealth or honors by unlawful actions, by deceitful and criminal arts, by rapacity and injury of our neighbors; but shall confine ourselves to the pursuit of those interests, which will not seduce us from the path of innocence."[15] He may have been more provocative than he knew in not ruling out the seizure of wealth and honors by industry, diligence, and dependability.

In any event, Calvinism imbued the work of the merchant and artisan, as much as the work of the priest or monarch, with all the values of religious service. It is no wonder that the sanctification of work by Calvinist Protestantism served to generate reliable patterns of behavior among its membership of a kind which were wholly compatible with a smoothly functioning capitalism: an intense commitment to work, dependability, diligence, self-denial, austerity, thrift, punctuality, fulfillment of promises, fidelity to group interests—in short, the "inner-worldly asceticism" that Weber contrasted with the "other-worldly asceticism" of the Catholic monk who, lacking the Calvinist belief that the world's everyday work is itself as sanctified as any other form of service to God, rejects the concerns of this world by retreating to a monastery. The "inner-worldly asceticism" of the Protestant, by contrast, led to an intense channeling of human energies into business affairs at the same time that it spurned the frivolous pleasures of the material world. Weber was not the first to observe the adverse secular consequences of other-worldly asceticism and monasticism. Edward Gibbon, in his *Decline and Fall of the Roman Empire*, published in 1776, had criticized the more ancient civic irresponsibility of the monastic movement in chapter 37, observing, in one of his milder comments, that "whole legions were buried in these religious sanctuaries; and the same cause, which relieved the distress of individuals, impaired the strength and fortitude of the empire."

In the prolonged debate over Weber's thesis, two counterarguments have been dominant.

First of all, capitalist institutions emerged in many places where Catholicism had prevailed, especially in such places as Italy, portions of Southern Germany, and portions of the Low Countries, though perhaps not so rapidly as in Protestant areas. It is perhaps useful also to keep in mind the complication that both Protestantism and Catholicism were heterogeneous. The Protestantism of the Church of England and the established Lutheran Church of the German principalities is sometimes considered closer to Roman Catholicism than to the Protestantism of Calvin or Knox or, later,

The Evolution of Institutions Favorable to Commerce

of John Wesley. One must therefore ask why England, probably the least Protestant of the Protestant countries and particularly repelled by ascetic Protestantism owing to its unhappy seventeenth-century experience with Cromwellian Puritanism, led in the development of capitalism. Perhaps a partial answer is to be found in the Calvinist tradition of the Scotch, who are popularly thought to play a role in British business out of proportion to their numbers. Catholicism also, from the time of the first missionary journeys to Ireland and other parts of Northern Europe, had shown substantial willingness to adapt to local circumstances and local customs. Without a close (and by now all but impossible) study of local Church practices in Catholic areas where commerce developed at a relatively early date, it is not safe to assume that the local religion was as out of touch with the needs of the merchant class as mainstream medieval Catholicism.

Second, many have argued that the causal relation between Protestantism and capitalism was far more complex than the rather simplistic interpretation attributed to Weber. One might argue, not that Protestantism created capitalism, but rather that capitalism created Protestantism.[16] By this, Weber's critics have essentially meant that Protestantism offered a set of beliefs which were highly congenial and flattering to the successful capitalist, who therefore embraced it. Or, less invidiously, one might argue that the new merchant and capitalist class felt religious and moral needs not satisfied by the religious institutions of feudalism, thereby creating a vacuum which Protestantism filled.

For it is hardly necessary to suppose that capitalists picked a religion to suit their financial interests. It would not be surprising if sixteenth-century individuals with a stronger moral sense than was common in Renaissance Europe were attracted, in numbers disproportionate to their number in the population, by religious reform movements and were useful, again in numbers disproportionate to their number in the population, in emerging capitalist institutions. Renaissance society is not noted for its high moral scruples, and the traits of character essential to an emerging capitalism may very well have been most common among those interested in religious reform.

It is not necessary to attempt to assess the merits of these positions.[17] Rather, we would emphasize some relatively uncontroversial aspects that bear more on our present concerns. Weber's interest was not so much in the specific doctrine or symbolic content of Protestantism as it was in the patterns of social behavior inculcated by that belief. Protestantism undoubtedly encouraged and legitimized specifically capitalist patterns of behavior or patterns which were highly conducive to success in the capitalist marketplace. Second, there can be little doubt that the long-term effect of the Protestant Reformation was the progressive removal of religion from intimate involvement in the sphere of business activity. Protestantism sanctioned a high degree of individual responsibility for moral conduct and reduced the authority of the clergy; and Protestant merchants were able to free themselves of clerical constraints which they found incompatible with their own experience. Under the circumstances, it would have been too much to expect the Catholic clergy to continue to stress doctrines which could only turn prosperous parishioners toward Protestantism. More and more, the religious world came to concede that what seemed right within the world of commerce was right for that world. Thus, with respect to the prohibition on usury, Sir John Hicks observed:

> [T]he appearance of banking, as a regular activity, is an indication that the bar against interest, at least in appropriate fields, is breaking down. This began to happen, it should be emphasized, long before the Reformation; in so far as the "Protestant Ethic" had anything to do with it, it was practice that made the Ethic, not the other way round.[18]

Thus, religious authorities, whatever judgments they might pronounce over the conduct of business affairs, gradually abandoned the position that the day-to-day conduct of business ought to be regulated by, or be directly subject to, ecclesiastical authority. In the course of the sixteenth and seventeenth centuries, the business sphere was, in a word, secularized. As it grew increasingly independent of ecclesiastic authority, it acquired a much higher degree of autonomy, this time from religious intervention, than it had previously possessed. Religion was gradually transformed from a restraining influence upon capitalist development to a force that both sanctioned and supported mercantile capitalism by precisely the moral teachings required for the smooth running of the rising commercial system. This was not wholly a question of the theological content of either Catholicism or Protestantism. It was partly a question of the competition inherent in the existence of several rival religions, which, like the existence of competition inherent in the existence of several rival national states, enabled a rising merchant class chafing under the restraints of one authority to take refuge with another more congenial.

A full appreciation of the historical relations between capitalism and religion requires an understanding of the dialectical relation between those two spheres but, in addition, a comprehension of the accommodation and change that occurred within the religious sphere itself. Tawney saw a "violent" contrast between the "iron collectivism" practiced in Calvin's Geneva and the "impatient rejection of all traditional restrictions on economic enterprise which was the temper of the English business world after the Civil War," a century later—a view that has been shared by others.[19]

The perception of inconsistency arises in part from two of the many different strains in Protestant thought and in part from a combination of changes in moral perceptions and a certain intellectual insensitivity to the meaning of the shift from an integrated to a plural society. Protestantism emphasized the belief that salvation was intensely individual and personal. Good works done under the compulsion of social control or compassionate transfers of wealth forced by the tax collector did not advance the pilgrim's journey to salvation by a single step. At the same time, Protestant preachers and churches viewed themselves as instruments of teaching and example, and they had no hesitation about lecturing their errant sheep on the errors of their ways and not much hesitation in excluding persistent wrongdoers from their communities. Between the sixteenth and nineteenth centuries, a burgeoning middle class came to view the "traditional restrictions on economic enterprise" as oppressions of a decadent aristocracy. Yet the two strains in Protestant thought continued, and the Protestant clergy did not allow to pass unnoticed what they saw as excesses of nineteenth-century businessmen. Indeed, the clergy played an appreciable part in the enactment of the first English factory acts. But by then the world of business had become highly specialized, and those who lived in it were no more receptive to correction by the moral judgments of the clergy than were those who lived in the worlds of science, art, music, or literature. Tawney might as aptly (or ineptly) have contrasted the "iron collectivism" of Puritan England with the "impatient rejection of all traditional restrictions" on literary enterprise, "which was the temper of the English" literary world "after the Civil War"—the age, be it remembered, of Restoration drama.

Protestantism, a product of the sixteenth century, did not anticipate Adam Smith's economic doctrines of the eighteenth century. It was, of course, not an economic doctrine at all. But it supplied the merchant class with both a highly individualized moral responsibility outside the control of its clergy and with moral dogmas that emphasized exactly the thrift, industry, honesty, and promise keeping needed for capitalist institutions. The emerging merchant class and its autonomous economic sector, like any other large and autonomous social system, needed a suitable moral and ethical system. To the degree that Protestantism was more suited to the need than Catholicism, it contributed to the rise of capitalism.

One other probable consequence of the Reformation should be mentioned. It has been argued that a reduction in expenditures for religion, like reductions in expenditures for war, is favorable to industrial expansion. Such a reduction followed, in England, Henry VIII's conversion to Protestantism, and it may have followed in other Protestant countries. A closely related point is that, in Catholic countries, a substantial portion of the land was owned by ecclesiastical foundations and so was not available for purchase in the usual course of trade. The dispossession of these foundations, in the countries that became Protestant, added appreciably to the land and mineral resources available for exploitation by the merchant class. John U. Nef put the point as follows:

> Henry VIII's break with Rome (followed soon by dissolution of the monasteries and other religious guilds) and the resulting reduction in the number and wealth of the clergy, provided conditions which were favorable to industrial expansion on the eve of the Elizabethan age, long before the constitutional struggle became acute. The proportion of the national income required to maintain ecclesiastical foundations was much smaller in England after the dissolutions of 1536 and 1539 than it had been for some eight hundred years. This was by no means true of the countries which remained Roman Catholic. In France the clergy retained their hold over property and remained as numerous as ever. In Spain and the Spanish Netherlands the combined number of priests, monks, and nuns increased.
>
> The partial dispossession of the clergy in England (and in other Protestant countries—Sweden, Denmark, Scotland, and Holland in particular) made it easier than during the Middle Ages for private businessmen to get possession of land and mineral resources on advantageous terms.[20]

Apart from dispossession of religious foundations, the Reformation had implications for the long-term growth of the respective wealth of the capitalist class and the Church, for Calvin's doctrines of predestination and sanctification of work implied that capitalists might just as well keep their property in the family instead of donating or willing it to the Church.

The Mercantilist Partnership

Here we take up an institutional invention which was important in smoothing the politics of the transition from feudalism to capitalism and in pointing the way toward modern capitalism: partnership or alliance between governments and their merchant classes. The partnerships were eventually rationalized in the collection of policies embraced under the rubric of mercantilism.[21] Historically, they were particularly significant in effecting an expansion of trade in circumvention of the established medieval traditions and institutions.

In the Europe of the emerging monarchies, governments were first of all military power centers, and the perceived economic prerequisite of military power was gold to buy arms (often abroad) and to pay the troops. Spain had a supply of gold from the New World. In the other countries, domestic supplies of gold were difficult to expropriate from the subject and, once expropriated and spent, were exhausted. The mercantilist solution was for the country to sell more goods abroad than it imported, taking the difference in gold. Raw materials capable of conversion into manufactured goods which could then be exported at a profit were desirable, even though mercantilists did not relish importing anything. If the raw materials could be obtained from colonial possessions with no outlay of gold to foreigners, so much the better.

To get the highest possible revenue from the export of any particular product, mercantilist theory implied that export of the product should be handled by a suitable monopoly, so that, for example, one French merchant would not end up bidding against another and thus lower the price of a French manufacture to a foreign buyer. Similarly, establishing a monopoly of the import of a product avoided the risk that domestic buyers might bid against each other, unnecessarily raising the price of imports. Grants of such monopolies made business partners of monarchs, their more influential courtiers, and merchants. The political authorities thus became substantial personal participants in the profits of the mercantile and manufacturing enterprises. The theory may sound odd and the practice corrupt, but mercantilism was strong enough, and widespread enough, to account for the decline of the Italian cities and the Hanseatic League from the commercial preeminence they had enjoyed since the twelfth century.

The practice is more understandable not as a product of the adoption of mercantilist principles (which were developed after the practice), but rather as a holdover from feudalism and an aspect of the battle over the power of the Crown to levy taxes without the consent of a parliament. In feudal society, trading rights were regularly granted by charter of the appropriate feudal lord. Fairs were held by grace of the lord's charter and the guilds gained their authority over their respective crafts in the same way. These charters were sold to provide revenues in situations where the power to tax was hotly contested. The revenue might be a lump sum, continuing payments of taxes for the privileges granted, or both. Taxes from the wool trade, administered by the Merchants of the Staple, were a principal source of revenue for the British Crown for a long time. But however strange the new nation-states' twin practices of restricting imports and granting exclusive trading privileges to their own nationals, these practices played a significant role in building a merchant class free to trade, within the scope of its numerous charters, on its own terms, because sufficiently influential members of the political class shared the profits.

One other observation should be made about the grants of monopolies. Many of them were designed to encourage the introduction of new industries. England, particularly, owed its conversion from an exporter of raw materials to a manufacturing economy in good part to monopolies granted to induce Flemish and other immigrants to bring their skills to England. Monopolies were granted to foreign weavers as early as 1331 and subsequently extended to many other trades. According to North and Thomas, fifty-five monopolies were granted under Elizabeth, and of these twenty-one were issued to foreigners or naturalized subjects.[22]

At the distance of centuries, it is not easy to evaluate the factors that entered into the grants of trading monopolies. They put the royal governments on the side of expansion of trade, not necessarily as a matter of principle, and perhaps wholly to enhance revenues. In a way, the trading monopolies served as a teaching device, as if they had been invented to supply the royal governments with a concrete, short-term demonstration that they shared with the rising merchant class an interest in the expansion of trade. By Adam Smith's day, the lesson had been taught, and he urged that the device be discarded. But partnerships between government and capitalists persist in forms ranging from patents to the peculiar institutions of military procurement, and they are a device not forgotten in today's Third World.

Europe's Political Division as a Source of Growth

In the light of the mercantilist practices discussed in the last section, it seems certain that the development of capitalism in the West owed a good deal to the fragmentation of Europe into a multitude of states and principalities. There was not one "Empire, Inc.," but a number of competing "Monarchies, Inc.," "Princes, Inc.," and "City-States, Inc." Competition among the political leaders of the newly emerging nation-states, each anxious to retain the revenues and credits available from a merchant class and each aware of the political danger of allowing neighboring states to increase their capacity to finance military power, was an important factor in overcoming the inherited distaste of the rural military aristocracy for the new merchant class. Had the merchants been dealing with a political monopoly, they might not have been able to purchase the required freedom of action at a price compatible with the development of trade.

Numerous empires have governed regions of economic and cultural diversity comparable to the West without relaxing their political control over trade. In these empires, characterized by fully consolidated political authority and less internal competition for mercantile patronage, there was no similar impairment of political control. One must also add that there was no similar development of trade.

In chapter 3, we referred to the Chinese empire, whose technology was superior to the West's and which had a highly developed civil service based on merit. One possible reason that its superior technology was not translated into economic growth of the sort achieved in the West is that the very rationality of the Chinese merit system led to a centralization of power, whereas in Europe power was diffused among the landed aristocracy.

In technology, the Chinese had a tendency to reach and hold plateaus. Once a good way of doing something was discovered and established, it seemed to harden into a custom immune to change. It is not correct to think of Chinese technology as limited to inventions designed to give pleasure or to satisfy the curiosity of the imperial court. Chinese junks, waterwheels, and the compass were practical tools widely applied. And in both China and the West, there were always those whose economic interests were adversely affected by technological innovation, and who from time to time bitterly resisted its intrusions. In China, however, they had the implicit support of a mandarinate satisfied with the status quo, unwilling for technological change to disturb anyone and with nothing to gain itself from troublesome innovations. Despite this conservatism, Chinese technology and the Chinese economy reached a level more advanced than the West of, say, the fifteenth century. But a policy of making only such changes as do not appreciably disturb anyone is a formula for glacially slow advance, both in technology and in economic growth.

In the West, the individual centers of competing political power had a great deal to gain from introducing technological changes that promised commercial or industrial advantage and, hence, greater government revenues, and much to lose from allowing others to introduce them first. Once it was clear that one or another of these competing centers would always let the genie out of the bottle, the possibility of aligning political power with the economic status quo and against technological change more or less disappeared from the Western mind. Thus, it may not be wholly a coincidence that modern Japan, which led in adapting Western institutions to its own economy, also grew out of a politically decentralized feudal society.

The Chinese experience allows us to conjecture that, in Europe, the late development of a civil service, the counterpart of the mandarinate, helped hold open the way to the rise of capitalism. The differences in values observed by Needham between merchants and mandarins are very much like the later differences of values between merchants and Prussian, French, or English civil servants. For the European civil servants, the timing was wrong; they came to power too late to prevent the rise of capitalism, and their only recourse for expressing mandarin values was a gradual, Fabian exertion of authority over the aspects of capitalism not too mercurial to elude their grasp.

The puzzle of the Chinese combination of advanced technology and lack of economic growth is an aspect of a larger question about the relation between imperial political structures and economic growth. The Chinese empire was only one of a number which failed to find the road from poverty to wealth. Unable to generate sustained growth, these empires always declined. Rostow sees in the declines a hubris which leads empires to undertake wars beyond their resources and to burden their economies to the point where growth turns to decline:

> The central fact about these traditional empires is that they were not capable of generating sustained growth. Their periods of expansion gave way to periods of decline. The most typical proximate cause of decline was war. While the possibility of war and, sometimes, limited military engagement encouraged policies which tended to modernize the society, large and protracted wars led rulers to grasp for more resources than the society could generate, and self-reinforcing processes of economic, social, and political decline ensued. The rapid decline of Athens in the fifth century B.C. and the slow grinding decline of the Roman Empire in the West are, of course, classic examples of this process. It can be seen also at work in the fall of some of the Chinese dynasties and elsewhere.[23]

It may be that a prerequisite to sustained economic growth is an economy trading across a geographical area divided among a number of rival states, each too small to dream of imperial wars and too fearful of the economic competition of other states to impose massive exactions on its own economic sphere. The United States had a federal system in the nineteenth and early twentieth centuries in which political intervention by the national government was narrowly restricted by political tradition and constitutional interpretation, while political intervention by the state governments was restricted by the fear of economic competition from other states. Whether the constitutional reconstruction of the United States as a classic empire is compatible with indefinitely sustained economic growth is, of course, a topical and controversial question. The same question can be asked about the Soviet Union, where the exactions required to support imperial ambitions have been a heavy drag on economic progress.

Conclusion

In assessing the sources of the West's economic development, the inventions of technology spring more readily to mind than the inventions of institutions. Yet the contribution of new institutions to Western economic growth was unmistakable, and in some cases essential. As an economic domain emerged in Western Europe, it had to devise its own institutions, sometimes alone and sometimes by interaction with the political realm.

A striking fact about the institutions that emerged as Western mercantile capitalism developed is the degree to which they were bound to the cities as their origin and context. The close linkage between trade and urbanization shows up again and again in the development of trading institutions which were urban as well. In an age when communications were slow, the development of enterprises based on ties other than kinship was inherently urban, presupposing a community of numerous individuals with the knowledge and skills needed to form and staff mercantile enterprises. Insurance is a striking example of an urban-centered development, for the spreading of risks among many merchants presupposes many merchants gathered in one urban market, whether Florence, London, or Amsterdam. Even the legal enforcement of mercantile contracts requires a community where the volume of such contracts and the volume of conflicts about them is large enough to support a specialized corpus of law, judges, lawyers, or arbitrators. The move from bills of exchange to deposit banking could hardly have occurred had not the deposit bankers enjoyed the confidence of the merchants in their own city before they gained credit elsewhere. The division of Europe into national states was not intrinsically an urban phenomenon, but the hospitality of the Italian city-states, and later of Amsterdam and London to trading not yet welcomed elsewhere, encouraged economic development.

The sixteenth-century changes in religious belief were not specifically urban, and their role in the emergence of mercantile capitalism has been much argued. Market institutions placed almost everyone in the dual position of debtor and creditor, and they required a moral system woven of obligation and responsibility in the fulfillment of one's commitments and of industry in the performance of one's work. The Protestant Reformation probably supplied a moral system somewhat better suited to economic growth than the older Catholic teaching. In the end, one may say that the merchants of London and Amsterdam eventually gained a degree of credit with merchants in other cities, and hence a scale of operations, never attained in Venice, Genoa, Florence, or Milan. But too many factors entered into the differences in achievement to enable us to attribute them solely, or even in great part, to a moral superiority not everyone would concede. The important point is that the economic sphere did acquire a moral system that, whatever its merits or shortcomings, allowed that sphere to function as an autonomous social group and furnished the merchant group with the morale it needed to be able to ignore, without awkward feelings of guilt, the preachments of outsiders. Each sphere of activity in a plural society requires its own moral system, similarly subject, and yet almost impervious, to outside criticism, informed and uninformed.

NOTES

1. Max Weber, *General Economic History* (New York: First Collier Books Ed., 1961), p. 252. Weber attributes to Judaism the fact that Christianity was free from the influence of magic:

> Since Judaism made Christianity possible and gave it the character of a religion essentially free from magic, it rendered an important service from the point of view of economic history. For the dominance of magic outside the sphere in which Christianity has prevailed is one of the most serious obstructions to the rationalization of economic life. Magic involves a stereotyping of technology and economic relations.

Ibid., p. 265.

2.

> The capitalist form of industrial organization, if it is to operate rationally, must be able to depend upon calculable adjudication and administration. Neither in the age of the Greek city-state (polis) nor in the patrimonial state of Asia nor in western countries down to the Stuarts was this condition fulfilled. The royal "cheap justice" with its

The Evolution of Institutions Favorable to Commerce

remissions by royal grace introduced continual disturbances into the calculations of economic life. The proposition that the Bank of England was suited only to a republic, not to a monarch, . . . was related in this way to the conditions of the time.

Ibid., p. 208.

3. David Landes, *The Unbound Prometheus* (Cambridge: Cambridge University Press, 1969), pp. 16–17.

4. William H. McNeill, *The Pursuit of Power* (Chicago: University of Chicago Press, 1982), p. 114.

5. John U. Nef, *War and Human Progress* (Cambridge: Harvard University Press, 1950), p. 15. The "early English industrial revolution" refers to Nef's claim that England had experienced such a revolution in the century after 1540.

6. Douglass C. North and Robert Paul Thomas, *The Rise of the Western World: A New Economic History* (Cambridge: Cambridge University Press, 1973), p. 7:

> The creation and enforcement of property rights are a prerogative of the government as the source of coercion. The locus of governmental coercion and decision-making shifted from local to larger political units. This movement was slow and halting, for everywhere it was circumscribed by conflicting authority. So even when the short-run fiscal interests of government coincided with the development of more efficient property rights (as in the protection of long-distance trade, which provided a new source of crown revenue) because of conflicts with rivals it could produce only imperfect enforcement. The most important factor in the development of new property rights is that the government created them only when it had a fiscal interest. As we saw above, the granting of the alienability of land (a key step in the development of fee-simple absolute ownership) was accomplished in England, France, Anjou, Poitiers and other areas to ensure that the Crown would not lose existing feudal revenues. Protection of property rights of alien merchants had a similar origin, as did the Burgundian establishment of fairs at Autun and Chalon. For identical reasons counter-productive actions, such as the multiplication of tolls, arbitrary confiscation, forced loans and many other similar devices, were taken, which made for greater uncertainty with respect to property rights. The direction the government took depended upon its fiscal interest.

7.

> Overall Burgundian and Hapsburg policy was to promote unification and trade, which redounded to the prosperity of the economy and hence of the Crown. Throughout the wars of Charles V in the sixteenth century, the seventeen provinces remained loyal and provided increasing revenue for the conquest of the growing empire. The Low Countries had because of their prosperity become the jewels of the Hapsburg Empire, furnishing the Crown with the bulk of its revenues . . . Although the Low Countries had tolerated Charles V, they were no longer willing to put up with the more exacting demands of his successor Philip II. Accepting the leadership of the House of Orange, the Low Countries revolted and a long struggle, complicated by religious controversy, ensued.

Ibid., p. 134.

8. Frederic C. Lane describes the Venetian family partnership in the context of the associated forms of enterprise organization in "Family Partnerships and Joint Ventures in the Venetian Republic," in Frederic C. Lane and Jelle C. Riemersma, eds., *Enterprise and Secular Change* (Homewood, Ill.: Richard D. Irwin, 1953), pp. 86–101. As a device for keeping a family fortune in one unit, the Venetian partnership of heirs bears comparison to the English land policy of primogeniture.

9. Werner Sombart, "Medieval and Modern Commercial Enterprise," in Lane and Riemersma, eds., *Enterprise and Secular Change*, p. 36. The chapter is an extract, in translation, from Sombart's major work, *Der moderne Kapitalismus*.

10. Speaking of developments in Italy, Weber stated:

> Originally there was no separation between the household and the business. Such separation gradually became established on the basis of the medieval money accounting

while . . . it remained unknown in India and China. In the great Florentine commercial families such as the Medici, household expenditures and capital transactions were entered on the books indiscriminately; closing of the accounts was carried out first with reference to the outside commenda business while internally everything remained in the "family kettle" of the household community.

General Economic History, p. 172.

11. Sombart, "Medieval and Commercial Enterprise," in Lane and Riemersma, *Enterprise and Secular Change*, p. 38. For a critique of Sombart's evaluation of double-entry bookkeeping, see Braudel, *The Wheels of Commerce* (New York: Harper & Row, 1982), pp. 573–75.

12. Max Weber, *Protestant Ethic and the Spirit of Capitalism*, trans. Talcott Parsons (New York: Scribner & Sons, 1930). The essay first appeared in 1904–1905 under the title, "Die protestantische Ethik und der Geist des Kapitalismus" (Tubingen u. Leipzig, J. C. B. Mohr [Paul Siebeck]).

13. David Landes (ed.), *The Rise of Capitalism* (New York: Macmillan, 1966), p. 7.

14. Calvin's views on predestination are in chapters 21–24 of book 3 of *Institutes of the Christian Religion* (Geneva: 1559; trans. John Allen, London, 1813), Seventh American edition (Philadelphia: Presbyterian Board of Christian Education, 1936), vol. 2, pp. 170–241.

15. Ibid., vol. 1, pp. 761–62.

16. See, for example, H. M. Robertson, *Aspects of the Rise of Economic Individualism* (Cambridge: Harvard University Press, 1933).

17. While the debate has raged over the connections between Protestantism and capitalism, a much more radical view has been expressed by Lynn White, who has contrasted Christianity generally with other religions. White argues that Christianity has cultivated a more active and manipulative attitude toward the natural world than any other major religion. In fact, White even attributes what he calls an "ecologic crisis" to Christianity:

Especially in its Western form, Christianity is the most anthropocentric religion the world has seen . . . Christianity, in absolute contrast to ancient paganism and Asia's religions (except, perhaps, Zoroastrianism), not only established a dualism of man and nature but also insisted that it is God's will that man exploit nature for his proper ends.

At the level of the common people this worked out in an interesting way. In Antiquity every tree, every spring, every stream, every hill had its own *genius loci*, its guardian spirit. These spirits were accessible to men, but were very unlike men; centaurs, fauns, and mermaids show their ambivalence. Before one cut a tree, mined a mountain, or dammed a brook, it was important to placate the spirit in charge of that particular situation, and to keep it placated. By destroying pagan animism, Christianity made it possible to exploit nature in a mood of indifference to the feelings of the natural objects.

It is often said that for animism the Church substituted the cult of saints. True; but the cult of saints is functionally different from animism. The saint is not *in* natural objects; he may have special shrines, but his citizenship is in heaven. Moreover, a saint is entirely a man; he can be approached in human terms. In addition to saints, Christianity of course also had angels and demons inherited from Judaism and perhaps, at one remove, from Zoroastrianism. But these were all as mobile as the saints themselves. The spirits *in* natural objects, which formerly had protected nature from man, evaporated. Man's effective monopoly on spirit in this world was confirmed, and the old inhibitions on the exploitation of nature crumbled.

Lynn White, Jr., "The Historical Roots of our Ecologic Crisis," *Science* 155 (10 March 1967): 1205.

18. John Hicks, *A Theory of Economic History* (New York: Oxford University Press, 1969), pp. 78–79. For a brief account of the measures taken by merchants to avoid the prohibition of interest, see Braudel, *Wheels of Commerce*, pp. 559–66. Braudel also discusses Calvin's acceptance of interest, about 1545, pp. 568–69.

19.

"The capitalist spirit" is as old as history, and was not, as has sometimes been said, the offspring of Puritanism. But it found in certain aspects of later Puritanism a tonic which braced its energies and fortified its already vigorous temper. At first sight, no contrast could be more violent than that between the iron collectivism, the almost military discipline, the remorseless and violent rigors practiced in Calvin's Geneva, and preached elsewhere, if in a milder form, by his disciples, and the impatient rejection of all traditional restrictions on economic enterprise which was the temper of the English business world after the Civil War. In reality, the same ingredients were present throughout, but they were mixed in changing proportions, and exposed to different temperatures at different times. Like traits of individual character which are suppressed till the approach of maturity releases them, the tendencies of Puritanism, which were to make it later a potent ally of the movement against the control of economic relations in the name either of social morality or of the public interest, did not reveal themselves till political and economic changes had prepared a congenial environment for their growth. Nor, once these conditions were created, was it only England which witnessed the transformation. In all countries alike, in Holland, in America, in Scotland, in Geneva itself, the social theory of Calvinism went through the same process of development. It had begun by being the very soul of authoritarian regimentation. It ended by being the vehicle for an almost Utilitarian individualism. While social reformers in the sixteenth century could praise Calvin for his economic rigor, their successors in Restoration England, if of one persuasion, denounced him as the parent of economic license, if of another, applauded Calvinist communities for their commercial enterprise and for their freedom from antiquated prejudices on the subject of economic morality. So little do those who shoot the arrows of the spirit know where they will light.

R. H. Tawney, *Religion and the Rise of Capitalism* (New York: Harcourt, Brace & Co., 1926), pp. 188–89. Braudel attributes the same view to Sombart in *Wheels of Commerce*, p. 568.

20. Nef, *War and Human Progress*, pp. 15–16.

21. For a fuller account of mercantilism, see Eli F. Heckscher, *Mercantilism*, 2 vols., 2d rev. ed. (London: George Allen & Unwin, 1955); and Charles H. Wilson, "Trade, Society and the Staple," in *The Cambridge Economic History of Europe*, E. E. Rich and C. H. Wilson, eds., vol. 4, *The Economy of Expanding Europe in the Sixteenth and Seventeenth Centuries*, chap. 8.

22. North and Thomas, *Rise of the Western World*, pp. 152–53.

23. W. W. Rostow, "The Beginnings of Modern Growth in Europe: An Essay in Synthesis," *Journal of Economic History* 33 (September 1973): pp. 548–49.

5 / The Development of Industry: 1750–1880

The belief that the wealth of the West springs from its technology is almost always coupled to the belief that the most important technology is mass production, embodied in the factory system. Thus, once the countries of the Third World were free of colonialism, their common impulse was to equip themselves with modern factories—an impulse with antecedents in the Soviet Union's five-year plans a half-century ago.

However, in the West, the development of commerce and commercial institutions, summarized in chapters 3 and 4, preceded the development of modern industrial institutions. Second, the factory has never been the dominant employer of Western workers. Workers in agriculture, forestry, mining, transportation, communication, the arts, the professions, banking, wholesale and retail trade, education, medical services, and government, have always matched or overmatched the number of factory workers.

We need also to keep in mind a far more complex qualification as we explore the development of industrial institutions in this and following chapters. In all Western countries, the inventory of physical facilities for economic production changes. The inventory at any given moment is unquestionably important, but it is like a single frame of a movie: taken alone, it misses all the action, and it is the action that we need to understand and that holds the promise of economic advance to non-Western countries. Western industry is a system for change, sometimes creating new markets and sometimes responding to them, adapting itself to changing sources of fuel and raw materials, reaching out for new technologies and sometimes creating them, and always modifying and reshaping its physical plant, which is far more transient than it appears to be. There is a fascination in the physical apparatus of giant factories, smokestacks, whirring machinery, and well-drilled workers. We need to keep reminding ourselves that what matters to economic expansion is the institutional system that made the apparatus—which is, however impressive, merely temporary. The deserted nineteenth-century mills on New England's rivers and the abandoned steel plants rusting in the Midwest, not to mention the occasional restoration, by a museum, of a smith's forge or a clockmaker's shop—what we have changed from—tell as much about the sources of the expansion of the West as the latest robotized plants— what we are now changing *to* and will no doubt be changing *from*. All are frames in the same film.

In this chapter, we will be concerned with the period from 1750 to 1880. Starting about 1750, the factory system of production gradually became dominant in most of Western industry. It changed relationships in the workplace and, probably with more drastic social effect, changed the location of the workplace from the household to the factory. The shift to the factory was practically complete by 1880, but most commercial and industrial enterprises continued to be organized as individual proprietorships or partnerships, with the exception of banks and railways. The industrial corporation and the diversity in size and structure of the enterprises characteristic of modern Western economies came after 1880 and will be examined in chapters 6 and 7.

Between 1750 and 1880, the respect of the Western governments for the autonomy of the economic sphere became virtually an ideology. Apart from such sporadic intrusions as the British Factory Acts and Bismarck's system of social insurance, governments were content to assist only when asked. Peacetime taxes were small and currencies comparatively stable. On the other hand, there were wars, especially the Napoleonic Wars from 1790 to 1815, and there was much social unrest.

Most, but not all, of the revolutionary changes in Western industry and transportation between 1750 and 1880 are traceable to one organizational development and two technological developments. The first was the change in the organization of production from the artisan's shop to the factory. The transition took different forms in different industries. In some cases, the transition to factory production involved the same firms and the same people that had previously functioned as artisans, usually to their benefit. In other cases, the factory's people and firms were different and their predecessors were replaced painfully. In a few industries, factories never did replace the artisan shop. Factory organization was not suited to the large sectors of the economy devoted to transportation, wholesale and retail selling, banking, insurance, publishing, the arts, and the professions, and they experienced the change primarily in increased business and declining prices of merchandise.

The first of the two technological developments was an enormous increase in the use of steam and water power in factory production and the application of steam power to land and water transportation. At least in the iron and textile industries, the hallmark of the Industrial Revolution was the production of goods by energy derived from coal and applied through steam engines and steam-powered machinery. The Industrial Revolution was a revolution primarily because of the increase in the sheer quantity of goods produced; the primary explanation of this explosion in quantity was a corresponding, and possibly even greater, increase in the amount of work, in the physicist's sense of the term. We will find that there is a good deal of room for doubt that the advantages of factory organization, qua organization, would have made the factory worthwhile in more than a few industries, but as a device for using mechanical power in the production of goods, the factory was unbeatable.

The second seminal technological change was the substitution of iron and steel for wood in fabricating machinery and other products. This substitution changed the size, longevity, precision, and mechanical complexity of a wide range of products, from sewing machines to ships.

The social and political consequences of these changes in industry and transportation were profoundly affected by two equally important changes that were going on in other parts of Western society. First, Western population was rising rapidly. Second, agricultural productivity was steadily improving, displacing agricultural workers and foreclosing agricultural employment—long society's principal source of work—to the rising population.

Had the rise of population in the towns outpaced the rise of population in the countryside by a sufficiently wide margin, it is conceivable that the demand for food might have risen faster than the supply of agricultural labor and so have led to a rise in agricultural wages, just as it had led to an increase in the land under cultivation and a rise in its price. But Western agricultural workers had no such luck. The rise in agricultural population was more than sufficient to meet the rising needs of the towns for food. In England, the downward pressure on agricultural wages was accentuated by the enclosure movement—that is, the fencing of agricultural land formerly available for the pasturage of animals owned by agricultural workers. The enclosure movement reflected the twin facts that the market price of land was rising as the population increased, while the market price of agricultural labor was declining: landowners had other uses for land more remunerative than its use as a fringe benefit for cottagers. The combination of a rise in agricultural population with a reduction in agricultural employment was a compelling incentive for the urbanization of Western society, but it also compelled many agricultural workers in England and other Western countries to endure long periods of economic and social adjustment. It was a combination that accounted for much social misery in England and other Western countries until well into the nineteenth century.

By now, it is quite clear that the new factories and towns were a large part of the solution to Europe's problem of employing a rising population outside of agriculture; they were not part of the problem. But they did not seem like part of the solution to contemporary observers who, finding them disturbing and disruptive of old social relationships and values, created a literature, centered on the British textile industry, which treated the factories themselves as sources of misery.

The account of Western industrial development in this chapter contradicts another conventional belief, that the economic gains of the period from 1750 to 1880 were achieved at the cost of enormous sacrifices, certainly by workers but also by many capitalists who saved and scrimped to supply the capital required for this great expansion of industry. In point of fact, there is good reason to think that the alternatives supposedly sacrificed by early factory workers were much less attractive than factory work—which is not to say that factory work was attractive otherwise than by comparison to the alternatives. As for capital formation, the wealth generated by new institutional and technological advances allowed capital formation to proceed concurrently with a rise in consumption by the capitalists—a sometimes spectacular rise that seemed more scandalous than sacrificial to contemporary social conservatives. The history of the Industrial Revolution gives no support to the view that a bleak present is a necessary, or even a plausible, preliminary to a glorious future.

Antecedents of Industry

By 1750, three hundred years of gradual expansion in markets had been accompanied by a corresponding expansion in production, both in agriculture and handicrafts. While there had been no such sharp change in methods of production as the factory system was to introduce, the putting-out system in the English textile trade, by which textile merchants supplied materials to cottagers and bought their products, was indicative of the growing pressures that expanding markets exerted on the organization of the older production processes.

Over this period of three hundred years, there had been no lack of change in the end products of the production process, though only here and there did the changes reflect a technological advance rather than a change in style. The changes were almost entirely in products used by sovereigns, the wealthy, and the churches. In architecture, for example, the shift from medieval to classical forms began in late-fifteenth-century Italy. By the end of the seventeenth century, the design of Northern European churches, palaces, mansions, barracks, and even storefronts had changed entirely, but not the design of cottages and huts. It is easy to trace the development of carriages from the clumsy springless wagons of the Elizabethan period to the far more graceful and comfortable vehicles of the late eighteenth century, but only a few rode in carriages. Dress changed, but the materials used were much the same in 1750 as in 1450.

Until about 1880, the principal technological achievements of Western industry were in the mechanical arts. The mechanical skills needed for these accomplishments developed in substantial part in response to a Western interest in horology. This interest in timekeeping was traceable to the town clocks of the Middle Ages. As early as the sixteenth century, clocks had their eager collectors: the Emperor Charles V is said to have had three thousand of them. The invention of the telescope and the Copernican revolution in astronomy in the seventeenth century supplied an impetus for improvements in the accuracy of clocks. In struggling with the problems of building accurate clocks and portable watches, clockmakers advanced Western knowledge of precision machining; the effects of changes in temperature on different materials; friction; the uses and misuses of gear trains, levers, ratchets, springs, and other elements of mechanical systems; selection of suitable materials; lubrication; and mechanical durability. By 1750, when the Industrial Revolution was about to impose immense demands on the skill and ingenuity of mechanical designers, Western clockmakers had already brought mechanical design to an advanced state of development.

Much of the early Western interest in clocks and watches was in no sense utilitarian. In order to fit their development—and the development of Western mechanical skills—to the causal pattern, economic need to technological response, one must allow economic need to include fad, fashion, fascination with complex mechanisms, and similar foibles. Much later, the timeclock became a symbol of factory discipline; but Western interest in clocks and watches long antedated the factory system. A non-utilitarian fascination with clocks was not limited to the West, for clocks proved welcome gifts from early traders to Chinese officials, who became avid collectors but made no practical use of them whatever. Even the medieval town clocks were as much ornamental as useful. For watches more than for clocks, the market consisted almost entirely of those who bought them as articles of jewelry, status symbols, or from collectors' enthusiasm. That the market existed was fortunate, for portable watches proved much more challenging to mechanical ingenuity than clocks, and hence were a substantial additional source of Western skills in the mechanical arts.

Horology was thus a jeweler's or astronomer's art, with one exception: the marine chronometer. Until nearly the end of the eighteenth century, navigators had no reliable or accurate way to find a ship's longitude, and as a result many lives, ships, and cargoes were lost in strandings on shores and reefs that had been thought to be many miles distant. Local noon, the time when the sun reaches its maximum altitude above the horizon, could be determined with reasonable accuracy by eighteenth-century instruments. What was needed was a clock accurately showing time at 0° longitude, for with such a clock mariners could determine their longitude by comparing local noon, as they observed it, to the time shown by the clock: each hour of time difference translated into 15° of longitude. Accurate eighteenth-century clocks depended, however, on the pendulum, which did not function on the unstable platform supplied by a ship. "Longitude, then, was the great mystery of the age, a riddle to seamen, a challenge to scientists, a stumbling block to kings and statesmen. Only such will-o'-the-wisps as the fountain of youth and the philosophers' stone could match its aura of tantalizing promise—and longitude was real."[1]

Later, in the nineteenth century, accurate watches were needed both for the operation of the railroads and for passengers, who had to get to the station on time.[2] High-grade watches became a status symbol, worn with pride by those who were far from the reach of factory discipline. Clocks, watches, and time came to mark the life of the factories as well. As the rhythm of machines established a working day measured in hours and paid by hours worked, time became money. It differed from the rhythm imposed by the farmer's seasons, the sun, the weather, and the needs of the farm's animals. It differed also from the working rhythm of the home weavers, to whom not time but their finished output was money.[3]

HOW THE WEST GREW RICH

In the seventeenth century, Western science had taken a turn that had much to do with the subsequent Industrial Revolution (that turn in science will be discussed at greater length in chapter 8). Scientific method became experimental, in that the savant expected to learn from personal observation, both of nature and of contrived experiments, and in that hypotheses were to be tested by experiment. The inventions of the Industrial Revolution, typically and not just occasionally, proceeded by experimental trial and error. The inventors, however, were often more patient and ingenious than learned. The inventor had to be prepared not merely for the "Eureka" experience of inspired discovery, but for the tiresome frustration of repeated small malfunctions which had to be corrected before the machine could be used productively. The Greeks were also inventive, but what has survived of the Greek experience offers no parallel to the thirty years John Harrison worked between his first and his fourth, and successful, chronometer. (Harrison was a carpenter who produced the first chronometer successfully tested at sea.) The notion that the pursuit of truth was incomplete without experimental verification made it respectable to persist until the inventor's ideas came to terms with the intractable behavior of cotton fibers, leaking pistons, minute variations in the chemical content of ores fed to blast furnaces and smelters, and metal parts of imprecise chemical composition that were of one dimension at one temperature and a different dimension at another.

The Overall Growth Required by the Factory System

The technology of a factory system and its sharply increased output could not be introduced in isolation. There had to be parallel changes in the production of raw materials, transportation of both raw materials and finished goods, and in wholesale and retail trade, insurance, and banking. We have just mentioned that changes in agriculture created a surplus of labor to which the new industries were in one sense an answer. At the same time, changes in agriculture were indispensable to the growth of other sectors of the economy, for the rising number of workers in these other sectors had to be fed.

Although the steam engine played a key part in the shift to the factory system of industrial production, its first widespread use was to increase production of coal by pumping water out of coal mines. It thus contributed to the expansion of fuel and raw materials production necessary to an expanded production of finished goods. Steam engines were also being used to power factory production by the time they were applied to expansion of transportation, that is, to ship propulsion and to locomotives. From about 1830 on, construction of railways and construction of factories moved in tandem. This was inevitable: the Industrial Revolution was of necessity also a revolution in transportation; in the supply of raw materials and food—in mining, forestry, and agriculture; and in trading specialties: wholesaling, retailing, commodity trading, and finance.

In the nineteenth century, it also became a revolution in communication. The invention of the telegraph, the laying of the Atlantic cable in 1859, and the application of steam power to the printing press (which led to cheaper books and daily newspapers whose readers numbered in the hundreds of thousands) revolutionized communication long before the invention of the telephone and radio.

We are far from suggesting that these multiple and mutually self-supporting revolutions in all departments of eighteenth-century economic systems, especially in England, occurred by delightful coincidence. They occurred in response to pressures from expanding markets, felt directly and indirectly all through the economy, and they occurred when and where the economic system not only encouraged invention and discovery but was quick to put them to commercial use. A good reason to attribute the growth of eighteenth- and nineteenth-century industrial technology in good part to economic forces is that mining, land and sea transportation, metallurgy, manufacturing, forestry, and agriculture each found a technology adequate to its part in the joint process of growth, so that no one of these fields is remembered as having checked Western growth. But it is also worth keeping in mind the degree to which the steam engine, applied across mining, transportation, metallurgy, and manufacturing, may explain the coincidence.

The Shift to Factory Production

The most conspicuous institutional development of the Industrial Revolution was one of degree: not the invention of the factory mode of production, but such a massive expansion of its use that almost no one could distinguish it from invention. Enterprises employing large numbers of workers in repetitive production can be found here and there before Europe shifted from a handicraft to a factory economy. The Arsenal at Venice, used for building ships, was an example; and we read of a Chinese ironmaster with two thousand employees long before the English Industrial Revolution. Also, we will see in a moment that the English pottery industry used factories some years before they began to spread to other industries. But if it cannot be said that the factory was an invention of the Industrial Revolution, it can be said that few Westerners ever saw one before 1750 and that few could avoid seeing them by 1880.

At the beginning of the nineteenth century, most finished goods in Europe and the United States still came from workshops in which the owner had not become wholly specialized to a commercial and financial role, but rather had personal knowledge of the production processes and kept a personal hand on production work. In the guild tradition, the workshop owner was called, for example, an ironmaster or a master potter with connotations of applied personal skill that did not become a mere figure of speech until the latter half of the nineteenth century.

Many of the workshops were no more than cottages where an individual worker and his or her family applied their skills to materials supplied by a merchant trader. Nor was this unity of the workplace and the household limited to rural cottage industry. In the towns, under the guild system, it was more typical than exceptional for the master to live and work in the same building and for the apprentices and journeymen to live in this same household. The factory owners who, a little later, supplied housing for their workers (in so-called company towns) were following an earlier guild practice on a larger scale. The degree to which a worker was treated less as a stranger and more as a member of the master's family must have depended partly on the size of the enterprise, as it still does on farms. The social distance between the owner and employees in these workshops was no doubt appreciable from the beginning, but the rise of factories sharply increased the gap, not simply by interposing a hierarchy of foremen and foreladies, superintendents, and managers between worker and owner, but by the differentiation of roles and by separation within the community. The owner no longer knew how to do the employees' many specialized tasks, and most of the employees were even further out of touch with the financial and commercial problems which preempted the owner's attention.

It is difficult to evaluate the effect of the factory's separation of workplace and household on the social gap between owners and employees. The formation of independent households by factory workers widened the gap, in that these households were in separate neighborhoods and their members soon began to form separate communities, with their own social and political associations and even their own religious sects.[4] Moving urban workers out of their employers' households and enabling them to form independent households of their own was an enormous leap toward greater personal independence and a less servile status, for which the factory has received, as an institution, much less credit than it deserves. But it had a price payable in the coin of greater social division. Both owners and employees began to form their conceptions of each other and of each other's character and goals less and less on the basis of personal acquaintance and more and more by acceptance of secondhand stereotypes, not to say caricatures. The consequences for economic organization are still not completely worked out.

Unhappily for social scientists' interest in generalization, what made the factory system an economically attractive alternative to the handicraft production system varied from industry to industry. Some industries, such as the tool and die industry, have never turned completely to the factory system. The best we can do toward generalizing is to stress the part played in the change to the factory system, by the shift from the use of mechanical energy on a small scale to the use of mechanical energy on a large scale. Then we will touch on the change to factory production in three key industries: iron and steel, textiles, and ceramics. The selection is not random. The first two were central to the Industrial Revolution, and the ceramic industry is of special interest because it turned to factory methods somewhat earlier than the others, primarily to improve the organization of work and without the impetus of any noteworthy mechanical invention.

Earlier Sources of Energy: Water, Wind, and Muscle

Until the invention of the steam engine, workshops depended for power upon watermills, windmills, draft animals, and human muscle, in ascending order of cost. The power available from a watermill or windmill varied with the site and the size of the mill, but until well into the nineteenth century a typical value was around 10 horsepower (HP).[5] A grouping of machines of a size and number to be driven by a total of 10 HP does not, as a rule, make a workshop big enough to warrant the separation of ownership and management from the manual work of production.

By the eighteenth century and for a long time before, England and Continental Europe had many workshops operated by water or wind. Waterwheels were used to drive pumps in mines, pump the London water supply, run Arkwright's waterframe spinning machine of 1769 (one of the first of the machines that revolutionized the textile industry),[6] and above all for milling grain. As early as 1086, the Domesday Survey had recorded over five thousand cornmills in England.[7]

In the early stages of industrialization, water was the main source of power, both in New England and in Britain. England resorted to steam power somewhat earlier than the United States—partly, one may suppose, because the slower pace of industrialization in the United States did not exhaust the water-power sites quite so early; partly because of the greater abundance of water power in New England, where United States industry was originally concentrated; and partly because the organization of the British textile industry into factories specialized to a single step in the production process favored their location in a small geographical area, that is, in a few towns. Methods of harnessing streams were greatly improved as a result of John Smeaton's experiments with waterwheels, which he published in 1759, and again as a result of the development of turbines after 1850. Thus water power continued to be competitive with steam for many purposes, and continued to be used long after the introduction of the steam engine.[8] More United States factories were powered by waterwheels and turbines than by steam engines as late as 1870; and the balance shifted in favor of steam only in 1880.[9] On the other hand, A. J. Taylor's estimates of the use of water and steam power by the English textile industry in Lancashire, Yorkshire, Derbyshire, and Cheshire in 1838 and 1850 show a clear dominance of steam power as early as 1838, with the gap widening by 1850. He estimates a decline in water power from 8,917 HP in 1838 to 7,518 HP in 1850, and a rise in the use of steam power from 39,579 HP to 61,586 HP.[10]

The Development of Industry: 1750–1880

The Steam Engine

The Newcomen steam engine came into use in England for pumping water from mines, as well as for some other purposes, about 1725. Its critical part was a piston, moving in a large vertical cylinder. The pressure of steam injected into the cylinder from a boiler raised the piston. The steam was next condensed by injecting cold water into the cylinder, leaving a vacuum. Atmospheric pressure then forced the piston to the bottom of the cylinder, and the engine was ready for the injection of more steam.

Despite the priority of the atmospheric engine, James Watt is conventionally credited with the invention of the steam engine. What he actually did, some fifty years after the Newcomen engine had come into use, was to change it in ways which reduced its coal consumption by some two-thirds. The principal source of this improvement in efficiency was the use of a separate cylinder for condensing the steam. The air in this cylinder, called a condenser, was evacuated by an air pump, leaving a vacuum which drew the steam from the main cylinder at the point in the operating cycle when, in the Newcomen engine, cold water would have been injected to cool the steam. The result was that in Watt's engine the main cylinder ran hot all the time, and the steam injected into it dissipated much less of its energy in reheating the cylinder.

Watt made a number of other changes and improvements in the steam engine, including the use of steam pressure to drive the piston in both directions (what is called the double-acting steam engine); the admission of steam to the main cylinder during only part of the stroke, allowing the expansion of the steam to drive the piston; the centrifugal governor to control the admission of steam under variable loads; and the development of mechanisms for converting the back-and-forth motion of the piston into a steady rotary motion, of the sort needed to drive textile and other machinery. By 1790, he had improved the design of the steam engine to the point where it became a widely useful and economical prime mover.

Watt did not believe in the use of steam at high pressures, because he feared explosions. Happily for the further development of the steam engine, there were others who did not agree with him and who were in a position to put the argument to the test of experiment. So it was that his early-nineteenth-century successors developed high-pressure steam engines and their corollary, the compound engine, in which steam was expanded in two stages, the first in a small, high-pressure cylinder and the second in a larger, low-pressure cylinder. They were also responsible for solving the considerable problems of designing furnaces, boilers, engines, and driving mechanisms suitable for locomotives and ships, beginning about 1815.[11]

The steam engine not only helped move production from the cottage to the factory, it helped change the location of the factories. The steam engine was not a device that could be installed in cottages or urban household shops. It required a specialized facility, preferably near a ready source of coal. In the textiles industry, it produced enough power to run a number of machines, and the machines that were to be powered by it had to be concentrated around it. No form of household industry could contain the steam engine and the complement of machines it drove.[12] This, in turn, changed the size limits of the machines that the steam engine might power; they no longer needed to be small enough to be installed in a cottage, but could be made as large and complex as seemed efficient.

It also changed the siting of factories. Until the development of the steam engine, the industrial use of power machinery was limited by the availability of sites for waterwheels. The steam engine opened the way to locating factories near sources of coal, transportation, labor, and markets.

Iron and Steel

The furnaces and smelters of the eighteenth-century iron industry, like other eighteenth-century shops, were small. There was little hint that they were to become the prototype of early-twentieth-century heavy industry.[13]

The output of eighteenth-century blast furnaces was modest, partly because they were operated only about thirty weeks a year. They closed down in the summer for lack of water power, because of the effect of summer humidity on the quality of the iron, and for the repair of furnace linings and bellows.[14] It was modest also because the chemistry of blast furnaces was not well understood, and their operation was more art than science:

> A furnace is a fickle mistress and must be humored and her favors not to be depended on. I have known her [to] produce 12 tons per week, and some times

but 9 tons, nay, sometimes but 8, the excellency of a founder is to humor her dispositions, but never to force her inclinations.[15]

During the eighteenth century, there was a marked increase in the output of blast furnaces. An output of 12 tons a week for a thirty-week working year would yield 360 tons at a maximum; but by 1805, Staffordshire's furnaces were averaging about 1,600 tons a year, according to Hyde's estimate.[16]

Limits of scale were imposed on the working of iron by the need for large quantities of charcoal, which had to come from extensive forests. The forests had to be close by, for the transportation of wood over long distances was prohibitively expensive and charcoal deteriorated when it was transported.[17] The size of the blast furnaces was limited also by the power available for pumping air—again a limitation not overcome until the introduction of Watt's steam engine.[18] Indeed, one of Watt's first two engines was built to power the blower for a blast furnace owned by John Wilkinson, an ironmaster in Staffordshire. The inevitable effect was to render a whole generation of blast furnaces (including Wilkinson's) uneconomically small.

The increase in both size and complexity of ironworks that followed throughout the nineteenth century was motivated by a desire to achieve economies in the use of fuel. As to size, within the practical limits of construction, large furnaces lose less heat by radiation than small furnaces and so are more fuel-efficient. As to complexity, preheating the air blast required ovens to heat the air. The addition of apparatus for capturing and using the gas escaping from the top of the furnace was a further complicating economy. There are also fuel economies in combining blast-furnace operations, which produce pig iron, with the further operations required to produce steel, thus saving the expense of reheating iron that has been allowed to cool after being drawn from the blast furnace. The integrated steel mill was another attempt to reduce fuel costs even further.

The increased output of iron and steel mills required a corresponding increase in mining both iron ore and coal. It also required that the mills be served by transportation networks on a correspondingly increased scale, both to supply raw materials to the mills and to distribute their output. Even internally, the mills came to require transportation systems of their own of a size and complexity not found in the eighteenth century.

The steam engine was central to the expansion of production of iron and steel and to lowering their cost, for it provided the power for mining, transportation by rail and water, and for the mills themselves. To some extent, the mills created the demand for their own product; iron and steel were essential to the construction of steam engines, railroads and, in the last half of the nineteenth century, to the construction of ships.

Until after the middle of the nineteenth century, the process of making steel, which requires adding to iron a small, carefully controlled amount of carbon, was slow and expensive, and output was small. Then, beginning with an announcement in 1856 and several years of subsequent experiment, improvement, and demonstration, Sir Henry Bessemer introduced his so-called converter, a flame-spouting device which surely produced, along with cheap steel, the most spectacular fireworks of the Industrial Revolution.

After Bessemer, the late nineteenth and early twentieth century came to be known as the Age of Steel. The machinery of the early Industrial Revolution had been built mostly of wood, with some iron and a very little steel for reinforcement. The substitution of iron and steel brought gains in longevity, feasible speed of operation, precision of construction, and possibilities of mechanical complexity. It made possible the building of larger ships, larger steam engines, larger bridges, steel-framed skyscrapers, and so on, through a whole range of products which are more economical in large sizes. Iron and steel were essential to the railway revolution in land transportation, supplying the material for locomotives, wheels, and tracks. The internal combustion engines later used in automobiles, airplanes, and Diesel locomotives and ships would hardly have been possible without an ample supply of iron and steel. Internal combustion engines needed iron and steel because they were essentially air pumps, so that they depended for their efficiency on virtually airtight pistons and valves, and they depended for their longevity on the ability of pistons and valves to remain airtight in prolonged use at what were, at the time, high temperatures and severe pressures. It was an Age of Steel in a political sense also, because national military power came to depend upon access to an advanced steel industry capable of staying abreast in the competition between guns and armor which began in the 1850s. Military power also depended on breech-loading rifles (adopted by the Prussians before the Franco-Prussian War of 1870 and by everyone else after that) and of breech-loading cannon, both of which required steel alloys and skills in precision forging and machining of steel.

The Development of Industry: 1750–1880

Textiles

The textile industry led factory development during the first decades of the Industrial Revolution, not only in England but also in the United States. Richard Arkwright, inventor of a spinning machine, came to be known as the "father of the English factory system," owing to the numerous cotton-spinning mills he promoted.[19] The early textile mills were also a principal object of the public agitation that led to the first English factory legislation.

In the early eighteenth century, spinning and weaving were conducted almost entirely on machines operated by hand or with pedals, and located in the operators' cottages. Textile merchants supplied the operators with materials and paid for their finished work. The irregular work habits of the cottage operators, the problem of theft of materials, and the desire to gain greater control of the production process were recognized incentives for the adoption of the factory system even before the invention of factory machinery.[20]

In the development of the cotton textile industry, powered machinery was introduced first for spinning yarn. Arkwright's patent for a spinning machine supplies an approximate date, 1769, for the beginning of the conversion. Since his machine required power, its use had at first the effect of decentralizing spinning to watermills located at the available dam sites. Chapman accepts a contemporaneous estimate that by 1788 there were 143 watermills in the cotton industry in the United Kingdom.[21] But with the invention of the steam engine, the spinning mills again concentrated in the cities where the textile industry centered, close to the weavers who were their customers.

For the organization of the British textile industry was unusual in that firms tended to specialize in a single step in the process of producing cotton cloth. Instead of building fully integrated plants of the type used in the iron and steel industry and (as we shall see in a moment) in ceramics, the British textile makers located highly specialized plants close to each other. The development of these regional textile complexes was facilitated by the substitution of steam for water power.[22]

Power machinery was longer coming to cotton weaving. Cartwright's basic design of a power loom dates from about 1787, but it was the early 1800s before corrections and improvements had made it a successful machine. It was, for a long time, efficient only in weaving cotton cloth of relatively poor quality. It expanded the supply of cheap, low-grade cotton textiles, a class of product welcomed by the many millions who could not afford anything better, but not one to cause handloom weavers to lose their traditional customers. In addition, there was a commercial factor that made power spinning somewhat more attractive than power weaving. The spinners' output was a more homogeneous product than the weavers', with simpler inventories and fewer market risks. The expensive machinery was less likely to have to stand idle through periods of slack demand. In England, as late as 1829, it was possible to doubt the economic advantage of power looms, even though they had increased in number from 2,400 in 1813 to 55,500 in 1829.[23]

Over the years, the power loom improved steadily, both in productivity and in its ability to weave cloth of the better grades. A. J. Taylor associates the decline of the handloom in England with an intense depression which began in 1838.[24] In the period 1829 to 1831, there were 225,000 handlooms and 60,000 power looms in the United Kingdom; in 1844–46, there were 60,000 handlooms and 225,000 power looms. In Taylor's words, "When it is remembered that the power-loom was by 1850 at least three times as productive as the hand-loom the clear dominance established by power-weaving in the middle forties is at once apparent."[25] By 1850 or a little later, the power looms had been made equal to the weaving of the better quality cotton textiles,[26] and the handloom practically disappeared.

The shift from handloom to power loom was a change in the *technology* of production that went hand in hand with a change in the *organization* of production, shifting work from cottage to factory. Though the history of the English textile industry has been studied to the point where much of the literature on the social and political effects of factories scarcely mentions any other industries, there is still room for controversy over the relative importance of advantages of organization and advantages of technology in the introduction of the factory system in the textiles industry.

Whether, as Chapman suggested in 1910, the textile factory would have been adopted as a more efficient device for the organization of work, had the steam engine and the machines for applying its power output to weaving not been invented, is necessarily conjectural. The point was raised more recently by Stephen A. Marglin,[27] and we will turn to it again at the end of this chapter.

In a deeper sense, British manufacturers of textile machinery, all through the nineteenth century, were taking advantage of an economic opportunity created by the ability of nineteenth-century British merchants to sell all the cotton cloth they could get, coupled with a downward pressure on prices that became more severe as the century wore on. It is arguably a mistake of nomenclature to call them "manufacturers of textile machinery," for their principal product was not machinery as such, but change in the technology and reduction in the costs of textile production. They made their profits not from their skill in manufacture, but from their skill in the design of machines that could spin and weave better and more cheaply than those of their predecessors and contemporary rivals. They were highly successful, though their names are all but forgotten.

Ceramics

The dependence of the adoption of the factory system on the circumstances of each industry is well illustrated by ceramics. The manufacture of ceramics is one of the most ancient of industries. We do not know for sure whether the ancient Greek vase painters—some of whom were first-rate artists whose individual work is readily recognizable by experts in ancient vase painting—designed their paintings to decorate an available article or caused articles to be shaped for paintings they had in mind. But by the eighteenth century there was no doubt: the size, shape, material, and the decoration of the product were jointly conceived.

This unity of design made it advantageous to combine in one shop the successive steps in the production process, for the realization of the design and quality intended for the final product begins with the selection, grinding, and mixing of the materials to be used and ends only with the final decoration and finishing. This would not in itself have precluded a master potter and apprentices in a cottage shop from performing all the steps, one at a time, but there were advantages in the division of labor into successive steps. In part, the advantages arose from the fact that some of the steps required more skill than others, and it was wasteful for workers with the more difficult skills to spend time on work that could be done by less skilled workers. In addition, some of the steps, such as the grinding and mixing of materials, were best done with machinery driven by water power (before steam became available), and this alone took ceramic production beyond the scale of the one-man loom powered by its own operator. In sum, by 1787, Staffordshire already had an industry of small ceramic factories; its two hundred master potters had an average of one hundred employees each.[28] The production of ceramics had been transferred from the small shop or cottage to the factory before Watt's engine came into general use.

The pioneer of factory production was Josiah Wedgwood. At his works at Etruria, he divided his factory into departments by type of product and, within each department, workers were classified according to numerous specialties. A. and N. L. Clow describe the division of labor at Etruria as follows:

> The gradual multiplication of the processes whereby ceramic products could be produced led, as in other industries, to a marked division of labour. Josiah Wedgwood's Etruria, where the principle of specialization was first introduced, was divided into departments according to the type of ware produced: useful, ornamental, jasper, basalt, and so on. In 1790 some 160 employees were engaged in the "useful" branch, in the following categories: slip-house, clay-beaters, throwers and their attendant boys, plate makers, dish makers, hollow-ware pressers, turners of flat ware, turners of hollow-ware, handlers, biscuit-oven firemen, dippers, brushers, placers and firemen in the glost oven, girl colour-grinders, painters, enamellers and gilders, and, in addition, coal getters, modellers, mould makers, saggar makers, and a cooper.[29]

In the textile industry, spinners produced yarn and weavers produced cloth, but in the ceramics industry, each product passed through the hands of many workers and no one worker produced a marketable product. The ceramic industry was typical of later industries in its elimination of any easily visible connection between what a worker does and the marketable product of the worker's efforts. We will return to the objections to this form of organization of work later in the chapter.

In ceramics, much of eighteenth-century innovation was directed toward the product rather than the apparatus for manufacturing it. If the industry ever experienced revolutionary change, it was the discovery of soft-paste porcelain and bone china. The English industry also had to make the shift from wood fuel to coal, and in consequence the industry became concentrated in Staffordshire, where both coal and clay were available.

In the use of that hallmark of the Industrial Revolution, steam power, potters were ahead of spinners in replacing waterwheels with steam power, which the potters used in the mixing and grinding of their raw materials and which they soon applied to lathes and other mechanical equipment. But it was less an industrial revolution than an application of steam power—in factories that already existed and to tools they already had. We read of no such radical changes in ceramic manufacture as Arkwright's spinning machine or Cartwright's power loom brought to the textile industry. The factory system came to ceramics because there were advantages to unified control of the step production process (which could have been realized in a shop with only one general worker), further advantages to specializing workers to each step in the process (that could be realized only with a number of workers), and yet further advantages in a central source of power—be it waterwheel or steam engine. But the invention of new machines specialized to the industry played no such part in bringing the factory system to the ceramics industry as it played in bringing factory organization to the textile and the iron-and-steel industries.

Higher Output and Lower Prices: A Cause of Growth in Markets?

Along with the problems of the social relationships between factory owners and employees, the development of the factory produced an enormous increase in output. Imports of raw cotton into England are perhaps the best available index of the physical increase in the output of cotton textiles. From 1791 to 1795, the British textile industry imported an average of slightly more than 27 million pounds of raw cotton a year, ranging from 19 million pounds in 1793 to nearly 35 million pounds in 1792. From 1896 to 1900, British imports of raw cotton averaged 1,799 million pounds—an increase of nearly sixty-seven times.[30]

Production of pig iron is another particularly useful index of the physical mass of industrial output in an age when iron and its derivative product, steel, were much more generally used in manufacturing than they are today. During the eighteenth century, British production of pig iron increased from 25,000 tons in 1720 to 125,080 tons in 1796 and perhaps 200,000 tons by 1800[31]—roughly an eightfold increase in the last eighty years of the century. Eighty years later, in 1880, British pig iron production was 7,749,000 tons—an increase of almost thirty-nine times.

Up to about 1800, it is easy to interpret the expansion of Western production as the producers' response to the demand created by opening new channels of trade. But these figures illustrating the growth of physical output after 1800, considered together with the striking changes in industrial production, make it seem likely that, at some point early in the nineteenth century, the causal relation between the growth of markets and the Industrial Revolution became a two-way relation or was even reversed. After 1800, there was a revolution in the means of supplying economic needs and, at least on the surface, this expansion in means centered more in production than in trade. But the relation between the expansion of production and the expansion of trade is complex enough to be worth a little digging below the surface.

A rise in trade due to the expansion of old markets and the opening of new ones can add to wealth even though there is no change in the physical volume, or even the physical character, of output. In orthodox economics, this positive effect is a corollary of the theorem that voluntary exchange does not occur unless each party thinks it advances his or her own interests, and the advance is a gain in the trader's economic welfare—that is, in the trader's wealth. The positive effect can be illustrated by reference to almost any one-product economy. The economic welfare of a country like Brazil is evidently much greater than it would be if all the coffee Brazil grows had to be consumed in Brazil. Brazil's wealth and welfare are immensely improved by exchanging the coffee it exports for the products it imports, and also by finding new markets in which to trade Brazilian coffee. It is also safe to assume that Brazil is better off to grow and exchange coffee for imports than it would be if it substituted other crops for the coffee it now exports.

There is no doubt that, from the fifteenth century to the present, the growth of trade and the expansion of markets contributed very substantially to the West's economic advance, as distinguished from simply mirroring, in trade, a rise in physical output. Trade would have improved economic welfare even if the total of physical output had not changed, and trade would have increased output in some degree even if technology had not advanced. And some of the changes in technology were straightforward responses to the requirements of a rising level of trade. Finally, trade increased output by providing many—indeed, most—of the conditions and incentives necessary to improving the technology and the organization of production, transportation, and distribution.

Until 1750 or 1800, it is thus possible to view the expansion of trade as a result of falling costs of transportation, mercantile initiative in building markets, and the introduction of new relations favorable to trade. These developments placed industry under pressure to produce enough to satisfy the new markets, but it was a pressure which implied an upward, rather than downward, trend in prices. During the nineteenth century, the picture changed. What one sees is a growth in trade stimulated by the appetite of the factories for raw materials and by new markets opened up more by the falling cost of factory output than by any change in the cost of transportation or the conditions of trade. The expansion in output was not stimulated by a rise in prices, for after one allows for the effect of wars and depressions, the nineteenth century was an era of declining prices. In short, as the century wore on, the economic pressure for the expansion of transportation and trade originated in the manufacture of an increased volume of goods. Goods were offered at lower and lower prices, reflecting the decline in manufacturing costs achieved mainly by technological advances.

Thus, after giving trade all due credit for advancing the material welfare of the West, one must likewise allow for the part played in the advance of economic welfare by the increase in the sheer physical volume of output. Some, possibly most, of the economic growth of the West during the Industrial Revolution was directly attributable to advances in the organization and technology of production. It is true that the increase in output would not have enhanced human welfare had there not developed also the warehouses, stores, merchants, financiers, and transportation systems needed for getting it into the hands of those who put it to use. Nor would it have occurred had there not existed market relations through which producers were duly paid for their efforts at rates generally consistent with the buyers' priorities. But warehouses, stores, merchants, financiers, transportation systems, and market relationships are not so unique to the West as is its output per capita.

In short, the Industrial Revolution was a period in which technological and organizational advances played a more conspicuous role in bringing about growth than they did before 1750. These advances were built on, and indeed depended on, trading, market, property relations, and other institutional foundations that were laid before that time. But for a change so sharp, we must be prepared to look beyond conventional economic incentives and to include, in our search for its sources, causal impulses and organizational relations specific to Western technology and organization. That search is the primary subject of chapter 8.

Meeting the Capital Requirements of Factories

A number of historical arguments have been built on the assumption that the Industrial Revolution, with its shift to factory production, required the accumulation of great quantities of capital. Indeed, if the simple arithmetic of the formula, Consumption = Output − Capital Accumulation, really captured the process of the accumulation of capital, it would mean that many people must have sacrificed current consumption in the interest of accumulating capital. Marx took the sacrificial burden of accumulation for granted but argued that the capitalists had managed to shift it from themselves to labor. Others attributed the accumulation to the Calvinist principles of the capitalists themselves. To this day, the leaders of the U.S.S.R. use the need to accumulate capital, in the form of industrial facilities, to explain their neglect of the production of consumer goods. Third World as well as socialist countries have assumed burdensome debts in order to provide capital for new industries, and orthodox Western bankers have supposed that such loans serve a useful economic purpose. There may be some truth to all this, but it has to be supported by evidence other than the history of the Industrial Revolution in England.

To begin with, the historical evidence suggests that the capital required for the early factories was modest. Arkwright's first Cromford mill was insured for 1,500, and his second for 3,000 pounds. The introduction of steam power and multistory plants, near the close of the eighteenth century, pushed the cost of a spinning mill as high as 15,000 pounds; but by then the early factory owners had behind them twenty years of operations, sometimes highly profitable. There is some suggestion of a need for outside funds in the fact that factory owners often joined banking partnerships, but these affiliations may have indicated that the factory owners had surplus funds to invest or that they needed close banking ties to provide working capital.[32]

Of course, the capital that supplied the Industrial Revolution was not created out of thin air. But neither was it painfully accumulated by the frugal habits of Protestant burghers, expropriated from labor by massive reductions of wages, or squeezed out of reduced consumption. No reduction in the real income of workers or landowners nor in their rate of consumption, no national resolve to increase the rate of saving, was needed to fund the new machines and the new forms of factory organization. Rather, the increase in output that was generated by the factories was more than sufficient to pay their capital costs over a short period of time, for the increase was large and the capital costs were modest.

The funding of the factories was facilitated by the English system of country banks which, by the usual effects of deposit banking, created the money supply needed for their factory customers' working capital—which roughly equaled the fixed capital embodied in the new factories. Undoubtedly, both the inventories and sales financed by working capital and the underlying plant financed by fixed capital were real assets which had to be drawn off the real stream of production somehow, perhaps by the inflationary effect of the increase in money supply created by this deposit banking. But since the period was one of stable or declining prices, the inflationary effects must have been offset by other factors. One such factor was the improved productivity of the new factories and the resultant downward pressure on prices. To put the same point in terms of the "real" economy rather than the "financial" economy, if the real stream of production was constantly expanded by a continuing stream of more productive capital investments, there need not have been any time at which consumers experienced a reduction in the consumption goods portion of the stream, for no such reduction need have occurred.

It is too late to reconstruct the process in detail, but it is quite clear that the capital financing of the Industrial Revolution required little or no lowering of the existing standards of consumption in the interests of accumulating capital. According to Feinstein's authoritative estimates, overall consumption per capita in Great Britain did not decline between 1760 and 1800, and it rose dramatically thereafter. Moreover, the share of gross investment in British gross national product remained basically constant from the 1780s to the 1850s.[33]

Another indication that the Industrial Revolution did not impose important strains on the ability of Western nations to generate capital is that corporations, the traditional institutional tools for assembling large amounts of capital, played only a limited and specialized part until quite late in the nineteenth century. Corporations were formed for the building of turnpikes, railroads, and canals, but, by and large, widespread adoption of corporate forms of organization in industry came after factory production had become the dominant mode of industrial output. In both Europe and the United States, the entrepreneurial capitalists of the early and middle period of the Industrial Revolution were merchants, bankers, and inventors, operating in partnerships and only rarely making use of joint-stock corporations for manufacturing firms.

The claim that a decline in income among handweavers paid for the new factories is, at best, a metaphor. Economic change implies a relative or absolute reduction in both the value of the resources devoted to, and the income derived from, activities which become partially or wholly obsolete, whether handweaving, sailmaking, hostling, glassblowing, or steelmaking. A reduction in the value of human skills committed to handweaving, because of a decline in demand for handweaving, did not create a fund of resources transferable to the purchase of power looms. The weavers' loss was a consequence of change, not a source of capital for change. The old activity was in no position to finance its successor.[34]

It would be wrong to leave a sense of paradox about the failure of the Industrial Revolution to create painful problems of capital creation. The reason the formula, Consumption = Output − Capital Accumulation, presents a misleading picture of the process of economic growth is that it misses the effect of time. One may readily concede that an increase in output implies an increase in working capital and fixed capital, or else in productivity. But the causal link is between the *present* rate of production and the *past* rate of capital accumulation. It is entirely possible that over a period of time, whether a year or a long period such as 1750 to 1880, output, capital accumulation, and consumption could each increase at the same rate, or with differences in rates which nevertheless allowed a continuous rise in consumption throughout the period. All that is required is that the *current rise* in capital accumulation absorb less than all of the *current rise* in output. In the West, increases in productivity have tended to make this condition easy to meet.

A comparison of Soviet and Western economies suggests also that capital accumulation can be overdone. There is much reason to think that work effort, and hence output, in Soviet bloc countries has been adversely affected by shortages of consumer goods. Since expansion of consumption is, after all, the main incentive for the effort required to increase output, it should surprise no one to find that too much capital accumulation, with too little output of consumption goods, may reduce the rate of economic growth.

Urbanization and the Concurrent Revolution in Agriculture

The Industrial Revolution of the nineteenth century was intimately related to a concurrent agricultural revolution. The revolution in agriculture made possible the urbanization of Western society by reducing the proportion of the population required for providing food from the medieval 80-to-90 percent to less than 5 percent. At the same time, the enforced displacement of agricultural workers to the cities provided labor for the factories.

As in industry, the agricultural revolution was in part a matter of utilizing mechanical energy on an immensely greater scale, but this was a change which came after 1880.[35] Apart from mechanical energy, the other major factors in the agricultural revolution were an increased use of fertilizers, improved seeds, improvements in methods of cultivation and animal husbandry, and, as a consequence of improved transportation, the development of regional specialization in agriculture. Many of these changes reflected the application of the experimental methods of nineteenth-century science and engineering to the processes of supplying food. The opening of the American Great Plains to agricultural development was also very important to the urban food supply, but, like the expansion in mechanical energy, it came about toward the latter half of the nineteenth century, and we need to look primarily to improved farming methods for the explanation of the earlier advances.

One might have expected the agricultural revolution, like the industrial revolution, to universalize the use of agricultural factories, akin to the Roman latifundia or the plantations of the Southern United States and some tropical regions. There are several reasons why the agricultural revolution did not produce agricultural factories in the West.

One reason was that, because of the seasonal character of much farm work, it is often more economical for farm owners to hire seasonal migrant labor than to employ a permanent work force. Also, the belief that factories offer major advantages in the organization and control of production work, net of the costs of supervisors, other overhead personnel, and capital charges, is not necessarily true even of indoor factories, where supervision is easier than on farms. Much farm work must be done by individuals or very small groups, at a distance from effective supervision, and self-supervision, motivated by an owner's or tenant's interest in the size of the crop, remains an important device for the efficient organization of agricultural production.

The Factories and Labor

We now turn to the effect of the introduction of factories on labor—on both those employed in the factories and those not so employed, including those who lost their livelihood as the result of the introduction of factories.

The Industrial Revolution marked the beginning of a dramatic period of improvement in the material welfare of Western European and American society, both of the whole and of the laboring class. It was also a period of improvement in biological welfare, as measured by growth of the human population, extension of the length of human life, the conquest of many diseases, and a decline in the death rate of infants in the first year of life. At least in some spheres, it was a period of remarkable intellectual advance. It was the era during which the social sciences were invented and in which the physical sciences advanced. It is best left to experts in literature to judge whether there was an advance on Shakespeare, but in music it was the era that added the works of Haydn, Mozart, Beethoven, and Brahms to the repertoire. In politics, the decades between 1750 and 1880 witnessed the American and French Revolutions and a considerable, if incomplete, expansion of voting and other civil rights.

There is, however, an extensive literature to the effect that the material advances were achieved at the expense of great sacrifices imposed on the laboring class, and that even the intellectual advances were clouded by inadequate sensitivity to the crying needs of the Western masses. Much of this literature was written to advance legislation intended to improve working conditions in nineteenth-century factories, and if objectivity suffered, at least it suffered in a good cause. But by now, it has become more important to understand the world of the nineteenth century than to change it.

This literature was focused on the British textile industry. In this much-studied industry, the introduction of the factory resulted in the fairly rapid displacement of cottage spinners and the much slower displacement of cottage weavers, which caused substantial hardship to many of those displaced. The textile factories employed some of the displaced workers, but they also drew on a landless rural population for whom factory employment was an advance rather than a sacrifice. In other industries, such as iron and steel, shipbuilding, chemicals, and machinery, the transition from artisan production to factory production came more easily to the artisans, whose shops more readily became the factories. In most of the rest of the pre-Industrial Revolution economy—including construction, retailing, wholesaling, transportation, insurance, banking, law, medicine, and education—there was only expansion, with no transition to the factory system. This is not to say that there were no pockets of displaced workers outside the textile industry, but only that the displaced textile workers dominated the others, at least in their literary importance. Agriculture was also undergoing a reduction of the portion of the labor force required for the production of food. It thus kept adding to the pool of labor in need of alternative employment, and on a scale that dwarfed the displacement of workers in the textile industry.

In order to judge whether factory employment was, from the beginning of the Industrial Revolution, progress or retrogression for the workers, we need to understand the circumstances from which these workers came to the factories.

The Development of Industry: 1750–1880

1. The Eighteenth-Century Labor Pool: The Enclosure Movement

Under the manorial system, agricultural laborers worked the lord's demesne in exchange for the right to use other land for their own benefit, either by cultivation or as pasturage. The best land was cultivated and the "waste" land was left open, as common pasturage for the cottagers' animals. These were the oxen used in plowing, the sheep raised for wool, the dairy cows, and perhaps a pig. This system enabled the cottagers to earn a living above the bare subsistence level, provided agricultural prices were strong and crops good; as early as the sixteenth century, the rising population of England, combined with improvements in agricultural methods, tended to satisfy both provisos much, if not most, of the time.

By the eighteenth century, the same conditions that had brought relative prosperity to small farmers also supplied landowners with a strong incentive for enclosing common lands and bringing them under cultivation. While legal title to the commons typically rested in the large landowners, the villagers had long since acquired a variety of customary rights (mainly pasturage) in the common lands, and it took an act of Parliament to accomplish each enclosure. In theory, the acts compensated the cottagers for the loss of their commons rights by giving them some of the enclosed land. But the cottagers were not effectively represented in Parliament, and there is much reason to believe that the compensation was in practice inadequate. In any event, animal husbandry was often essential to the villagers' margin of prosperity over the barest subsistence, and the commons were essential to animal husbandry. Thus, quite apart from any question of the inadequacy of compensation, the long-term effect of enclosure was an impoverishment of agricultural labor—an impoverishment that, anomalously, accompanied a rise in the demand for food and an expansion of its production.

Writers on the enclosure movement usually claim that it came at a time of considerable prosperity among agricultural laborers, but it is worth remembering that periods of prosperity among agricultural workers tended to be short-lived. Even the fencing in of open lands was not new to the eighteenth century. The first act of Parliament dealing with the subject was the Statute of Merton, enacted in 1235. During the troubled times of the plague in the fourteenth century and of the Wars of the Roses in the fifteenth, the growth of the wool trade, in combination with a shortage of labor, led many landowners to remove their land from cultivation altogether and use it for raising sheep instead.

The shift from open-field agriculture, in which each villein cultivated a number of small strips, to small holdings agriculture was an enclosure movement of yet another type. It tends to be viewed with approval, for it worked to the advantage of the agricultural laborers who acquired interests in their own land. But it is a mistake to think of agricultural laborers as a homogeneous class, for the shift was not necessarily of benefit to those who ended as tenants of large landowners, and it was a disaster for the agricultural laborers it left wholly landless.

There was, in point of fact, widespread poverty of the most abject kind in England and other countries of eighteenth-century Europe, and it was from this pool of the forgotten poor that the early factories drew many of their workers. Braudel treats the phenomenon of poverty as nearly universal, characterizing as a "brake on social unrest ... in all past societies" the existence of "an enormous sub-proletariat."[36]

We may define a subproletariat in terms of a threshold of poverty, even though such a criterion is notoriously imprecise. By a test used in sixteenth- and seventeenth-century Lyons, it was crossed when daily income was less than the daily cost of the minimum bread requirement. In the last quarter of the sixteenth century, Lyons's casual laborers crossed the line, downward bound, in twenty-five out of twenty-five years, and unskilled laborers crossed it in seventeen out of twenty-five years. A quarter to half the population is said to have been near or below a state of poverty in Stuart (seventeenth-century) England, and comparable percentages were reported in Cologne, Cracow, and Lille.[37] Were the U.S. Bureau of Labor Statistics to adopt a similar standard of poverty, Americans below the poverty line would be those with incomes below approximately $18 a month, or $216 a year—the exact figure depending on the local price of bread. It is difficult for us not to view such figures as an absurd joke, something that never could have been tolerated. But a large proportion of the world's population still lives in pre-industrial societies where per-capita incomes are of that very order.

Perhaps Braudel's most striking statistic is the estimate that there were, in the Paris of 1776, about ninety-one thousand persons without a fixed abode or employment.[38] He does not present the situation as a transient phenomenon, but as one that had persisted since the eleventh or twelfth century:

> What appears to have happened in the West was that the great division of labour between town and countryside that took place in the eleventh and twelfth centuries, had left a permanent mass of unfortunates unprovided for, with nothing left to do. The fault lay in society no doubt and its usual evils, but it was perhaps even more to be found in the economy, which was powerless to

create full employment. Many of the unemployed eked out a living somehow, finding a few hours of work here and there, a temporary shelter. But the others—the infirm, the old, those who had been born and bred on the road—had very little contact with normal working life. This particular hell had its own circles, labelled in contemporary vocabulary as pauperdom, beggary and vagrancy.[39]

The romantic view that workers in pre-industrial Europe lived well may safely be dismissed as pure fantasy. Perhaps Braudel exaggerated a little; after all, people did live, though not very long on average. But if early factory work was oppressive, the alternatives open to those who voted with their feet for factory work were worse. The early factories were able to attract workers with low wages because the wages were still well above the poverty level, at least by the Lyons definition, and better than anything available elsewhere to an impoverished agricultural population. Victorian England was revolted by the fact that children labored in the factories for a few shillings a week, but when Parliament prohibited child labor, their places were quickly taken by landless Irish immigrants equally eager to work for a few shillings a week. The low wages, long hours, and oppressive discipline of the early factories are shocking in that the willingness of the inarticulate poor to work on such terms bespeaks, more forcefully than the most eloquent words, the even more abysmal character of the alternatives they had endured in the past. But this was not the way the romantics of the nineteenth century read the message of the factories.

2. Superseding the Apprentice System

To evaluate the impact of the factory on Braudel's "sub-proletariat" or, in current terms, the least-advantaged members of eighteenth-century society, it is necessary to consider the part played by the antecedent apprentice system in the antecedent artisan industry. There, it was customary to train workers through a long apprenticeship. Access to an apprenticeship was frequently restricted at the outset by the necessity of paying the master a substantial sum in advance, both for the support of the apprentice and for the master's instruction. Access was also restricted by guild rules limiting the number of apprentices a master might teach at one time.

An even more fundamental restriction was the practice of prolonging the apprenticeship. The usual term of the medieval apprenticeship was seven years. One purpose was to teach the apprentice all aspects of the craft. In some crafts, this meant acquiring skill in every step of producing the final product. In crafts where there was no specific product to be produced repetitively, it meant acquiring a range of skills defined in some other way, perhaps by the material being shaped (gold, silver, wood, leather, for examples). A second purpose of the prolonged apprenticeship was to give the master the benefit of the apprentice's labor for a period of time. This unpaid labor was rationalized as part of the master's compensation for instructing the apprentice.

The apprentice system restricted access to employment and it also restricted the production of goods. Its effect on the prices exacted of those outside the system—often buyers poorer than the guildmasters—was monopolistic, resulting from the restriction of access to the guild trades and the consequent restriction of the supply of goods. Secondarily, it reflected the wastefulness of unnecessarily prolonged training. Its persistence can be attributed to the fact that the guilds exercised combined political and economic functions, and so had the power to enforce uneconomic arrangements highly beneficial to themselves and highly injurious to the other members of society, including the very poor. Happily, the guilds were typically municipal political agencies, so that their writ did not run to the countryside. When factories were introduced, the legal power of the guilds was evaded by locating them in areas outside the guilds' jurisdiction. The medieval flight to the cities to escape the oppression of the manors ended as a return to the countryside to escape the oppression of the guilds.

There were, in the eighteenth century, a numerous subproletariat who had no funds to buy tools, no skills in their use, no possibility of supporting themselves through the years of an apprenticeship, none of the personal influence needed to obtain an apprenticeship, and no money to buy one. It was from this subproletariat that the early factories often drew their labor, even to the point of emptying an occasional poorhouse en masse.

Neither the entrepreneurs who built the factories nor anyone else supposed that they were engaged in a work of charity or an exercise of social conscience. But whatever the moral quality of their intentions, their actions advanced the interests of a down-trodden subproletariat—a subproletariat in part, perhaps, characteristic of pre-industrial societies and, in part, drawn from an agricultural work force hard pressed by the enclosure movement and a high rate of growth in agricultural productivity.

The reaction of the English middle class to all this remains a fascinating case study in social pathology. Having for centuries seen no better use for the poor than supplying an opportunity for their betters to exercise, with due moderation and modesty, the virtues of charity and compassion, much of middle-class England perceived the factory system not as a significant social advance, but as ruthless exploitation of the poor. Just below the middle class were the artisans, whose guild rules had long blocked all but privileged access to much of the everyday world of work. They did not think of themselves as monopolists at long last caught up with, but as victims of a new and highly unfair form of competition. Literary England, by and large, shared the opinion of both the middle class and the artisans. The reality could hardly have been more absurdly caricatured.

3. The Overall Effect on Workers

If the way the early factory workers voted with their feet is evidence that the textile factory system improved *their* condition, it cannot be assumed that the factory system improved the condition of the cottage workers whom it displaced. The decline in their earnings, followed by new employment in circumstances not of their own making, could have been beneficial only for a lucky few. It may well be that the factory system improved the *average* condition of workers from the beginning, but the issue is complex, because, as T. S. Ashton has pointed out, the initial years of rapid growth of the factory system were also years of the Napoleonic Wars, which had a material impact on the cost of living and on the distribution of income.[40] Ashton's general conclusion is that the distribution of income changed adversely for workers during the Napoleonic Wars and that their real income fell. By about 1820, the effects of the Napoleonic Wars on the British economy had worn off, and the conditions of the workers' lives began to improve steadily. The improvement was not uniform for all workers, and there were some, notably those skilled in crafts made obsolete by the factories, who suffered loss rather than benefit. Ashton summarized the matter as follows:

> During the period 1790–1830 factory production increased rapidly. A greater proportion of the people came to benefit from it both as producers and as consumers. The fall in the price of textiles reduced the price of clothing. Government contracts for uniforms and army boots called into being new industries, and after the war the products of these found a market among the better-paid artisans. Boots began to take the place of clogs, and hats replaced shawls, at least for wear on Sundays. Miscellaneous commodities, ranging from clocks to pocket handkerchiefs, began to enter the scheme of expenditure, and after 1820 such things as tea and coffee and sugar fell in price substantially. The growth of trade-unions, friendly societies, savings banks, popular newspapers and pamphlets, schools, and nonconformist chapels—all give evidence of the existence of a large class raised well above the level of mere subsistence.

There were, however, masses of unskilled or poorly skilled workers—seasonally employed agricultural workers and hand-loom weavers in particular—whose incomes were almost wholly absorbed in paying for the bare necessaries of life, the prices of which, as we have seen, remained high. My guess would be that the number of those who were able to share in the benefits of economic progress was larger than the number of those who were shut out from these benefits and that it was steadily growing. But the existence of two groups within the working class needs to be recognized.[41]

While it is widely assumed that factory workers in the early textile mills earned less than handloom weavers had earned under the putting-out system, the reality was complicated by large differences in earnings among cottage weavers—a phenomenon still associated with piece rate systems—and a tendency to compare the earnings of skilled weavers with those of unskilled factory workers. Moreover, the statistics need to be interpreted carefully. Bythell found evidence that Scottish adult men worked as handloom weavers for about 10 or 12 shillings a week in the 1790s. By comparison, adult males working at power looms in Manchester in 1842 (still a time of transition) were earning about 20 shillings a week. Adult women were earning 8 to 12 shillings, and girls of twelve to sixteen years of age earned 5 to 7 shillings.[42] Bythell found that piece rates for handlooming fell steadily all through the early nineteenth century, especially after the depression of 1826, causing severe hardship among handloom weavers. But the question whether handloom weavers earned more or less, before the advent of power looms, than the workers who ran the early power looms, can be answered either way, depending on how much one allows for differences in skills and on one's choice of handloom weaver—the average worker or the Stakhanovite.

The passage of time and changes in values, attitudes, assumptions, and expectations make it difficult to evaluate what was happening in the transition from the pre-industrial to the industrial era. Consider, for example, the fact that hours of work in the factories were longer than those of most workers before the advent of factories. The longer hours may imply either a retrogression in the worker's welfare or a gain in opportunities for employment.

There is, however, a third possibility that may lie closer to the truth. It is based in part on observations of present-day conditions in Third World countries. The hours of work in pre-industrial economies are likely to be short simply because an undernourished population lacks the energy to work any longer. Shorter hours are not necessarily a choice of leisure over work; they may be compelled by the need to limit one's activity to what an inadequate diet can support. Considering the marginal standards of subsistence in Western Europe in the eighteenth century, and for long before, it is not clear that the hours of labor were short because the workers preferred leisure over wages; they may have been short, as in Third World countries, because of malnutrition.[43] The improvement in English agriculture before the Industrial Revolution, and the resulting improvement in the English national diet, may have been a contributing cause of the Industrial Revolution and a possible explanation of why it occurred first in England. The thought that increased hours of labor can be an indication of improved worker welfare seems nearly incomprehensible today, but then neither are we accustomed to assume in our thinking that workers as a class may not be fed enough to work very long, or very hard.

The conditions faced by Western European working classes were harsh before the Industrial Revolution; they were harsh during the Industrial Revolution; and they were harsh for a long time afterward. But the balance of evidence is that even though the Industrial Revolution did not initially benefit all workers, it did not, even at its beginning, make matters any *worse*, on average,[44] and once the effects of the Napoleonic Wars were shaken off, it led to major advances in the welfare of the working class.[45] This point has a bearing on late-twentieth-century economic problems, in that the Industrial Revolution is not, as many have thought, a precedent for imposing sacrifices on the living generation (especially its working members) in the hope that things will be better for later generations. So far as this primary historic example of rapid economic progress teaches us anything about the need for social sacrifice, its lesson is that economies progress rapidly when the fruits of progress are widely and contemporaneously enjoyed.

It is appropriate to evaluate the effect of the West's economic growth, in the early stages of the Industrial Revolution, on the welfare of factory workers in narrow terms of material well-being, simply because one is dealing with the transition of a subproletariat on the edge of starvation to a working population with at least the beginnings of some small amenities. The pre-1750 subproletariat suffered in a silence which leaves us little knowledge of what sort of social community may have existed among paupers, beggars, and vagrants, but it was surely not worth starving for. For people who can just begin to afford a little sugar, the social and political consequences of the change hardly matter, short of such extremes as a switch to a slave system. No such extremes occurred. In England, workers in the cities became independent householders rather than members of the household of a master worker. They gained in literacy and, by the Reform Act of 1897, most gained the right to vote. Granted that the working, urban life resulted in the loss of the community of pauperdom, beggary, and vagrancy, whatever it may have been, or even of the community of apprentices and journeymen in the household of a master worker, it substituted its own working-class community, signaled by the formation of unions, cooperatives, savings funds, and even, under the leadership of John Wesley, founder of Methodism, what amounted to a working-class church. In France, Germany, and the United States, the story was not much different.

Of course, we cannot settle the ages-old argument between the proponents and opponents of urban living, who include Old Testament prophets ancient and contemporary. The terms of the debate have changed in the context of modern transportation and communication, which have made it possible to move much of industry back to the countryside. Cities are becoming more and more centers of services and commerce rather than of manufacture, and urban life is no longer lived in the nineteenth-century cities of smokestack industries, primitive housing, and undeveloped health and sanitation services. However, two observations are in order. The first is that, given the growth of its population and the decline in the need for agricultural labor, the West never had a humane choice between pastoral and urban life. The second observation is that urban life was primarily a consequence of an agricultural revolution, not of the Industrial Revolution— a point sadly illustrated in our own times by the analogous struggle of Third World metropolises to cope with a flood of desperate immigrants from the countryside. The question then, as in today's Third World, was whether displaced rural workers and new workers would find some kind of non-farm employment capable of sustaining life. In this sense, the Industrial Revolution and Western economic growth were not an initiating cause of urbanization and its associated social problems, but rather a solution to its most pressing problem. Not even a Malthusian solution would have met the problem of the excess rural population, for a decline in the number of mouths to feed would have resulted in a further decline in the number of workers needed to provide food. Finding other forms of employment was simply imperative, and the factories and cities were the response.

4. Were Factories Introduced to Reduce Wages or to Achieve Efficient Production?

As A. J. Chapman pointed out some seventy years ago,[46] the introduction of factories was influenced by organizational as well as technological factors. From the viewpoint of the promoters of the early factories, an improvement in the organization of work was a change that reduced the cost of labor without reducing output. Recently, Marglin, in comparing factory work to work under the putting-out system, principally as practiced in the British textile industry, has specified the following advantages of the factory to its owners: (1) stealing of materials and work in process by workers could be reduced; (2) unskilled women and children were capable of doing the narrowly specialized factory jobs and accepted lower wages for equivalent output than the more highly skilled adult male labor used in the putting-out system; (3) factory hands could be induced, by the threat of dismissal for absenteeism, to work regularly for a full week instead of working the partial and uncertain week common among cottage workers.[47]

These gains were not cost free. In order to realize the reductions in labor costs from factory organization, the early factory promoters had to incur the costs of building a factory, equipping it with looms, and hiring supervisors for their work force. Since interest and depreciation on the investment in the factory continued in slack times as well as in good times, the factory mode of organization also implied greater financial risk than the cottage mode of organization.

In textile weaving, the saving in labor costs from the change to factory organization, after one deducts the cost of realizing them, were small or negative, as evidenced by the long history of gradual displacement of handlooms by power looms, closely correlated as it was with the slow extension of the capabilities of power looms to the weaving of better-grade fabrics.[48] Had the net savings been positive, the change from cottage weaving to factory weaving could as well have occurred in the 1790s as the 1840s. There is also the complication that during the time that factory weaving and handweaving coexisted, they were producing products of different qualities for different, and expanding, markets, so that the number of handweavers actually reached a peak between 1821 and 1831, several decades after the introduction of factory weaving.[49]

The inference seems unavoidable that, in the particular case of textile weaving, a general change to factory from cottage weaving would not have occurred had the only gains to the factory promoters been those attributable to savings in wages, longer hours, reduced theft, and other improvements in organization. Improvements in the productivity of the machines and in their ability to produce textiles of high quality were a necessary condition. Whether change in technology was also a sufficient condition at the time the changes occurred, we do not know. By then, competition between factory and cottage had dissipated some, perhaps all, of the organizational advantages of the factory. Later, the gap in productivity between a technologically contemporary weaving mill and cottage weaving widened to the point where, without consideration of organizational savings, cottage weaving had become an economic anachronism.

5. The Worker, the Division of Labor, and the Tools of Production

The introduction of the factory system has conventionally been treated as changing certain important relations between work and reward and between the workers and their tools. It is convenient to begin by outlining the orthodox view of the changes, reserving until the end a very substantial question as to the degree to which Western pre-industrial economies actually exemplified the orthodox pre-industrial model of production.

The conventional model of pre-industrial production emphasizes the independent artisan who bought parts and materials and personally transformed them into a visibly different end product with uses and a market of its own. The relations among the worker's effort, the value of the product, and the worker's reward were close and highly visible. The introduction of factory division of labor made the relation collective rather than individual. The product of the individual worker's efforts became a contribution to the final value of a product, often so attenuated and melded with the contributions of others that it became indiscernible, leaving its value with no visible link to the value of the product. This breaking of the line from the worker's effort to the value of the product to the worker's reward left no completely satisfying way to connect effort with reward.

In the present state of knowledge of group psychology, it seems conceivable that collective relations among work, the quality and value of the product, and the worker's reward could be made even more satisfying than individual relationships. But even in Japan, the translation of our knowledge of group psychology into factory practice is still far from complete. There is little doubt that, to date, the collectivization of the relation between the worker and the product is a cost to be entered on the debit side of an evaluation of the factory system.

The factory system was also incompatible with the workers' ownership of the tools they used. An essential feature of the factory system is that a large number of workers share at least part of the apparatus of production in common, and in practice almost all production equipment is now so used. At the outset, the factory building itself, its waterwheel or steam engine, and the system of drive shafts and pulleys for delivering power to the machines had to be used jointly by all who worked at the machines in the factory. The entity that owned the common parts of the factory also owned the machinery, historically because the individuals employed in the factories could not afford their own machines and as a matter of economics because the calculation of the marginal costs and benefits of buying each machine had to be made by and for the factory as a single entity.

Ownership of tools by someone other than the individual worker has economic efficiency implications, in that workers may be likely to take better care of their own tools than of someone else's. Marx made a great deal more of it than that. He saw it as a central objection to the capitalist system, arguing that the status of a worker who used someone else's tools was less akin to that of the guild master than to that of an apprentice, or even of a slave. The worker who did not own his own tools was a *proletarian*, a term derived from the Latin *proletarius*, a Roman citizen who was propertyless and hence of the lowest class of citizens. In Marx's day, it was not a practical objection to this terminology that, though wage earners might not own their own tools, they might nevertheless own appreciable property of other kinds. That problem came later. Similarly, Marx shared the tendency of intellectuals of his day to perceive the factory as reducing the status of independent artisans rather than as advancing the status of a class which had never owned its own tools—or much of anything else, for that matter.

Much the same limits to true individual ownership inherent in the factory system are inherent in partnerships and other forms of group ownership. Even in a partnership of two individuals, it is essential to distinguish partnership property and individual property. When the partnership includes hundreds of individuals, control of its property has to be delegated to an authority structure of managing partners, committees, accountants, and auditors, and any one partner's sense of interest in a particular asset becomes so much more abstract and attenuated than an individual owner's sense of dominion over personal property as to amount to a change of kind. In much the same way, given that a large number of workers are to use the factory, there is no way for each one who uses it to own it in fact.

It is, however, possible for each worker to own a minute share in the entity that owns the factory. Purchases of stock by employees, either planned or unplanned, employee cooperatives, and public ownership (where everybody is an owner) are ways of removing wage earners from the propertyless status of the *proletarius* and are possible ways of restoring to workers a form of the artisans' link to their tools. But ownership of any other kind of property would also lift the wage earner out of the proletariat, and the strategy of diversification of risk would suggest that the worker should not stake both savings and career on one enterprise. Also, it is controversial to just what degree any such arrangements give workers feelings of attachment to the factory and an interest in caring for it akin to the feelings of artisans for their own tools. True feelings of ownership may be intractably individual, making collective ownership a pyschological contradiction in terms. The loss of the artisans' feelings for their tools may thus be another debit entry in the evaluation of the change to the factory system.[50]

The foregoing discussion sets out the conventional view of the problems occasioned by the shift to factory production from production in the shop of an individual artisan, typified by the much-discussed cottage weaving industry. It is necessary to recognize, however, that once we move away from the cottage weaving industry, we find owners of pre-industrial mills, shops, and farms who employed helpers, apprentices, and hired hands who used tools they did not own and who received wages in amounts hardly more visibly linked to the market value of a product than the wages of a modern Detroit assembly-line worker. In fact, the use of helpers was not unknown even among the weavers. And the artisan-owners were an elite among the work force. In the towns, they were the leading citizens, not the rank and file. In agriculture, the visible link between one's income and the market price of one's product existed (as it still does) for a numerous class of small farmers, including tenants. But there was still a large body of agricultural workers who possessed no land, who rarely supplied their own tools, and whose wages were by no means a simple function of their employers' revenues. Also, the link between work and the product is not easily demonstrated in the services furnished to the lord of the manor by the villeins. Like so many other golden ages, the age when goods sold were everywhere the product solely of the seller's own hands and the price received was the reward of the seller's own efforts, is a product of imagination only loosely constrained by acquaintance with the facts.

The Development of Industry: 1750–1880

Conclusion

There were many changes in the technology of production, transportation, and communication in the nineteenth century that were dramatic enough to be called revolutionary. We look back on it as the period when the West established at least six elements of its growth economies:

1 Invention, technology, and change became fundamental features of economic activity. In 1750, there were still guilds and artisans who actively sought to preserve old ways of making old products, to the point of expressing their opposition to the new by arson and sabotage. By 1880, such attachment to existing practices had become anachronistic. The social stereotype of the maker of goods as an artisan practicing an ancient craft in the received ways had given way to the social stereotype of the manufacturer of goods as an entrepreneurial inventor trying to create a new world.

2 By 1880, market relations had so far submerged economic relations based on custom, usage, and law that the latter were nearly forgotten, and markets were taken for granted as a basic feature of modern economies. Supply and demand became more and more important even in relations between employer and employee. The change to a money nexus was accelerated as the shift to the factory separated workplace and dwelling, so that fewer and fewer workers lived in their employers' households. It was reinforced also by the division of labor and the shared use of common tools, which totally obscured the relations between the individual worker's efforts and the price realized from those efforts on the sale of the finished product. Up to the close of the feudal period, wages and other terms of employment had been determined principally by guild and manorial custom, usage, and law. By 1880, the change to market relations was substantially complete. By then, terms of employment were determined by employer offers of terms and employee acceptances, and, as in any other market, both offers and acceptances were influenced by the state of the supply of, and the demand for, labor. In industry and commerce, the domination of employment by market relations was qualified only by the occasional successes of the early trade unions, by a few statutes setting outer limits on conditions of work, especially for women and children, and by the survival of some obligations imposed by maritime law as compulsory incidents of the employment of sailors.

3 The earlier relaxation of overarching religious and political authority in Western societies bore fruit in the form of a plural society of comparatively autonomous spheres of industry, trade, finance, science, politics, education, art, music, literature, religion, and the press. It was as if Western society had set out to extend the advantages of the division of labor and specialization to all the major aspects of social life.

4 Urbanization proceeded rapidly, impelled by the displacement of agricultural workers by advances in agricultural methods and, in England, by the enclosure

movement, and facilitated by the introduction of factories in which relatively unskilled workers could be employed.

5 Modes of economic organization were as subject to the regime of change, market relations, and experiment as were individual purchases and sales. Unevenly, but eventually over most of industry, the factory organization of the work place superseded the artisan's shop. Some factories, like those making ceramics and, eventually, iron and steel, were highly integrated, embracing several steps in the process of production from raw material to finished product. Others, especially in the textile industry, tended to specialize in a single step of the production process. Factories were built where there was water power, or coal, and they needed also to be near customers, sources of raw materials, and transportation: they had unprecedented appetites for all three. The governing principle was the use of the most economical form, place, and scale of production. Since the controlling circumstances differed from industry to industry, so did the mode, location, and scale of production organizations.

6 In some ways, the most fundamental change in economic organization was the realization that the deeper function of a manufacturing enterprise was not simply to operate its factory (or, rarely, factories) efficiently, but to create or discover changes—in product, production, raw materials, distribution, or organization—that would increase the margin between costs and revenue. The concepts of an enterprise and enterprising became distinct from the concepts of a factory and manufacturing.

Like more recent eras of progress and change, it was also a period with many elements of continuity. The factory, with its engines and machinery, was brought into being by the merchants and bankers, miners and ironmasters, shipwrights and founders, of the late eighteenth and early nineteenth centuries. Their firms were organized as partnerships or proprietorships, and they worked within a system of exchange institutions that had already received its intellectual framework from Adam Smith. The railroad system was different: it required the corporate form of organization for its financing and management and produced competing centralized and decentralized systems of management whose relative merits were still unsettled a century later. In general, however, the types of enterprise organization that had sufficed for merchants and artisans of the 1750s sufficed also for merchants and manufacturers of the 1870s.

It is understandable that Marx, writing in 1848, should speak of modern industry as already a century old, for many of the institutions of industry in 1848 were already that old. Yet the greatest advances in the output of the capitalist engine of production, and the greatest changes in its modes of organization, still lay ahead.

The Development of Industry: 1750–1880

NOTES

1. David S. Landes, *Revolution in Time* (Cambridge: Harvard University Press, 1983), p. 111.

2.

> The railway companies themselves and their employees were destined to become a major market for watches, but even more their riders, who not only wanted to know the hour and minute in order to catch trains but found their entire consciousness of time altered by the requirements and opportunities of a railway world.

Ibid., p. 285.

3. See E. P. Thompson, "Time, Work-Discipline, and Industrial Capitalism," in *Past and Present*, no. 38: 56–97. The home work week in the textile industry concentrated in the last three or four days of the week; "Saint Monday" was a holiday. "The work pattern was one of alternate bouts of intense labour and idleness, wherever men were in control of their own working lives." Ibid., p. 73. For "idleness," the moralists of the day were ready to read "drunkenness," apparently with some basis in truth.

4. E. P. Thompson, *The Making of the British Working Class* (New York: Vintage Books, 1966).

5. See R. J. Forbes, "Power to 1850," chap. 5 in vol. 4 of *A History of Technology*, C. Singer, J. R. Holmyard, A. R. Hall, and T. J. Williams, eds. (New York: Oxford University Press, 1958), p. 148.

> From the figures available for eighteenth-century water-wheels we can conclude that their energy-output was seldom better than 10 hp, and on the average only 5 hp ... The largest series of water-wheels was the colossal "machine of Marly" built for Louis XIV by the Liege carpenter Rennequin in 1682. ... It had a potential capacity of 124 hp and delivered at least 75 hp in actual work. (Ibid., p. 155.)

As to windmills, which were popular along the windy coasts of the North Sea and the Baltic but less so in England, "the eighteenth-century mill would produce an average of 10hp." Ibid., p. 159. Louis XIV's Marly machine was built to pump water for the fountains of Versailles; it was not necessarily of the most economical size for supplying power, since the design of Versailles was not dominated by cost considerations.

6. Julia de L. Mann, *Oxford History of Technology*, "The Textile Industry: Machinery for Cotton, Flax, Wool, 1760–1850," chap. 10, vol. 4, 277 at 278.

7. A. Stowers, "Watermills *c* 1500–*c* 1850," chap. 7 in Singer et al., *A History of Technology*.

8. See the discussion in Robert B. Gordon, "Cost and Use of Water Power during Industrialization in New England and Great Britain: A Geological Interpretation," *The Economic History Review*, 2d Ser. 36, no. 2 (May 1983): 240–59. As late as 1869, less than 30 percent of the power employed in New England manufacturing establishments was derived from steam. Nathan Rosenberg, *Perspectives on Technology* (London: Cambridge University Press, 1976), p. 177.

9. Jeremy Atack, "Fact in Fiction? The Relative Costs of Steam and Water Power: A Simulation Approach," *Explorations in Economic History* 4 (October 1979): 409–37, and table 1, 412.

10. A. J. Taylor, "Concentration and Specialization in the Lancashire Cotton Industry, 1825–1850," *Economic History Review* 1, no. 2: 115.

11. For a convenient short account of the development of steam engines, see H. W. Dickinson, "The Steam Engine to 1830," in *A History of Technology*, vol. 4, 168–98. See also his *A Short History of the Steam Engine* (Cambridge: Cambridge University Press, 1939).

12. Later in the nineteenth century, with the development of smaller and more mobile steam engines, steam power became a good deal more domesticated and urbanized. Mobile steam engines were used on farms to drive farm machinery, and New York's elevated railway trains were drawn by steam locomotives. The steam launch became a recreational vessel for those not rich enough to own a steam yacht and, for a while, early in the

twentieth century, there was some doubt about whether the future of the automobile lay with steam or gasoline power.

13.

Iron smelting did use by and large the same basic processes as it does today—blast furnaces and power-hammers—but the difference was one of scale. Whereas a blast furnace today "can consume the equivalent of three train-loads of coke and iron ore in twenty-four hours," the most perfected of these furnaces in the eighteenth century only functioned intermittently; then, flanked by a forge and two fires, it barely produced 100 to 150 tons of iron a year. Today, production is calculated in thousands of tons.

Fernand Braudel, *The Structure of Everyday Life*, trans. Sian Reynolds (New York: Harper & Row, 1981), p. 373.

14. Charles K. Hyde, *Technological Change and the British Iron Industry, 1700–1870* (Princeton: Princeton University Press, 1977), p. 10.

15. Ibid., p. 9. The quotation is from a letter, 30 July 1754, of John Fuller to the Prince of San Sorrino, as quoted in H. R. Schubert, *History of the British Iron and Steel Industry, c. 450 B.C. to A.D. 1775* (London: Routledge & Kegan Paul, 1957), pp. 237–38.

16. Hyde, *Technological Change*, p. 30.

17. Braudel, *Structure of Everyday Life*, pp. 362–67. England restricted the cutting of forests for making iron as early as the reign of Elizabeth, in 1558.

18. The requirement of a stronger air blast was associated initially with the shift from charcoal to coke. See H. R. Schubert, "Extraction and Production of Metals: Iron and Steel," chap. 4, part I, in *Oxford History of Technology*, vol. 4.

19. S. D. Chapman, "The Transition to the Factory System in the Midlands Cotton-Spinning Industry," *Economic History Review* 17: pp. 526–43, at pp. 531–32. Chapman points out, however, that the Nottingham hosiers had preceded Arkwright in organizing factories. Chapman lists ten Arkwright-organized mills in the Midlands, and Arkwright later established others in Manchester and Scotland:

Apart from water power, the most important asset of Derbyshire for Arkwright and his imitators was the labour supply. Though a poor agricultural area, the Peak District nevertheless supported a relatively dense population because of the mining industry, one of whose centers was at Wirksworth, 2 miles from Cromford. The contraction of this industry toward the end of the eighteenth century created a pool of female and adolescent labour searching for employment.

20.

First emphasis must be laid upon the point that it was not mechanical change alone which constituted the industrial revolution. No doubt small hand-looms factories would have become the rule, and more and more control over production would have devolved upon the factory master, and the work to be done would have been increasingly assigned by merchants, had the steam-engine remained but the dream of Watt, and semi-automatic machinery not been invented. The spirit of the times was centralizing management before any mechanical changes of a revolutionary character had been devised. Loom-shops, in which several journeymen were employed, were not uncommon: thus "in the later part of the last (18th) and the beginning of the present (19th) century," says Butterworth, describing the state of affairs in Oldham and the neighborhood, "a large number of weavers possessed spacious loom-shops, where they not only employed many journeymen weavers, but a considerable proportion of apprentice children."

S. J. Chapman, "Cotton Manufacture," in *Encyclopaedia Britannica*, 11th ed. vol. 7, pp. 281–301.

See also his article on "Cotton: Marketing and Supply," ibid., and his *The Lancashire Cotton Industry* (Manchester: University Press, 1904).

21. Chapman, "Cotton Manufacture," p. 285c. And according to A. J. Taylor: "By 1850 the cotton industry was tending to contract into the area of the Lancashire coal-field or into districts served by it; but within that area the country-mill was able to survive,"

The Development of Industry: 1750–1880

"Concentration and Specialization in the Lancashire Cotton Industry, 1825–1850," *Economic History Review*, no. 2: 114–22.

22. Forbes refers to cotton as "the steam industry *par excellence*" ("Power to 1850" in *A History of Technology*, p. 156). S. J. Chapman discussed at some length the unusual organization of the British textile industry in his articles in the *Encyclopaedia Britannica*, "Cotton Manufacture," and "Cotton: Marketing and Supply."

23. Chapman, "Cotton Manufacture," in *Encyclopaedia Britannica*, p. 287b.

24. A. J. Taylor, "Concentration and Specialization," p. 117. B. R. Mitchell, in *Abstract of British Historical Statistics* (Cambridge: Cambridge University Press, 1962), pp. 185–87, writes that the number of handloom weavers peaked at 240,000 between 1821 and 1831 and then declined to 110,000, less than half the number, by 1841. In 1851, their numbers had fallen to 40,000 and, by 1861, to 7,000, according to Mitchell. He numbers the power looms at 110,000 in 1835; 250,000 in 1850; and 400,000 in 1861.

25. A. J. Taylor, "Concentration and Specialization," p. 117.

26. "As late as 1853, in spite of improvements in the power-loom and its steady encroachment on the classes of work hitherto monopolized by the domestic weaver, it was still observed that the hand-loom was 'in fancy goods, more used than the power-loom.' " Ibid., p. 118. G. N. von Tunzelman, *Steam Power and British Industrialization to 1850* (Oxford: Clarendon Press, 1978), states: "Lower costs of power in the 1850s permitted the economical spinning of yarns and weaving of cloths of substantially higher qualities . . . [C]heaper power led to a faster rate of output from the machines, and this consolidated their advantage." P. 202. Tunzelman details the changes in power looms which gradually increased their advantage (pp. 195–202), noting that handlooms were also improved, but in ways that made them more expensive and tended to bring them into factory rather than cottage use. (Pp. 200–202.)

27. Stephen A. Marglin, "What Do Bosses Do? The Origins and Functions of Hierarchy," in *Review of Radical Economics* (Summer 1974): 60–112, discussed on p. 178 of this chapter.

28. A. and N. L. Clow, "Ceramics from the Fifteenth Century to the Rise of the Staffordshire Potteries," chap. 11, in *A History of Technology*, p. 353.

29. Ibid., pp. 356–57.

30. Mitchell, *Abstract of British Historical Statistics*, pp. 178, 181. These figures are subject to small corrections for re-exports of raw cotton. Corrected, growth in the nineteenth century might be 60:1 instead of 67:1.

31. Ibid., pp. 131–32; and H. R. Schubert, "Iron and Steel," in *A History of Technology*, p. 107.

32. The figures cited are from S. D. Chapman, "Transition to Factory System," pp. 540–42. He lists other spinning mills built between 1778 and 1792 with comparable values.

33. C. Feinstein, "Capital Accumulation and the Industrial Revolution," in Roderick Floud and Donald McCloskey, eds., *The Economic History of Britain since 1700*, vol. 1, *1700–1860* (Cambridge: Cambridge University Press, 1981), p. 136. Feinstein's estimates do show a rising share of gross investment in GNP, but this appears to have occurred before the years of most rapid industrialization, that is, before the 1790s.

34. For a brief discussion of the effect on growth of imperfect transferability of labor between industries, see John Hicks, "Structural Unemployment and Economic Growth: A 'Labor Theory of Value' Model," chap. 2 in *The Political Economy of Growth*, Dennis C. Mueller, ed. (New Haven: Yale University Press, 1983), pp. 53–56. When improvements in productivity result in reductions in prices, the distribution of the consumer's expenditures will change in favor of the industry with the greater relative reduction in prices (except in very special circumstances). If resources from other industries are not fully transferable to the favored industry, from others, then (using Hicks's assumption that additional resources are not available from other sources), there is an adverse effect on the rate of growth. Hicks does not go into the effect on the nontransferable resources, but it could hardly be otherwise than adverse.

35. Even then, it was not at first a question of substituting mechanical energy for animal energy, but of adding both. Between 1880 and 1920, mechanical horsepower on U.S. farms rose from 668,000 to 21,443,000. But the number of work animals in rural and urban use also rose throughout the same period, though at a much slower pace: from 11,580,000 to 22,430,000. The nearly total substitution of mechanical for animal power took place even later, after 1920. The data are from Department of Commerce *Historical Statistics of the*

United States (Washington, D.C.: Government Printing Office, 1975), pt. 2, ser. S 1–14, p. 818.

36. Fernand Braudel, *The Wheels of Commerce* (New York: Harper & Row, 1979), p. 506.

37. Ibid., p. 507. Braudel's figures for cities outside of England are from P. Laslett, *The World We Have Lost* (London: Methuen, 1965).

38. Braudel, *Wheels of Commerce,* 510.

39. Ibid., p. 506.

40. T. S. Ashton, "The Standard of Life of the Workers in England, 1790–1830," in F. A. Hayek, ed., *Capitalism and the Historians* (Chicago: University of Chicago Press, 1954), pp. 123–55. "During the war, then, there took place a whole series of transfers of income—to landlords, farmers, houseowners, bondholders, and entrepreneurs—and these almost certainly worsened the economic status of labor." P. 131.

41. Ibid., pp. 154–55.

42. Duncan Bythell, *The Handloom Weavers: A Study in the English Cotton Industry during the Industrial Revolution* (Cambridge: Cambridge University Press, 1969), pp. 133, 135.

43. This point is developed in Herman Freudenberger and Gaylord Cummins, "Health, Work, and Leisure before the Industrial Revolution," *Explorations in Economic History* 13 (1976): 1–12. They suggest that advances in British agriculture in the seventeenth century made possible improvements in diet whose social consequences became apparent in the eighteenth. Their hypothesis is not altogether consistent with the work of Bythell, who found that, by the last half of the eighteenth century, English weavers were working less than a full six-day week—more like four days—apparently as a matter of choice, and earning more than a subsistence income. See *The Handloom Weavers,* pp. 116, 130–31. At the beginning of the Industrial Revolution, all indications are of a classic disequilibrium between a rising demand for textiles, without a corresponding rise in the supply of weavers, resulting in high piece rates until ways were found to bring weavers' wages closer to those prevailing in the English labor market generally.

44. The factories were bitterly attacked in nineteenth-century England by many individuals of high intellectual capacity, from John Stuart Mill to Frederich Engels, with a view to obtaining legislation to improve working conditions. For a brief comparison of some of the political rhetoric with the evidence on which it purported to be based, see W. H. Hutt, "The Factory System of the Early Nineteenth Century," in Hayek, ed., *Capitalism and the Historians,* pp. 156–84.

45. Peter H. Lindert and Jeffrey G. Williamson, "English Workers' Living Standards during the Industrial Revolution: A New Look," *Economic History Review* (February 1983): 11.

46. S. J. Chapman, "Cotton Manufacture."

47. Marglin, "What Do Bosses Do? Origins and Functions of Hierarchy."

48. See this chapter, 159–60.

49. See Mitchell's estimates in *Abstract of British Historical Statistics.*

50. In most Western countries today, employee cooperatives enjoy tax advantages and access to public or institutional financing. The incremental value that workers attach to worker ownership, in comparison to purchase of stock in their corporate employers, is very roughly indicated by the relative size of the employee cooperative sector. As a mode of economic organization, however, employee cooperatives have disadvantages in comparison to publicly held corporations. See chapter 10.

6 / Diversity of Organization: The Corporation

From the fifteenth century on, Westerners, as individuals, gained an increasing degree of freedom to choose the economic activities in which they would engage, despite the inheritance of manorial obligations and the pervasiveness of guild restrictions on an individual's choice of livelihood in the towns. But more than individual choice was required. Much of economic life has always been a group rather than an individual matter, and the introduction of the factory in the eighteenth century made production not simply a group activity, but an activity of increasingly large groups. For Western economies to develop comparatively autonomous economic spheres within which authority over economic decisions was decentralized to multiple decision centers, it was no longer enough for individuals, or even for small groups, to enjoy the freedom to select their own ways of making a living. With the growth of large-scale transportation, merchandising, and manufacturing, it became essential to extend a similar freedom to the formation and operation of larger groups. By the close of the nineteenth century, Western societies needed institutions in which large commercial groups could organize to engage in economic activity, and yet remain relatively free of political control.

The publicly held corporation was the West's principal answer to this institutional need. It was not, of course, the only possible answer, and there was nothing inevitable in the specific forms that the corporation actually took. Large-scale economic activity could be, and was, still conducted under the older forms of proprietorship and partnership organization. But the publicly held corporation had two important advantages, worth mentioning here in anticipation of their exploration in the next two chapters. The first is familiar: it enabled investors to spread the commercial risk of investment by buying small, and quickly marketable, shares in a number of enterprises. The second is a little more complex. Increasingly large enterprises were forced to imitate the hierarchical organization structure of armies, governments, and churches. In a way, this was an unfortunate development, for hierarchies have always been subject to what has come to be called the agency risk—that is, the risk that managing hierarchies would, however honorable their intentions, tend to operate organizations for their own welfare at some cost to the organizations' ostensible purposes. When, as with armies, size has obvious advantages that outweigh the agency costs (that is, the loss due to waste of organization resources by hierarchies' pursuit of their own goals at the expense of organization interests), the problem of organization is not how to dispense with hierarchies, but how to keep agency costs from getting out of hand. In the case of the publicly held corporation, the ease with which stockholders could express their dissatisfaction with the hierarchy by selling their shares and reinvesting somewhere else turned into a formidable control device that had no equivalent in the older forms of hierarchical organization.

Though corporations were familiar to Roman law, chartering them to conduct economic activity, as distinguished from regulating it, was, except perhaps in Italy, a late-sixteenth- or early-seventeenth-century development. The guilds were older, but their purpose was to regulate the conduct of a trade by their members and to exclude interlopers from practicing the trade, not to engage in the trade themselves. Most of the early corporations chartered to engage in economic activity also had political powers, an exclusive right to engage in the activity for which they were chartered, or both. The grant of such charters was a source of substantial revenue to the sovereign.

By the beginning of the eighteenth century, in England at least, some voluntary groups of investors were attempting to operate joint-stock companies as purely economic entities without benefit of a royal charter and without political powers or exclusive rights to any trade. They differed from partnerships in that their shares were freely transferable. The legal status of these enterprises was not regularized until the nineteenth century, when the chartering of corporations ceased to be a matter of obtaining a formal delegation of political powers from the sovereign and became a matter of making a public record, by registration, of the fact that a group of people wished to trade as an entity, through agents acting for the entity.

In this chapter, we deal with the origins of the corporate form of enterprise organization and with its development through the period of widespread adoption of laws providing for incorporation by registration, up to the development of a market for industrial stock in the 1890s. We concentrate on the experience of the United States and England, but, to emphasize the pervasiveness of the forces leading to the adoption of the corporate form, it has seemed worthwhile to include a comparative note on the growth of corporations in France and Germany. The adoption of laws providing for incorporation of economic groups by simple registration did not in itself supply the West with the institutions it needed for group organization on the scale required by the emerging enterprises of the turn of the century. But it did set the stage for the revolution in economic organization which took place in the period from 1895 to 1914, when a growing public discovery of the advantages of investment in corporations with readily marketable shares led to the reorganization of American and, considerably later, Western European, industry into publicly held corporations. But that is a story as much of technological revolution and the development of securities markets as of the development of corporations, and we leave it for chapter 7.

Roman Antecedents

The need for group ownership of property and group economic activity is so ancient and universal in human society that it becomes easy to play the game of tracing the genesis of corporations to exotic sources, along with the opposite game of showing that the modern corporation had no antecedents. Some primitive legal systems treated the family (or rather the household) as a body corporate, represented for most legal and political purposes by the head of the household. In Rome, this was the paterfamilias. But membership in the household was not usually voluntary, and the paterfamilias was not an agent of the members of the household in anything like the sense that the managers of a modern corporation are agents of its owners collectively.

The Romans did, however, leave to both common law and civil law the collegium, an institution hardly distinguishable in form from the later Western corporations. With proper official permission, it could be formed by three or more persons, hold property, and sue and be sued through the agent of its members. It survived changes in its membership and was governed by its own by-laws. Conventionally, the Roman collegium is viewed as the ancestor of the modern corporation, though the blood lines are clearer in governmental and religious corporations than in business corporations.[1]

Guilds and Regulated Companies

After the fall of Rome in the fifth century, the corporation, as a legal institution, was kept alive by the need of municipal and ecclesiastical bodies for an entity with the power to receive and hold title to property and to sue in the courts to redress violations of their property rights. Then, in the Middle Ages, the merchant and craft guilds took on the character of corporations, frequently by formal charter. They came to own considerable property, both guild halls and charitable funds accumulated for the welfare of their members. They needed, therefore, the basic corporate power to maintain the continuity of title to corporate property irrespective of the death of individual members or accession of new members. But if the guilds were economic institutions, they were economic institutions with a strong mix of governmental powers. As a rule, membership in the guild appropriate to his trade was compulsory for each free townsman; and the wardens of the guilds had extensive powers of search, inspection, and punishment. The English government also used the guilds as convenient instruments for the collection of taxes into the sixteenth century.

Diversity of Organization: The Corporation

Chartered Trading Companies

Beginning in the sixteenth century, England, as well as France and Holland, granted numerous charters to joint-stock companies. Typically, a company was chartered to carry on a defined trade, and the charter gave it a monopoly of that trade. The distinction between commerce and politics was not clearly drawn—a point perhaps best exemplified by the role of the East India Company (chartered in 1600) in the British conquest of India. In an age when merchant ships carried cannon for their own protection, it was not surprising that merchant companies chartered to trade with India and other far distant places received the authority to protect their warehouses and counting rooms by building and arming forts. The Russia Company (chartered in 1554) and the Turkey Company even paid the expenses of the embassies sent by the British Crown to the Russian and Turkish courts.

The chartered company mode of organization was also used extensively for colonization projects. The Virginia Company, the Massachusetts Bay Company, William Penn's Free Society of Traders, and the Hudson's Bay Company are familiar reminders that some of the American colonies were originally established by groups organized as chartered companies.

Adam Smith divided these companies into those which traded on a joint stock and "regulated" companies. The regulated companies were in effect merchant guilds, to which a merchant had to gain admission, on payment of a fine, as a condition of participating in the trade of which the regulated company held a chartered monopoly. Probably the original, and certainly the largest, English regulated company was the Merchants of the Staple, which was responsible for the export of wool (including collection of the export taxes), mainly to the Netherlands. The regulated companies did not trade with their own assets, nor did they issue shares of stock transferable independently of membership in the company. Smith noted that many European cities had similarly incorporated their trades. Chartered joint-stock companies traded from a common stock, each investor sharing in the profits according to his or her interest.

Smith's opinion was simple:

> These companies, though they may, perhaps, have been useful for the first introduction of some branches of commerce, by making, at their own expense, an experiment the state might not think it prudent to make, have in the long-run proved, universally, either burdensome or useless, and have either mismanaged or confined the trade.[2]

HOW THE WEST GREW RICH

The French chartered more than seventy trading companies between 1599 and 1789, including their own East India Company. The French companies were not generally successful, and eventually they disappeared in the reforms of the French Revolution. The Dutch also chartered companies extensively, treating them as national enterprises and paying for their colonial wars with the revenues they generated.

Franchised Corporations

By the early decades of the nineteenth century, chartered trading companies had declined in importance, but another form of corporation was engaged in building turnpikes, bridges, canals, and railroads and, at least in the United States, in operating banks. Later, these corporations also operated public utilities supplying gas, water, electricity, and street railway transportation and, toward the end of the nineteenth century, telephone service. Until well after the Civil War, transportation, utility, and banking corporations were the prototypical large American corporations. As late as 1929, about half of Berle and Means's[3] two hundred largest American corporations were in the transportation or utilities industries.

These corporations resembled the old chartered companies in that they had essentially governmental powers. Canal and railroad companies had the power of eminent domain,[4] and banks had the power to issue paper money on their own credit.[5] Except perhaps the banks, they were public agencies also in that they had a legal obligation to serve all comers without discrimination. Some, such as the transcontinental railroads, enjoyed substantial governmental subsidies in the form of land grants.

Franchised corporations were not necessarily monopolies, but many (like water companies and the early street railway lines) were so in law or fact. They are still not among the business corporations which can be formed by mere registration. Some regulatory authority has to pass judgment on each request for a franchise charter, although the practice of requiring a special act of the legislature has died out.

It is possible that the need to assemble large amounts of capital for construction of such projects as railroads and canals furnished an economic reason for using the corporate form, but the significance of the economic reason is submerged by the fact that most of them could not have conducted business without the power of eminent domain, and to acquire that power they had to have a governmental charter. It would, for example, have been virtually impossible for a railroad or a canal company to assemble the necessary right of way if each landowner whose property was needed had the power to defeat the whole project by refusing to sell or by holding out for a prohibitive price. The power to compel the sale was essential.

Franchised corporations were pioneers in large-scale corporate management and finance. Railroads led in developing techniques of management for far-flung enterprises through professional managers; they could not have survived without finding ways to control work done a long way from the home office. Their success was epitomized in the phrase, "Run it like a railroad."[6] And in the United States at least, the market for corporate stocks developed originally as a market for the shares of franchised corporations. As we will see in chapter 7, extensive trade in industrial stocks developed only after 1890, in securities markets established earlier to trade in the shares of franchised corporations.

Joint-Stock Companies

Neither chartered trading companies nor franchised corporations were the direct ancestors of the modern business corporation. That distinction belongs to the joint-stock company, a form of business association developed by English merchants from the seventeenth century on. It differed from the corporation in that it lacked a royal charter, and it differed from the partnership in that financial interests in the enterprise, represented by stock certificates, were freely transferable. Unlike partners, holders of the certificates were not authorized to act as each other's agents; only the managers of the company were authorized to trade on behalf of the association.

These joint-stock companies, formed without benefit of royal charter, were subject to three major infirmities. The first arose from the fact that the common law divided commercial associations into partnerships and corporations; since the joint-stock companies lacked charters, they were, by default, partnerships. Hence their members were liable without limit for the debts of the company. This was no great matter if the company prospered, but it mattered a great deal if it did not. Their second infirmity was likewise related to the fact that the courts did not recognize them as legal entities, so that they could enforce rights in property and contracts only by resort to comparatively awkward legal expedients.

The third infirmity was inherited from Roman law and enhanced by the interest of the Crown and Parliament in the revenues to be derived from granting corporate charters. The Roman notion was that any association among subjects was a potential conspiracy against the state; consequently, no private association whatsoever was recognized as lawful unless it was duly licensed by the imperial authorities. Robert Nisbet refers to ". . . Roman Law's notable doctrine of *concession,* under which no group or association, however deeply rooted in history and tradition, however profoundly structured in human allegiances, could claim to have legal existence, legal reality, indeed, except insofar as this existence and reality had been conceded by the sovereign."[7]

The idea of the corporation as a legal fiction, created entirely by a political act of the state, was a constant obstacle to the development of corporations as economic institutions. Sir Frederick Pollock also associated this idea with the doctrine of concession: "the assumption, which runs through the whole of continental public law, that associations of any kind must not be formed without being authorised by the State."[8] Only when association in political parties, churches, social clubs, and similar voluntary groups, as well as in partnerships and joint-stock companies, came to be accepted as a matter of common right did it become easier to view incorporation less as an act of creation than as an act of legal recognition of a group whose existence originated outside the political sphere.

Registered Corporations and General Corporation Laws

The most serious attempt to check the use of joint-stock companies was the act of 6 Geo.I. c.18, known as the Bubble Act of 1720, which made joint-stock companies indictable as a common nuisance. On the surface, this was not an application of the doctrine of concession, for there is no doubt that companies of this type had been utilized for fraudulent purposes. But joint-stock companies, with the corporate features of readily assignable ownership interests, continuity of management, and management by agents of the owners rather than by the owners themselves, were sufficiently popular that neither the history of fraud nor the risk of indictment seems to have served as more than a nominal check on their continued use.[9] In 1825, nearly half a century after the publication of *The Wealth of Nations*, the Bubble Act was repealed, and the question became one of designing laws appropriate to joint-stock companies created by merchants, rather than whether the state should, by concession, create legal fictions in the form of joint-stock companies.

With the doctrine of concession thus out of the way, there remained the two other legal problems with unchartered joint-stock companies. The first was that since they were not recognized as legal entities, they had difficulty in holding title to property, in bringing suits to enforce their legal rights, and in entering into binding contracts. The second was that each of their members was personally liable without limit for all the debts of the company.

Parliament addressed the first of these two difficulties in 1834, when it authorized the Crown to grant joint-stock companies "letters patent" conferring the privilege of suing or being sued through the agency of a public officer. The "privilege" of "being sued" is not an ironic one; a joint-stock company that wished to incur indebtedness or enter into contracts had a strong incentive for subjecting itself to the ordinary creditors' remedies. The letters patent were a corporate charter in all but name since, for legal purposes, the definition of a *person* (natural or artificial) can be shortened to the capacity to sue and be sued. The right to sue is a necessary and sufficient condition to holding enforceable rights in property and contracts, and the capacity to be sued is a necessary and sufficient condition to incurring legally enforceable duties and obligations by contract.[10] The result is that the 1834 act, while resolutely denying that it was making joint-stock companies into legally recognized bodies corporate, in fact did exactly that.

There still remained the problem of the unlimited liability of shareholders for the debts of the company. In 1844, Parliament established a Registrar of Joint Stock Companies and required registration of all "partnerships" with more than twenty-five members and transferable shares. There is evidence that joint-stock companies were more used in trade than in industry: of 910 companies registered under the 1844 act between 1844 and 1856, only 106 were industrial.[11] Even yet, however, the liabilities of the stockholders of the registered companies were not limited to the amount of their stock subscriptions. According to Cottrell, three parliamentary inquiries in the first half of the 1850s produced no other reason for allowing free incorporation, with limited liability, than the fact that a "small but growing number of companies . . . were establishing themselves abroad in order to obtain the privilege of limited liability."[12] A more fundamental reason may have been the English practice of accommodating the rules of commercial law to commercial usage. The English upper classes may have shared the disdain of their French and Prussian counterparts for persons in trade, but, unlike the French, they did not try to elevate commercial morals, nor did they have the Prussian Junkers' concern that corporate development might raise agricultural interest rates.[13] At any rate, Parliament extended limitation of liability to registered corporations in 1856.

The desirability, from the point of view of investors, of not incurring personal liability for the debts of an enterprise is often thought of as the major reason for incorporation. The historical evidence, however, is ambiguous. Joint-stock companies were common before limited liability was available to them. Even after Parliament authorized free incorporation with limited liability, the promoters of corporations frequently provided an impressively large nominal capital and issued shares to subscribers who paid only part of the par value. In the event of insolvency, the subscribers remained liable for the balance of that value; thus, the promoters did not take full advantage of the statutory offer of limited liability. Over the years 1856 to 1882, the average percentages paid in by shareholders varied from a low of 13.30 percent in 1869 to a high of 57.81 percent in 1858.[14] Limitation of liability was thus not an absolutely controlling consideration.

The history of forming corporations by registration under general corporation laws in the United States paralleled England's in some respects. It was, in both countries, a third step, after a first experience with corporations formed for religious, charitable, and local governmental purposes[15] and a period of the extensive formation of franchised corporations. There is even a certain parallelism between the British use of informal joint-stock corporations and the American use of the business trust.[16]

Limited liability seems to have been more emphasized in the United States than in England.[17] At least in New York, by the early nineteenth century the practice of the legislature in granting corporate charters took limited liability for granted, but it also reflected the belief that incorporation was inappropriate if the corporation intended to compete with partnerships because limited liability was thought to give the corporation an unfair advantage. In time, the view that partnerships were at a disadvantage was eroded by the introduction of limited partners—that is, individuals who invested in a partnership business but who had no authority to act for the partnership and whose liability for its debts was limited to their investment in it.[18]

In the United States, allowing the formation of corporations by registration, without obtaining a charter by special act of the legislature, began with statutes limited to specified lines of business.[19] Such charters, whether granted by legislatures or under general incorporation laws, led to the development of a singularly arid but nevertheless active branch of corporation law, *ultra vires* acts. The English language is not well adapted to defining the limits of a line of business in a few words, and neither the draftsmen of corporate charters nor their clients could foresee precisely how those limits might change in the future. So the question of whether a particular business proposal or transaction was beyond the powers of (*ultra vires*) the corporation was sometimes answerable only by a decision of the court of last resort. But even the sterility and occasional gross injustice of litigation over *ultra vires* actions of corporations was overshadowed by the political favoritism and crude corruption spawned by legislative grants of charters, of the sort described by Ronald Seavoy with regard to the chartering of New York banking corporations.[20]

The path of reform lay in the same direction as in England: allowing unincorporated business associations to achieve status as legal entities by simple public registration. Beginning in 1837 in Connecticut, some of the American states adopted broad general incorporation laws applicable to most lines of business activity, enabling firms to obtain corporate charters without procuring a special legislative enactment.[21] The exceptions to these general incorporation laws included corporations requiring powers of eminent domain, monopolies, or banking. The laws did not spread rapidly. Berle and Means list Delaware, which adopted a general incorporation law in 1899, as only the twelfth state to do so.[22]

Not until the latter half of the nineteenth century did England and the United States recognize that the old tradition of maintaining strict governmental control of the formation of corporations with exclusive rights in a particular trade, or with powers of eminent domain, had no proper application to joint-stock associations, whose origins were economic and whose legal powers were similar to those of an ordinary partnership. The only real public interest came to be seen as making sure that those who dealt with such an association were given fair warning that the liability of its members was limited to their interest in the association. It thus became possible to adapt the incorporated mode of enterprise organization to an increasingly wide variety of business situations.

The Spread of General Incorporation Laws

There were hundreds of incorporations under the early general corporation laws. The years from 1864 to 1870, in particular, were a peak period for incorporation in American industrial states. The interest in incorporation was presumably associated with the ending of the Civil War and the accompanying economic changes, but the links are not easy to see.[23]

In spite of the considerable number of incorporations, unincorporated enterprises continued to be common, and probably dominant, in American manufacturing until after 1890. The reasons for holding to the old forms probably differed somewhat between small and large enterprises.

1 Smaller business firms, trading locally, had little to gain by incurring the expense of incorporation. There remained appreciable prejudice against an individual proprietor or partner who, being actively in charge of a business as well as its owner, sought to limit responsibility for its debts by the device of incorporation. Such individuals were (and still are) commonly asked to assume personal responsibility for the corporation's major debts. In the late twentieth century, incorporated small businesses acquired tax advantages that made incorporation very popular, but in 1890 these advantages were still far in the future.

2 Business firms large enough to trade interstate found the early incorporation laws excessively restrictive of the lines of business for which incorporation was allowed, of the corporation's capital, and of ownership of stock in other corporations—that is, in subsidiaries set up to trade in other lines of business or in other states. These restrictions were tolerable in the nineteenth century because there were not many firms that had places of business in several states (as distinguished from a factory in one state that sold to merchants in several states). The few that had multiple places of business could try to obtain legislative charters: as late as 1892, the promoters of General Electric Company, formed to acquire factories in New York and Massachusetts, took the trouble to obtain a New York legislative charter rather than use the New York or the recently liberalized New Jersey general incorporation laws.

3 Ready marketability of corporate shares offered investors very important advantages. These advantages were evident from experience with railway stocks, which were regularly traded on the New York Stock Exchange. But there was no well-developed market for industrial stocks in the United States until after 1890. An active and continuing market in the shares of a corporation cannot exist in practice unless the corporation has a large number of stockholders, and most late-nineteenth-century industrial firms did not have a large number of stockholders. As we shall see in the next chapter, it took the share certificates issued by the unincorporated trusts of the 1880s to create the modern market for industrial securities. In England also, and for the same reasons, relatively few industrial stocks had a ready market.

Diversity of Organization: The Corporation

Despite these limitations, the statistics leave no doubt that there were situations where late-nineteenth-century entrepreneurs saw sufficient reasons for using the corporate form. One important use was to raise venture capital. Even if late-nineteenth-century securities markets were unreceptive to industrial enterprises, there were, in France, the post–Civil War United States, and post-unification Germany, wealthy individuals and investment banks that constituted a venture capital market capable of funding such new and inherently speculative ventures as Edison's development of the electric lamp. For venture capitalists, limitation of liability was (and remains) distinctly desirable and quite possibly essential. In addition, the corporate board of directors was useful as a mechanism through which venture capitalists could retain general control and supervision of the venture.

Also, when the heirs of founding proprietors or partners were not active in the enterprise, limitation of liability by incorporation was an act of simple prudence. Limitation of liability could also have been obtained by using a limited partnership, but as in the case of venture capitalists, the corporation combined limitation of liability with a board of directors through which the heirs or other investors could exercise general supervision and control over the enterprise, even though they were not prepared to act as full-time partners or managers.

Given the effect of one factor that encouraged the incorporation of new enterprises and another that encouraged the incorporation of those old enough to have passed to a new generation of owners, one might have expected incorporation to become, in time, the dominant mode of enterprise organization. We will find in the next chapter that the opening of securities markets to industrial securities compressed what might have been a long-term shift into not much more than a decade.

Liberalization of General Corporation Laws

Alfred Chandler is of the opinion that the modern industrial corporation resulted from the integration of mass production with mass distribution, beginning in the 1880s.[24] Whether because of this integration or because of the completion of the transcontinental railroads and the development of the telegraph and telephone, it was by then becoming increasingly clear that the United States comprised a single market for many products, and that incorporation laws framed only for local operations were no longer adequate. It is conceivable also that the 1880s spectacle of large enterprises organized as trusts for lack of suitable incorporation statutes may have been a factor in the adoption of broader corporation laws. During the period from 1888 to 1896, consolidations large enough to affect market structure took place in mining, food, tobacco, textiles, lumber, furniture, paper, printing, chemicals, petroleum, leather, glass, primary metals, fabricated metals, machinery, electrical machinery, transportation equipment, and miscellaneous manufacturing.[25] A business movement that widespread might expect to find friends who would view the makeshift trust form of organization as reflecting more on the archaic character of corporation laws than on the purposes of the trusts.

In 1889 it found them in New Jersey, which amended its incorporation law to allow the formation of holding companies—that is, corporations that could hold stock in the trusts' constituent companies. This was exactly the legal function of the trustees and the trusts which gave the movement its common name. In 1891, New Jersey went on to adopt a general incorporation statute that contemplated interstate operation, permitted corporations to own stock in other corporations, and provided roughly the same degree of freedom of choice, in forming corporations, that England had provided some decades earlier. The trusts were then reorganized as corporations, some as operating companies, and the rest as holding companies. Standard Oil, the first of the trusts, was the last to incorporate, in 1899.

Incorporation of Cooperatives and Nonprofit Enterprises

The diversity of modes of economic organization in Western countries manifests itself in a number of enterprises which, though they are definitely and unequivocally corporations, are rarely referred to as corporations in political and economic discourse. Nonprofit groups are usually incorporated: churches, unions, hospitals, schools, and charitable agencies, and the several types of cooperative enterprise—consumer (including clubs), employee, and supplier. All have limited liability, the right to own property, and the right to sue and be sued. There are both similarities and differences between conventional business corporations and nonprofit or cooperative corporations of equivalent size and function. To the extent that they are all economic enterprises, operating under economic constraints, the similarities are more pervasive than the differences. There are, however, schools of political thought that view the differences as very important.

So-called nonprofit corporations usually operate under a board of directors or trustees, which may be self-perpetuating or which may be elected by some defined group—for example, the graduates of a university. The term *nonprofit* means only that profits are added to the assets of the corporation and used in furtherance of the corporation's objects, not that there are no profits. However, neither the owners of a nonprofit corporation nor its agents derive personal financial benefit from its profits (except indirectly, when the board of trustees may consider profits in setting the manager's salary)—a major point of difference from conventional business corporations.

Cooperative corporations are much closer to conventional business corporations, in that they are intended to operate for the financial benefit of a specified class of members. The differences among cooperatives rest, initially, on the question of which group of participants in the enterprise is entitled to its profits and the right to select its management. The main groups of participants are stockholders, employees, suppliers, and customers or dealers, and each group contributes something to the enterprise in exchange for some return from it. In conventional business enterprises, investors contribute capital in exchange for the right to its profits, and the others contribute in exchange for specified payments. But there are many enterprises to which employees contribute their services in exchange for the right to profits, or from which consumers buy at a price adjustable by the amount of its profits, or to which suppliers sell at a similarly adjustable price. Given the contingent nature of profit and its dependence on the way management operates the enterprise, it is nearly inevitable that the group that makes its contribution primarily in exchange for this contingent return will insist on the right to select management and require management to operate the enterprise with a view to producing a profit. It is convenient to refer to the participant group that has the right to select management and receive the profits as owners of the organization, though shared ownership by numerous individuals is so different from individual ownership that the use of the same word for both can be deceptive.

In other forms of enterprise organization, ownership is vested in management itself, and in socialist systems it is vested in government. This gives us six kinds of cooperatives, depending on whether the profits, and the associated right to select the management, go to investors, employees, consumers, suppliers, the management itself, or the state. This classification scheme is muddied a little in profit-sharing plans, but it is almost always possible to identify a dominant group that shares profits with others only to enhance its own returns, at least in the long view. The investor cooperative is unique only in that the right to receive a share in profits and cast a vote is transferable by itself, without being coupled to one's status as an employee, customer, or supplier. Free transferability is usually extended to the point of allowing one individual to acquire any number, up to a majority or all, of the shares in profits and voting. Somehow, free transferability of ownership interests has to harbor the answer to two questions of considerable practical interest. Why are investor cooperatives the prevalent form of enterprise organization wherever there is anything like open competition among the six forms? And why are investor cooperatives the object of so much more hostility and distrust than the other forms? We shall return to these questions in chapter 10.

Western legal systems have produced a diversity of forms of corporation corresponding to the diversity of circumstances in which people wish to engage in economic (or other) activity as a group, distinguished in its legal rights and liabilities from its individual members. The distribution of economic activity among nonprofit corporations and the several forms of cooperative corporations must be attributed to economic, political, or social forces other than legal restrictions on the variety of permissible modes of organization. Such restrictions are, in Western countries, of little significance.

The Development of Corporations in France and Germany

During the nineteenth century, the same economic forces that encouraged England and the United States to adopt general incorporation laws and leave the details of forming enterprises to their promoters produced much the same result in France and Germany. The same need for a convenient form of group ownership of economic enterprises, adapted to a multitude of different lines of business and to countless variations in the size and distribution of ownership, slowly overcame initial opposition and eventually resulted in a system of incorporation by registration. Continental experience even had its national parallels to the attempts of American states to withhold recognition from corporations chartered by other states.

In France, the reluctance to allow free incorporation arose from a conflict of philosophy between French statesmen and businessmen. In the words of one 1863 commentator, "The *Conseil d'Etat* sees in the business world only dupes to be protected, charlatans to contain, and abuses to prevent." And again, "In wishing to regulate everything to the last details . . . more good is prevented than abuses avoided."[26]

Until 1856, France had two modes of incorporation. One, the *société anonyme*, could be formed only with the approval of the government. The other, the *société en commandité par actions*, could be freely formed, but in it the stockholders ceded all control over the enterprise to its management, somewhat as limited partners ceded control to the active partners in a partnership. In the early 1850s, France's economy expanded rapidly. The promotion of *commandités par actions* boomed, and there was widespread fleecing of stockholders and creditors.

Before the enactment of the English Company Act of 1856, a number of English firms incorporated in France as *commandités* in order to obtain the benefits of limited liability—a practice cited in England as a reason for the liberalizing Act of 1856. In the same year, however, France sharply restricted the terms on which *commandités* could be formed. The year before the 1856 law, *commandités* capitalized at 581 million francs had been formed in the Paris area; the year after, the corresponding figure was 74 million.[27] This was also the year in which the French economic expansion of the early 1850s ran its course, and some thought the two events were connected. The other argument used for liberalization of the French corporation laws was that French investors, deprived of the opportunity to buy shares in French companies, were investing in foreign companies instead.

European governments, like the American states, had to face the fact that, if their incorporation laws were unduly restrictive, their citizens would incorporate under the laws of neighboring countries. It did not prove feasible to prohibit corporations formed under comparatively liberal foreign corporation laws from operating within the jurisdiction of a more restrictive government. In the United States, corporations formed under the laws of one state had to be recognized as corporations under the laws of all states, under the "full faith and credit" clause of the Constitution. Even so, the states were not required to permit corporations of other states to transact business within their borders.[28] But eventually it became the universal practice to allow foreign corporations to register (or "qualify") to transact business in each state. The outcome in Europe was the same.

In 1849, the Belgian Court of Cassation decided that French corporations could not exist as legal personalities under Belgian law, but in 1854 the two countries agreed by treaty to adopt legislation permitting French companies to operate in Belgium and Belgian companies in France. Reciprocity became the general rule in the 1860s.[29] And in 1867, after three years of debate, France adopted a law under which the *société anonyme* could be formed without specific government consent and on terms which were otherwise consistent with widespread use of the corporate form.[30]

In Germany, the industrial Rhineland came under the political control of Prussia as a result of the 1815 peace treaties that ended the Napoleonic Wars.[31] Politically, Prussia was dominated by a landed aristocracy, the Junkers. The government was administered by a middle-class bureaucracy that was, however, sensitive to the Junkers' interests. As a result, the development of the Rhineland after 1815 was slowed by the Junkers' opposition to projects that might raise agricultural interest rates by drawing savings into railroads and industry. The Prussian bureaucracy used its power to refuse incorporation to obstruct the chartering of railroad companies and, a little later, of banks. Private bankers in the Rhineland took on the dual role of political intermediaries and promoters of railroad and industrial projects. Their projects were promoted by syndicates of bankers, a practice which enabled the Rhinelanders to recruit help in Berlin and Frankfurt from other bankers with closer links to key government officials. On occasion, key officials were made stockholders on favorable terms—a form of persuasion with Tudor antecedents. By the 1840s, privately financed railroad building was in full swing in the Rhineland.

The private bankers undertook similar roles as promoters and intermediaries in developing industrial corporations in the Rhineland and Ruhr. They placed the corporations' long-term securities (bonds and stocks), maintained a limited market in the securities through private sales (there was little trading on stock exchanges), supplied the corporations with short-term capital for their current needs, sat on boards of directors, and sometimes acted as managers of purchasing. By keeping in touch with purchasing, the bankers were able on occasion to establish new firms with ready-made customers. Industrial stocks were listed on German stock exchanges well before the 1880s, but as elsewhere, railroad stocks and government securities were the principal subjects of trading.

The close affiliation of German corporations with their banks did not, however, have the decentralizing effect it had in England, partly because the German banking system was less decentralized. Industrialization came later to Germany, and the banking community was too close-knit to encourage the development of numerous competing industrial firms. There were early German industrialists—Krupp for one—who founded their own firms without depending on a close affiliation with a bank. But by the time Germany was industrialized, capital requirements had become far larger than in the early days of the Industrial Revolution, and relatively few firms were able to finance themselves without association with a bank.

Conclusion

By the closing decades of the nineteenth century, the use of the corporate mode of organization in the West had been extended beyond the types of economic activity for which it was politically necessary—that is, beyond enterprises that had to have a power of eminent domain, a grant of monopoly, or some other governmental powers. The concept of manufacturing and trading enterprises, group-owned and conducting their business affairs through agents elected by the owners, had achieved general acceptance.

In its purely economic form, the incorporated enterprise was derived more from the partnership (especially the limited partnership), the business trust, and the joint-stock company than from the politically chartered town, guild, public utility, or monopoly. And not until the mid-nineteenth century was the West ready to confer the legal status of persons on groups formed for economic purposes without requiring an act of the legislature or other political authority.

The circumstances that gave rise to a need for group ownership varied from one enterprise to another and from one period to another. In a world in which enterprises had good reason to incorporate as they grew old and their heirs took the founders' places, and in which enterprises formed with the help of outside capital had good reason to incorporate at birth, a steady increase in the use of the corporate mode of organization was to be expected. This happened in all Western countries after the 1850s. Nevertheless, the tendency was far from universal, and many enterprises, including some that were very large, continued to operate as proprietorships or partnerships. In legal form as much as in economic form, the organization of Western enterprise continued to be diverse, proliferating, and adapting ad hoc to the different circumstances of different enterprises.

In the long run, corporate law was innovative and supplied the legal framework for meeting the organizational needs of emerging nineteenth-century enterprise. But the line of causation ran from economic need to legal response, often long-delayed and embarrassed by the need to resort to such interim makeshifts as unincorporated joint-stock companies, partnerships with hundreds of inactive partners, and trusts.

In the late 1880s and 1890s, at least in the United States, securities markets were opened to industrial corporations. This development supplied a new reason both for using the corporate mode of organization and forming corporations of considerable size. The effect on economic organization is examined in the next chapter.

NOTES

1. Sir Henry Maine, in emphasizing that primitive societies viewed themselves as aggregations of families rather than as aggregations of individuals, described primitive law as "adjusted to a system of small independent corporations." See "Primitive Society and Ancient Law," chap. 5 in *Ancient Law*, 3d ed. (New York: Henry Holt & Company, 1888), pp. 121–22. For a convenient discussion of the Roman collegium, see "Corporation," *Encyclopaedia Britannica*, 11th ed., vol. 7.

2. Adam Smith, *An Inquiry Into the Nature and Causes of the Wealth of Nations*, vol. 2 (New York: Oxford University Press, 1976), p. 733. He goes on to discuss the shortcomings of particular companies with investigative zeal (pp. 733–58). He expresses the opinion that the only trades which it seems possible for a joint stock company to carry on, without an exclusive privilege, are those reducible to a routine: banking, insurance, canals, and water supplies for a city, pp. 756–57.

3. Adolf A. Berle, Jr., and Gardiner C. Means, *The Modern Corporation and Private Property* (New York: Macmillan & Co., 1932).

4. The power of eminent domain is the power to acquire property needed for corporate purposes by compulsory purchase, at a value fixed by a court in case negotiation fails. It is a power peculiar to government and franchised corporations.

5. For a brief account of the bank chartering mania and the impact of the very loosely controlled issue of bank notes, see "Banks and Banking: United States," by Charles Arthur Conant, in the *Encyclopaedia Britannica*, 11th ed., vol. 3. For fuller accounts, see Fritz Redlich, *The Moulding of American Banking* (New York: Johnson Reprint Corporation, 1968), chap. 3; and Bray Hammond, *Banks and Politics in America from the Revolution to the Civil War* (Princeton: Princeton University Press, 1957).

6. For an account of the development of railroad management, see Alfred D. Chandler, Jr., ed., *The Railroads: The Nation's First Big Business* (New York: Harcourt, Brace & World, 1965). Chandler also discussed railway management and the role of the financiers in *The Visible Hand* (Cambridge: Harvard University Press, 1977), pp. 175–87.

7. Robert Nisbet, *Twilight of Authority* (New York: Oxford University Press, 1970), p. 170.

8. Sir Frederick Pollock, *A First Book of Jurisprudence*, 5th ed. (London: Macmillan & Co., 1923), pp. 115–16.

Diversity of Organization: The Corporation

9. See Oscar Handlin and Mary F. Handlin, "Origins of the American Business Corporation," in Frederic C. Lane and Jelle C. Riemersma, eds., *Enterprise and Secular Change* (Homewood, Ill.: Richard D. Irwin, 1953), pp. 102–24. The Handlins state:

> Partnerships of many degrees were unaffected by the Bubble Act; by 1800, unincorporated joint-stock companies, though conducted as partnerships and lacking the legal characteristics that could be obtained only by special charter, "had reached the point where the financial interest was almost if not entirely as liquid as it was with the incorporated companies." One need only think of the company mills in the woolen industry or the Banking Company of Aberdeen, in which 446 partners got on without incorporation, to measure the flexibility of the old forms.

P. 1041. The Handlins were quoting Armand B. DuBois, *The English Business Company after the Bubble Act, 1720–1800* (New York: Commonwealth Fund, 1938), pp. 36, 38, a study which demonstrated at length the ineffectiveness of the Bubble Act in preventing the spread of joint-stock companies.

10. Today, we like to say that all human beings are natural "persons" with the right to sue and be sued; and to take care of minors and individuals under guardianship, who can sue only through a "next friend" or guardian, we treat the latter as agents of the principal for whose benefit the suit is prosecuted. The law was not always so insistent on the personhood of individuals. See Maine, *Ancient Law*, pp. 128–41.

11. P. L. Cottrell, *Industrial Finance, 1830–1914* (New York: Methuen, 1980), p. 44.

12. Ibid., p. 40.

13. See pp. 205 and 206, this book.

14. Cottrell, *Industrial Finance*, table 4.3, p. 85.

15. Ronald E. Seavoy, "The Public Service Origins of the American Business Corporation," *Business History Review* 52 (Spring 1978): 30–60.

16. In New England, they were often called "Massachusetts trusts."

17. Under the legislative charters of some of the earliest American business corporations, there seems to have been no limit to the power of corporate management to assess the members of the corporation for funds to pay corporate debts. In consequence, if the corporation became insolvent, its receiver could exercise this power to assess its members in proportion to their share interests. See Handlin and Handlin, "Origins of American Business Corporation," pp. 111–18. In the United States, the liability of stockholders of national banks for an assessment equal to the par value of their shares, in case of insolvency of the bank, was not ended until the 1930s.

18. Braudel traces the limited partnership in Europe as far back as 1532, to Florence, in Fernand Braudel, *The Wheels of Commerce*, trans. Sian Reynolds (New York: Harper & Row, 1982), pp. 438–39.

19. Thus the loss of textile imports from England under Thomas Jefferson's Embargo and the looming War of 1812 led the New York legislature, in 1811, to adopt a general incorporation law for textile companies. Other products were later added. New York was not, however, the first state to authorize incorporation of a particular line of business without a formal act of the legislature; Massachusetts had provided a general corporation law for aqueduct companies as early as 1798. Handlin and Handlin, "Origins of American Business Corporation," p. 106.

20. Seavoy, "Public Service Origins," 49–54. Bank charters in New York were apparently granted with a view to keeping control of credit within New York in the hands of those who controlled the legislature. Martin Van Buren, Jackson's second vice president and successor, had labored mightily in the bank charter vineyard in New York. Ibid., 52–53.

21. The Louisiana constitution of 1845 included a provision to the effect that whatever corporate charters were granted should be granted under general corporation laws, rather than by individual acts of the legislature. See G. H. Evans, Jr., *Business Incorporations in the United States, 1800–1843* (New York: National Bureau of Economic Research, 1948), p. 11.

22. Berle and Means, *Modern Corporation*, p. 127. In New York, at least, the state legislature had granted corporate charters freely, in pursuit of a policy of industrial and commercial development, so that the adoption of a general incorporation law was not a revolutionary change. See the history of New York's legislative policy in Ronald E. Seavoy,

The Origins of the American Business Corporation, 1784–1855: Broadening the Concept of Public Service During Industrialization (Westport, Conn.: Greenwood Press, 1982).

23. Evans, *Business Incorporations*, chart 1, p. 13, and chart 3, p. 23.

24. Chandler, *The Visible Hand*, pp. 287–89.

25. Ibid., table 6, pp. 340–44. Chandler drew on Shaw Livermore's "The Success of Industrial Mergers," *Quarterly Journal of Economics* 50 (November, 1935): 94.

26. The definitive account of the struggle is Charles E. Freedeman, "The Coming of Free Incorporation in France, 1850–1867," *Explorations in Economic History*, 2d ser. 4, no. 3 (Spring-Summer, 1967): 212. Freedeman attributes the first quoted sentence to Adolphe Blaise and the second to Charles Lescoeur. Ibid., 220, 227.

27. Ibid., 217–18.

28. The leading case was *Bank of Augusta* v. *Earle*, 13 Pet. 519, 10 L.ed. 274. In the nineteenth and early twentieth centuries, the case led to much litigation over the questions of what constituted sufficient transaction of business within a state to require qualification as a foreign corporation, and of whether the requirements for qualification as a foreign corporation infringed the constitutional rights of the foreign corporation.

29. Freedeman, "The Coming of Free Incorporation in France," 218–19.

30. Freedeman notes that the 798 *sociétés anonymes* formed between 1868 and 1876 exceeded the number formed during the sixty-year period when government consent was required. But incorporation was apparently just getting under way; in 1881, 976 *sociétés anonymes* were formed in France. Ibid., 223–27.

31. The basic source for an account of the development of Rhineland industry and finance up to German unification is Richard Tilly, *Financial Institutions and Industrialization in the Rhineland, 1815–1870* (Madison: University of Wisconsin Press, 1966).

7 / Technology, Trusts, and Marketable Stock

At the end of the period discussed in chapter 6, we left the corporate mode of enterprise organization widely used by railroads and other forms of franchised industry. Elsewhere in trade and industry, its use was growing but it was still far from dominant, and the West had still not found an institutional answer to the growing need for large-scale economic organization outside the sphere of franchised corporations. The modern, publicly held industrial corporation was an innovation that still belonged to the future. We explore how it came about in this chapter.

In the United States, the 1880s were a time of change in many ways. Industry began to contribute more to economic output than agriculture. Thus, not quite a hundred years after Yorktown, the United States became a predominantly industrial economy, no longer economically a colony of the Old World. A number of technological and organizational developments in the United States favored an increase in the size of enterprises. The period was one of expanding output and falling prices—a combination so unfamiliar to late-twentieth-century observers that their interpretations of it often seem naive. It was a combination that posed severe financial problems for small manufacturing firms caught with obsolescent plants in a world of declining prices and poor financial prospects—that is to say, for virtually the whole manufacturing economy of the 1880s.

Against this background of economic difficulties, two beliefs came to be widely held by investors. One was that the suppression of competition through the consolidation of competing enterprises was profitable. The other was that larger enterprises were more efficient than smaller enterprises as a rule, and not just occasionally. It did not matter that these two beliefs were at best half true: crossed with the severe financial problems of many enterprises, they led to the widespread formation of "trusts" in the United States.

Among the many economic and political consequences of the trusts, one of the least noticed had the greatest importance in shaping the organization of Western enterprise: the trusts created a market in industrial stocks and, with it, the publicly held industrial corporation. Before 1890, few industrial stocks were publicly traded, if for no other reason than that few industrial enterprises were large enough to support regular public trading in their shares. The trusts, however, were large enough, and they were popular with investors. By 1914, after a quarter-century of mergers and consolidations, most major American industrial enterprises were publicly held corporations. By then, few, if any, of them were trusts in the sense of cornering the whole of an industry, for most of the trusts had proved financially unsuccessful. But these enterprises were large enough to support regular public trading in their stock, and this proved to be of very appreciable advantage to investors in reducing risks and controlling agency costs (a type of cost discussed later in the chapter, at p. 231).

Whatever their merits from the viewpoint of investors, large corporations could not have survived had they not somehow managed to cope with the difficulties of organizing work forces of unprecedented size. This was no easy matter, for large enterprises unsettled the relationship between employees and employers in ways still by no means resolved, nearly a century later. The confrontational aspects of the relationship, probably inherent in the division of their joint product between capital and labor (there is no "fair" way to divide a joint product), supplied corporations with an incentive to substitute capital-intensive production for labor-intensive production wherever possible and discouraged their use in labor-intensive sectors of the economy. Thus large corporations have come to be used primarily in the organization of capital-intensive production, with the very important result that most of the labor force in Western economies works within the framework of other modes of economic organization.

We begin our account of what happened to the size of American manufacturing enterprises after 1880 with a summary of the technological background and then touch briefly on some of the changes in the organization of enterprises associated with the development of mass production and urban, national, and international markets. With this background in mind, we can see how the emergence of a market in

industrial securities interacted with the earlier development of free incorporation to bring about a reorganization of industry into publicly held
corporations, the basic institutions of Western economies for large-scale,
capital-intensive industrial enterprise.

Changes in the Technology of Production

The period after the American Civil War saw a number of striking advances
in the technology of production, measured, as they should be, by reductions
in the cost of production. Chandler has collected several examples.[1] Using
the Bessemer process, Andrew Carnegie reduced the cost of making steel
rails from close to $100 a ton in the early 1870s to $12 by the late 1890s.
In the early 1880s, Standard Oil consolidated its refining in three new
refineries, bringing its average cost of production of a gallon of kerosene
from 1.5¢ a gallon before 1882 to 0.54¢ in 1884 and 0.45¢ in 1885. The
introduction of a cigarette-making machine in England and the United
States reduced the cost of making cigarettes, in England, from almost $1 a
thousand to about 6¢ a thousand. The first three German firms to produce
the blue dye alizarine on a large scale brought production costs from 200
marks per kilogram in the 1870s to 9 marks by 1886. The Hall process for
refining aluminum reduced the price of aluminum from 87.5 francs per
kilogram in 1888 to 3.75 francs in 1895. Overall, the American wholesale
price index declined from 100 in 1880 to 82 in 1890—a change for which
advances in technology were in good part, though not wholly, responsible.

Underlying these few examples were advances in metallurgy, the
substitution of steel for cast iron, improvements in machining, and progress
in mechanical engineering. The combination of steel with controllable
metallurgical properties and advances in machining made possible the
interchangeability of parts, which in turn made possible the mass production of agricultural machinery, sewing machines, typewriters, cash registers,
bicycles and, a little later, automobiles.

In the United States, the number of steam engines in industrial use
doubled between 1860 and 1880, and it doubled again between 1880 and
1900. Since the use of steam power was characteristic of factories in the
latter part of the nineteenth century, this rise gives a good idea of the
magnitude of the post–Civil War rate of growth of investment in industrial

plant. The increase in number of steam engines was attributable to an expansion of industrial plant, and not to mere replacement of waterpower with steam power in existing factories, for until at least 1880 the industrial use of waterpower also increased.[2] In judging the demand for capital implied by this rate of expansion, one must remember that the capital required for a steam engine was typically less than the capital required for the accompanying land, buildings, the machinery the steam engine was bought to operate, and the working capital required to finance a growing volume of production and sales.

Though the use of steam power did not peak until 1910,[3] the availability of electric power began to render both steam- and water-powered plants obsolete as early as the 1880s.[4] Before the introduction of electricity, the distribution of power to factory machines depended on drive shafts, gears, and pulleys. Whether the source of power was a waterwheel or a steam engine, the only way to get the power to the spindle, shuttle, lathe, hammer, saw, or bellows was with shafts, pulleys, belts, and gears. As transmission systems grew in size, they grew also in complexity and in transmission losses of power. The layout of the machinery in the factories was governed by the need to locate the machines with the greatest power demand closest to the engine. The efficient flow of work was a secondary consideration.

About 1890, it became possible to provide each machine with an electric motor and to transmit power to the motor through an electric wire. Many factories attached an electric generator to their steam engines and provided their own electricity, but in addition it became possible to draw almost any amount of power from the new central stations. The substitution of electric wires and motors for shafts and pulleys was at first justified by easily calculable savings in maintenance, fuel consumption, and interest and depreciation on investment. But the calculable savings were not the most important: what mattered most was that the wires could be bent to any shape and run to almost any desired length, for transmission losses in wire were small. This introduced new flexibility into the design of factories,[5] and the efficient flow of work between successive steps in the production process claimed its natural priority in plant layout.

Substitution of electric for mechanical power transmission made it efficient to build larger factories, but it also had an important effect of just the opposite character: it made it efficient to retain and expand small plants. Small manufacturing shops, being without waterpower or their own steam engines, had been forced to depend on machinery operated by hand or pedal. Now they had the opportunity to draw power from one of the new central electric plants and to replace hand and pedal drives with electric motors. The effect was not simply to check the displacement of small-scale manufacturing by large-scale manufacturing, but to enable industries still dominated by small-scale production to reduce their costs and prices and to expand their output and employment. It is not easy to imagine how the New York and Los Angeles garment industries (for example) could have evolved to their present sizes without electric power. In sum, the introduction of electricity in the 1890s outmoded an appreciable part of the West's manufacturing plant. The large-scale plants were suddenly the wrong size and layout, and the small-scale plants needed to electrify.

The development of the internal combustion engine and the early experiments with automobiles or, as they were then called, horseless carriages, also occurred between 1880 and 1900. The electromagnetic spectrum was just being discovered, from Roentgen's X-rays to Marconi's first radio transmissions. The first development contained the seeds of a second industrial revolution, based not on the steam engine but on the internal combustion engine, which was to be used in automobiles and airplanes; the second sparked a revolution in communications. Perhaps the American financiers whose merger movement peaked out in 1900 were just lucky, but they created an economy ready to build and supply an auto industry that, by 1914, had become a new giant with the most far-reaching economic, social, and political consequences.

In summary, between 1880 and 1900, the United States was increasing its industrial capacity and altering manufacturing technology in ways that required extensive replacement of obsolete plants, often with plants of considerably greater size. There were serious obstacles to finding the required capital. From 1880 on, there was a general fall in the prices of manufactured goods, and a long and severe depression followed the panic of 1893. Under the circumstances, existing firms could not generate the required capital internally, nor did many of them appear as attractive places to invest further capital, even to their owners. There was a serious need for new forms of enterprise better able to attract capital—that is, forms that promised investors some combination of higher profits and lower risk. In an economy where financial promoters profited from the sale of securities of new enterprises which could be portrayed as likely to be more profitable, or safer, than past enterprises, the plausible expedients were tried many times: incorporation, the formation of trusts, and, after 1894, mergers, which peaked in 1900 or 1901. Although these promotions produced many enterprises that failed, they also produced a number of large enterprises that proved able to raise the capital required for reconstruction and expansion. As with other kinds of experiment, it was the successes that counted, and a burgeoning American economy emerged from the merger movement ready to take off on a second industrial revolution, powered by the internal combustion engine and electricity.

Changes in the Organization of Enterprise

If changes in technology were reshaping the size of American enterprises between 1880 and 1914, they were no more important than a second factor: an expansion in the range of functions performed by the single enterprise. This second factor requires explanation. Manufacturing enterprises may either perform themselves or buy from others any of the following general functions, each of which embraces a good many subfunctions:

- Product design.
- Raw materials production.
- Parts fabrication.
- Product assembly.
- Local or regional marketing.
- National marketing.

The sheer size of an enterprise depends partly on how many of these functions it performs itself. Its efficiency depends even more on how judiciously it selects these functions. We shall return to the subject of the sources of enterprise size in chapter 9.

1. Integration in Assembly, Parts Fabrication, and Raw Materials

The mass-production factories possessed rapidly increasing appetites for raw materials and components of all kinds. This was not a novel development. During the nineteenth century, the British textile industry multiplied its demand for raw cotton by sixty times, as we saw in chapter 5. The needs of the industry for raw cotton were supplied by the cotton merchants of Liverpool and Manchester, and there is no record of any tendency on the part of the Lancashire spinning mills to integrate backward into growing cotton.

Technology, Trusts, and Marketable Stock

In the United States, a number of industries of the late nineteenth century differed from the British cotton industry in that they did not have dependable, competitive markets in which to buy all of their parts and raw materials. Sometimes the answer was backward integration—that is, producing their own raw materials. The combination of mine and refinery, often at the same site, was common in the nonferrous metal industries, and it became common in the steel and petroleum industries as the raw materials required by the new steel mills and oil refineries increased. The cost of transportation tended to divide the national and international raw materials markets into regional markets, and these regional markets might or might not be able to supply the expanding needs of a single mill or refinery without sharply increasing their prices. The problems of grading and quality, especially of coal, were endless. And there was always the danger that producers of raw materials might form troublesome cartels.

Steelmakers and oil refiners, in particular, undertook the production of their own basic materials—that is, iron ore, coal, and petroleum. In addition, they learned from their experience with the railroad cartels to undertake much of their own transportation. The oil companies built their own pipelines and operated barges and tankers. The steel companies established their own ore carriers. (It should be added that refiners and steel companies that did not produce their own raw materials continued to function, but more successfully when raw materials were in ample supply than when they were not.) In addition, the introduction of refrigerated cars and ships induced some meat-packers and food processors to integrate backward into transportation and, in a few cases, to grow their own produce, such as bananas.

In some instances, notably in oil and steel, backward integration resulted in complex flow production processes under control of a single management. These were major organizational innovations: John D. Rockefeller's invention of the integrated petroleum company is still in wide use throughout the world. But flow production processes were far from taking over the American economy. By and large, suppliers of raw materials successfully (and, no doubt, cheerfully) expanded to supply the needs of the new factories. Even in the steel industry, integration stopped with the refining of metal. General Motors was a massive user of steel, but it did not integrate backward into steel. Henry Ford experimented with backward integration into steel among other things, but the experiments seem to have been unsuccessful in reducing Ford's costs. Indeed, with the exception of gasoline and heating oil, it is still not easy to think of consumer products whose manufacturer began by producing the raw material.

2. *Integration in National, Local, and Regional Marketing*

It is sometimes said that the modern industrial enterprise was born when the mass manufacture of a line of products was first combined with their distribution in one enterprise. There is some basis for this viewpoint, but it needs qualification.

In the age of artisan manufacture, selling the product was an incidental part of the artisan's work, taking place across the counter or from a booth at a local fair, not a specialized occupation. Interregional trade and regional specialization were developed by merchants who bought from local artisans and sold in other regions. Thus distribution as an occupational specialty—getting output from producer to user—developed in mercantile enterprises that were themselves excluded from manufacturing by guild charters and rules.

The change from artisan to factory production did not result in combining production and distribution in a single enterprise—at least not at first. In the early British textile industry, for example, there were still merchants and brokers with the resources to act as middlemen for the early factories. Much of the output was exported, and the local market was geographically compact.

In the United States, beginning in the 1880s, a number of manufacturing enterprises reached a point where their production was sold nationwide in substantial quantities. Few of these enterprises depended on a single merchant or broker to sell their output. They were more likely to sell to numerous wholesale distributors and to direct accounts—that is, to buyers who, though not wholesalers, bought in wholesale quantity: other manufacturers, government agencies, or construction companies. National distribution through wholesalers required a factory selling department, often with field offices, field warehouses, and sometimes field repair facilities. Also, the work of supplying information to customers was centralized, for wholesalers or dealers could rarely prepare and distribute catalogs, instruction books, and service manuals as cheaply as manufacturers. Advertisements might be printed in local publications with a dealer's or wholesaler's logo, but the cost of preparing the advertisement was reduced when the factory (or its advertising agency) did the work for all its wholesalers. And national advertising had to be done by the factory, since no one wholesaler had a sufficient financial interest in supporting it.

Despite the importance of these activities, the integration of manufacturing and distribution was incomplete. Mass production enterprises continued to use independent wholesalers and retail dealers for the final steps in the distribution of their products. Exceptions were few, though some were conspicuous. In consumer goods, direct selling to the user has been common in the petroleum industry. It has also been used here and there by manufacturers of products ranging from vacuum cleaners and sewing machines to radar detectors. Some mass production manufacturers set up their own wholesaling warehouses to deal directly with retailers. Sometimes owned wholesaling was used nationwide, while other manufacturers might use independent wholesalers in some sales regions and their own wholesale operations in others. Many mass manufacturers established their own export organizations. The permutations and combinations were myriad, but for the most part getting a product to consumers, in the quantities and at the time and place consumers would buy it, proved to be more costly if done entirely by the manufacturer than if done with the help of independent wholesalers and retailers.

Most direct selling by manufacturers occurred when customers bought in large enough quantities to make it feasible for the factory to deal with them directly. Some examples could be found among manufacturers of capital and producer goods, who sold machinery, factory supplies, and product components to other manufacturers, and there were other examples among manufacturers of professional supplies, who sometimes sold directly to physicians, lawyers, accountants, and photographers. Technically complex products were often sold directly, partly because specially trained sales representatives were needed to answer customers' questions, partly to avoid furnishing customers with an unsuitable product, to the injury of its reputation, and partly in the belief that the manufacturer's specialists could handle installation, repairs, and operator training better than independent dealers could.

The distribution departments of many national manufacturers grew larger than the leading mercantile enterprises had been in the eighteenth and nineteenth centuries, and the combination of these distribution departments with manufacturing was unquestionably an important development in the organization of enterprises. In their late-nineteenth-century origins, however, most of the selling departments of mass manufacturers seemed little more than necessary expedients for getting their products to their wholesalers and dealers. The distribution of the products of mass manufacture was not transferred from the existing wholesalers and retailers to new national marketing organizations. Singer, Standard Oil, and National Cash Register were conspicuous exceptions, but they remained exceptions. Although the existing distribution system had never handled the products of mass manufacture and the old arrangements had to be modified ad hoc, the wholesale and retail trades made out very well, if we may judge from their growth during the period of introduction of mass manufacture.

The value added to the national income by wholesale trade rose from $220 million in 1879 to $810 million in 1899 to $1,300 million in 1909. For retail trade, the corresponding figures are $560 million for 1879, $1,340 million for 1899, and $2,320 million for 1909.[6]

Stock Markets

We have seen that developments in technology and organization enlarged the fields of economic activity in which the costs of enterprise size were offset by economies of production or distribution. Next we turn to the factor that made publicly held industrial corporations the preferred form of enterprise whenever they were not uneconomical, namely, the development of a market for industrial securities.

Publicly held industrial corporations were very rare in the United States before 1890, and major industrial enterprises that were not incorporated and publicly held were almost equally rare after 1914. The shift required changes not only in corporations, but also in the trading conducted on stock exchanges. These changes were of fundamental importance to twentieth-century capitalism.

The earlier history of stock exchanges was mixed. They trace their origins to trading in government securities and the securities of chartered companies. Braudel gives the Amsterdam market, formed at the beginning of the seventeenth century, credit for novelty of volume, fluidity, publicity, and speculative freedom, though he finds antecedents for it in Italy, France, Spain, the Hanseatic towns, and the trading of shares in German mines at the Leipzig fair as early as the fifteenth century.[7] In London, securities traders formed their own exchange in 1773. In New York, systematic trading was conducted on the street (literally), beginning in 1792. Securities exchanges are thus much older than the general practice of trading stocks in industrial corporations.

Investors in the United States were made thoroughly familiar with a wide variety of stock exchanges during and immediately after the Civil War. Marian V. Sears found that some 250 local stock exchanges were established in the United States from 1860 to 1930, and much of that activity was early in the period. In the West, mining stocks were traded on local exchanges. They left behind an unenviable record of investor losses, often due to the crudest forms of fraud. Gold was popularly traded. In New York, the variety of exchanges was epitomized by an exchange established to trade in shares of the Erie Railroad, after the Erie had been delisted by the New York Stock Exchange.[8]

In periods of economic expansion, stock exchanges, not only in the United States but in Europe as well, were centers of optimism and get-rich-quick expectations, sometimes called speculative fever. They were also centers of operation for sophisticated hustlers adept at exploiting this excessive optimism. During periods of contraction, the pricking of these bubbles caused widespread loss and a good deal of personal suffering. Stock exchanges, in short, accumulated an unsavory reputation among prudent investors, somewhat less well-earned by exchanges that attempted to exercise a measure of control over the shares traded than by those with no control at all.

Until the 1890s, the stocks traded on public exchanges in the United States were principally shares of railroads and utilities. The Pullman Palace Car Company was the only manufacturing enterprise traded on the New York Stock Exchange, and most of its assets were railroad sleeping-car companies.[9] The New England textile companies were sometimes incorporated, fairly widely held, and were traded on the Boston Stock Exchange. But only about 25 percent of the spindles in the New England industry were owned by incorporated firms and their shares were priced at levels (of the order of $1,000) that later experience showed to be too high for any widespread trading; in fact, the volume of trading was very small. Some of the largest enterprises were not incorporated at all: for example, Andrew Carnegie operated his extensive steel interests as a partnership until 1892, when they were finally incorporated.

England was somewhat ahead of the United States in developing markets for industrial stocks. There was a wave of incorporation of textile firms in the 1860s, promoted principally by local financial interests.[10] They were responding to pressures comparable to those that appeared later in the United States: a need for plant modernization in the face of financial stringencies attributable, in Britain, in part to the cutting off of cotton supplies during the American Civil War. By 1882, manufacturing firms with a capital totaling 54 million pounds were listed on the London exchange, and the total grew to 872 million pounds over the next twenty years.[11]

Lance Davis has argued that England had better-developed capital markets than the United States, with the consequence that, when technological opportunities arose for realizing important economies of scale within an industry, existing English companies more easily financed the necessary expansion.[12] A curious exception was the brewing industry, which, beginning in 1886, resorted to public flotations of securities to finance the breweries' acquisition of public houses in order to assure outlets for the breweries' products.[13] These flotations were, for the time, very large and were promoted by the leading London merchant banks. American companies, in contrast, were dependent for finance on informal personal contacts with wealthy individuals or banks. Davis suggests that those who had such contacts were in a position to preempt opportunities for economies of scale and capital-intensive systems of production. Davis may well be right in believing that one reason why American manufacturers were more willing than their British counterparts to merge or sell out was their comparative inability to obtain financing.[14] But in considering the usefulness of financial contacts in the effort to take advantage of economies of scale, certain reservations should be kept in mind.

First, if one visualizes an industry whose manufacturing facilities evidently need to be replaced by larger-scale facilities operated by fewer firms, investment will seem very risky until the survivors are identified. Some consolidation of existing firms may be a rational condition for attracting capital for larger-scale plants, and the fact that it occurred in the United States is not necessarily an indication of weakness in American capital markets.

Second, there are two different kinds of economies of scale. With their well-developed capital markets, the British were in a position to grasp those that were apparent in advance of large-scale operation. This type of advantage is especially likely to develop in industries (such as the British textile industry or agriculture) where most advances in production originate with manufacturers of machinery or others outside the industry.

But the Americans' propensity for consolidation of firms put them far ahead in grasping economies of scale that became apparent only as a result of large-scale operation or that were developed only because a high volume of orders furnished the necessity that was the mother of the invention. The low-cost Rockefeller refineries were built to supply the needs of a trust already formed, and mass production of automobiles was almost entirely Ford's response to orders too numerous to be filled any other way. Those who believe that innovation tends to be a response to existing needs will view this second class of scale economies as in general the more important of the two.

It is also quite clear that a great many industrial corporations were formed in England on too small a scale to create an effective market in their shares. And the leading London financial houses exhibited little or no interest in the promotion of industrial corporations; it was second-class or provincial business.[15] Thus, English capital markets may not bear so favorable a comparison to the American as Davis suggests.

The Trusts and the Marketability of Industrial Stock

Why did it take so long for investors in industrial enterprises to discover the advantages of publicly traded stock? After all, franchised corporations existed, and were publicly traded on the New York and other stock exchanges, for more than a half-century before it became common for industrial corporations to be publicly traded. The anomaly is compounded by the fact that some industrial corporations—the New England textile companies—had been publicly traded in Boston.

The likely answer is that most nineteenth-century manufacturing enterprises were too small to sustain an active market in their shares. The emergence of larger enterprises had to precede the shift to incorporation and marketable securities. But it was not feasible to form a large enterprise merely to gain the advantages of marketable securities; the experience of the trusts showed that smaller competitors without marketable securities but with lower costs could and did undercut the prices, profits, and market shares of larger firms: size in itself was of little advantage. The move to larger enterprises was not sustainable before the economies that could be realized from larger-scale operation offset the additional costs of larger-scale organization—the agency costs which we will discuss later in this chapter. Trusts and mergers could speed up the realization of the required economies, but if the organizational costs of the consolidated companies exceeded their economies of scale, they did not survive.

It is thus not altogether surprising that large-scale trading in American industrial stocks traces its origins to trading in the trust certificates issued by the trusts of the 1880s.[16] Some of the trusts were large enough to support an active market in their shares, and the popularity of their shares reflected the view that the suppression of competition was both practical and profitable and that larger-scale manufacturing was more economical than smaller-scale manufacturing. By the end of the 1880s, trading in trust certificates had become extensive. The New York Stock Exchange permitted its members to trade in them as unlisted securities, since their uncertain legal status was thought to preclude them from listing on the Exchange. While trust certificates were regarded as speculative, they nevertheless created a history of market prices and dividends for industrial securities, as distinguished from railroad and utility stocks. After 1891, when New Jersey's new incorporation law enabled the trusts to regularize their legal status, their shares were fully listed on the New York Stock Exchange as quickly as the trusts were legally incorporated.

The capital structure of the incorporated trusts differed markedly from modern financial practice. A common, though not universal, pattern was to capitalize the established earnings record of the trust's component companies in the form of preferred stock, designed as a security of investment grade.[17] The common stock was issued to reflect both the risk of loss and the prospect of increased future profits. While the same pattern had been followed in the capitalization of railroads, a good many outside observers characterized the common stock of corporations so capitalized as "watered" or representing "nothing but the blue sky." To these observers, for a corporation to earn profits on its common stock was not so much a happy outcome of a risky speculation as the result of over-charging its customers.

Navin and Sears list 28 industrial preferred stock issues during the years 1890 to 1893.[18] At the time, investment bankers, whose experience had been primarily with railroad securities, seem not to have been fully persuaded of the investment quality of industrial securities, and they marketed only 5 of the 22 issues which were actively promoted. J. P. Morgan, the largest of the railroad investment bankers, did not become active in the underwriting of industrial securities until the formation of Federal Steel, in 1898. The promoters of six of the 28 companies listed by Navin and Sears made no special effort to market the preferred stock. General Electric Company, for example, was formed in 1892 by a merger of Edison Electric Company of Schenectady, New York, with the Thomson-Houston Electric Company of Lynn, Massachusetts, using a New York legislative charter. J. P. Morgan and some associates had invested $300,000 in Thomas A. Edison's Edison Electric Light Company in 1878, before the invention of the Edison lamp, and although the Morgan firm was instrumental in the merger of the Edison and Thomson-Houston interests in 1892, its role seems to have been more that of an investor than of an underwriter or securities dealer. The suitability of industrial securities for public distribution was still an open question in 1892.

The panic of 1893 proved to be a turning point. First, it put a temporary end to the issuance of new industrial securities. Second, it provided a testing ground for a comparison of the performance of industrial securities with the performance of railroad securities in four years of depression. The industrial securities passed the test reasonably well. Third, although there were few mergers during these depression years, the number of industrial corporations whose shares were listed in the financial journals grew from 30 in 1893 to 170 in 1897.[19]

The Postdepression Merger Movement

If the trusts were responsible for introducing publicly traded industrial securities to American markets, it is evident that the pressures of the depression of 1893 to 1897 reduced the earning power of large numbers of firms and set the stage for their owners to sell out at the first convenient opportunity. The most remunerative way to sell out turned out to be neither sale to a successor partnership nor simple incorporation and sale of the corporation's securities. What brought the highest sales price was incorporation as part of a group of firms large enough in total to sustain a market in publicly traded stock. The reason was simple. The rule of thumb for the sale value of individually owned businesses was "three times earnings" and marketable securities could be sold for seven to ten times earnings. Navin and Sears explain the difference as follows:

> To run a business, particularly a specialized manufacturing enterprise, required peculiar skills in addition to capital. These skills were usually possessed only by persons already operating in the industry. Consequently, potential buyers generally were to be found only among competitors . . .
> The infrequent opportunity to complete a sale had kept the going price of industrial concerns at a low level. A common sales figure was "three times earnings" . . . By comparison a man who owned part of a sound railroad or textile mill could sell his share at a price ranging from seven to ten times earnings. Clearly the owner of industrial capital was at a serious disadvantage because of the lack of an established and recognized market for industrial securities.[20]

It is important to emphasize that *marketable* securities meant securities issued in sufficient quantity that there was regular trading in them, not securities that changed hands only once in a while. The advantage enjoyed by large issues was not merely an economy of scale in legal, accounting,

225

and underwriting costs; the advantage was that a security issue which is large enough and widely enough held to generate frequent sales at an easily observable price is more valuable to investors than one which is not.

Beginning in the fall of 1897, a postdepression merger movement virtually completed the shift of most American industries to organization in the form of publicly held corporations with listed shares. At first, these mergers were simply promoters' buy outs, the payment to the former owners taking the form of stock in the merged company. The usual merger plans contained no provision for adding cash to the merged company, either for working capital or for new plant. But to later economists, looking back, the hallmark of a successful merger was the reorganization of the production and selling operations of the participating companies into an integrated system rather than a mere confederation of the former companies' separate operations. Such reorganizations required a plan, financial resources, and the managerial leadership to carry the plan through. All three were lacking in the typical promoter merger.

When J. P. Morgan joined the movement in the late 1890s, his firm remedied these deficiencies. He formed Federal Steel Company in 1898 in accordance with a plan that included the sale of preferred stock to provide additional working capital and funds for new plant. He also acted as underwriter, agreeing to buy any of the preferred stock not purchased by other stockholders or by the public. There were Morgan nominees on the board of directors to see that the organizing plans were carried out. Finally, the British practice of using independent, "chartered" accountants to audit the corporation's accounts, which had been extended to the United States in the late nineteenth century at the instance of British investors in American enterprises, was used by the Morgan companies— and one may be sure that the accountants selected were acceptable to the bankers.

The American practice of issuing preferred stock, though the object of much criticism, paralleled contemporary British practice. Writing of England, Cottrell has described how ordinary shares had come to be regarded as "very risky securities to hold" as a result of adverse experience with shares of industrial companies bought during the boom of the first half of the 1870s. Common shares also bore the brunt of a "long-term decline in the profitability of English industry between the mid-1870s and the mid-1890s." A parallel decline in the profitability of American industry contributed to the development of the trust movement. Still speaking of England, Cottrell notes:

Technology, Trusts, and Marketable Stock

The type of securities issued by public companies changed completely during the 30 years before the First World War. In 1884 only 227 out of the 1,585 public companies listed in *Burdett* had more than one class of capital but by 1915, 75% of all public coal, iron, and steel companies had issued both preference shares and debentures, 75% of "other" public commercial and industrial companies had issued preference capital, and 50% of the latter group had issued debentures.[21]

Cottrell also notes that, on the other hand, the practice of issuing shares that were not fully paid disappeared between 1895, when the average unpaid liability on shares listed in Sir H. Burdett's *Official Intelligence* (first issued in 1882) was 33.2 percent and 1915, when it had ceased to exist for all but financial and insurance shares.

There was evidently a belief among late-nineteenth-century investors that industrial consolidation offered promise of monopolistic profits—a belief no doubt exploited by the promoters of the trusts. George A. Stigler has summed up the case for monopoly motives in the earlier mergers as follows:

> Why was merger preferred to collusion? Part of the answer lies in the prima facie illegality of collusion after 1890. This point should not be pressed, however. The effectiveness of the Sherman Law in dealing with conspiracies was not clear until 1899, when the *Addyston Pipe* case was decided; and there was a contemporaneous wave of amalgamations in England, where conspiracies were unenforcible but not actionable. Mention should also be made of the conflicting tendencies of the greater durability of mergers and the ability to avoid diseconomies of scale through collusion. I am inclined to place considerable weight upon one other advantage of merger: it permitted a capitalization of prospective monopoly profits and a distribution of a portion of these capitalized profits to the professional promoter. The merger enabled a Morgan or a Moore to enter a new and lucrative industry: the production of monopolies.[22]

If the consequences of economic action could safely be judged by the motives and intentions, or even the hopes, of those who initiate it, the American manufacturing economy might well have been permanently transformed into a set of industrial monopolies in the last two decades of the nineteenth century. But, as happens so often in economic history as to verge on a law, the eventual consequences owed little or nothing to anyone's intentions.[23] The merged companies were seldom able to maintain their initial market shares.[24] Sometimes they were unable to keep up with the rate of growth of their industries, sometimes they learned the hard way that maintaining their share of the market was incompatible with attempting to control prices.[25] In Stigler's words, "Almost invariably the share of the merger in the market declined substantially as time went on."[26] The trusts had other problems than a decline in their shares of the market. Even so prototypical a trust as Standard Oil made its profits principally by reducing its own costs and then charging the same price as its competitors[27]—and the trusts that lacked a way of reducing costs fared badly.[28]

The relevant point is that the early-twentieth-century promoters, whatever their motives or expectations, organized much of American industry into corporate enterprises large enough to issue shares that could be widely held and frequently traded. The American manufacturing economy thereby became largely an economy of publicly held corporations. This type of enterprise organization spread more slowly in England, France, and Germany, but it became general after World War II.

Were Corporate Securities More Valuable Than the Enterprise?

Whatever motives may have led investors to favor marketable stock, this form of investment offered investors two real advantages. Marketable stock was a form of insurance of long-term investment risks, and it brought agency risks under better control. In terms of social values, marketable stock made possible the decentralization of investment decision making, which had substantial organizational advantages of its own. We shall explore these points in the next three sections.

1. Marketable Stock and Investment Risk

The large enterprises that evolved after the Industrial Revolution, during the period from 1880 to 1914, required the tying up of capital in amounts, and over a period of time, unprecedented in medieval or Renaissance commerce. The key phrase is "tying up." Such enterprises as railroads, steel mills, and electric power networks required enormous amounts of capital, and only the rare projects with extremely high expectations of profit could be expected to pay for themselves in any short period of time. If the enterprise turned out badly, there was seldom any prospect that these highly specialized assets could be liquidated at a reasonable price. The risk was underscored by the fact that the life of the assets (and the time needed to recover the investment through profit and depreciation) often exceeded the life expectancy of the mortal charged with their management, and there was no assurance that a successor would be either competent or honest.

To the medieval merchant accustomed to keeping wealth in a form easily buried against the hazards of political extortion, war, revolution, and other forms of banditry, such a tie-up of capital for a period far beyond the range of foresight would have seemed insane. There was simply no way to calculate the future stream of benefits. It is hardly too much to say that no investor had ever voluntarily accepted such risks. The irrigation works of the hydraulic empires were comparable in scope and time, but payment for their construction was not voluntary—it was imposed by political force.

As risks are perceived by investors, the corporation with transferable shares converted the underlying long-term risk of a very large amount of capital into a short-term risk of small amounts of capital. Because marketable corporate shares were readily salable at prices quoted daily (or oftener), their owners were not tied to the enterprise for the life of its capital equipment, but could pocket their gains or cut their losses whenever they judged it advisable. Marketable shares converted the proprietor's long-term risk to the investor's short-term risk. The ownership of the underlying assets was divided into two levels: first, the corporation as an entity; second, the shareholders who supplied it with capital. The first-level risks remained as severe as ever, but the second-level risks were entirely different and were widely acceptable. The division was analogous to the redistribution of risk between an owner of property and an insurance company.

The size of many late-twentieth-century enterprises is such that it would be almost impossible to conceive of their functioning as proprietorships or partnerships, unless a government were the proprietor. It was not simply that new technology requires investment on a huge scale, for some investors' fortunes are very large. Rather, the need for a new way to raise capital for large enterprises arose from the desire of investors to apply insurance principles to investments. Many wanted to spread their risks by diversification, investing only a small fraction of their funds in any one enterprise or project. Marketable securities provided the means for doing so.

The investor in corporate shares could further reduce risk by hedging the dangers inherent in any one enterprise or, for that matter, in any one industry, by investing in a number of different enterprises in the same or different industries. This diversification of risk was particularly valuable to investors who were unable to follow the strategy, "Put all your eggs in one basket and watch that basket," because they were unable to watch a basket that was under someone else's direct management and control—or to understand what they were seeing even were they in a position to watch. The total system risk of business losses did not change, but investors were able to achieve an insurance effect by sharing the risk widely and reducing the likelihood that it would fall disproportionately on any one investor.

Kenneth Arrow has linked risk, insurance, and limitations on the use of insurance in a way that is particularly helpful in clarifying the role of risk in the rise of the corporation with marketable securities. Many bearers of business risks (including investment risks) would like to insure against the risks, but no such insurance is available in conventional insurance markets. Uninsurability is attributable to the moral hazard: "The insurance policy might itself change incentives and therefore the probabilities upon which the insurance company has relied.... Either [the insurer] will refrain from insuring or he will resort to direct inspection and control, to make as certain as he can that the insured is minimizing all losses under the latter's control."[29] But there are ways of spreading risk other than going to the conventional insurance markets. During the nineteenth century, as Arrow points out, many owners of businesses divested themselves of some of the risks through sale of common stocks, opening opportunities for reducing aggregate risk by portfolio diversification.[30]

The result of investors' interest in spreading their risks is that no matter how large the fortunes of some investors, by comparison to the size of needed investments, very large investments are unlikely to be made (except by government) without some institutional arrangement for spreading the risk. Since the seventeenth century, the capitalist device for spreading the risks of large capital investment has been the corporation with marketable shares. As we have seen, it was used to raise large blocks of capital for railroads, canals, bridges, toll roads, and the like early in the nineteenth century, and it was widely used by industrial enterprises at the end of the century. All this is not to deny that some individuals, such as Carnegie and Ford, accumulated great fortunes and large undiversified holdings. Their accumulations proceeded largely, however, through a sequence of *small* investments with very successful outcomes. Carnegie was one of many entrepreneurs who, in the end, sold their businesses and diversified their holdings; Ford's successors eventually did likewise.

To pursue Arrow's insurance analogy one step further, the marketable stock put the holders of common stock in the position of insurers whose assumption of risk had changed the incentives of owners or management in possession of the enterprise, creating a situation where it was appropriate for holders of common stock to insist on what Arrow called "direct inspection and control."[31] This brings us to the agency problem.

2. Agency Risk

In modern economic studies of the organization of enterprises, much importance is attached to what has come to be called the agency risk or agency costs.[32] Whenever the owners of an enterprise delegate its conduct to agents and employees, there is a risk that the agents and employees may fail to act diligently or may, consciously or subconsciously, act in their own interests rather than in the interests of the owners. Agency costs in larger enterprises are increased not merely by the cost of additional employees, but by the tendencies of hierarchies to make decisions in their own interests rather than in the interests of the owners and to depreciate the quality of decision making by dividing responsibility, taking time to obtain numerous approvals, buck-passing, and moving authority to individuals comparatively remote from immediate knowledge of the subject matter. Allocation of the resources of the enterprise among its specialized functions—research and development, engineering, manufacturing, advertising, marketing, purchasing—is made especially difficult because the managers in charge of each of these functions almost inevitably become biased in favor of allocation to that function. A parallel problem of expert bias occurs in governmental, educational, and other nonprofit hierarchies. In large organizations, the corrupt elements in agency costs—excessive perquisites, salaries, bonuses, and expense accounts, and empire-building through hiring unneeded personnel—tend to be trivial by comparison to the costs of decisions badly made because of bureaucratic politics and conflicts of interest among decision-making agents and between decision-making agents and their principals.

Despite all this, large hierarchical organizations exist because they have advantages that offset their agency costs. The advantages include not simply the economist's economies of scale, but the advantages of specialization and division of labor in the management function. An owner may have better incentives, but properly chosen professional managers are likely to have greater competence. Thus the practical reason for emphasizing agency costs is not so much to argue against hierarchies as to stress the importance of linking hierarchy to effective devices for controlling or minimizing agency risks.

231

In politics, the familiar democratic device for controlling the risk that the citizens' agents may act in their own interests is voting. The same device is used in corporations. But it has two major inadequacies. The first is that it depends on verbal persuasion, and incumbent officeholders have every advantage of access to and control of information, plus the ability to hire public-relations firms that are expert in rationalizing their clients' conduct. The second is that it does not give the individual citizen any control over public agents, but instead transfers that control to a shifting majority of other citizens with diverse interests of their own. It thus creates a second form of agency risk to compound the first. The individual citizen's only ultimate resort is migration—voting with the feet. The inadequacies of voting as a control device are notorious; like democracy, it survives only because no one has thought of a less unsatisfactory substitute.

The individual corporate stockholder is much less dependent on the outcome of verbal battles and election contests, because voting with the feet is very easy. If the investor does not like the way affairs are being conducted, he or she can switch holdings from one company to another almost instantly and at very low selling cost. This form of voting, with its depressing effect on the market value of the stock of the corporations that are losing stockholders and its positive effect on the stock of corporations that are gaining stockholders, places corporate managements into mutual competition in serving owners' interests.

A considerable part of the history of corporations could be written as a history of efforts to deal with the problems of agency risk. Originally, the investment bankers who had promoted a corporation had a strong incentive for controlling agency risk on behalf of their own and their clients' interests. They exercised this control through membership in boards of directors, selection of outside auditors, employment of law firms acceptable to the bankers, and participation in choosing chief executive officers through what some have appraised as an "old-boy network." Later, as corporations founded in the early part of the century matured and became less dependent on their investment bankers, federal securities laws took over much of the work of reducing agency risk, principally by requiring publicly held corporations to make a great deal of information available to securities markets, better enabling investors to avoid corporations with high agency risk.

In recent years, the takeover bid has become another significant control device. Failure of management to perform adequately will depress the stock's price, and depressed stock prices make management vulnerable to a takeover bid, leading in this way to its direct replacement. The development of a market for companies and of experiments with conglomerate and diversified enterprises have produced full-time professional specialists in looking for firms that would be more profitable with a change in management. Before the takeover bid became common and readily financed, inadequate management could continue in office for a long time, resisting buy-out offers that might displace it, while the enterprise gradually deteriorated as its investors left it. The takeover bid is also a noteworthy aspect of the two-level division of ownership in corporations—the underlying assets having one value and the shares another. The industrial corporation became popular because the shares tended to be worth more than the assets. But the difference reflects in part the competence with which the assets are managed, and sometimes the assets are worth more than the shares. Takeover bidders have become a serious factor in controlling agency risk partly because they are looking for exactly such situations.

Agency risks and costs are a matter of concern wherever societies employ hierarchical forms of organization. In publicly held corporations, it has become almost as easy for stockholders to exit as for customers to do so. Both are in a far more powerful position than the political voter, if one measures power by the individual's ability to act effectively when his or her agents do not fulfill their preelection commitments.[33]

3. Marketability of Stock and the Social Risk of Investment

To the extent that the corporation with marketable stock reduces investor risks and hence the cost of capital, it serves both a private and a social purpose. The likelihood is, however, that the principal social benefits of this institution have a different source. A system of economic organization that decentralizes investment decision making is likely to be appreciably more efficient than one that does not; and for investments larger than any one investor might be willing to risk, decentralization requires the publicly held corporation, or some similar organizational mechanism, for consolidating the interests of a number of investors. Let us see why.

The present value of an investment is a forecast of the timing and amount of the earnings (or other benefits, however measured) the investment will produce in the future, hedged by an equally future-oriented estimate of salvage value in case of a failure to produce earnings. In any economic system, a decision to reduce consumption—and any diversion of economic resources to physical or human capital investment must be expected to reduce consumption to less than it would be without the diversion—is irrational unless the deferment is expected to produce future benefits, with a present value in excess of their cost.

In an economic sense, the cost of an investment is the sacrifice of the most advantageous available alternative use of the invested resources. For this reason, whether an estimate of the future benefits of a given investment proves correct depends not just on the usefulness of that investment, but on the usefulness of alternative investments. One method of making steel may be technologically admirable, but it will be a poor investment if some other method of making steel turns out to be more economical.

The uncertainty inherent in estimates of present value and cost is not peculiar to capitalism. There is no way for either a capitalist or a socialist system to escape the risk of making the wrong investments, and the losses flowing from inaccurate prediction of the benefits of various ways to use capital are unfortunately, even tragically, as familiar to students of modern socialist and Third World economies as to students of capitalism.

Because predictions of the future are partly subjective, the quality of the predictions and thus the quality of the decisions regarding a society's capital investments are likely to be substantially affected by the penalties and rewards provided for the decision makers. Capitalism has dramatically rewarded decision makers for investment decisions that were validated by future events and just as dramatically penalized those who made wrong decisions.

This system of personal rewards and penalties is not, however, the crucial point. It is even more important to successful economic organization that those who select investment alternatives not be given the power to prevent their decisions from being invalidated by future events. A condition of economic change in the direction of growth is that there exist somewhere investors with no financial or bureaucratic interest in preserving an industrial status quo less economical than an available successor. To get social decisions made on the principle that sunk costs should be disregarded in considering future economic behavior, it is necessary that there be decision makers to whom those sunk costs truly have zero value.

This need to expose investment decisions to the risk of being proved wrong implies the decentralization of decision-making authority, since any central authority will be highly motivated to withhold financing from those who are bent on proving that the central authority made a mistake, or on imposing on the central authority the cost of scrapping splendid-looking facilities whose only fault is that some interloper has devised more productive facilities or discovered that the work done in the facilities can be accomplished more cheaply in some other country—or perhaps need not be done at all. The social cost and risk of such moves might be well worth financing, but the private cost and risk to centralized decision makers are prohibitive.

Historically, one of the most distinctive features of capitalist economies has been the practice of decentralizing authority over investments to substantial numbers of individuals who stand to make large personal gains if their decisions are right, who stand to lose heavily if their decisions are wrong, and *who lack the economic or political power to prevent at least some others from proving them wrong.* Indeed, this particular cluster of features is among the stronger candidates for *the* definition of *capitalism.* Its importance in Western growth turns on the point that the choice of capital investments includes the selection of the proposals for innovation that are to be funded. The diffusion of authority to select programs for capital expenditure and the diffusion of authority to select projects for innovation thus cover much the same ground.

The Organization of Employees

There is one problem that could have checked the formation of large, publicly held corporations and that, in any event, left industrial enterprises preoccupied with the development of capital-intensive methods of production and the minimization of the use of labor. The problem was the organization of large numbers of workers.

The economic organization of large numbers of people has almost always proceeded by a combination of coercion, reward, and persuasion, in varying proportions. In major economic enterprises such as the irrigation agriculture of the hydraulic empires, the Roman latifundia, or the medieval manor, political force and religious persuasion were appreciably more common than reward. Economic organization was not distinguished, in this respect, from political or social organization. The military services were the prototypes of large organization and, in achieving discipline within them, political and religious persuasion, group psychology, and coercion played at least as large a part as reward. Corporal punishment was thought necessary to the administration of both naval and merchant vessels until well into the nineteenth century. We have already explored the status of the medieval lord of the manor as both the political and economic chieftain.

The prospect that large numbers of employees in factories could be organized into a cohesive body on the basis of reward alone must have seemed, to anyone who thought about it beforehand, incompatible with past experience. It was not that the wage system lacked punitive elements, such as the docking of wages and dismissal for infractions of discipline. But these punitive elements, amounting to a withholding of a reward, were of a different character from the physical punishment and religious penalties formerly used to organize large groups.

Some of the early factories backed into the problem very slowly. Marx's discussion of the shift from handicraft to factory production treats the change as unplanned—an accident. He describes early factories in which a capitalist provided the tools and the workers (sometimes with apprentices) saw the product through the successive stages of its production in very much the way they always had. But then, for example, an "increased quantity of the article has perhaps to be delivered within a given time" and, to speed things up, the successive operations are each "assigned to a different artificer. . . . This accidental repartition gets repeated, develops advantages of its own, and gradually ossifies into a systematic division of labor."[34]

David Landes records that the leasing of space and power in a mill to individual artisans, "each conducting his own enterprise," was common in nineteenth-century England.[35] Another way of avoiding direct employment was through "inside contracting," by which the owner of a factory bought the required input of labor from contractors who hired and supervised their own employees in exchange for a piece rate from the factory.[36] If the contractor's employees could be organized into a union, it was no great step to substitute a union president for the contractor in dealing with the factory; and some of the early unions perceived themselves as operating the factory in their own way, under a production contract with the owner. The notion that management (= the owner) has no business trespassing on the workplace remained alive until recently in the printing trades.

The most spectacular battle over union control of production took place in the steel industry, at Andrew Carnegie's steel mill at Homestead, Pennsylvania, in 1892. The Amalgamated Association of Iron, Steel, and Tin Workers, said to be the strongest union of its day, controlled every aspect of production at the mill. In time, its accumulation of rules about methods of production, restriction of output, and opposition to labor-saving machines opened a considerable gap between the actual and potential costs of production. The upshot was that Carnegie and his partner Henry Clay Frick locked out the union, hired replacements, and, with the assistance of the state and federal governments, established a nonunion operation under their own control.[37]

Now that large enterprises are almost always large employers, it is surprising to find that as late as 1892, so substantial a plant as Carnegie's Homestead Works avoided the problems of organizing and managing the work of its manufacturing employees. Perhaps the willingness to use contract labor reflected the factory owners' lack of personal experience in production work, either because they were originally merchants (as in the textile industry) or because they were originally financiers. It is easier to see how, in the publishing industry, managements more concerned with what should be printed than with how to print it might cede control of their plants to their employees' unions.

Part of the puzzle may stem from an inadequate understanding of hierarchical managements. The pyramided table of organization disguises much differentiation and specialization of managerial functions. This is in part a difference between specializing on formulating future plans and programs and specializing on executing existing plans and programs. It also conceals differences in function. The organization of the work of large numbers of employees was a new management function, and direct employment could not have become a general practice until recruiting, organizing, and supervising factory workers had been sorted out and fitted into the hierarchical scheme.

There has been a long history of confrontation, often angry and sometimes bloody, between Western industries and their employees. The search for a substitute for the clear link between artisans' work and their income has been only partially successful. Employees still are not sure if they are being properly compensated, and employers have almost as much difficulty telling whether they are getting the work they pay for. Given these two defects of information that are central to the bargain between employers and employees, it is a wonder that their relations, especially those conducted on a large scale and of necessity impersonally, are not worse than they are. The problem is compounded by the fact that some types of factory work are at best harsh, exhausting, noisy, repetitive, and dirty.

The confrontational character of employer-employee relations has encouraged the use of labor-saving, capital-intensive methods of production throughout the West. The effects of using these methods include a reduction of the number of employees in manufacturing industry, the substitution of machine effort for human effort in many of the more strenuous jobs, and an increase of the marginal productivity, and hence the compensation, of the remaining workers. All three effects have made the underlying relationship less confrontational in the long run, though the introduction of labor-saving machinery has often been bitterly resisted in the short run.

In any case, it proved possible to control large numbers of workers without religious and political coercion, even though the quality of the administration of industry was never entirely satisfactory to either employers or employees. Otherwise, an early change to a command economy, with its implied command political structure, would have been unavoidable, particularly in Europe, where industrialization was essential to military power.

Conclusion

Between 1880 and 1914, there was a reconstruction and expansion of the American and, to a lesser degree, of other Western economies. The trusts, mergers, financial promotions, and stock-market speculations that supplied the capital for reconstruction were almost as controversial as the slightly earlier post–Civil War political Reconstruction—and their aftermath still generates almost as many rebel yells. These controversies are interesting, but we will defer consideration of them to chapter 9.

In retrospect, the accomplishments of the Western economies during this period were striking enough to merit being called a second industrial revolution. During the years of what may be taken as an extreme and sometimes brutal exercise of freedom of experiment, the United States and other Western countries made massive gains in economic welfare. The United States, which experimented most, also made the greatest economic gains. Whether this growth might have occurred as soon, or in the same degree, had the trusts and merger movement, along with the changes in economic organization which flowed from it, been repressed as soon as it started, depends on what the capitalists of the time would have done instead to adapt to the new technologies, the new markets, and the urbanizing world unfolding before them. To such counterfactuals as these, history provides no definitive answers.

NOTES

1. Alfred D. Chandler, Jr., in a case prepared for class discussion, entitled "The Emergence of Managerial Capitalism."

2. Jeremy Atack, "Fact in Fiction? The Relative Costs of Steam and Water Power: A Simulation Approach," *Explorations in Economic History*, 2d ser., 4 (October 1979): 412.

3. Ibid., 412–13.

4. For a short study of the electrification of factories, see Richard B. Du Boff, "The Introduction of Electric Power in American Manufacturing," *Economic History Review*, 2d ser., 20, no. 3 (1967): 509–18.

5. Du Boff tells us that printing and publishing was the leading industry in electrification. "And it is worth noting that printing and publishing was also the leader in productivity increases . . ."—Ibid., 516. Of particular interest was the experience of the Government Printing Office, where "better arrangement of machinery, intensification of work loads, and elimination of belts and shafting resulted in 'at least a ten percent increase in production from presses.' " Ibid., p. 513. These initial savings were probably small compared to those resulting later from the redesign of printing equipment to take advantage of electrification.

6. U.S. Department of Commerce, Bureau of the Census, *Historical Statistics of the United States* (Washington, D.C.: Government Printing Office, 1975), ser. T 1-14, 839.

7. Fernand Braudel, *The Wheels of Commerce*, trans. Sian Reynolds (New York: Harper & Row, 1982), pp. 100–101.

8. Marian V. Sears, "Gold and the Local Stock Exchanges of the 1860's," *Explorations in Economic History* (Winter 1969): 198–231.

9. Thomas R. Navin and Marian V. Sears, "The Rise of the Market for Industrial Securities, 1887–1902," *Business History Review* 24 (June 1955): 105–38, to which credit for recording the shift of much of U.S. industry to the form of the publicly held corporation belongs.

10. See P. L. Cottrell, *Industrial Finance, 1830–1914* (New York: Methuen, 1980), pp. 108–109. As in the United States, the promotion of industrial companies was at first the business of second-rank financial houses; the first-rank houses in England promoted primarily foreign issues until after 1914. Ibid., pp. 144–45.

11. Lance Davis, "The Capital Markets and Industrial Concentration: The U.S. and U.K., a Comparative Study," *The Economic History Review* 19, no. 2 (1966): 255. Davis refers to testimony given in 1877 by David Chadwick before the Select Committee on the Companies Act of 1862 and 1867, to the effect that his firm had by then sold over 40 million pounds of corporate shares, mostly industrials (262, and n 5). Davis points out that the British markets for short-term credit and long-term borrowing by industrial concerns were also better developed than the American (260–61). Philip Mirowski, in "The Rise (and Retreat) of a Market: English Joint Stock Shares in the Eighteenth Century," *Journal of Economic History* 41 (September 1981): 561–78, notes that there were full-time specialists in share trading in England as early as 1690, complete with current information about share prices in newspapers and magazines. He shows, however, that this market went into a long-term decline.

12. Ibid., 263–68.

13. The brewery flotations are described in Cottrell, *Industrial Finance, 1830–1914*, pp. 168–71. A shortage of public houses resulted from a British temperance movement and restrictive licensing policies, making it desirable to the breweries to gain control of the surviving outlets for their products.

14. Davis says of the comparable situation in Germany:

> In the case of Germany, for example, it appears that the connexion was even more direct. With few established financial institutions, the "D" banks were responsible for a large proportion of the total capital mobilized for industry. This central control of finance soon produced central control of pricing and output decisions and the cartelized market structure that we know today. Given the much shorter industrial history and more primitive financial institutions it was impossible to compete without external finance.

"Capital Markets," 271.

15. Cottrell, *Industrial Finance, 1830–1914*, pp. 149–52, recounts the problems created by the unmarketability of small issues: "With regard to a summary of the Official List of 19 October 1877, a broker indicated that 1,082 out of the 1,367 securities which had a quotation were unmarketable" and:

The joint stock company form of organization was adopted rapidly in only a few areas of industry before 1885, namely cotton spinning and iron, steel, and coal ... In the cotton industry the incorporated form was adopted to establish large and efficient, by contemporary standards, new spinning mills, while in iron it provided a way to raise extra finance required for new investment, including the introduction of the Bessemer process. Most flotations were the products of either local or regional capital markets in which formal financial institutions played very little part ... The institutions of the metropolis would appear to have played not merely a passive but a negative role by allowing unscrupulous company promoters to have free rein.

(P. 154.)

16. Navin and Sears, "Rise of the Market," 112–21.

17. A similar practice was followed in British incorporations. See Cottrell, *Industrial Finance*, 164–67.

18. Navin and Sears, "Rise of the Market," table 1, 118.

19. Ibid., 127.

20. Ibid.

21. Cottrell, *Industrial Finance*, p. 167.

22. George A. Stigler, "Monopoly and Oligopoly by Merger," chap. 8 in *The Organization of Industry* (Homewood, Ill.: Richard D. Irwin, 1968), pp. 102–103.

23. Thomas Schelling took much of the mystery out of the fact that the collective consequences of individuals' actions are frequently quite different from any individual's intentions and from the individual consequences, in his *Micromotives and Macrobehavior* (New York: W. W. Norton and Company, 1978). The "invisible hand" is a familiar facet of the same phenomenon.

24. Yale Brozen, *Concentration, Mergers and Public Policy* (New York: Macmillan Publishing Co., 1982) pp. 214–18.

25. The technique by which a dominant firm can control prices is to restrict its own output. Maintaining one's market share in growing markets requires expanding one's output.

26. Ibid., p. 102.

27. See F. M. Scherer, *Industrial Market Structure and Economic Performance*, 2d ed. (Chicago: Rand McNally, 1980), pp. 336–37.

28. For the trusts' record of success and failure, see Alfred D. Chandler, *The Visible Hand* (Cambridge: Harvard University Press, 1977), pp. 337–44, where he reviews the earlier work of Shaw Livermore, "The Success of Industrial Mergers," *Quarterly Journal of Economics* 50 (November 1935): 94.

29. Kenneth Arrow, *Aspects of the Theory of Risk Bearing* (Helsinki: Suomalaisen Kirjallisuuden Kirjapaino Oy, 1965), especially lecture 3, "Insurance, Risk, and Resource Allocation," pp. 45–56. The quoted sentences are on p. 55. There is also a selection hazard, in that at any given level of premiums, there would be a tendency to insure the most severely risky businesses and not insure the safer businesses. Early marine insurers coped with the selection hazard by negotiating premiums ad hoc.

30. Arrow describes the diversification process on p. 47, ibid. To cite marine insurance again, diversification is reminiscent of the old practice of the individual underwriters at Lloyd's, each of whom accepted only a fraction of the risk on each ship. Other marine underwriters diversify their risks by reinsuring.

31. Ibid., 52–53. Arrow also treats vertical integration as a device for dealing with risks of poor performance by a vendor. It is worth noting that pooling the risks of loss entails pooling the risks of unusual gains. This implies a reconsideration of the sense in which the profits of any one firm or industry, as distinguished from the economy as a whole, might be regarded as excessive.

32. For example, the literature on "satisficing" includes James G. March and Herbert A. Simon, *Organizations* (New York: John Wiley & Sons, 1958), pp. 140–41; and Harvey

Leibenstein, *Beyond Economic Man* (Cambridge: Harvard University Press, 1975), who poses the concept of "x-efficiency." For other examples of studies of the problems posed by agents with interests not necessarily identical to those of their principals, see the papers prepared for a conference at the Hoover Institution on the fiftieth anniversary of the publication of Berle and Means, *The Modern Corporation and Private Property*, a book which may fairly be credited with first popularizing issues related to the separation of ownership and control in the corporate mode of organization. Among them, published in *Journal of Law and Economics* 26 (June 1983), are Eugene F. Fama and Michael C. Jensen, "Agency Problems and Residual Claims," 327–49; idem, "Separation of Ownership and Control," 301–306; and Oliver E. Williamson, "Organizational Form, Residual Claimants, and Corporate Control," 351–66. Other articles in the field include Michael C. Jensen and William H. Meckling, "Theory of the Firm: Managerial Behavior, Agency Costs and Ownership Structure," *Journal of Financial Economics* 3 (1976): 305–59; R. Joseph Monsen, Jr., and Anthony Downs, "A Theory of Large Managerial Firms," *Journal of Political Economy* 73 (June 1965): 221–36; Eugene F. Fama, "Agency Problems and the Theory of the Firm," *Journal of Political Economy* 88 (April 1980): 288–307; Armen A. Alchian and Harold Demsetz, "Production, Information Costs, and Economic Organization," *American Economic Review* 62 (December 1972): 777–93; and Louis De Alessi, "Property Rights, Transaction Costs, and X-Efficiency: An Essay in Economic Theory," *American Economic Review* 73 (March 1983): 64–81.

33. For a discussion of the relative merits of political and economic voting, see Charles E. Lindblom, *Politics and Markets* (New York: Basic Books, 1977), chap. 11. Ordinarily, stockholders buy into corporations of whose management they approve and sell out of corporations of whose management they do not approve. The result is that any corporation's stockholders tend to become a self-selected body of adherents of incumbent management; opposition stockholders who wish to express their opposition by voting, rather than by selling, face an uphill struggle.

34. Karl Marx, *Capital*, vol. 1 (London: Lawrence and Wishart Ed., 1974), 319. Oliver E. Williamson, "The Organization of Work: A Comparative Institutional Assessment," *Journal of Economic Behavior* 1, no. 1 (1980): 5–38, describes a number of nineteenth-century experiments in factory organization and their eventual outcome.

35. David Landes, *The Rise of Capitalism* (New York: Macmillan, 1966), p. 14.

36. See John Buttrick, "The Inside Contracting System," *Journal of Economic History* 12 (Summer 1952): 205–21.

37. Williamson, in *The Organization of Work*, makes use of the account of the Homestead strike in Katherine Stone, "The Origins of Job Structures in the Steel Industry," *Review of Radical Political Economics* 6 (Summer 1974): 61–97. He differs with Stone in arguing that the change in the structures of jobs after the strike furthered efficient work organization and that the pre-strike methods of operation were not a promising precedent for the workers' control of the workplace.

8 / The Link between Science and Wealth

In the West, science and industrial technology have always flowed in separate streams, easily distinguishable and yet linked here and there and replenished from common sources. Both the separateness and the linkages have been vital to the contribution of technology to economic growth.

The West surpassed other societies in the systematic study of natural phenomena by learned specialists—that is, in science—by the time of Galileo, say, 1600. The gap has been widening ever since. But the wealth of Western economies did not clearly draw ahead of the wealth of their predecessors and other economies for another hundred and fifty or two hundred years. Evidently the links between economic growth and leadership in science are not short and simple.

Western scientific and economic advance are separated not only in time, but also by the fact that until about 1875, or even later, the technology used in the economies of the West was mostly traceable to individuals who were not scientists, and who often had little scientific training. The occupational separation between science and industry was substantially complete except for chemists who were engaged in analyzing, testing, and measuring some industrial processes.

This situation changed in the last part of the nineteenth century. By then, basic science had developed explanations of electrical, chemical, and other natural phenomena which were no longer obvious to the common sense of untrained inventors, however gifted, nor even capable of expression save in the language of mathematics. These scientific explanations were not, for the most part, responses to economic needs. They seldom had direct economic application, and they arose mainly among academic and independent scientists whose incentives were not primarily economic and who constituted, collectively, a scientific sphere with an autonomy of its own. The derivation of new or improved products and processes from the esoteric explanations of science became the work of industrial scientists, whose efforts were driven and shaped by estimates of their potential economic value.

It would be a mistake to assume that the exploitation of these new intellectual resources was a merely automatic response of the economic sector to the appearance of fruit ripe for the picking. Neither in the West nor in other societies has the economic sector routinely exploited ideas originating outside that sector. China was by no means unique. In the West itself, the explanations of natural phenomena given by Aristotle and his successors were not used in Hellenistic mining, trade, transportation, agriculture, warfare, building, or manufacture. In the postfeudal West, the situation was at first very little different. The ideas of basic science, under development from about 1600, were 275 years in finding broad economic application. Here and there, an unusually perceptive industrialist would see reason to employ a scientist. But for most of history, in the West as elsewhere, science and industry might as well have lived in different worlds. The practical man or woman had no use for the scientific visionary—an attitude often reciprocated in full.

There is reason to believe that over most of human history industry had some justification for paying little attention to scientific explanations: the explanations were more imaginative than truthful. Be that as it may, there are thus two parts to the explanation of the role of technology in Western economic growth. First, Western basic science created explanations of nature that possessed unprecedented potentialities for practical application—an achievement one may credit partly to the genius of Western scientists and partly to the constraints of the experimental method, which held their explanations closer to reality than the more freewheeling explanations of other societies. Second, the West bridged the traditional gap between science and the economic sphere and translated scientific explanations into economic growth.

To bridge the gap, the West developed what amounted to a system for innovation, first at the level of the firm and then at the level of the economy as a whole. The bridge was anchored at one end in industrial-research laboratories invented to apply scientific methods and knowledge to commercial problems and, at the other end, in consumer purchase and use of a product or service embodying that knowledge. The West was unique in combining the manufacturing and marketing functions of the traditional business firm with centers of scientific knowledge under common management and with common goals and incentives.

This combination had ample opportunity to demonstrate its immense capabilities as an instrument of growth, for it arose while Western countries were still allowing a high degree of autonomy to the economic sphere. It was an effective device for identifying new situations where science might be of value to consumers—and profiting from them. By associating scientists and managers in a common enterprise, it improved recognition of the possibilities of change, reduced the risks of attempting change, and increased the probable rewards of change. It thus altered the goals and incentives of Western economic systems toward more change and growth.

Let us see how this bridge came into being. We will then examine some of the reasons for the West's successes in basic and industrial science and their part in Western economic growth. Finally, in pursuit of our objective of identifying the sources of the West's unique economic growth, we will consider briefly some of the policies of non-Western societies that might reasonably be expected to block innovation, or at least slow it down.

Industrial Science to 1875: The Chemical Age

Western industry has always made use of scientific explanations and scientific knowledge, albeit with some delay and only to the degree that scientific explanations helped to solve the industrial problems of producing goods economically and devising new kinds of goods. Yet, at the beginning of the nineteenth century, most industrial technology, including the technology of the Industrial Revolution, was the work of artisans and engineers with little or no scientific training. Shipbuilding, engineering construction, architecture, mining, smelting, weaving, and the other industrial arts of 1800 were based on experience, rules of thumb, and craft tradition. They had made important strides in developing their own technologies, but the developments were internal to the crafts and not part of a larger structure of technological knowledge. They owed some debt to the scientific advances of the two preceding centuries, but it was small.

The different patterns of prescientific and postscientific development can be illustrated by the case of food processing, a field crucially important to urban society. The transformation to an urban society created a need for the preservation of food so that it could be transported over long distances, stored for sale, and stored yet awhile longer by the buyer before being eaten. In 1810, Nicholas Appert, a Parisian confectioner, invented canning, that is, the preservation of food in glass bottles that had been immersed in boiling water and sealed airtight. For this, he won a prize of ten thousand francs that had been offered in 1795 by Napoleon's Society for the Encouragement of Industry. The interest of the donors of the prize was in provisioning armies, but provisioning cities presented similar problems. Appert used glass; but tin-coated steel cans came into use only two decades later, in the 1830s.

Neither Appert nor anyone else could explain why the process worked. The scientific explanation came much later. In 1873, Pasteur discovered the role of micro-organisms in food spoilage, thereby establishing the new science of bacteriology. With this knowledge in hand, chemists, biochemists, and bacteriologists studied the effects of the multiple factors in food spoilage: its composition; storage conditions; and the specific micro-organisms, their concentration and sensitivity to temperature, oxygen concentration, available nutrients, and the presence or absence of growth inhibitors. For the inspiration or lucky accident that made Appert the inventor of the process, scientists substituted analysis, measurement, and testing. There has followed a gradual expansion in the varieties of fruits and vegetables suitable for canning and in knowledge of the relations among the characteristics of the fruit or vegetables to be canned, the canning process, and the flavor and nutritional properties of the final product. This knowledge has, in turn, stimulated plant breeders and geneticists to develop varieties of fruits and vegetables adapted to the requirements of the food processors.

Among the various branches of science, chemistry was the first to be widely utilized by industry. It was the dominant discipline in nineteenth- and early-twentieth-century research and the first scientific discipline to produce results unmistakably useful in industry. Old though it was, with roots in medieval alchemy, it made immense strides in developing general explanations of chemical phenomena, starting early in the nineteenth century, when John Dalton, an English chemist, devised his atomic theory. By the 1860s, Dmitri Mendeleev's work on the periodic law, which led the Russian chemist to his periodic table of the elements, had gone far to systematize an understanding of chemical processes built around Dalton's atom.

Chemistry was used to analyze the properties of a wide range of commercial materials whose characteristics were not visible to the naked eye, including ores and metals. It thus was helpful in the protection of both buyers and sellers of materials. It could also be used in the analysis of traditional industrial processes with a view to better understanding how they worked and how they might be improved. So it is hardly surprising that the first industrial research laboratories in the United States were established by chemists: Charles T. Jackson in Boston, in 1836, and James C. Booth in Philadelphia, at about the same time.[1] These laboratories, not being affiliated with chemical manufacturers, were akin to modern independent research laboratories. A half-century later, in 1886, Arthur D. Little and another chemist opened a consulting laboratory in Boston. Chemical laboratories established by chemical manufacturers came later, in Germany, toward the close of the 1800s.

The first phase of the application of science to industrial processes and products consisted in testing, measuring, analyzing, and quantifying processes and products already in place. In the steel industry, scientific testing and measuring had simple beginnings. When the first Bessemer converter in the United States went into operation at Wyandotte, Michigan, in 1864, there was a chemical laboratory located alongside it to measure the composition of the ores fed to it, for experience in England had shown that the output of a Bessemer converter is highly sensitive to minute variations in the chemical composition of the ore. The railroads were also concerned about the longevity and reliability of the iron and, later, the steel rails supplied to them by industry. The Pennsylvania Railroad established a chemical laboratory at Altoona in 1874, and the Burlington Railroad established a testing laboratory of its own in 1876.

Andrew Carnegie was one of the first steelmakers to employ a chemist. The chemist, Dr. Fricke, applied himself to ascertaining the iron content of the ore from the mines that supplied Carnegie's mills. Carnegie's biographer quotes him as follows:

> We found . . . a learned German, Dr. Fricke, and great secrets did the doctor open up to us. [Ore] from mines that had a high reputation was now found to contain ten, fifteen, and even twenty per cent less iron than it had been credited with. Mines that hitherto had a poor reputation we found to be now yielding superior ore. The good was bad and the bad was good, and everything was topsy-turvy. Nine-tenths of all the uncertainties of pig iron making were dispelled under the burning sun of chemical knowledge.
>
> What fools we had been! But then there was this consolation: we were not as great fools as our competitors . . . Years after we had taken chemistry to guide

us [they] said they could not afford to employ a chemist. Had they known the truth then, they would have known they could not afford to be without one.[2]

The concrete industry was another early user of industrial laboratories. Concrete is far from a new product; it was used by the Romans. But in the late nineteenth century, systematic chemical analysis was applied to the raw materials employed in the manufacture of concrete: lime, silica, alumina, iron oxide, impurities. They were then tried in various proportions.[3] The chemist learned to design special kinds of cement to suit each of a wide range of end uses, and both success and failure challenged the scientist to arrive at a deeper understanding of the material, its characteristics, and its hardening properties. Reversing the usual conception of the application of science to industry, understanding followed practice. The economic result was an expansion of the use of concrete in American construction, to the point where more concrete is used, by weight, than all other building materials combined.

David Mowery has counted 139 research laboratories that were established in American industry before 1898, 112 of them in manufacturing, and another 553 that were established by 1918.[4] Almost always, in their early years the research output of these laboratories consisted in greater knowledge about materials and processes already in use by the firms that established them. Like Carnegie's Dr. Fricke, or like the chemists working in cement factories and meatpacking establishments, they analyzed, measured, and standardized. They tested and graded materials, measured their characteristics and related the measured characteristics to the requirements and performance of manufacturing processes. Their work extended from the few fields we have used as examples into many others, such as agriculture; pharmaceuticals; flour milling; the construction of dams, bridges, and tunnels; and, of course, chemistry-related industries: paints, paper, and petroleum.

Their laboratories contributed principally information rather than invention or new scientific insights, but, to cite only one example, with their aid, the life of a rail increased from two years to ten, and the car weight it could bear from eight tons to seventy in the forty years between the end of the Civil War and 1905. Only a very few new technologies have had equal economic significance.

Besides the understanding chemistry brought to the workings and problems of older industrial processes, nineteenth-century chemists also produced new products of great commercial value. One of the most important nineteenth-century product discoveries was accidental. In 1856,

William Henry Perkins, an English chemist, unintentionally synthesized a brilliant mauve dye from aniline, a derivative of coal tar. His discovery was taken up with special vigor in Germany, where it supplied the basis for a valuable dye industry and for an investigation of the properties of organic molecules (that is, molecules built around the carbon atom). Organic chemistry became the source of twentieth-century synthetic materials. Of still greater importance, all living matter is composed of molecules built around the carbon atom, so that modern biochemistry as well has its roots in organic chemistry.

Research in the industrial chemical laboratories extended to metallurgy and to the broader field of materials in general. Often the easiest way to improve a product is to improve the materials of which it is made. In some branches of industry, the hotter the temperature and the higher the pressure, the better the product performs—and improving the product becomes, willy-nilly, a problem of finding metals or ceramics that will withstand higher temperatures and pressures. For this reason, much of the technology of steam boilers, steam engines, and, later, steam turbines stemmed from metallurgy. The same requirements of temperature and pressure were important in the development of internal-combustion engines and, eventually, in aircraft jet engines and space rockets. The era of plastics and synthetic fibers is another outgrowth of the extension of chemistry to materials research.

Our own age was shaped by materials research of a different kind. Bell Laboratories, which was established in its present form in 1925, soon launched a program to improve the reliability and longevity of vacuum tubes, then a component of many products used in the telephone system. The frequent replacement of tubes is expensive, and some telephone equipment is so inaccessible as to make replacement very inconvenient. Eventually, in the 1940s, William Shockley, a physicist, and his associates at Bell undertook to solve the problem by making an electronic amplifier of semiconductive material instead of using vacuum tubes. Their solution involved an advance in the understanding of electron flow in semiconductor materials and of the "holes" in their crystalline structure. Even though their research grew out of an intensely practical problem in the improvement of telephonic transmission, their advance was a sufficiently fundamental contribution to basic science to earn a Nobel Prize.

The Link between Science and Wealth

Industrial Technology: The Utilization of Physics

Physicists had developed an important body of reliable knowledge before Dalton made it possible to systematize chemistry, but it was a body of knowledge whose applications to astronomy were a good deal clearer than its usefulness in everyday life. The full impact of physics, as a scientific discipline, did not strike industrial technology until after 1875.

The seeds, however, were planted earlier. In the early nineteenth century, the scientific investigation of electricity produced a series of discoveries of fundamental importance to modern physics. These early discoveries related to magnetism, the flow of current, batteries, capacitors, and electromagnetic induction. They were used in the practical business of telegraphy by Samuel F. B. Morse before the American Civil War. After the Civil War, Thomas Alva Edison, George Westinghouse, Elihu Thomson, Charles Steinmetz, and many others developed electric lighting and other uses for electricity, including, by the 1890s, electric motors for factory power.

The later investigations into electrical phenomena were part of the history of modern theoretical physics. In 1864, James Clark Maxwell predicted, in a mathematical formulation, the existence of electromagnetic waves propagated through space. Gustav Hertz experimentally confirmed Maxwell's prediction in 1886, and in 1895 Wilhelm Konrad Roentgen discovered X-rays. In the same year, Guglielmo Marconi transmitted messages by Hertz waves—that is, by wireless telegraphy. Seventeen years later, in 1912, Marconi's wireless telegraph was carried on enough ships in the North Atlantic to enable it to summon help for the sinking *Titanic*.

Edison is usually credited with pioneering the organization of invention in 'he field of communications and electricity, particularly by establishing, at Menlo Park, New Jersey, in 1876, an "invention factory" with fifteen employees. Edison was trained as a telegraph operator, and by the time he was twenty-one he had been granted his first patent, for a telegraphic vote-recording machine. The machine was not a commercial success. But Edison went on to more valuable inventions in telegraphy, including, by 1874, a system for "quadruplexing" that enabled Western Union to send two messages in each direction over a single circuit, thus multiplying the capacity of its lines by four.[5]

The Menlo Park laboratory soon became deeply involved in the development of a system of electric lighting. Daniel Boorstin stresses the point that Edison did not merely invent an electric lamp; he invented a *system* of domestic lighting and incorporated a company to produce and market it. Its elements included the central station generator (or dynamo), a distribution system for delivering electricity from the central station to the office or home, and a system of wires, switches, and receptacles for distributing electricity within the office or home.[6]

Edison's Menlo Park laboratory was conceived to bring scientific knowledge to bear on industrial innovation and, in doing so, to match and better the patience, ingenuity, and originality of independent inventors. Its inventions were goals chosen with a careful eye to their marketability; a factory, after all, does not last long if its products cannot be sold. But Menlo Park was not rapidly imitated: even the pioneering manufacturing companies did not establish industrial research laboratories until nearly a quarter-century later. The German chemical industry, with its virtual monopoly on dyes, did not begin establishing its own research laboratories until the 1890s.[7]

In 1892, General Electric Company succeeded Edison's electric company, by merger. It retained Charles Steinmetz as a consulting engineer. Steinmetz had been educated in German universities in mathematics, electrical engineering, and chemistry. He had emigrated to the United States in 1889, because of difficulties with the German authorities generated by his attachment to socialism. Steinmetz was primarily interested in mathematics and the theory of electricity, to which he made significant contributions. Also, working very much as an individual inventor he produced more than two hundred patented inventions. A little later, in 1900, General Electric hired Willis R. Whitney, who was teaching chemistry at the Massachusetts Institute of Technology, to organize a formal research laboratory.[8] The company's emphasis on chemistry stemmed in part from the need to find improved materials for lamp filaments, competitive with those that were being made in Germany.

After 1880, industry was moving toward a closer synchronism with pure science, if we may judge by the fact that the intervals were growing shorter between scientific discovery and commercial application. Faraday discovered electromagnetic inductance in 1831, but it was a half-century before transformers and motors became significant commercial products. Similarly, Bessemer's converter was based on knowledge of the chemistry of steelmaking that was at least a half-century old. By comparison, Marconi developed an apparatus for using Hertz's waves commercially nine years after Hertz discovered them. Roentgen's X-rays were in medical use within even less time, partly because apparatus development from Roentgen to medical offices was more straightforward.

The Link between Science and Wealth

By the early years of the twentieth century, industrial research had clearly turned toward the development of new products and processes. If the knowledge required for innovation lay on (or even a little beyond) the frontiers of science, the industrial laboratories worked the frontiers. In recent years, the electronics industry has been particularly successful in pushing its commercial products so close to the frontiers of science that the interval between a scientific discovery and its commercial application has become a matter of getting it into production, as distinguished from bridging a learning gap. As good an illustration as any of the more recent conversion of this time gap into overlap is supplied by the work at Bell Laboratories, undertaken for prosaic commercial reasons, which again led to the award of a Nobel Prize for a discovery that could hardly be surpassed for its purely scientific interest: the residual radiation from the Big Bang.[9]

Natural Science: The Visible, the Invisible, and Professionalization

The new technologies of the late nineteenth century completed the change in the relation of basic science to industrial technology begun by the chemists. The nature of this change is worth exploring.

So long as industrial technology was focused on the visible world of the mechanical arts, where lines of cause and effect were matters of direct observation, advances in technology originated almost entirely with artisans who were surely more imaginative, ingenious, and persistent than most of their contemporaries, but who were in no sense learned scientists. There is a scattered, but only a scattered, historical record of pre-nineteenth century contributions by scientists to the development of pottery, textiles, agriculture, land reclamation, waterwheels, windmills, mining, metallurgy, metalworking, plows, architecture, construction, clocks, armor, weapons, harnesses, saddles, stirrups, wagons, coaches, tools, glassmaking, dyes, shipbuilding, sailmaking, cordage, and printing—in short, to the long list of what anthropologists would call cultural artifacts, which proliferated in the West beyond any earlier society well before the Industrial Revolution. Even the borrowing from other cultures, Chinese, Indian, or Islamic, was more often the work of a merchant or soldier than of a scientist: what was probably the most important single example of cultural borrowing, the Hindu-Arabic number system, was imported by a merchant, Leonard of Pisa, rather than by way of a scientist.

About 1875, the frontier of Western industrial technology began to move from the visible world of levers, gears, cams, shafts, pulleys, and cranks to the invisible world of atoms, molecules, electron flows, electromagnetic waves, inductance, capacitance, magnetism, amperes, volts, bacteria, viruses, and genes. The consequence was to change the main source of advances in Western industrial technology. The new sources were the interaction between work done by basic scientists, functioning in what amounted to an autonomous sector of their own, pursuing knowledge for its own sake, and funded by grants and subsidies not directly linked to economic values, on the one hand, and work done by industrial scientists, functioning in the economic sector, and funded on the basis of the economic value of their work, on the other.

We think of the scientific method as invented by Galileo and Bacon in the early seventeenth century. Their insistence upon observation, experiment, and reason as the path to truth and Galileo's use of experiment to demonstrate the falsity of then-accepted theories were of basic importance. But the use of observation, experiment, and reason easily became part of the artisan's commonsense approach to invention. By itself, Galileo's method neither separated basic and applied science nor professionalized industrial technology. That required two things: first, natural phenomena where human understanding and utilization depended wholly or in part on scientific explanation, and, second, a mode of scientific explanation that could be understood easily, or perhaps at all, only by those specially trained in it.

The natural phenomena were in abundant supply: electricity, electromagnetic waves, genes, and the behavior of atoms and molecules in chemical processes, for examples. The mode of scientific explanation was based on postulating entities and processes that could be observed only indirectly, by their effects, and that could be understood only by trained scientists. It is important to understand why these invisible entities of science could be more useful than the common sense of skilled mechanics and artisans in designing and manufacturing industrial products. After all, for thousands of years, humankind had explained natural phenomena as acts of invisible entities, from leprechauns to gravity to phlogiston to Dalton's atoms. But the invisible entities of scientific explanation had one overwhelming advantage over leprechauns and their companions of myth and fable: experimental test could show that they were nonexistent as well as invisible, as Antoine Lavoisier demonstrated of phlogiston and as the discovery of more elementary particles showed of Dalton's atoms.

Constrained as they were by experimental test of their invisible entities, scientific explanations proved to be reliable guides to the commercial development of new processes and products. Unlike the unrestrained inventions of myth and fable, they could not be ignored by industrial firms except at the risk of being displaced by rival firms. But to understand and apply scientific explanation required years of training in the theology of an invisible pantheon of scientific entities. That requirement professionalized industrial science and diminished the role of artisan invention.

By the latter part of the nineteenth century, it became possible to redefine basic or pure science, without reference to the motives (intellectual or financial) of those who engaged in it. Basic science came to be seen as the testing and development of the explanatory structure of the natural sciences. It had become several full-time professional specialties, including physics, chemistry, astronomy, biology, and mathematics, to mention only the major divisions. The use of these explanations in the advancement of human welfare, whether from motives benevolent or selfish, became applied or industrial science.

Explanations of Western Technological Success: Basic Science

There is an immense gulf between societies in which science was the domain of a handful of wise men, often with individual agendas running not much beyond the devising of a calendar and the treatment of the sick, and, on the other hand, Western society's thousands of specialized scientists seeking to contribute to a coherent understanding of all natural phenomena. The contrast is so striking that it becomes hard to resist the belief that Western science has succeeded out of all comparison simply because it was conducted on an unprecedented scale and was very efficiently organized. This is not to deprecate the part played by genius and dedication, but there was genius and dedication in Hellenic and other societies that recorded nothing like the scientific achievements of the West. The most obvious differences are in scale and organization.

The differences in scale and organization are closely related to a difference in method. In the early seventeenth century, Galileo and Francis Bacon spelled out the uses of experiment to test and verify scientific explanations or theories. Experiment is, of course, inherent in the work of the artisan inventor who seeks to produce a novel product. But in the science that the Renaissance inherited from Greek and Hellenistic sources, the explanation of natural phenomena was deductive. The reasoning was, like Euclid's geometry, from supposedly certain axioms to equally certain conclusions. In substituting reason for fantasy, Greek deductive science was itself a great advance on the use of myth and religion to explain natural phenomena. Unhappily, one of its supposedly certain axioms was that the speed of a falling body is proportional to its weight; and by demonstrating the falsity of this axiom, Galileo established the priority of experiment. His conclusions could not be ignored as a scientific oddity, for they had to be used in the practical business of pointing cannons at the correct upward angle to compensate for the fall of cannonballs in flight.

The Western scientific community thus became a community of practitioners of the experimental methods of Galileo and Bacon. The importance of the method as a way of winnowing scientific wheat from chaff was immense; a large community of astrologers and alchemists could not have created Western science. What made the difference to the creation of *organized* science was that the experimental method was adopted by a number of researchers, and their common method united them in a community of working scientists. Post-Galilean natural science could specialize and departmentalize into physics, astronomy, chemistry, geology, biology, and a host of narrower specialties because all of them shared a common method of determining scientific truth. A geologist or biologist could use the teachings of physics or chemistry in geological or biological research without feeling the need (or even the possibility) of checking their validity. The general acceptance of the experimental method made it possible for hundreds and even thousands of specialists to build the results of their individual research into a single store of information, usable across all sciences. The introduction of the printing press greatly speeded the cumulation of this body of knowledge—as it had earlier speeded the dissemination of the ideas of Galileo and Bacon. Thus the West, alone among the societies of which we have knowledge, succeeded in getting a large number of scientists, specialized by different disciplines, to cooperate in creating an immense body of tested and organized knowledge whose reliability could be accepted by all scientists.

The West's advance can be clarified by the experience of Galen, a physician-philosopher of the second century A.D. who anticipated Galileo's insistence on observation, experiment, and reason. But Galen was only one among many Greek and Hellenistic savants, each pursuing his own methods of investigation. An earlier Greek thinker, Democritus, even suggested a form of atomic theory, but no one followed it up with experimental testing, either of Democritus's theory or of the more conventional Greek view, which he challenged, that the basic elements of matter were earth, air, fire, and water. Galen's contemporaries included no one working in physics and chemistry with the same system of observation, experiment, and reason that he advocated, and in consequence Galen's medical achievements reflected no such infrastructure of physical and chemical theory as the nineteenth century created for modern medical researchers.

The West successfully organized its scientists with very little use of hierarchical management, except perhaps for the relationship between the individual scientist and the apprentices, students, and assistants he or she might employ. The scientific community functioned well without a hierarchy, simply because the organizational tasks normally delegated to a hierarchy were, in science, far better left undelegated. Working toward a shared goal of achieving explanations of natural phenomena truthful by the tests of observation, experiment, and reason, individual scientists exercised their own judgment as to the field in which they could best contribute to this goal—a judgment they would have strongly resisted delegating to a management hierarchy. In the aggregate, these individual judgments produced professional specialization and division of labor no less effective for the lack of managerial approval.

Individual scientists likewise planned their own work, and again the lack of planning by a management hierarchy, attempting to put definitions, times, and costs on the achievement of scientific goals, was not missed. The rewards and penalties of scientific activity were less monetary than intellectual—a combination of approval or disapproval by one's peers and the satisfaction of success in a highly intellectual and deeply respected form of puzzle-solving activity. These rewards and penalties were not open to allotment by a hierarchy. The resolution of conflicts on points of professional controversy was also a process of achieving professional consensus; no scientist would willingly have delegated the settlement of scientific disputes to a hierarchy. On the whole, it is apparent that the Western scientific community was more, rather than less, efficiently organized by reason of its lack of a hierarchy. And where hierarchy has prevailed, there have been results ignominious to the cause of science— an ignominy memorialized in the eponym "Lysenkoism."

Hierarchical organization might have been unavoidable had Western societies been so organized that the funding of basic science could have come from only one source. Basic science is not expected to be commercially marketable, and it is not self-supporting. At first, and well into the nineteenth century, scientists without private funds were sometimes given government employment with no duties, or else had to depend on the generosity of wealthy patrons. Others were themselves wealthy. Later funding was formalized in university budgets, government grants and subsidies, and the endowments of nonprofit research institutes. The result of this diversity of sources of funding is that Western societies have sustained, on a large scale by comparison to other societies, basic scientific activity that could not have paid its own way, and they have done so without imposing a centralized hierarchical organization on the scientific community.

We are so far accustomed to think of organizations solely in terms of hierarchical bureaucracies like armies, governments, or corporations that it is difficult to realize that an enterprise so individualistic and nonhier-archical as modern science can properly be said to be highly organized. But such a narrow impression of *organization* would have to be dismissed as misleading on the basis of the history of science alone. Without a hierarchy, Western scientists formed a scientific community within which they pursued shared goals of understanding natural phenomena with dedication, cooperation, competition, collective conflict resolution, division of labor, specialization, and information generation and exchange at a level of organizational efficiency rarely matched among large groups, hierarchical or nonhierarchical.

Western science had many other advantages over contemporary and antecedent sciences. It arose at a time when political and religious authorities lacked the power to suppress new ideas incompatible with conventional explanations of natural phenomena, though they often tried to do so. The invention of the telescope and the microscope in the seventeenth century gave the West an advantage in instrumentation which it has never stopped extending. Beginning with the invention of the calculus, Western mathematics gave the West a further advantage in intellectual instrumentation as well. Mathematics also supplied scientists with a common language of immense value in communicating across specialized lines.

But these developments seem more like consequences than causes of the West's unique and original institutional invention: a large, highly organized body of scientists, seeking explanations of all natural phenomena by a common method based on observation, experiment, and reason.

The Link between Science and Wealth

Explanations for Western Technological Success: Industrial Science

There is no doubt that basic science contributed to the success of Western industrial science, but its contribution is not a complete explanation of industrial science. As we have already seen, industrial science did not begin to draw heavily on basic scientific explanation until about 1875. By then, Western industrial technology was far ahead of that of any other society. Even after 1875, and in the industries that drew most on basic science, industrial scientists had to solve problems of application that presented intellectual challenges comparable in difficulty to the theoretical work of basic science.

Neither is the comparative success of Western industrial science readily explained by the scale of the Western effort. The gap between the scale of Western industrial science and the industrial science of other societies probably became as overwhelming as the gap in basic science early in the twentieth century. But Western industrial technology had attained a lead over other societies by 1800, and it is questionable whether artisan inventors were more numerous in the West before 1800 than in China or Islam or Hellenistic Europe. We need to examine more closely the way the West organized industrial technology, if we are to find the differences that may explain its success.

Three points of difference seem particularly important: the decentralization of the selection of innovation projects, the incentives for innovation, and the diversity of research agencies.

1. Selection of Innovation Projects

Let us begin with the obvious point, explored briefly in chapter 1, that in order to add to industrial technology, there must be a supply of ideas sufficiently advanced that their validity is not determinable without experimental test. It is necessary also to have some process for screening and testing such new ideas, so that relatively few ideas with appreciable promise will be rejected without test.

This second requirement poses real difficulties, because the ultimate test is the acceptability, in the marketplace, of goods or services embodying the idea. Such a test is never cost-free and may be very expensive, requiring years of painstaking effort. And, for a fair test, the product has to be competently manufactured and competently marketed. Industrial technology is thus a part of innovation, and that consists not simply in

257

generating new ideas, but in generating new products, services, or processes which consumers will buy. Innovation is a product of the organized enterprise, not just of the individual with an idea.

The difficulty of predicting the success or failure of proposals for innovation is twofold. Until a product or service has actually been produced, there is uncertainty about its technological feasibility, its cost, or both. There is also uncertainty about the consumer's response. The two are related, since the consumer's response depends in part on what the cost turns out to be. The relatively short history of the computer industry is an example of the unpredictability of both cost and the consumer's response.

The Western method of dealing with these uncertainties is basically statistical. Western economies authorize a large number of enterprises, as well as individuals who might form new enterprises, to make decisions to accept or reject proposals for innovation, their own or others'. The rejection of a meritorious proposal by a half-dozen decision-making centers is presumably less probable than its rejection by only one. The system is thus biased toward the acceptance of proposals, but with the cautionary qualification that the costs of unsuccessful programs are borne by the decision maker, and all the rewards go to the programs which succeed. The advantage of having proposals for innovations considered by many decision centers is illustrated by the microcomputer, which was *not* undertaken by any of the leading American computer manufacturers, nor by the Soviet Union, nor by the French Commissariat du Plan, nor by MITI in Japan, but which has nevertheless proved widely useful.

The microcomputer illustrates also the importance of the formation of new enterprises. Innovation often originates outside existing organizations, in part because successful organizations acquire a commitment to the status quo and a resistance to ideas that might change it. The adoption of the factory system in British textile weaving is an example of major historic significance. Even though the merchants who participated in the putting-out system had nothing like the commitment of artisans to artisan manufacture and could well have pioneered factory production, the "father of the factory system" was Richard Arkwright, a wigmaker by trade. His technical contribution lay not in the originality of his ideas, but in turning ideas borrowed from others into workable textile machinery and promoting the factories that used them. Edmund Cartwright, the inventor of the power loom, was by training and occupation a clergyman. It is entirely safe to generalize: innovation is more likely to occur in a society that is open to the formation of new enterprises than in a society that relies on its existing organizations for innovation.

The Link between Science and Wealth

2. Incentives: Penalties and Rewards

This openness to new enterprises, or to a change in the activities of existing enterprises, has put Western enterprises under chronic threat of injury from new technologies developed by rivals. In considering a proposal for innovation, an existing enterprise well satisfied with itself and content to forgo an uncertain prospect of gain has to take into account the risk that some other enterprise (either existing or potential) will carry through the innovation successfully, with the result that the otherwise satisfied enterprise would lose business to the innovator. In this way, the openness of Western societies to the formation of new organizations and to changes in the activities of existing organizations encourages innovation by the threat of penalty for failure to innovate.

The rewards of innovation go primarily to enterprises, rather than to inventive individuals. The payment of a reward is dependent on the commercial success of the innovation. Since commercial success requires the manufacturing and marketing resources of an enterprise, the rewards of innovation can be captured only by enterprises, not by individuals with ideas. The individual inventor has sometimes founded an enterprise or, more often, obtained a share in an enterprise or its rewards by agreement with other members of the enterprise, and in some instances individuals with ideas have obtained rewards through patents. But in an institutional sense what the West rewards is innovation, not the idea, and in consequence the payees are as a rule enterprises, not individuals with ideas.

The size of the rewards depends primarily on the commercial success of the innovation and on the commercial skills of the enterprise in extracting returns from commercial success. An innovator's monopoly will be more quickly eroded by rivals if the innovation is easily imitated than if it is difficult to imitate, and the rewards will be smaller. Factors irrelevant to the size of the reward include the intellectual merit of the innovation, the diligence of the innovators, the amount of money spent on it, and the degree of risk incurred in undertaking it—except as they may influence commercial success or ease of imitation. In the West, the rewards are not subject to offset for the losses sustained by those injured by an innovation, such as workers whose skills are made obsolescent or capitalists whose investment in superseded enterprises becomes worthless.

The size of the market is evidently an important determinant of the magnitude of the potential rewards of innovation. The uniquely large American market of the late nineteenth and early twentieth centuries offered the innovator much greater potential returns than, say, a medieval market limited to a single city and its surrounding countryside. The comparative technological conservatism of European industry at that time reflected, probably correctly given the smaller size of European markets, the smaller size of the potential rewards for innovation. Since then, the relaxation of political barriers to trade and advances in transportation and communication have tended to increase the potential rewards of innovation, without a proportional increase in the costs and risks, both in Europe and in the United States.

3. Diversity of Research Organizations

The organization of the scientific side of Western innovation has taken the form of a proliferation of research laboratories widely different in size, sponsorship, goals, personnel, and facilities. Several factors have contributed to this diversity of organization.

One factor has been a natural reluctance on the part of innovating enterprises to rely on external research facilities, especially facilities with a conflict of interest between preserving the status quo and changing it; openness to new enterprises is openness to new laboratories. Another factor is the focus on the needs of small groups of consumers, which has extended the search for the rewards of innovation into a multitude of nooks and crannies of the economy. A third factor has been the variety inherent in technology itself, as well as the inherent variety of scientists.

The West has interposed few ideological obstacles to this proliferation of research agencies. The lack of ideology may be illustrated by the lack of opposition to government ownership of research and development facilities. As long ago as the first years of the nineteenth century, when the Du Pont family established its powder mill in Delaware, it drew on the French royal powder factories for manufacturing information. Later, American government arsenals, particularly those at Watertown, Springfield, and Harper's Ferry, pioneered in the development of precision methods of manufacture of interchangeable parts. The twentieth-century expansion of government research facilities is only partly chargeable to national defense. To take but three examples, the long-standing work of the National Bureau of Standards, the National Institutes of Health, and state agricultural experiment stations has been both valuable and peaceful.

Within industry, laboratories differ widely in function (from comparatively routine testing to work overlapping pure science), in size, and in the scope of the scientific disciplines represented in them. Some are owned by industrial corporations; some are separate, independent businesses. A number of these different ways of organizing innovation and linking science and industry have met the test of economic survival. Their variety parallels the variety of the needs of those who finance them and who are unwilling to rely on some larger, more distant, consolidated facility to meet those needs. The elements of this capitalist research network both cooperate and compete with each other, within and between universities as much as within and between rival corporations or rival government agencies.

Innovation is itself a form of revolt against convention, and it may be assumed that innovators are more individualistic than most other people. If so, the variety of organizations for research and development in the West may reflect a degree of individualism that may not have been duplicated, or that may have been suppressed more effectively, in China or Islam. Even in feudal Europe, or perhaps because Europe was feudal rather than fully centralized, there existed people who were more ambitious and more willing to take risks than most others—including the serfs who fled the manors for the freedom of the towns; the merchants and mariners who undertook long and perilous trading voyages; the devout who dared the pilgrimages, armed or unarmed, to Palestine or shrines closer by; and even the scholars who devised theological doctrines that skirted the limits of Catholic tolerance. The breakdown and diffusion of political and religious authority in postfeudal Europe widened the range of activities over which this minority could expend its energies, and beginning in the fifteenth or sixteenth century there followed what some have viewed as an attack of human hyperactivity—scientific, literary, musical, dramatic, military, political, and commercial—from which the West has never wholly recovered. Innovators must be, by self-selection, more willing to take risks than the average individual, more given to dissent from the status quo, more willing to upset applecarts. They are therefore more likely to flourish in a society that either fails to inculcate a complete respect for authority or that offers a number of competing authorities to its members. Individuality has found expression not simply in Western innovation, but in the multiplicity of ways the West went about the work of innovation.

Historians often like to revel in the diversity of the past and the inability of simple models or monocausal explanations to capture the past. The point worth making here, with respect to the emergence of the industrial research laboratory and its industrial technology, is a different one. The origins and forms of industrial research in the United States *were* diverse. What seems to have been most significant in the American experience was precisely the institutional flexibility that ensued. There was no attempt to pursue a single model. Rather, laboratories arose in a variety of ways and took a variety of forms. That is precisely what was needed—a flexibility that allowed the special requirements of different sectors to shape institutions according to their own special needs.

Technological Growth as a Cause of Economic Growth

There is a long-standing controversy about the sources of innovation. Some believe that technological advance is predominantly a fortuitous spin-off from that branch of scientific research which is guided only by a desire to add to knowledge. Others believe that technological advance is a systematic response to human needs, mediated through economic markets that promise large rewards for successful innovation.[10] Some historians have viewed Western technology as a natural response to the development of needs and opportunities arising primarily from the decline of feudal authority, the rise of a merchant and capitalist class, and the expansion of trade.

We have emphasized the long persistence of a geometric expansion in economic output as the most puzzling aspect of the West's rise to wealth. The growth of Western technology has roughly paralleled economic growth, persisting over an equally long time in what, to observers outside science, seems a similarly geometric expansion. Unlike most forms of geometric expansion, there is no reason to believe that the expansion of knowledge has any inherent limits, so that the growth of technology is especially appealing as an explanation of the persistence of Western economic growth. This persistence cannot very well be attributed to a strengthening, in the twentieth century, of such capitalist institutions as the autonomy of the economic sector, freedom of trade, or property rights, for the trend has been in the other direction. The case for a causal relation between technology and economic growth has thus been strengthened by the events of the latter half of the twentieth century, but this does not necessarily resolve the question for earlier periods of growth, nor does it tell us which is cause and which is effect.

The West has clearly benefited from a broad class of technological achievements that virtually created their own economic opportunities, their own industries, and even their customers' awareness of their own needs. These achievements normally began as relatively crude devices that, in their original form, had no more than moderate economic utility, but that demonstrated the feasibility of an idea and served both as a starting point and as a stimulus for a long process of further technical development. The beginning is, typically, a marked discontinuity in technological development, while the later development flows more smoothly and can more plausibly be interpreted as a response to economic or social needs.

Thus, Western oceangoing transport, whose consequences include the discovery of America, can be traced to the full-rigged, carvel-built ship that originated in the fifteenth century. These first Western oceangoing ships were the more remarkable, as a technological discontinuity, because their builders used materials and components most of which had been available for more than fifteen hundred years, without having been put to similarly good use. But these first ships were only the beginning of a long process. They were no more efficient, perhaps even less efficient, than the Chinese junks of the time. But while Chinese junks changed little from the twelfth century to the nineteenth, Western ships developed from Columbus's late-fifteenth-century carracks to the Spanish galleons of the sixteenth century and the East Indiamen of the eighteenth. The whole course of development both stimulated oceangoing trade and was stimulated by it. Even in the nineteenth century, the Western oceangoing ship entered upon a new phase of development, based on the application to shipping of Watts's late-eighteenth-century invention of an efficient steam engine and the nineteenth-century development of cheap wrought iron and steel.

A generally similar pattern—an initially rudimentary device, then a long period of development, often extended into a period of extensive borrowing of components and materials from other technologies—characterized such other achievements, vital to Western economic growth, as the development of the steam engine and powered textile machinery, beginning in the eighteenth century; advances in land transportation (the railroad) and iron and steelmaking (beginning with the Bessemer converter) in the nineteenth century; and the twentieth-century development of antibiotics, synthetic materials, air and highway transportation, communications, and computers. In short, major innovations typically consist of an initial development that sets up a causal loop in which the initial commercial success stimulates further development, which in turn stimulates further commercial success—and so on. Alternatively put, truly major innovations provide the framework for much subsequent innovative activity.

Much of Western technology lies in the loop, requiring only patient technical work that can be readily accomplished when an economic need for it arises and that can therefore be regarded as a consequence of economic needs. However, routine technical work is routine only because it is an application of an existing body of knowledge, and the origins of existing knowledge are rarely routine. Agricultural technology tended to be evolutionary, for in an old industry one does not find many of the discontinuities that create new industries. But much agricultural technology appeared of routine origin only because it was part of a causal loop originally set up outside agriculture. For example, the introduction of mechanical power to agriculture was a comparatively obvious application of the far from obvious steam engine. Later, the combination of the internal-combustion engine with a proliferation of agricultural machinery was relatively straightforward, but it rested on far less straightforward nineteenth-century advances in producing and working iron and steel.

The major technological advances initiated economic opportunities that were themselves causes of capital formation and expansion of trade. The economic consequences followed rapidly and in the normal course of economic activity, giving every appearance of being routine consequences of the technological achievements. The major inventions, on the other hand, were far from routine. Retrospectively, they could always be located in a more or less continuous stream of technological development, but prospectively most of them occurred at irregular intervals—their exact nature, place of occurrence, and timing unpredictable—and, even with the advantage of hindsight, not easily explicable.

If there is a persuasive case for holding that Western technology was the lever that moved Western economies upward, there is an equally strong case for holding that some familiar Western institutions supplied the fulcrum. Economic growth results from innovation—the introduction of new products, processes, and services—and while technology is vitally important to innovation, it is not the sole responsible agent. The long growth in scientific and technical knowledge could not have been transformed into continuing economic growth had Western society not enjoyed a social consensus that favored the everyday use of the products of innovation. Also, the West allowed innovators a degree of freedom from political and religious interference that was unusual among major societies, if not unique. The practical power to innovate was widely diffused—a diffusion made possible by another Western economic institution: the freedom to form new enterprises and change old ones, in whatever sizes and shapes seem best adapted to the task at hand. And it was through its markets, which many economists regard as its most basic economic institution, that the West conferred great rewards on those who innovated successfully and penalized those who did not.

The Link between Science and Wealth

How to Hinder Innovation

Western technology developed in the special context of a high degree of autonomy among the political, religious, scientific, and economic spheres of social life. Is this high degree of autonomy indispensable to the successful application of technology to economic welfare?

Few Western scientists would disagree with the proposition that a high degree of autonomy of the scientific sphere from political or religious control is essential to scientific advance. It is almost as clear that a similar autonomy, in much the same degree, is essential to the economic process of translating scientific advances into goods and services.

The technological capability of a society is bound to be degraded if control of either scientific inquiry or innovation is located at points of political or religious authority that combine an interest in controlling the outcome of technological development with the power to restrict or direct experiment. In all well-ordered societies, political authority is dedicated to stability, security, and the status quo. It is thus singularly ill-qualified to direct or channel activity intended to produce instability, insecurity, and change.

We often underestimate how drastic change stemming from novel technology can be, because it occurs slowly and is not an immediate and obvious consequence of readily identifiable inventions. It is too easy to forget that not much more than a century ago, the average European was an illiterate villager who never went beyond walking distance from the village, from birth to death, and who had little idea of what was happening outside it. It was not the power of an idea that urbanized and educated the Western masses and put them in touch with the whole world, but the proliferation, within the economic sphere, of innovations in transportation, communication, and production that enabled, and indeed compelled, the Western masses to exchange the darkness of village life for the lights of the city.

The first condition of this proliferation, as in basic science, was that the innovations did not require the assent of governmental or religious authorities. The division of political authority among a number of national states may well have been at the heart of this failure of authority to prevent innovation. Innovations were of course opposed, both informally and legislatively. Labor-saving machinery was sabotaged, early factories were burned, English legislation required someone with a red flag to walk ahead of the early automobiles. But though the English legislated against automobiles, the French, the Germans, and the Americans did not, and the automobile revolution was not contained, even in England.

In recent years, the degree to which a society may hope to control innovation has become a subject of controversy in both the United States and the Soviet Union. The potentialities for control may be greater than they once were, partly because the safety valve that immigration used to offer to scientists harassed by political authorities is no longer as open as it was for Steinmetz or Einstein, and partly because the possibility of catastrophic accident in some types of scientific research and high-technology production generates more widespread political concern than it once did. Still, so long as the world is politically divided, prudent planners will assume that, while attempts to control innovation may delay it, the attempts will not ultimately succeed. Bottles will continue to be uncorked, the genies can never be put back, and the polities that take the uncorking in stride will prosper at the expense of those that try to prevent it.

Conclusions and Conjectures

Growth is a form of change. Change implies innovation; and the Western system of innovation has depended upon wide diffusion of the power to undertake and use innovations, coupled with ample rewards for success and penalties for failure. Innovation and change imply also insecurity and risk, for few changes fail to affect some people adversely. Indeed, the Western system of innovation has made use of the adversities of change to penalize those who fail to keep abreast of their times.

Innovation in the economic sphere was successful for reasons similar to the reasons for its success in basic science. As the growth of markets increased the rewards for economic innovation, it came to be conducted on a very large scale, as an explicit or implicit goal of a great many enterprises. Its incentives were measured in money rather than honors or personal satisfaction, but they supplied the needed motivation. The laboratories in which innovative industrial technology was developed were tailored to the diversity of circumstances which brought them forth.

Because commercial innovation is inherently a cooperative undertaking of specialists in technology, manufacture, and marketing, much of it was conducted in organizations with a management hierarchy. But hierarchical control of industrial technology was never pyramided anywhere near all the way to the top in any Western economy, as it is in the Soviet Union. Their diversity helps accommodate the prickly individualism of those upon whose professional skills their success depends. And it has another use. Industrial laboratories are part of the network of decision centers on which Western economies rely to evaluate proposals for innovation, and their diversity is one source of assurance that the evaluations reflect multiple viewpoints and are not merely multiple carbon copies of a single viewpoint.

We have, in this chapter, considered the Western system of decentralized economic organization in the context of technology and innovation. It is evident that there is no way to imitate the Western organization of innovation without also imitating the Western decentralization of enterprise, with the authority to make economic decisions diffused into a multitude of enterprises of diverse size, ownership, internal structure, objectives, and situs. For enterprises to realize the rewards and suffer the penalties that go with the selection of programs of innovation, they have to be responsible for selecting their markets, determining the prices at which they will buy and sell and the wages at which they will hire, hiring and dismissing their employees, and investing capital. They have to keep the benefit of their rewards and bear the burden of their losses.

These are difficult conclusions for Eastern European and the majority of Third World countries, whose modes of economic organization allow little autonomy to the economic sphere and which pyramid the hierarchies of economic organizations all the way to the top. To internalize the Western processes of growth in technology and economic output, these countries would have to extend a high degree of autonomy to existing enterprise units and permit the formation of new ones. This remains true, even allowing for the possibility that the successful transfer of technology may require conditions rather different from those that generated the technology in the first place. A relinquishment of power by entrenched hierarchies may seem too much to expect, at least so long as they can persuade themselves that they have a viable alternative road to wealth. But whether they would be relinquishing or gaining power is a matter of perception, for there can be little doubt that the nineteenth- and twentieth-century Western political hierarchies that refrained from exercising authority over their economies thereby added enormously to their own wealth and political power.

NOTES

1. Daniel Boorstin, "The Social Inventor: Inventing the Market," chap. 56 in his *The Americans: The Democratic Experience* (New York: Vintage Books, 1974), pp. 538–39.

2. H. Livesay, *Andrew Carnegie* (Boston: Little, Brown and Company, 1975), p. 114.

3.

The major constituents—tricalcic silicate, dicalcic silicate, and tricalcic aluminate—which impart to Portland cement its valuable cementing properties, were determined as the result of extensive research, involving the preparation and study of all compounds formed when lime, alumina, and silica are fused together in various proportions.

G. A. Rankin, "Portland Cement," chap. 15, in H. E. Howe, ed., *Chemistry in Industry* (New York: Chemical Foundation, 1925), vol. 2, p. 271.

4. David Mowery, "The Emergence and Growth of Industrial Research in American Manufacturing, 1899–1945," Ph.D. diss., Stanford University, 1981, p. 51.

5. Boorstin, *The Americans*, p. 529.

6. Ibid., pp. 533–35.

7. For a concise account of the German development, see J. J. Beer, *The Emergence of the German Dye Industry* (Urbana: University of Illinois Press, 1959).

8. Boorstin, *The Americans*, pp. 540–42.

9. The discovery arose out of an effort to survey sources of radio interference with satellite communication systems. A receiver developed for this purpose was applied to "a rather prosaic survey of radio sources that lie outside the plane of our own galaxy." James S. Trefil, *The Moment of Creation* (New York: Charles Scribner's Sons, 1983), p. 16. "Penzias and Wilson . . . found that there was an inexplicably large level of 'noise' on their readings, equivalent to static on your radio or snow on your television screen. They spent a great deal of time trying to get rid of this signal, because they believed it came from the instrument and not from the sky . . . [N]o matter how many extraneous effects were removed, the unexpected signal persisted . . ." Ibid. Eventually, it was concluded that their noise was the residual radiation left over from the Big Bang. For another popular account of the discovery, see Joseph Silk, *The Big Bang* (San Francisco: W. H. Freeman & Company, 1980), pp. 75–77.

10. See Nathan Rosenberg, "How Exogenous Is Science?" chap. 7, in Nathan Rosenberg, *Inside the Black Box* (Cambridge: Cambridge University Press, 1982).

9 / Diversity of Enterprise

Large publicly-held corporations in mass-production industries are the most conspicuous type of economic organization in the West. Some proponents of Western capitalism attribute its growth to these corporations, and critics of capitalism interpret their emergence as a reason for thinking that the period of capitalist growth is coming to an end. Socialists have at times perceived giant corporations as the last phase of capitalist evolution, facilitating the transfer of the means of production to the state. Both socialist and less-developed countries have often taken it for granted that to imitate Western economic growth is to organize their economies along the lines of the giant enterprise—only state-owned.

The large publicly-held corporation arrived on the scene too late to qualify as a fundamental explanation of Western economic growth. We saw, in the last three chapters, that Western economies had been growing with striking success for more than a century before the large industrial corporation emerged in the United States, and for even longer before it became prominent in Europe. Likewise, as a fundamental explanation of a decline in Western economic growth, the large corporation suffers from having been a prominent part of the American economic system for upward of sixty years before signs of a slowdown in growth appeared.

Undue emphasis on the role of large corporations in Western economies implicitly understates the role of smaller enterprises. Large enterprises are the predominant users of capital in Western systems, but smaller enterprises are the predominant employers of labor—a point often forgotten in countries with limited capital and massive unemployment. Large corporations have participated very little in agriculture, and yet advances in agricultural output were basic to urbanization and the increase of population in the West. Agriculture is only one of the sectors of Western economies in which the economies of large-scale organization seldom offset the agency costs. And much innovation in the West has succeeded by trying out new ideas in enterprises newly organized on an experimental scale, with little commitment to the status quo.

To bring both the historical record and contemporary data into a better balanced perspective, the point worth stressing is that Western systems have employed enterprise organizations of all types and sizes, depending on the nature of the economic mission for which the enterprise was organized. Many types and sizes of enterprise are useful under the right circumstances, but what we would emphasize is the *diversity* of economic organization in Western systems—the variety of the system's organizational repertoire rather than the size of particular enterprises. This diversity is a matter of tailoring organization to different kinds of economic activity, especially to innovation.

In the first three of the seven sections of this chapter, we explore some of the sources of diversity in Western industry, beginning, in the first section, with competition as a source of diversity in enterprise organization. Differentiation is central to the strategy of competition, and so it is not surprising to find that a competitive economic system produces enterprises differentiated in many ways, size among others.

In the second section, we discuss the role of new, usually small, enterprises in bringing about change—a role whose importance may well depend on the degree of inertia accumulated in older enterprise bureaucracies. An interesting point is the part new enterprises play in replacing jobs lost in declining enterprises.

Size is, of course, far from the only way to differentiate Western firms. This point is considered in the third section, a discussion of industries in which a few very large enterprises and a large number of smaller enterprises coexist. The differences in size are great enough to suggest that the large and smaller firms must be engaged in different activities, even though they are in the same industries.

The general view that Western economies have shaped enterprise size to enterprise mission is often challenged by those who insist that the size of Western enterprises is the result of merger manipulations of Western financiers. This controversy is discussed in the fourth section of the chapter, which deals with the comparative roles of mergers and competition in determining the size of enterprises. Our view is that financiers may frequently propose enterprise size, but—if one may judge from outcomes— competitive forces sooner or later dispose.

Diversity of Enterprise

In the fifth section, we consider enterprise size as a factor in the development of Western technology. Again, large size seems important to certain types of technological development and not to others. It can be argued that the most useful innovations are likely to produce one or more giant enterprises, simply because *useful* often means "widely used" and *widely used* may well mean "mass-produced." There are large enterprises in chemistry, electronics, drugs, and electrical products that have remained large over a long period of time by operating as systems for developing new products. There are other large firms that owe their size to a single innovation that occurred while the firm was still small.

It is probably inevitable that diversity and experiment in enterprise organization will produce some sectors where the factors that determine prices, profits, and wages appear monopolistic rather than competitive. In the sixth section, we review the long-standing controversies over this problem, primarily in the United States, and the question whether industries where most of the output originates in a few large firms are more like monopolies than multifirm industries. The evidence is complex, but at least in the United States it falls short of supporting claims that a society which allows freedom of enterprise organization necessarily pays a high price in monopoly. In recent years, the issue has become less cogent than the question of whether American giant enterprises will survive in competition with Japanese and West European firms and with firms in low-wage Third World countries.

In the closing section, we reiterate the point that in the United States, the original home of giant corporations, most people make their living in comparatively small enterprises. The Western strategy of growth has been to fit the enterprise to its mission, using entities ranging from giant corporations to self-employed individuals, depending on the task in hand. That small enterprises have played a large part is not accidental; it can be explained, at least in part, by their smaller agency costs and their special suitability to the experimental stage of innovation.

Competition and Variety

The competition that occurs in capitalist systems arises from rivalry among enterprises for scarce resources and for the patronage of buyers, unrestrained by controls on the entry of new firms or by a management

271

hierarchy extended above the level of the individual enterprise (as it is in the Soviet Union and other planned economies). The absence of higher authority capable of restraining inter-enterprise rivalries is a corollary of the relative autonomy of the economic sphere from political control.

It is characteristic of competition of all kinds (not business competition alone) that success is achieved by identifying the factors most important to winning and somehow differentiating oneself from competitors, favorably, on some of these factors, without suffering offsetting losses on other factors. Because the fundamental strategy of competition consists in each competitor's differentiating itself from its rivals, competition has been the principal source of diversity in the organization of Western enterprises. The types of differentiation that contribute specifically to economic growth and innovation are the development of unique products, methods of production and distribution, and forms of organization.

Competition, in the sense of purposefully competitive conduct among rival enterprises, is not emphasized in traditional economics, and only in the 1970s and '80s have scholars developed comparatively systematic formulations of the competitive strategies used by business firms.[1] These formulations have provided insights into the ways firms come to differ in size and other respects as a result of adopting different competitive strategies. This literature emphasizes the strategic importance of achieving costs lower than competitors' for any given level of product quality and service. The emphasis on costs is somewhat at variance with the common view that competition primarily involves price, quality, and service, or that the economically significant tactics of differentiation involve products and brand names. Lower costs are important because they give the enterprise that attains them a number of strategic options, ranging from cashing in its lower costs in the form of higher dividends, increasing its sales by reducing prices, improving quality or service, or increasing promotion in ways its competitors cannot afford to match.

Most ways of reducing costs can be used by firms of all shapes and sizes and so have little bearing on the diversity of enterprises. Three, however, have played a large part in differentiating firms one from another: economies of scale, specialization, and flow process management. To reduce costs by capturing economies of scale, a firm has to design its products and selling organization to serve a high-volume market. To reduce costs by specialization, firms tend to concentrate on a narrower market with a narrower product line. Economies of scale tend to go with large firm size, and specialization with smaller firm size. Which achieves the lower costs depends on the production and distribution technologies and customer requirements of the specific industry. It depends also on the rate of change in product and distribution technologies, since the maximum achievement of economies of scale tends to require freezing product designs and production methods and so sacrifices the ability to adapt to change. Also, consumers who are willing to pay higher prices for specialized variety, in preference to mass-produced sameness, may constitute a submarket in which the economical production of small quantities is more important than the economies of large-scale production.

Flow process management is typified by the integrated petroleum company invented by John D. Rockefeller in the 1880s. Petroleum is the largest industry where there are economies in common management of some or all of the stages of the production and distribution process from mine (or oil well) to consumer. The effect of combining several stages in one firm is to increase the size of the firm, whether measured by number of employees, assets, or value added.

The choice of strategies leads to firms that, while in the same general industry or market, differ in their size, in the products they make, in the customers they seek to serve, and in the functions they perform. Porter classifies firms into "strategic groups," a classification intermediate between the "industry" and the "firm."[2] In most large industries manufacturers can be classified among the following groups, though not always without overlap:

1 Contract manufacturers that do not sell under their own brand names.
2 Full-line manufacturers that do sell under their own brand names.
3 Manufacturers specializing in the requirements of a limited geographic area, or in products of a specific type or quality.

Contract or full-line manufacture tends to require large-scale manufacturing and to result in relatively large firm size. Specialization is more likely to produce smaller firms. Brand-name manufacturers usually gain in size by using some degree of forward integration, including a marketing and perhaps a service organization.

The tactical art of competing against rivals resides, almost by definition, in devising moves from which the firm can gain advantage without an offsetting loss to rival firms' imitative or retaliatory moves. Some aspects of the art, like the television promotion of consumer goods, are professional specialties in their own right. Of the many other competitive tactics available to rival enterprises, three are of special importance in the differentiation of firms: innovation, prediction, and pricing.

Changes in products and in methods of manufacturing and marketing can be particularly profitable forms of competition, because they can be initiated without the knowledge of rivals. After they become known, they may be imitated by rivals, but imitation takes time, and the change may confer a temporary advantage, perhaps the first in a long-continuing series. Sometimes rivals will judge the changes not worth imitating, or they may lack the resources to imitate, and the advantage may be long-lasting. In the 1920s, Alfred P. Sloan offered customers automobiles in a wider variety of models and colors, as well as annual model changes, and he strengthened General Motors' dealer network. These changes were not matched by Henry Ford, then the market leader, apparently because, without benefit of hindsight, Ford thought they were mistakes. Different degrees of success in innovation are probably the most important single source of differences in size among firms in the same strategic group.

Other differences in the success of firms originate in their skill in predicting the volume and product content of future sales. Given the inherent uncertainties of the future, different firms are likely to make different predictions. Some may end up with insufficient facilities to meet actual demand, and others will be burdened with excess facilities, in both cases with adverse effects on costs and profits. Those skilled or lucky enough to forecast correctly will have an advantage.

Price competition also has an effect on a firm's size. Firms that can produce at least cost can price their products at, or a little less than their competitors' costs as a way to expand sales indirectly—that is, by discouraging competitors from expanding and encouraging their ultimate departure from the industry. The fact that such prices are immediately imitated does not matter tactically, for they are meant to be imitated. Specialist firms also have a degree of pricing flexibility that helps explain their survival, because the direct effect of a change in a price or product by a specialist firm is limited to the firm's own segment of the market, and other specialized or full-line firms may not find it worth matching.

When we investigate the causal relations among competition, diversity of enterprises, and the growth of Western economies, several possibilities come to mind. In the West, different firms have had different motives and criteria for undertaking new developments. The point may be illustrated by Shockley's development of the semiconductor for the purpose of improving the reliability of the telephone plant. Bell Laboratories' interest in the improvement of semiconductors and in the exploration of their application to other uses was considerably more limited than that of the individuals who had worked on the development of the device, and before long independent semiconductor companies had arisen by spin-off of Bell personnel. The use of semiconductors was appreciably accelerated and broadened as a result of the ready formation of enterprises with different development criteria than Bell's. Other major developments, from the steam engine on, have been reshaped, speeded, and expanded by enterprises with different objectives, interests, and ideas from those of the original inventor. In the absence of interfirm differences in the criteria for financing innovation proposals, many innovations would not have occurred at all or would have been long delayed.

The natural world, as perceived through the lens of Western technology, contains a very wide variety of possibilities for the satisfaction of human needs and wants, and economic enterprises formed to explore these possibilities must almost inevitably differ in goals, functions, size, and other aspects of organization. Consider the relatively limited possibilities offered to Eskimo cultures by the natural world of the Arctic. The available sources of food, clothing, and most tools were fish and a few animals, and the forms of economic organization required for utilizing these narrowly limited resources were comparatively simple. In contrast, economic growth in the West has consisted in successfully widening the range of search, both geographically and technologically, for new possibilities of meeting human needs. If the economic entities that search out and utilize these new possibilities are aptly adapted to their missions, they will be as various as the missions. Had Western enterprises been restricted by fixed rule to uniform black box firms, each enterprise would have been less well adapted to its mission, and growth would have been slower, though how much slower it is quite impossible to guess. At the extreme, it is unlikely that Western growth would have occurred at all had the forms of enterprise organization been restricted, as they were among the Eskimos, to family and tribal cooperation.

The diversity of the forms of Western enterprise organization are closely related, both as cause and as consequence, to diversity of Western products and services available to consumers. This diversity is linked to the system of incentives that drives Western economies. Observers who have compared the very limited variety of products available in East European economies to the much more extensive variety available in the West find the difference profoundly impressive—a difference between a gray world of monotony and a brighter world of wide-ranging choices and prospects. The differences affect the rewards and incentives for work, which are not measured so much by cash paid as by what can be bought with that cash. Marked differences in the variety of available products bring about a qualitative, rather than a merely quantitative, difference in these basic rewards and incentives.

To put the point another way, *wealth* can be defined as a wide range of choice of what to buy. The individual perceives growth in wealth as a widening of his or her range of choice. The extension of choice cannot be purely quantitative, because, by ordinary notions of marginal utility, too much of a good thing speedily loses its value. The extension has to be qualitative as well. In this sense, economic growth is in part a growth in the qualitative range of the consumer's choice, and it would be a weaker incentive if it were growth only in the quantity of available goods. The diversity generated by competition is itself an aspect of the West's wealth.

One last, seldom-praised function of competition in economic growth, is that it eliminates obsolete forms of economic activity, clearing away the underbrush or, if one prefers, burying the economically dead. This function is not to be taken for granted: consider the difficulty experienced by the political sphere in getting rid of programs that are obsolete or that have simply failed.

The Role of New, and Small, Enterprises in Change

Economies growing at the rate to which the West has become accustomed duplicate themselves every quarter-century, give or take five years. Because change is continuously producing obsolescence in older lines of business, the new economic activity required to achieve a net duplication considerably exceeds the activity being duplicated. This new activity arises in part from the expansion of some older enterprises (others are static or die), in part from the conversion of old enterprises to new lines of activity, and in part from the formation of new enterprises.

While all three sources of new activity are important, the formation of new enterprises plays a particularly important part in growth by innovation. New enterprises are useful devices for experimenting with innovation, because they can be established on a small, experimental scale at relatively low cost and therefore in large numbers, and their efforts can be intensely focused on a single target. The experimental aspect of new enterprises is reflected in the facts that they usually start small, their number is large, and, as with other kinds of experiment, most of them fail. But those that succeeded have been an important source of Western innovation, and the amount of growth attributable directly to new enterprises is large in its own right.

The easy formation of new enterprises also acts as a disciplinary device for older enterprises. The same human forces that produce bureaucratic rigidities in mature government agencies are also at work in mature economic enterprises, in both cases opposing the forces that produce change and growth. But in Western economic sectors the forces of change can express themselves in the formation of new enterprises, thereby circumventing bureaucratic rigidity and supplying older enterprises with an incentive—self-preservation—for taking internal measures to avoid the habits and practices that eventually lead to rigidity.

The practice of forming new enterprises for novel ventures is no doubt as old as the prudent merchant's desire to limit the amount at risk on unfamiliar transactions. In the West, a prominent feature of the Industrial Revolution was the formation of new enterprises to establish factories, almost always initially small. It was their growth in numbers and size that displaced artisan manufacturing and greatly increased the total production of goods. The diffusion of the Industrial Revolution from England to the Continent, to the United States, and eventually to Japan and other countries was effected far more by the formation of new enterprises than by the establishment of branches of old enterprises. The decay of the American trust movement of the 1880s and 1890s was attributable partly, and probably principally, to the inability of the trusts to check the formation of new enterprises. New enterprises, specializing in new technologies, were instrumental in the introduction of electricity, the internal-combustion engine, automobiles, aircraft, electronics, aluminum, petroleum, plastic materials, and many other advances. This is not to say that older companies played no part; on the contrary, some of them kept abreast of the times very well indeed. It is to say that the part played by new enterprise formation was indispensable to the total result, both directly and because of its effect on incentives in older companies.

Some economists and publicists have stressed the importance of large enterprises in Western economies to the point of arguing that the giants are all that matters in the modern West. Such arguments greatly understate the importance of smaller enterprises in a modern Western economy. The mistake is endemic among Marxists who see monopoly capitalism as a stage of development leading to nationalization of the monopolies and so to monopoly socialism. The effects of the mistake have been tragic, insofar as it has misled socialist and Third World countries into seeking growth by imitating the largest mature Western enterprises rather than by imitating the Western practice of growth through experiment with a wide variety of initially small enterprises. It is a mistake of a type that, ironically, Marx often attributed to his critics—a failure to distinguish being from process.

One can get a fair indication of the part played by new and small enterprises in growth processes from the number of jobs lost and created in firms in different age and size classes. In the West, economic growth has tended to arise from improvements in the efficiency of older industries or from the displacement of old industries by new industries. Either way, growth has often required a shift of employees from old to new industries. In any given region, employment declines in declining businesses and expands in expanding businesses. In the United States, the rate of job shrinkage, as a percentage of total employment, varies among regions. David Birch gives an annual rate of 8 percent as typical.[3] By analogy to population statistics, this may be called the job death rate. The job death rate is a rough measure of the speed with which an economy is moving away from its past and toward its future.

In the 1970s, the job birth rate reflected the post-World War II baby boom and the shift of women from domestic to paid employment. The net increase in jobs was approximately 1.8 million annually, but the total number of new jobs required to offset job deaths and produce this net increase must have been in the neighborhood of eight or nine million.

New jobs can be created either by the expansion of existing firms or by the formation of new firms. Between 1954 and 1970, the *Fortune* 500, which is composed of industrial firms as distinguished from retail, wholesale, financial, transportation, and service firms, approximately doubled their employment. During the 1970s, their expansion of employment changed to contraction, and Birch estimates their present employment at 1.2 million less than it was ten years ago.[4] The change may be explained by normal improvements in productivity in combination with the absence of a corresponding rise in the demand for industrial products—an absence attributable to increased consumption of nonindustrial products, mainly medical care and education.[5]

Birch's study of the years 1979 to 1980 indicates that the formation of new firms was crucial in keeping the birth rate above the death rate. The existing firms that expanded employment did not keep ahead of contractions by other existing firms. The formation of new firms was essential.[6] Approximately three-quarters of the new jobs were in business establishments (whether independent or branches of larger enterprises) that were less than four years old.

Birch finds that a disproportionately high percentage of new job creation occurs in small firms. Whether one interprets this finding as indicating that small enterprise size per se is favorable to the growth of employment, or as a statistical reflection of the tendency of new firms to start small in what appear to be fast-growing industries, it argues strongly against development strategies that ignore, or even discourage, the formation of small enterprises. It argues equally against attempts to understand capitalist systems solely in terms of their largest enterprises.

Diversity of Size in the Same Industry

One of the more striking instances of the diversity of enterprise organization is the coexistence of firms of greatly different size and function within the same Census industries. The important point about size differences is that they reflect other, less easily measured differences in the structure and function of firms. For example, the very largest manufacturing corporations, as measured by assets, size, and sales, are in the petroleum and automobile manufacturing industries. Yet the Bureau of the Census reported that, in 1972, there were 152 companies in petroleum refining, 165 companies in motor vehicles and car bodies, 1,748 in motor vehicle parts and accessories, and 788 in automotive stampings. There were 245 companies in the classification, blast furnaces and steel mills. The same pattern occurred in the electrical and chemical industries,[7] though the numbers are less striking because they are divided among several product classifications.[8]

Since the capital assets of these industries are heavily concentrated in the very largest firms, it is apparent that the smaller firms are engaged in activities that must differ appreciably from those of the larger firms. The smaller enterprises apparently require less capital, and their operations do not involve economies of scale worth the costs of large-scale organization. In the American automobile industry, for instance, there are four very large corporations that design, assemble, and market complete passenger automobiles. But the formidable sales statistics of these firms reflect their purchase of a large volume of parts and materials fabricated by other firms. Many makers of repair parts and accessories also function independently of the central design-assembly-marketing firms. And there are many makers of specialized vehicles, such as campers, limousines, hearses, and so forth, who use chassis supplied by one of the Big Four.

In short, each industry with large firms tends to have niches for smaller firms, the result of the grouping of the industry into contract, brand-name, and specialized manufacturers along the lines described earlier in the chapter. Conceivably these smaller firms might owe their existence to some weakness on the part of the giants—laziness, oversight, timidity, or incompetence—but it is more likely that they have found specific functions they can perform at a profit at a price lower than the giants can profitably meet.

Some economists have developed theories of industrial organization that offer generalized explanations of how this mutual coexistence could happen. For example, Oliver Williamson has approached the question of organization as a matter of choice between market and hierarchical modes of organization.[9] Suppose one takes as primitive the division of labor by direct exchange among specialized workers, which can hardly be improved upon under the conditions of perfect competition. Then one needs to explain why command, through hierarchies, sometimes supersedes exchange. Williamson looks for explanations in transaction costs and in limits on the amount and reliability of information available to traders. One must take into account also the agency costs associated with the shift from markets to hierarchical organization. Williamson suggests that it will not pay a large firm to incur the administrative costs of any given production activity, in preference to buying it from outside suppliers, unless it has no other way of assuring itself that the outside market is functioning competitively. The outcome is that the companies that market final products make extensive use of independent suppliers, fabricators, and assemblers.

The cost of acquiring information and conducting a multiplicity of transactions explains why consumers buy complex products, like automobiles and television sets, from one enterprise rather than in multiple purchases from their designers, fabricators, and assemblers. The hierarchical enterprise serves much the same function as a general contractor in the construction of a house; the owner of the house *can* do the work of the general contractor, but usually at greater cost. Given the nearly infinite variety of degrees of difficulty of access to information and the variations in the costs of negotiating and coordinating a multiplicity of transactions, it is not surprising that the corresponding degrees of resort to hierarchical modes of organization differ widely from industry to industry and, within industries, from function to function: design, fabrication, parts, assembly, advertising, and wholesale and retail distribution. These are the differences that allow living space for a wide variety of specialized firms of various sizes, almost always small by comparison to the firms that package the industry's output for a mass market.

Mergers and Competition among Large Enterprises

There are several schools of thought about what forces determined the size of the American corporations that emerged between 1880 and 1914. One polar school emphasizes the role of promoters and financiers in creating large enterprises through trusts, holding companies, mergers, and consolidations. According to this school, the present structure of American industry is largely the handiwork of these turn-of-the-century "robber barons." The other polar school asserts that the technologies of production and distribution, together with developments in enterprise organization, had come to favor larger enterprises under the circumstances of some industries, and that the only lasting effect of the trust and merger movement was to identify those industries by practical experiment. This second school concedes that the experiments had short-term social costs in the form of welfare losses due to monopoly, but argues that these short-term losses were offset by the welfare gain resulting from the identification of industries in which large-scale production was economical. The number of intermediate positions is nearly as numerous as the students of the subject.

The general position that the size of enterprises depends on the nature of the processes of production and distribution that they undertake finds support in the massive and painstaking researches of John D. Glover, who explored a number of aspects of corporate size.[10] He divided American industry into fifty-four categories, not unlike the Department of Commerce Standard Industrial Classification. He then placed, in these categories, "large" corporations, which he defined as corporations with $250 million or more in assets (in 1971 dollars). He first classified the large corporations of 1929 and then the large corporations of 1971. The 1929 list nearly coincided with the list of the 200 largest corporations used by Berle and Means in *The Modern Corporation and Private Property*,[11] while the 1971 group numbered 559. In each category, he calculated:

1 The number of large corporations in the category, which he called their "occurrence."
2 The total assets held by large corporations in the category, or their "presence."
3 The average size of the large corporations in each category.
4 The percentage of all assets in each category held by large corporations, or their "relative presence."

It was then possible to arrange the fifty-four categories in order of occurrence, presence, average size, and relative presence of large corporations, according to the definitions just given.

If large corporations possessed appreciable economic power simply by virtue of being large, one would expect them to be distributed more or less evenly throughout the economic system. In fact, Glover found that 86.6 percent of the large corporations' assets in 1971 were concentrated in twenty of the fifty-four categories. The remaining 13.4 percent was distributed over thirty categories. In the remaining four categories, there were no large corporations.

Eleven industries were among the Top 20 by all four measures of the large firms' role in the industry:

- Electricity, gas, and sanitary services.
- Petroleum.
- Telephone and telegraph services.
- Motor vehicles.
- Rail transportation.
- Chemicals.
- General merchandise.
- Iron and steel.
- Office and computing equipment.
- Radio communication equipment and electronic supplies.
- Air transportation.

In 1971, these eleven industries accounted for 71.4 percent of all the assets of large corporations. Another 10.7 percent was accounted for by six additional industries which were in the Top 20 by three of the four measurements: nonferrous metals; lumber and paper products; aircraft; pharmaceuticals; rubber and tires; and tobacco. Most of these categories employ some production systems that cost more than $250 million each, so that enterprises that administer them are necessarily "large" by the standard Glover used.

Glover's comparisons of 1929 with 1971 are interesting evidence of the extent to which the role of large corporations is determined by their managers and the extent to which that role is a response to larger economic forces. One might suppose that if economic power means anything, it means the ability to survive and to protect one's turf from interlopers. Applying this test of economic power, one finds forty-three railroads on the list of the two hundred largest corporations of 1929; by 1971, only thirteen survived as large corporations. Of 21 large corporations in railroad transportation in 1971, 8 were newcomers, not yet on the list of large corporations in 1929. Another eight of the two hundred largest in

1929 were transit companies; they had disappeared, via bankruptcy, into municipal ownership by 1971.

Aside from railroads, utilities, and transit companies, there were 102 large American corporations in 1929; and of these twenty-two did not survive until 1971. However the economic power of the top two hundred may be specified, it was not sufficient to protect their turf, for an influx of newcomers after 1929 displaced many of the old large corporations and brought the total number to 559 by 1971. This was the period of a major shift in the American economy, away from railroads and utilities and toward automobiles, trucks, and petroleum—a shift the railroads tried to discourage, but without success.

This comparison between 1929 and 1971 bears in another way on the evaluation of the link between merger movements and structure of industry. The composition of the economy changes over time, so that a generalization about the effect of mergers on the structure of industries that existed in 1900 cannot safely be applied to the industries of 1929, 1971, or 1985. The computer industry did not exist in 1929 and IBM, its leading firm, had no history of significant mergers until the 1980s. The aircraft industry, the pharmaceutical industry, and the medical care industry in its present form, all developed after 1914.

Even in industries that existed around the turn of the century, time has greatly changed the structures left by the merger movement. General Motors, the leading firm in the auto industry, was formed by a merger of companies which, at the time, had an 11 percent share of a market dominated by Ford. It is quite clear from Chandler's history of Ford and General Motors that mergers played no real part in the results of their continuing rivalry.[12] The modern petroleum industry resembles Rockefeller's business of supplying kerosene from tank wagons in little more than name. The Du Pont of the turn-of-the-century mergers was a gunpowder manufacturer; it has, however, made many acquisitions in the course of becoming a diversified chemical company. The two early electrical companies, General Electric and Westinghouse, still supply a large part of the market for electrical generation and distribution equipment; but both draw the greater part of their revenues from businesses they were not in, mainly because they did not exist, in 1900.

The largest U.S. nonfinancial corporation of 1929, as measured by assets, was United States Steel, with assets of $7,012.6 million. (All of the 1929 figures in this paragraph have been corrected to allow for inflation between 1929 and 1971.) By 1971, its assets had declined to $6,408.6 million. On the other hand, the largest petroleum company of 1929 was Standard Oil of New Jersey, with assets of $5,421.2 million. By 1971, its assets had risen more than three times, to $20,315.2 million. A similar increase in assets occurred among the largest auto companies. General Motors' assets rose from $4,294.5 million in 1929 to $18,241.9 million in 1971; Ford's, from $2,334.4 to $10,509.8 million; and Chrysler's from $643.3 million to $4,999.7 million. Another example of the effect of the change in the structure of the American economy is the category, "Office, computing, and accounting machines." This category had no firms among the "large" corporations of 1929, but by 1971 it had seven, with total assets of nearly $20 billion.[13]

Glover viewed the economy as much like an ecosystem in which enterprises, as the price of survival, adapt and interact with changing technologies, shifts in consumer taste and life-styles, and changes in the structure of society. After the Civil War, the United States became principally an urban economy. To support an urban economy, it had to create basic systems for:

- The production of raw materials for urban industry.
- The transportation to the urban centers of food and raw materials.
- The transportation of their manufactured output from and among the urban centers.
- The development of a communications network for commercial transactions among cities.
- The development within the cities of power, lighting, sanitation, and transit systems.

More difficult still, each city had to develop a complex of internal industries and markets to support its population and give it the means of maintaining an even balance of trade with the rest of the world. The urbanization of the United States between 1880 and 1930 required a massive, infinitely complicated reconstruction of the economic system. The reshaping of the economic system made urbanization possible; but it also was compelled by urbanization. Both processes were facilitated by advances in technology; and again the advances in technology were stimulated by the needs of urbanization and the restructuring of the economy.

Glover put to rest the more extreme forms of the claim that the present structure of American industry is a historical product of mere merger manipulation by the financiers and promoters of the era from 1880 to 1914. Both the upper and lower limits of firm size evidently vary from industry to industry, depending on the nature of the processes of production and distribution. While these limits are undoubtedly real enough to cause severe losses to unwary entrepreneurs, there is no sure way to ascertain what they are except by experiment. The uncertainty is in part due to the limits of present-day organization science. But it is also in part intrinsic because any present estimate of the right enterprise size that will produce the maximum future stream of profits for an enterprise depends entirely on the future—that is, on future patterns of distribution and consumption, future moves by rival firms, future technology, and future politics. On any given date, an industry will have a largest firm and a smallest firm, and one may infer that the sizes of these two firms and the sizes between have recently been compatible with enterprise survival. But only experiment can determine whether enterprises of a size larger or smaller than the existing extremes might also survive. Some of the experiments are undertaken as byproducts of the pursuit of growth as an enterprise objective; others are undertaken deliberately, by way of acquisitions or mergers, to increase the size of the enterprise; and some are spin-offs undertaken to reduce the size of an enterprise.

Before we leave the subject of mergers as a determinant of the size of enterprises, we should add a word about merger movements after 1900. The long history of American antitrust legislation has been intertwined with extensive economic studies of mergers.[14] One of the findings of these studies has been that mergers occur in cycles. A rise in the number of mergers accompanies an expansion of business activity and a fall in their number accompanies a general business contraction.[15] What has been learned from these later merger movements may shed some light on the probable sources of the earlier, turn-of-the-century mergers.

The simplest explanation of the cyclical nature of merger activity is that there exists a market for firms. The supply of firms of any given size comes in part from the stock of existing firms and in part from the formation of new firms. During periods of economic expansion, the number of firms bought and sold increases because buyers have both the money and the inclination to pay higher prices, and the higher prices draw more sellers into the market.[16] Thus the merger wave of 1899 to 1900 in the United States was paralleled by similar, though less extensive, merger waves in England and Germany.[17] In England particularly, mergers were not only fewer, but also concentrated in fewer industries.[18] The tendency of transactions to peak during periods of expansion is analogous to what occurs in the housing market, where an increase in the sales of existing houses regularly accompanies economic expansion.

A related fact is that merger waves are virtually never accompanied or followed by a reduction in the number of enterprises, either in total or in the various size classes for which we have statistics. The reason is that during periods of economic expansion, both the formation of new firms and the growth of older firms into larger size classes increases the number of firms more than mergers diminish that number. The literature contains many references to the "disappearance" of firms through merger. Taken alone, these disappearances might well arouse concern. But the individual firm disappearances in major merger waves occur as part of a process of economic expansion which increases the total number of enterprises. In the United States, for example, the number of business enterprises increased from 1,209,000, in 1895, to 1,617,000, in 1913, a net increase of 408,000 concerns during the period when Tilly noted 3,964 "disappearances."[19] During economic contractions, there are few mergers, and their effect on changes in the number of firms is again minor compared to the effect of the contraction—its liquidations, bankruptcies, and a fall in the rate of formation of new firms.

The concept of a market for firms is helpful also in understanding another surprising phenomenon. In 1950 Congress passed the Celler-Kefauver Antimerger Act, prohibiting mergers which caused any substantial lessening of competition. As enforced, it eliminated all but negligibly small mergers between competing firms. To those who believed that the elimination of competition was the underlying reason for mergers, the merger wave of the late 1960s came as a surprise. The Antimerger Act redirected the market for firms away from sales to competing firms, but the Act had no discernible effect on the total number of mergers. The market seemingly reflects many reasons for buying and selling other than the elimination of competition.

The Size of Enterprises and Technology

Technology and large enterprises have a reciprocal causal relationship. The technology of mass production and economies of scale are almost always a causal factor in the survival of large enterprises other than conglomerates, and sometimes were a factor in their origin. Conversely, large enterprises have played a substantial part in the development of technology, though the nature of that part has been the subject of much debate. Some claim that large enterprises are too bureaucratic to do more than copy the work of more entrepreneurial individuals or inventors; others claim that virtually everything of any technological significance originates in the large laboratories of giant corporations.

Among economists, the most common method of trying to settle the issue is through comparative studies of research and development (R&D) expenditures, employment of technical personnel, and procurement of patents by corporations of different size classes. The results are inconclusive, for a mix of statistical and theoretical reasons.

Statistically, interindustry comparisons of R&D expenditures by large and small corporations suffer from the fact that such expenditures depend on the potentialities of the current technology. This potentiality varies from one industry to another, and it is likely to be greater in the early history of a technology than when it is nearing obsolescence. In industries where the potentiality is judged to be small, neither large nor small companies spend heavily on R&D. In industries where the perceived potentiality is great, both large and small corporations are more likely to spend heavily. Hence, the outcome of a statistical comparison may easily turn on the degree to which the samples of large and small companies, respectively, are biased toward industries in which the potentialities of R&D are great. The bias is not easily removed.

Even within the same industry, modern concepts of business strategy severely complicate comparisons between rates of R&D expenditure by large and small corporations. The percentage of sales revenue spent by a small specialist automobile manufacturer on R&D may exceed that of a mass manufacturer, simply because a strategy of serving a relatively small number of enthusiasts may require relatively more R&D than one of serving a large number of buyers with only average interest in the product. When two enterprises differ markedly in size and rate of R&D expenditure, they may also differ so much in business strategy and in economic function as not to be comparable.

The minimum inference to be drawn from the statistical studies is that enterprises of all sizes engage in R&D. The rates of expenditure by medium-size companies are somewhat higher than those of small companies and approximately equal to those of large. However, rates of expenditure do not tell the whole story. Some R&D is most efficiently conducted through programs that require expenditures that are large in an absolute sense, not simply as a percentage of sales. Such programs are more likely to be carried out in large enterprises than in small.

First, one would expect to find R&D projects that involve large financial risks, or that require extensive facilities, in the larger corporations. A project may require concurrent investigation of a number of alternative possibilities, the coordination of research work in different scientific disciplines, the coordination of design of a multiplicity of component parts, or the use of expensive test equipment. Technological advance would be hindered in some degree if an industry had no enterprises capable of undertaking such projects when they are suggested by the state of its technology. This is, however, a factor to be considered with caution. It is possible for competing companies to engage in joint development programs on a scale beyond the resources of a single company, although conflicts of interest among joint venturers and other management problems may be a serious handicap. Also, as a rule much the greater part of the costs of an innovation are costs of production and marketing, so that costs may be brought within the resources of a relatively small company by limiting its market. As an example, bringing a new large-scale computer to the general business market is an extremely costly project, beyond the resources of any but the largest computer manufacturers. Yet three different computer manufacturers (Control Data, Amdahl, and Cray) started from scratch by designing giant computers and offering them to a narrowly limited market.

Second, the economic and social significance of an innovation ordinarily arises from its use by large numbers of people. In turn, products and services that are used by large numbers of people frequently lend themselves to mass production and mass distribution. In such cases, corporations of a size suited to mass production or mass distribution are needed to achieve the widespread use which gives the innovation its importance. The mass-production enterprise sometimes grows from a small pioneering firm, as happened in the case of Ford. Or a large enterprise may switch its production and marketing organizations to a new field, as IBM did with computers. Large corporations invented neither the airplane nor the automobile, but they contributed both technologically and commercially to filling the gap between the horseless carriage and the everyday family car, and between the plane of Kitty Hawk and the commercial airliner.

Until relatively recently, such innovations never originated in an existing giant enterprise, simply because giant industrial enterprises and industrial research laboratories are themselves of relatively recent origin. Thus there are many major innovations whose story can be told as that of an invention taken over from a pioneering individual or a small firm and exploited by a giant enterprise with vast financial, technological, manufacturing, and marketing resources. Such stories miss the point; they describe invidiously what is, in many instances of innovation, exactly the economically efficient and sometimes indispensable role of large enterprises. For better or worse, neither Western economies nor innovative individuals were designed to assure that the best innovators would also be the best qualified administrators of enterprises large enough to exploit their innovations—a lesson easily learned from the biographies of Henry Ford and Thomas A. Edison.

Technologies of mass production have been particularly important to Western growth, and they are almost inevitably large enterprise developments, simply because only large enterprises have any reason to develop them. Even builders of machine tools and other capital equipment have little or no incentive to develop production equipment designed for operation on a scale larger than their customers can use. The most striking and familiar example is, of course, Ford's step-by-step development of assembly-line production methods under the pressure of more orders than could easily be filled. Ford is entitled to full credit as a pioneer, for the more conventional response would have been to raise the price of the Model T. More recently, the development of robots for use in manufacturing has centered in the automobile and other mass-production industries that use highly repetitive, assembly-line operations, for that is where robots are economically useful.

Are Industries With Large Corporations Monopolistic?

Marx predicted that capitalism would eventually become monopolistic,[20] and the belief among Marxist economists that this prediction has been fulfilled is reflected in their use of the term *monopoly capitalism* for the economic system prevailing in Western economies.

There is general agreement among economists that an appreciable amount of monopolization exists in the American (and other Western) economies. Some of it stems from governmental action. This type of monopolization may be either unavoidable or justified for noneconomic reasons, and it may seem inappropriate to apply the term *monopolization* to it. Unfortunately, there is no alternative term. We still use franchised monopolies extensively in regulated industries, such as the local distribution of gas and electricity, telephones, and mass transit. American economic and political history includes a long chapter on regulation of railroads, which some now attribute to an effort to provide government enforcement of cartel agreements that were being chronically violated.[21] There are other industries in which some monopoly is unavoidable, but regulation often extends monopoly to related industries. For example, multiple systems of urban electricity distribution would be very unwelcome; but the reasons for monopolizing the generation of power are less compelling.

There is a similar extension of an unavoidable monopoly in the combination of broadcasting and programming.

An extension of the literal meaning of *monopolization* carries us to government action that serves to raise the price of certain services by restricting their supply—the usual modus operandi of monopoly. Our inheritance from the guilds is reflected in the fact that most states have licensing laws, administered by individuals themselves in the business of supplying the licensed services, that restrict the supply of legal, medical, taxi, plumbing, electrical repair, burial, tonsorial, and many other services—to the considerable financial advantage of the licensed suppliers.[22] Trade unions also seek to restrict the supply of labor to employers in order to increase wages. The most effective way for employers to resist monopolistic wage demands is to refrain from employing members of unions, but the National Labor Relations Act of 1935 made this tactic unlawful, and some industrial unions have experienced a high degree of success.

Some local governments (for example, New York City) impose taxes on public utilities sufficient to push regulated utility rates to monopoly levels or higher. Such instances make one wonder whether the possibility of realizing monopoly returns ever goes wholly unexploited. Whether the entity in a political or economic position to exploit the monopoly is or is not a capitalist, the effects on consumers are much the same.

But these are not the forms of monopoly envisioned by Marx. His concern was with monopoly by capitalists, arising from the internal workings of capitalism in the autonomous private sector. In a literal sense, the term *monopoly* applies to vanishingly few unregulated markets in that sector. There is almost always more than one seller available to buyers, so one's first impression might be that events have not fulfilled Marx's prediction.

However, there are many markets with comparatively few sellers, and from the time of the Great Depression of the 1930s, a considerable number of non-Marxist economists, working in the field of oligopoly (that is, few sellers) theory have explored the hypothesis that, in a market with few sellers, prices and sellers' profits will fall somewhere between those that would prevail in a market with many sellers and those that would prevail in a market with only one seller.[23] There has by now been a half-century of debate about whether fewness of sellers confers an imperfect monopoly, akin to that enjoyed by the beneficiaries of licensing laws,[24] in that they may be able to restrict output somewhat, though probably not enough to achieve the profits of a perfect monopolist. All Western economies contain a number of markets with few sellers, whether as a result of the merger movement of 1880 to 1914 or because the quotient, Sales in the Market/ Minimum Efficient Firm Size, is not a large number.

A detailed review of the post-1933 history of the theory of oligopoly would carry us much too far away from our account of the emergence of market institutions and into a field well mined by others.[25] For our purposes, the following limited points must suffice:

1 The system that generated the unique growth of the Western economies may have considerable merit, even though it departs materially from the heuristic model of perfect competition. Not all departures from the model are undesirable: virtually no one, for example, would forgo the economies of scale in modern industry to increase the number of selling firms. Moreover, the concept of competition used in the models is typically more restrictive than the concept of Adam Smith and other early advocates of market systems.[26] Most important, the simpler models do not take account of competition from new products, new methods of production, and new modes of organization. Joseph Schumpeter was the leading spokesman for the view that these forms of competition are far more important than the competition embodied in static models.[27]

2 The empirical evidence on the effect of fewness of firms on profits (and, inferentially, on prices) indicates that profits in oligopolies average so close to those in multifirm industries that it is difficult to distinguish the two.[28] The interpretation of the statistical evidence has been complicated in recent years by studies of the relation between a firm's profitability and its share of its market.[29] These studies show that the profits of a firm with any given share of the market do not vary significantly with the concentration of the industry in which it operates.[30]

3 The profits associated with market share must, as a matter of arithmetic, be due either to a correlation between higher prices and greater sales (which seems to reverse the fundamental economic expectation, at least if prices are corrected to allow for differences in product) or to an association between lower costs and larger sales.[31] The findings about market share thus appear to suggest that large corporations learned that the most reliable path to above-average profitability is to achieve costs less than competitors' and hence less than the prices at which competitors *must* sell in order to continue in business. Since the models of competition predict prices equal to the costs of the highest cost firms whose output is necessary to supply the market, the inference is that, in terms of statistical averages, oligopolies are fully competitive. This conclusion leaves room for the possibility that individual industries with few firms may not perform competitively, but the same caution applies to industries with many firms.

4 The hypotheses that large firms take advantage of their monopoly power to refrain from competing energetically or that they waste their economic opportunities on unnecessary agency costs lose much of their force in view of the evidence that the profits of large firms are greater than those of smaller firms in the same industry. A large hierarchy incurs more agency costs than a small hierarchy, but if the large hierarchy also achieves greater economies

and lower overall cost, it is economically more efficient than the smaller hierarchy.

Probably the most widely accepted argument for the hypothesis that oligopoly is important was advanced by George J. Stigler.[32] Stigler reasoned that monopoly prices maximized sellers' profits, that sellers therefore had an incentive to collude, and that the obstacle to collusion was that increased sales at prices slightly below the monopoly level were highly profitable, so that some sellers would violate the collusive agreement by making such sales *unless they were fearful of detection*. Stigler then analyzed the problem of detecting a competitor's lower price from evidence of loss of customers to a competitor, failure to gain customers from that competitor, and gravitation of new customers to it. His conclusion was that fewness of competitors reduced the amount of "cheating" any one firm could do without detection.

Stigler's theory was designed to explain the finding that profit rates of firms in industries with few firms exceeded those of firms in industries with many firms. The more recent findings about market share have changed the phenomenon to be explained, because the profit rates of firms in concentrated industries do not exceed those of similar firms in unconcentrated industries. But the theory explains the new findings just as well as it explained the old: a firm with a high share of the market and lower costs than its rivals could conclude that there is an unacceptable risk of erosion of its market share if *any* cheating is allowed to proceed undetected. It could then decide (as did Standard Oil) that the more prudent course is to price at (or, if it wishes to increase its market share, below) its rivals' costs.[33] What leading firms actually do differs from one industry to another; but the studies that relate profit, market share, and concentration in broad cross sections of industry provide a basis for inferring that pricing otherwise than according to one's rivals' costs is exceptional rather than typical.

Some have thought that Stigler's assumption of overt collusion, as an explanation of higher profits in concentrated industries, was unnecessary. They posited an interdependent pricing theory, arguing that, in an industry whose firms have no prospect of improving their sales by reducing prices (since the reduction would immediately be imitated), prices will tend to be somewhat above competitive levels—perhaps not much above, but the differences to be explained were not great, either.

One of the implications of the interdependent pricing theory is that firms in concentrated markets respond to a drop in demand by reducing their output rather than their prices, anticipating that a reduction in price would merely be matched by competitors, and so would not improve sales. Similarly, they would respond to a rise in demand by increasing their output rather than their prices, since they stand to lose heavily if a price increase is not immediately followed by rival firms. The evidence bearing on this point was extensively studied by Phillip Cagan, in a project sponsored by the National Bureau of Economic Research. He concluded that there was no difference between concentrated and unconcentrated industries in their responses to changes in demand, because in *both* types of industry, firms respond to such changes by varying their output and inventory first and their prices later.[34] Another implication of the interdependent pricing theory is that price changes should occur less frequently than in unconcentrated industries, but again the empirical evidence indicates that their frequency does not differ significantly between concentrated and unconcentrated industries.[35]

Cagan's work suggests that the important change in pricing behavior occurs when we move from formal, organized markets to the informal markets that exist in most industries, rather than when we move from industries with many firms to industries with few. There is a fundamental difference between the flows of information in an organized market, where changes in demand are reflected in the continuous changes of posted prices, and in the informal markets where (except for mining and agriculture) almost all firms sell. In informal markets, a firm's first indication of a change in demand is usually a rise (or fall) in sales or orders received and a fall (or rise) in inventories—an indication made ambiguous by the possibility that it might be due to changes in competitive factors other than prices. Even news of a price change by a rival firm has to be evaluated as consistent or inconsistent with the state of market demand before the firm decides whether to follow it. In the absence of an unambiguous price index of demand, firms in informal markets respond to changes in sales and inventory first by adjusting their output and inventory; then by experimenting with increased (or decreased) selling effort and limited or temporary price reductions, promotions, and similar tactical moves, reserving general changes in price until the demand situation has become clear. The empirical evidence mentioned in the preceding paragraph suggests that sellers in unconcentrated markets generally cope with the ambiguities of informal markets in about the same way as sellers in concentrated markets—that is, by varying their output, inventories, and price in that sequence.

One other problem with the econometric approach to the monopoly issue is that of accounting for innovation. There are two principal difficulties. In economic theory, expenditures for innovation are a capital investment.

293

In determining its profits, a firm should deduct from revenues an allowance for depreciation of its accumulated investment in innovation, rather than its current expenditures for innovation. In accounting practice, however, innovation expenditures are not capitalized, but deducted currently, and firms do not even attempt to estimate an appropriate allowance for depreciation—and the data available to economists are almost entirely accounting data.

The other difficulty is that successful innovation results in a temporary monopoly, either for the time required for imitation or for the term of a patent. There is no real quarrel with the idea of rewarding innovation from the profits obtainable from such temporary monopolies. But for either a firm or an industry, it is hard to tell how much of its profits are attributable to innovation. Many enterprises derive revenues partly from the sale of familiar products and partly from a continuing series of innovations. The production of innovative and noninnovative products and services by one enterprise has the consequence that, as a rule, no one can tell how much of its profits come from innovation and how much from conventional operations. The difficulties stem partly from the impossibility of allocating joint revenues and joint costs and partly from displacement in time: current profits may be in part a consequence of earlier innovations. There is thus no clear way to divide the profits of the enterprise between sales of familiar products, possibly at excessive prices, and revenues from innovation. Nor is there any way to standardize industry data so as to eliminate revenues from innovation. The result is that in order to find any significance in broad cross-section comparisons between the profits of concentrated and unconcentrated industries, or between firms with high shares of the market and firms with more modest shares of the market, one must make the highly questionable assumption that on average firms achieve high market shares without being more innovative than firms that do not.[36]

It must be remembered that industries with few firms are relatively small segments of much larger economic systems and that the trends discussed in earlier chapters describe a world that is becoming more, rather than less, competitive. Among these trends are urbanization and improvements in transportation that eliminated many local, regional, and even national monopolies and a rise in discretionary income that has made interindustry competition more significant. Urbanization, improvements in transportation, and the growth of the national income have combined to increase the size and complexity of markets, with the result that market positions are more difficult to defend against attack by specialized competitors. Organizational changes, such as the introduction of mass merchandisers and diversified manufacturers, have facilitated entry by newcomers and have restricted sellers' ability to exploit market positions. The increasing introduction of products manufactured in foreign countries with radically different cost structures has also intensified competition. In many industries, the most important trend of all has been the systematic use of innovation as a competitive tool. It is quite plain that the events of 1880 to 1914 did not restructure American industry into monopolies. On the evidence of the cross-sectional studies, industries average a good deal closer to the competitive than the monopolistic end of the oligopoly spectrum, even to the point where the existence of *any* average departure from the competitive pole is doubtful. It is not likely that the events of 1880 to 1914, although they reduced the number of firms in some industries, left Western industry as a whole any less competitive than it had been, once we allow for other trends that were, concurrently, increasing competition.

Importance of Small Enterprises

We are so accustomed to thinking of Western economies generally, and of the American economy especially, as dominated by large enterprises that there may be a certain novelty to the question, Why does most of the American economy consist of relatively small enterprises?

The simple answer is that a main thrust of the publicly-held industrial corporation, as an institution, was to use high technology, capital-intensive, and hence labor-saving methods of manufacturing. This approach was successful; as a result, most of the labor force is employed outside the manufacturing sector. The long-term decline of the agricultural sector has been offset by growth in the tertiary sector, services. In June 1984, manufacturing accounted for only 19.8 percent of the American labor force, a labor force that is now predominantly employed in the service sector. In addition, the largest and most successful manufacturing corporations also tend to be capital-intensive. Thus the two hundred largest firms, which account for roughly 43 percent of manufacturing value added, account for only 31 percent of manufacturing employment. Put another way, the work of only about 6 percent of the work force is organized within the two hundred largest manufacturing corporations, as size is measured by assets. There are roughly twelve million proprietorships and partnerships in the American economy: almost twice as many people work as individual proprietors or partners as work as employees of the industrial giants.

Because they are capital-intensive, large industrial corporations organize a higher proportion of the economy's capital resources than of its labor resources. However, of the two, labor is much the more important, as measured by its social significance, the difficulty of organizing its contribution to production, and its share of output. Marxists argue that all value is attributable to labor. It makes no difference to the argument whether labor is credited with 100 percent of output or the 70 to 75 percent found in the capitalist distribution of income between capital and labor: either way, what economic organizations organize is principally the performance of labor, and industrial giants are not the institutions mainly used to organize labor.

There are, of course, large corporations in fields other than manufacturing, such as banking, insurance, retailing, mining, transportation, communication, and public utilities. But only a few of them are comparable in size to the industrial giants, as measured either by number of employees or by capital resources. Enterprises in Western economies come in a diversity of sizes, from the very small to the very large. The belief that very large industrial enterprises dominate Western economies is simply mistaken, as a matter of where most of the work of producing and distributing goods and services in these economies gets done. Large enterprises are adapted to work in manufacturing, transportation, and public utilities where the economical scale of operation is such that any enterprise that uses it is bound to be large. Such work is less than a quarter of the total work of the economy.

Conclusion

Two conclusions are particularly pertinent.

First, experiment is almost always best conducted on the smallest scale necessary to prove or disprove a point; and experiment so pervades Western economies as to assure that a great part of their economic activity will be conducted on a small scale. One must keep in mind that growth implies change and adaptation, and that much of the adaptation takes place through the formation of enterprises that are, at least initially, small.

Second, a fundamental characteristic of organization in Western economies has been decentralization—a diffusion of authority and responsibility and a limitation of the pyramiding of managerial hierarchies to cases where the hierarchy clearly pays its way. The resistance to agency costs and the complexities of controlling those costs are not limited to that part of the pyramid that extends from a government board of planning and control down to individual enterprises; they are reflected in the organization of economic activity at all levels. The organizing principle is that the costs and benefits of hierarchy must be balanced out. That the benefits outweigh the costs in comparatively few situations is a fact of social life, as evidenced by the predominance of relatively small hierarchies in Western economies. The strength of the tendency to decentralization in Western economies is chronically underestimated, if one may judge from the many prophesies that capitalism would end in the centralization of Western economies in the hands of a few capitalists—prophecies repeated by now for more than a hundred years and still unfulfilled.

NOTES

1. Michael E. Porter, *Competitive Strategy: Techniques for Analyzing Industries and Competitors* (New York: Free Press, 1980) includes a selective bibliography (382–87) and has itself become required reading for business planners. Two other recent and widely read books on the subject are Kenichi Ohmae, *The Mind of the Strategist: The Art of Japanese Business* (New York: McGraw-Hill Book Co., 1982); and Thomas J. Peters and Robert H. Waterman, Jr., *In Search of Excellence: Lessons from America's Best-Run Companies* (New Yo. :: Harper & Row, 1982).

2. Porter, *Competitive Strategy*, pp. 129–55.

3. David Birch, "The Contribution of Small Enterprise to Growth and Employment," unpublished manuscript, Massachusetts Institute of Technology.

4. Ibid., p. 27.

5. Yale Brozen, in "Industrial Policy," unpublished manuscript, University of Chicago, states:

> In 1966, we spent 5 percent of the national income on medical services. By 1982, spending on medical services rose to 12 percent of national income. In 1966, we spent 5 percent of national income on education. By 1982, spending on education rose to nearly 8 percent of national income. If we allocate more income to non-industrial uses, less is left to spend on industrial products.

Brozen attributes the rise in spending for education and medical care to the policy of providing them at less than their cost.

6. Birch, "Contribution of Small Enterprise," fig. 2, 25 and table 3, 12. Birch's data

indicate that in the year 1979 to 1980, the existing firms lost more jobs than they created. To find a positive growth in jobs, one has to add the new firms formed during the period under study. Then all sizes of firms gained jobs. Apparently, the net rate of loss of jobs in existing firms is highest in those with 0–19 employees.

7. The figures in this paragraph are from U.S. Department of Commerce, Bureau of the Census, *Statistical Abstract, 1979* (Government Printing Office: Washington, D.C.), 813–14, table 1429.

8. It is not too much to say that all of the industries which include the very largest firms also include a number of relatively small firms. There were, for example, 141 firms in the aircraft industry; 518 firms in the electronic computing industry; and 555 firms in photographic equipment and supplies. The only arguable exception is the cigarette industry, with only 13 firms. Ibid.

9. Notably in his *Markets and Hierarchies* (New York: Free Press, 1975).

10. John D. Glover, *The Revolutionary Corporations* (Homewood, Ill.: Dow Jones-Irwin, 1980). One of the present authors wrote a summary and commentary for Professor Glover's book. The present summary is drawn from it, especially from pp. 10–12.

11. Berle and Means, *Modern Corporation and Private Property.*

12. Alfred D. Chandler, *Giant Enterprise: Ford, General Motors, and the Automobile Industry* (New York: Harcourt, Brace & World, 1964), especially pt. 1, "Ford—Expansion through Mass Production," and pt. 2, "General Motors' Innovations in Management" and "General Motors' Innovations in Marketing."

13. Glover, *Revolutionary Corporations,* exhibit 1, 73–92.

14. For example, the subject was extensively discussed in *Mergers and Economic Concentration,* Hearings before the Senate Committee on the Judiciary, Subcommittee on Antitrust, Monopoly and Business Rights, pts. 1 and 2, 96th Cong., 1st sess., March–May 1979. Other sources, presenting a similar diversity of viewpoint, include Peter O. Steiner, *Mergers: Motives, Effects, Policies* (Ann Arbor: University of Michigan Press, 1975); Ralph Nelson, *Merger Movements in American Industry, 1895–1956* (Princeton: Princeton University Press, 1959); Jesse Markham, "Survey of the Evidence and Findings on Mergers," in *Business Concentration and Price Policy* (Princeton: Princeton University Press, 1955), pp. 141–82.

15. See Steiner, *Mergers: Motives, Effects, Policies,* p. 6, fig. 1–2. Nelson, writing before the merger wave of the 1960s, found a correlation between rising stock prices and rising mergers in *Merger Movements.*

16. A merger wave will occur when a rise in the price of firms sharply increases the number of owners willing to sell. The wave, an unusually large number of sales of firms, may be due to the magnitude of the price rise, to an elastic supply of firms within the range of the price rise or, as seems likely in 1899 to 1900, to a combination of the two. It should be added that, like any market, the market for firms is affected by numerous idiosyncrasies, some of which may contribute to particular merger movements independently of the expansion or contraction of the economy. These idiosyncrasies are extensively discussed by George Benston in *Mergers and Economic Concentration,* pt. 2, pp. 163–273.

17. Richard Tilly describes the German experience in "Mergers, External Growth, and Finance in the Development of Large-Scale Enterprise in Germany, 1880–1913," *Journal of Economic History* 42 (September 1982): 629–55. Tilly found that mergers were concentrated in the boom years of 1889, 1898 to 1900, and 1904 to 1905. Mergers were seldom the main avenue for the growth of enterprises; more often, "the key acquisition quickly magnified an enterprise's scale of operations, saved it from becoming an industrial also-ran, but never insured it market dominance." (Ibid., p. 643.) Tilly estimated that, from 1895 to 1913, 3,964 firms "disappeared" through merger in the United States; 1,439 in Great Britain; and 650 in Germany. (Ibid., table 10, p. 652.) He suggests that the reason for the differences "lies in the differential willingness and ability to exploit the corporate form of business enterprise."

18. P. L. Cottrell, *Industrial Finance, 1830–1914* (New York: Methuen, 1980), pp. 176–77. As in the United States, the merger movement extended into the coal, iron, and steel industries.

19. U.S. Dept. of Commerce, *Historical Statistics,* pt. 2, ser. 5: vol. 20, 912. Similarly, Steiner pointed out that the number of U.S. corporations with assets in excess of $10 million increased from 2,403 in 1965 to 2,659 in 1967 and to 2,930 in 1970, during the merger wave of the late '60s, which reached its peak in 1968 and 1969. Steiner, *Mergers: Motives, Effects, Policies,* p. 290, table 11–1.

20.

As soon as this process of transformation has sufficiently decomposed the old society from top to bottom, as soon as the labourers are turned into proletarians, their means of labour into capital, as soon as the capitalist mode of production stands on its own feet, then the further socialisation of labour and further transformation of the land and other means of production into socially exploited and, therefore, common means of production, as well as the further expropriation of private proprietors, takes a new form. That which is now to be expropriated is no longer the labourer working for himself, but the capitalist exploiting many labourers. This expropriation is accomplished by the action of the immanent laws of capitalistic production itself, by the centralisation of capital. One capitalist always kills many. Hand in hand with this centralisation, or this expropriation of many capitalists by few, develop, on an ever-extending scale, the co-operative form of the labour-process, the conscious technical application of science, the methodical cultivation of the soil, the transformation of the instruments of labour into instruments of labour only usable in common, the economising of all means of production by their use as the means of production of combined, socialised labour, the entanglement of all peoples in the net of the world-market, and with this, the international character of the capitalistic regime. Along with the constantly diminishing number of the magnates of capital, who usurp and monopolise all advantages of this process of transformation, grows the mass of misery, oppression, slavery, degradation, exploitation; but with this too grows the revolt of the working class, a class always increasing in numbers, and disciplined, united, organised by the very mechanism of the process of capitalist production itself. The monopoly of capital becomes a fetter upon the mode of production, which has sprung up and flourished along with, and under it. Centralisation of the means of production and socialisation of labour at last reach a point where they become incompatible with their capitalist integument. Thus integument is burst asunder. The knell of capitalist private property sounds. The expropriators are expropriated.

Karl Marx, *Capital* (London: Lawrence & Wishart Ed.), chap. 22, "Historical Tendency of Capitalist Accumulation," pp. 714–15. See also chap. 15, ibid.

21. Paul MacAvoy, *The Economic Effect of Regulation* (Cambridge: M.I.T. Press, 1965).

22. There is a discussion of the high cost of occupational licensure, using principally the medical profession as illustration, in Milton Friedman, "Occupational Licensure," chap. 9 in his *Capitalism and Freedom* (Chicago: University of Chicago Press, 1962), pp. 137–60.

23. The early theoretical works were Edward H. Chamberlin, *The Theory of Monopolistic Competition* (Cambridge: Harvard University Press, 1933); and Joan Robinson, *The Economics of Imperfect Competition* (London: Macmillan & Co., 1933). John Kenneth Galbraith has applied Chamberlin's thesis that each firm has a monopoly of a market of its own to the special case of very large firms: see, for example, *The New Industrial State* (Boston: Houghton, Mifflin, 1967). All three works are in the literary, rather than the empirical, tradition.

24. The power of a licensing authority to restrict output arises from its legal monopoly of the right of entry. An industry with few sellers has to find its power to restrict output in some other way, and the existence or nonexistence of such other ways is near the heart of the controversy about oligopolies.

25. See F. M. Scherer, *Industrial Market Structure and Economic Performance* (Chicago: Rand McNally, 2d ed., 1980). For an exposition of the view that oligopoly is not significant, see Yale Brozen, *Concentration, Mergers and Public Policy* (New York: Macmillan Publishing Co., 1982).

26. See Paul J. McNulty, "Economic Theory and the Meaning of Competition," *Quarterly Journal of Economics* 82 (November 1968): 639–56; and idem, "A Note on the History of Perfect Competition," *Journal of Political Economy* 75 (August 1967): 395–99.

27. In *Capitalism, Socialism and Democracy* (New York: Harper, 1942), Joseph Schumpeter expressed the belief that intellectual and middle-class hostility to capitalism, generated in part by its very success, would lead to socialism. Forty years later, the conspicuous gap between Western economic performance and the performance of Eastern economies that claim to be socialist suggests that the path to a new economic order is likely to be longer and more devious than Schumpeter expected.

28. The empirical case for the effect of oligopolies on profits rested on a series of correlations of average industry profit rates with ratios of industry concentration. Leonard Weiss surveyed forty such studies, plus six others using single-firm profits, in "The Concentration-Profits Relationship and Antitrust," in *Industrial Concentration: The New Learning*, H. G. Goldschmid, H. M. Mann, and J. F. Weston, eds. (Boston: Little, Brown & Co., 1974), pp. 204–17. Not all studies found such correlations, and they were usually statistically weak, indicating that the differences in profit were much less striking than one would expect from a monopoly. For a critique of some of the leading studies of concentration and profits and a replication finding no significant correlation, see Yale Brozen, "The Antitrust Task Force Deconcentration Recommendation," *Journal of Law and Economics* 13 (October 1970): 279–92.

29. The great majority of statistical studies sought to relate industry concentration to profits. The individual firms' market shares were not available in Census statistics. They were available in data furnished by associated firms to Strategic Planning Institute, of Cambridge, Mass., and, recently, in data collected by the Federal Trade Commission under its Line of Business Reporting Program. The finding that, when firm profit rates are regressed simultaneously on market share and concentration ratio, market share is significant and concentration ratio is not significant, is of particular interest because it serves as the "correct test for the hypothesis that high concentration merely reflects high market shares which derive from the same source as high profits . . . Market share should capture the effect of economies of scale, superior products, or superior management—and then some. At least in the case of dominant firms, it would also show the effect of control over price. If there is any effect left for concentration, this would surely show the ability of concentrated industries to act collusively." (Weiss, "Concentration-Profits Relationship and Antitrust," pp. 225–26.) The early studies based on the data available at the time enabled Weiss to argue, on p. 226, that they showed a residual effect of concentration. For the later studies, see n. 30, following.

30. Michael Gort, "Concentration and Profit Rates: New Evidence on an Old Issue," *Explorations in Economic Research* 3 (Winter 1976): 1; Harold Demsetz, "Two Systems of Belief about Monopoly," in *Industrial Concentration*, pp. 177–78. Work done at the Strategic Planning Institute is summarized in Bradley T. Gale and Ben S. Branch, "Concentration vs. Market Share: Which Determines Performance and Why Does it Matter?" *Antitrust Bulletin* 27 (Spring 1982): 83. Work using the Federal Trade Commission's line-of-business data includes David J. Ravenscraft, "Structure-Profit Relationships at the Line of Business and Industry Level," Federal Trade Commission, July 1981, *Review of Economics and Statistics* 65 (February 1983): 22–31; Stephen Martin, "Market, Firm, and Economic Performance: An Empirical Analysis" (July 1981); and Leonard W. Weiss and George Pascoe, "Some Early Results on the Concentration-Profits Relationship from the FTC's Line of Business Data," Federal Trade Commission, September 1981.

31. Gale and Branch found that the effect of market share on profits was attributable to lower costs, and that the achievement of lower costs followed, rather than preceded, the achievement of a larger share. See "Concentration vs. Market Share," pp. 94–95. Instead of relying on an assumption that buyers would not purchase a firm's products in greater quantities than other firms' products if they thought its prices, corrected for quality differences, were higher, Gale and Branch compared prices directly, but allowed for buyer-perceived differences in quality as reported by client firms' marketing personnel.

32. George A. Stigler, "A Theory of Oligopoly," *Journal of Political Economy* 72 (February 1964), chap. 5 in *The Organization of Industry* (Homewood, Ill.: Richard D. Irwin, 1968).

33. Stigler wrote "A Theory of Oligopoly" after puzzling over the antitrust conspiracies in the electrical equipment industry and the anomalous behavior of the leading firms in that industry. About 1968, he concluded that legislation to deconcentrate oligopolistic industries was inadvisable and, in 1969, testifying before the House Special Subcommittee on Small Business, he said: "I worry about the fact that where we have substantial large economies of scale, deconcentration puts burdens on us. Where the economies are not large, private rivals have a tendency to enter and eliminate (excess) profits themselves." Stigler is quoted by Brozen, *Concentration, Mergers, and Public Policy*, pp. 391–92. His change of view is recounted in ibid., 391–92, and by Richard Posner in *Industrial Concentration*, p. 414.

34. Senate Committee on the Judiciary, Subcommittee on Antitrust, Monopoly and

Business Rights, "Prepared Statement of Phillip Cagan," *Mergers and Economic Concentration*, pt. 1, 96th Cong., 1st sess., 25 April 1979, 474–75.

35. P. David Qualls, "Market Structure and Price-Cost Margin Flexibility in American Manufacturing, 1958–70," *FTC Working Paper no. 1* (March 1977); and "Market Structure and Price Behavior in U.S. Manufacturing, 1972–1976," *FTC Working Paper no. 6* (March 1977).

36. The differences between accounting rates of return and economic rates of return have always cast doubt on the economic significance of profit-market share–concentration studies that used accounting data. One analysis concludes that "the belief that they [the differences] are small enough to make accounting rates useful for analytic purposes rests on nothing but wishful thinking." Franklin M. Fisher and John J. McGowan, "On the Misuse of Accounting Rates of Return to Infer Monopoly Profits," *American Economic Review* 73 (March 1983): 82–97.

10 / Implications and Comparisons

A knowledge of the origins of Western wealth may help us to understand what economic, political, and social policies are likely to lead to the continuance of Western economic growth, what policies are likely to help less-developed countries grow, and what policies are likely to stop growth or lead to a decline. In this chapter, we can do no more than explore a few aspects of the trends that seem likely to affect growth one way or the other.

In the first three sections of this chapter, we discuss the relations between the political sphere and the economic sphere on the assumption that it is in the interest of the political sphere to exercise its monopoly of coercive force in such a way as to maximize the wealth it extracts from the economic sphere. There is room for difference of opinion as to how likely the political sphere is to act in its own interest, but on the further assumption that it will so act, we offer some grounds for doubting that the experimental method the West has used in advancing human welfare is compatible with reuniting the political and economic spheres of life under the hegemony of the political sphere. The fourth section is an exploration of the reasons that the investor-owned form of enterprise organization is more widely used in Western economies than employee or other forms of ownership. In the fifth section, we briefly consider the problem of comparing the economies of different countries and, in the sixth section, we discuss some of the dilemmas faced by developing countries that attempt to imitate the West's economic achievement.

The reader will sense that we raise a number of issues of social, moral, and political values without attempting to deal with them. A word of explanation is in order.

Our focus has been on a single widely shared value—the value of advancing the material welfare of human beings, as measured by the means available to the great majority of individuals to choose and shape the quality of the lives they lead. The success of the West in serving this value is still modest in absolute terms, but it has been overwhelming by comparison to the performance of other societies, past or present. For the most part, the question of how the West has differentiated itself from other societies in order to achieve a comparatively high level of material welfare has not raised many questions about such values as social justice, equality, and a concern for the environment, simply because these values have not dominated life in any of the past societies from which the West differentiated itself. There has been no reason to consider the hypothesis that a departure from modern moral values played an appreciable part in the Western achievement; indeed, it is only as a result of the material success of the Western world that the pronounced shift in values occurred. Besides, the question of how the West did it has seemed sufficiently puzzling to merit examination in its own right, reserving for another day complex questions about the consistency of the Western approach with its own and other value systems.

However, in recounting the ways the West differentiated itself, we have commented on one of the principal moral criticisms that was leveled at the growth process of a rising West, namely, that the West was achieving its advance by oppressing its workers. Our comments rested on the premise that the transition to capitalism was not costly to workers unless they were oppressed more than in the past. The early-nineteenth-century assumption was Malthusian, to the effect that the growth in population would forever condemn workers to the lowest level of material welfare compatible with surviving long enough to reproduce. It was thus taken for granted that the added output of the capitalist system could not accrue to the benefit of the working class. In retrospect, it is clear that the workers' gains were substantial in total, but that they were spread thin and easily overlooked by those who saw them through Malthusian glasses. Later in the nineteenth century, Karl Marx likewise believed that workers did not share in the gains from the transition to capitalism and saw this lack of participation as injustice. He viewed the advance in output as arising from a transformation of individual labor into the collective labor of the factory system, in which workers use tools they do not own to make products they do not sell. He found injustice in the very process of transformation, charging, in chapter 32 of *Capital,* that the "magnates of capital . . . usurp and monopolise all advantages of this process of trans-formation."[1] The word "all" is much too strong, and the substitution of "some" shifts the issues from moral absolutes to one of "how much."

The Western achievement has surely opened new possibilities of ad-vancing many other values, among them those embraced within the connotations of social justice, environmentalism, and equality. But anyone who seeks to advance them needs to understand the sources of Western achievement in order to avoid cutting off at the source the opportunities future generations may have to develop a society which can afford yet higher aspirations.

The Political Sphere

The postfeudal autonomy of the economic sphere implied a political sphere, likewise autonomous. We should say a little more than we have about the functions thus excluded from the economic sphere.

The minimum defining characteristic of government is a claim to a monopoly of the use of coercive force within some defined territory. As a first approximation, the core problem of the relation between those who hold military power and those in the economic sector is the division of economic output between the two.[2]

In Western countries, the underlying link between civilian and military authority is both adorned and concealed by a political and religious symbolism so elaborate as to constitute a field of study in its own right. Unhappily, Western political scientists usually treat this seminal problem of politics—establishing and maintaining control of the military by persons who are not generals by occupation—as if it were as nonexistent in fact as it is in political symbolism. Even a casual glance at the history of the Latin American states suggests how myopic such omissions can be.

Even in the Middle Ages, the military conceded some of the work of government to civilian officials, including raising money, whether from taxes, borrowing, or the sale of charters, and administering justice in the royal courts. As professional armies superseded the feudal militias, the soldier-kings of France and England, who led their armies in person as late as the battle of Agincourt in 1415 and in the English Wars of the Roses later in the same century, were succeeded by monarchs whose skills were political rather than military, such as Louis XI, king of France from 1461 to 1483, and Mary and Elizabeth in the England of the next century. Civilian monarchs and civilian officials took care of exactions from the economic sector and handled supply and pay for the military forces, receiving in exchange obedience from the military and authority over promotions in the upper ranks. It was a division of labor no doubt almost as welcome to the military as to the civilians. Thus those who extracted government revenues from the economic sector used the money to buy the obedience of the professional armies and so became themselves the effective holders of military power for most purposes, including dealings with the economic sector and all other spheres of society except the military itself. The civilian officials were also occupied with political administration, and in time they became more and more interested in the appropriation of economic output for other purposes besides direct support of their military power base. In France especially, earlier than in England, the royal revenues were used for public works, the development of industry, and drawing the landed aristocracy into a glittering and luxurious life at the royal court at Versailles and away from their former lives as feudal magnates and significant holders of political power. Later, the growth of democratic political institutions made the ballot box the immediate source of political power and created a new art of gaining and holding power by appropriating economic output to the subsidization of a wide range of political interest groups.

The relation of the political to the economic sphere may be analyzed by the methods of politics or by the methods of economics. Frederic C. Lane has offered a succinct version of the economic analysis:

> Men specializing in warfare appear very early in the history of the division of labor and were at an early date organized into large enterprises. In the use of violence there were obviously great advantages of scale when competing with rival violence-using enterprises or establishing a territorial monopoly. This fact is basic for the economic analysis of one aspect of government: the violence-using, violence controlling industry was a natural monopoly, at least on land. Within territorial limits the service it rendered could be produced much more cheaply by a monopoly ... A monopoly of the use of force within a contiguous territory enabled a protection-producing enterprise to improve its product and reduce its costs.[3]

From the viewpoint of economics, one would expect the division of output between the holders of political power and the economic sector to encounter some maximum point: the level of expropriation beyond which further exactions would diminish political revenues.

The search for such a point begins with the observation that some government services increase economic output, net of their costs, and that exactions necessary to pay for these services should not have a net adverse effect on economic output. The economic sector requires, for example, protection from banditry and an orderly way of settling its internal disputes, and to the extent that governments provide these services less expensively than they might be provided by the economic sector itself, government services benefit output. On the other hand, historically, holders of a monopoly of military force have tended to exact tribute appreciably in excess of the cost of supplying protection or obtaining it elsewhere.

Governments also affect economic growth by the nature of the property rights that they establish and enforce.[4] People are, for example, not very likely to invest in expensive enterprises unless they have some assurance that the fruits of the investment will accrue to the investor. Property rights are not a simple matter of supplying police protection, but rather of formulating legal rights and liabilities in such a way that the benefits and costs of economic action accrue, so far as possible, to the actor. Though this service, if well performed, is of great economic benefit, its cost is nominal, and a government that charges appreciably for it is exercising the power arising from its monopoly of force.

Government also contributes to economic output through measures to encourage trade. We have touched earlier on the importance of trade to economic growth. North and Thomas have summarized its wealth-creating effect:

> The very process of trade creates wealth as goods move from persons who value them less to persons who value them more. Both parties in a voluntary exchange become better off. Furthermore, the opportunity to trade allows specialization and lowers the cost of inventing and innovating which further increases the wealth of society. . . . If trade is possible, fewer resources would be required to maintain subsistence than in its absence. Ever since paleolithic times man has been improving his economic lot by trade. The gains from trade must be the cornerstone of serious study of man's economic past.[5]

Governments engage in a wide variety of activities to encourage trade, beginning with issuing the money used as a medium of exchange and ranging from product standardization to maintaining harbors and light-houses to building highways.

A fourth type of governmental contribution to economic output consists in providing schools and colleges which enhance output by raising the educational level of the work force.

Political exactions may be expected to affect economic activity adversely when the political sector exacts tribute for activities that do not add to economic output. Also, part of the economic cost of government is the cost of regulations imposed on the economic sector by the political authorities. Such regulations, designed to benefit one segment of the public, may impose additional costs on other segments of the public. In addition, economic growth can be hindered by overregulation. By reason of their control over the military, the political authorities have the power to appropriate any share of economic output they desire, subject to certain adverse consequences if they appropriate too large a share.[6] Total output may decline, perhaps with a shift of output to less demanding political jurisdictions, and a resulting decline in military power relative to the less demanding polities.

It does not necessarily follow that there is a calculable rate of exaction by government that maximizes the wealth of holders of political power, in the sense that either higher or lower rates of exaction would reduce government revenues. The difficulties of calculation aside, the maximum rate is clearly much higher in the short run than in the long run. In fact, the experience of the West suggests that, except in periods of war, this rate of exaction may be almost entirely a short-run concept: for after a generation or two, a government that charges the economic sector less than government services contribute to output may very well be receiving greater revenues than a government which charges its economic sector a good deal more.

Economists are accustomed to think of economic systems as having an outer limit of output which they might achieve under the most favorable conditions known to economics and technology. We have been discussing an ultimate constraint on governmental power to appropriate the output of the economic sector—the tendency of economic output to fall further and further short of its outer limit as governmental exactions increasingly exceed benefits, up to a theoretical extreme where complete appropriation of economic output by the holders of the monopoly of coercive force would result in zero output, zero revenues, no pay or supplies for the troops, and political and social chaos. But in practice, postfeudal Western governments have dealt only intermittently with their economic sectors on any such confrontational or exploitive basis. There was much the same desire then as today in the political sectors to advance economic welfare, but the mutual assumption was that the political sector would contribute by facilitating commerce and manufacture rather than by imposing political control over, or simply annexing, commerce and manufacture. This assumption furnished the basis for a relationship more cooperative than confrontational, and political and economic leaders frequently formed alliances for their mutual benefit.[7]

Following the Great Depression and World War II, relations between the political and economic sectors have become less cooperative and more confrontational, mainly because the old assumption no longer clearly prevails in the political sector. Much of the world has experimented with the complete absorption of the economic sector into the political sector, and democratic Western societies have turned to a version of interest group politics, in which the achievement of political power depends on the formation of a coalition large enough to vote itself the power to tax the rest of society for the benefit of the members of the coalition. There may be merit, economic or otherwise, in the arguments advanced for consolidation of the political and economic spheres and for the claims of interest group coalitions—a merit exceedingly difficult for anyone to evaluate without escaping the structure of his or her own belief system. Those skeptical of the arguments will view the trend that they rationalize as a move from democracy to kleptocracy, others as a move from greed to justice. Either way, the earlier chapters of this book supply reasons for thinking that the effect on the material welfare of the populations concerned will be adverse, even (or particularly) on the welfare of many of the ostensible beneficiaries.

Strong though the trend toward expansion of the political sphere has been, history supplies many examples where a tide of the future has receded without trace, and there are reasons to suspect that this may be another. The framework of democratic societies permits members of the economic sector to offer political resistance to the consolidation of the economic and political spheres or to coalitions of interest groups. In both democratic and totalitarian societies, there are the further, and ancient, possibilities of resistance through migration, evasion, smuggling, black markets, and the like. In a world of multiple national entities, there is also a possibility that the positive examples of societies that hold their exactions from the economic sector safely below the maximum, in conjunction with the negative examples of societies that allow them to exceed the maximum, will constitute political arguments too insistent to ignore, even when government has control of public information.

It is entirely possible that an exaggerated belief in the capacity of government to enhance economic welfare has created more havoc in the political sphere than in the economic. The nineteenth-century autonomy of the economic sphere reflected a division of labor between political and economic leadership that must seem almost idyllic to modern political leaders who are enmeshed in economic responsibilities that they cannot possibly discharge and who are harassed by their inability to finance and manage the traditional governmental functions. The management of economies entails so much frustration and futility, repeated year after year, that they must eventually exhaust the energies, initiative, morale, and effectiveness of those who attempt it. The silent intuition of such truisms may explain why Western European socialists in political office are already redefining *socialism* to reduce their personal involvement in, and responsibility for, administering production and distribution. The future will show whether this tendency is an aberration or the start of a trend.

Organizational Experiment and Politics

It is not coincidental that the proliferation of modes of organization that is characteristic of Western capitalism developed alongside a high degree of autonomy of the economic sphere from political intervention. There seems to be a perverse incompatibility between political and economic criteria of organization. Many innovations that have passed economic tests successfully have been met by efforts to make them unlawful: the joint-stock company; the department store; the mail-order house; the chain store; the trusts; the integrated process enterprise; the branch bank; the conglomerate; the multinational corporation. At the same time, forms of organization which have been only marginally successful by economic criteria frequently receive political preference, even at obvious and large cost to the economy. This is particularly true of cooperatives, certain types of financial institutions, and in Western Europe and Japan, small farms and small retailers.

One general reason for the adverse political response to organizational innovation is inherent in democratic politics. An organizational innovation tends, initially, to benefit a small number of innovators a great deal and a large number of consumers a great deal in total but very little individually. On the other hand, it may threaten the displacement of a number of people committed to the status quo. The more important the innovation is to consumers as a whole, the more serious the threat it presents to existing firms and their employees, and the more likely they are to organize for political action. By political criteria, it is acceptable to react favorably to the demands of small groups that want something enough to organize and work for it, even at the expense of larger groups not

309

sufficiently interested to organize. In command economies, organizational innovations face a particularly perverse political test. Organizational innovations are, virtually by definition, changes in the distribution of authority and responsibility within the organization. In command economies, such changes must be expected to meet effective opposition unless they add to the authority and responsibility of those already in control.

The fact that political decision making, at least in democracies, is a highly verbal process is another source of differences between political and market tests of innovations. The verbal method of decision making allows extended debate, further experiment, a weighing of costs and benefits, conflicts of expert opinion, successive resort to different political jurisdictions each with the authority to obstruct change, pleas for reconsideration, and other familiar exercises in decision making and law. Even if the criteria of decision were the same in politics and markets, a society which delayed innovations by the amount of time required to reach a political consensus would fall further and further behind a society which did not. But the criteria cannot be the same, for the use of verbal decision making is not solely a procedural device. It implies the substantive criterion that the benefits of the innovation are sufficiently understood and predictable that they can be persuasively verbalized in advance of its adoption— that is, that everything is too clear to need the test of experiment. It is questionable whether many of the West's significant innovations in organization (or elsewhere, for that matter) could have met such a criterion in political debate with those interested in opposing them. Thus, despite the great merits of political modes of decision making, their application in the economic sphere would have been an enormously costly impediment to Western growth.

The organizational experiments which have played a large part in the development of Western economic institutions have been not just any sort of experiments, but experiments of a special kind, modulated by profit and loss results from enterprise operations in capitalist markets. Initially, enterprises adopt or reject proposed organizational changes on the basis of expectations as to their effects on costs or sales. The changes survive and spread if the enterprises that use them survive and grow, as the more profitable enterprises are likely to do in capitalist markets. Thus the successful experiments are self-diffusing; they displace preexisting forms of organization without the delays associated with verbal modes of decision making. The substitution of political tests for the success or failure of organizational experiments would be a substitution of an entirely different mode of decision, one that experience suggests would be much less likely to introduce new forms of organization and retire old forms in a timely way.

As between two economic systems, one using market methods of decision making to adopt or reject organizational innovations and another using political-verbal decision making, the latter will almost inevitably lag behind the first in adopting innovations and will, as well, often reject innovations which would have advanced material welfare.

Organizational Experiment after 1914

It is not to be supposed that organizational experiment came to an end with the invention of the publicly-held corporation. The process of experiment in organizational form seldom produces a change as important as the publicly-held corporation, but neither does it ever entirely stop. The multidivisional corporation, the conglomerate, and the takeover are more recent, post-1914, organizational experiments that have had some success.

The organization of large industrial corporations underwent a major change between 1920 and 1960, when it became the practice to separate strategic decision making and control from the operating parts of the enterprise.[8] The operating functions were "decentralized" to more or less autonomous divisions of the parent corporation. From there, it was a comparatively short step to a "conception of the firm as a governance structure rather than as a production function." Williamson suggests that this conception led to the conglomerate form of enterprise, which emerged in the 1960s. In his view, the conglomerate "is usefully regarded as an evolutionary refinement, whereby the organizational principles responsible for checks on managerial discretion and the operating integrity of the original multidivisional structure have been extended beyond their immediate applications to include a competence to manage newly acquired assets as well."[9]

The corporate takeover became a significant factor in the control and structuring of economic organizations during the 1970s, about a decade after the development of the conglomerate. The takeover was possible because firms that have developed effective "governance structures"

311

frequently believe that they can administer operating divisions acquired in the open market as effectively as those already included in the firm. The takeover follows the conventional pattern of significant organizational innovations, in that it has generated controversies whose outcome seems likely to depend on whether they are settled in political forums or in markets. It has already produced an additional innovation in enterprise organization: the corporation with bylaws which so far protect its directors and officers from removal by takeover as to reduce substantially their accountability to stockholders. Such corporations compete in capital markets with others whose managements are less well entrenched, and their comparative success may shed light on long-standing questions as to the importance of control of corporations by their stockholders.

The divisional form of organization, the conglomerate, and the take-over bid are all developments in the organization of comparatively large publicly-held corporations. They are in the main tradition of organizational innovation, in that all have been actively opposed by incumbent power holders, both political and economic.

The most striking developments in the organization of smaller-scale businesses have been franchise systems and high-tech corporations. Of the two, franchise systems are the more significant in numbers of people employed. They combine the low agency costs of proprietor management with the low information costs of national marketing.

The high-tech corporation, whose goal is to exploit a new technology, is managed by scientists or engineers, and financed by investors willing to venture. As a form of economic organization, such corporations seem ideally suited to minimizing the social risk of experiment in developing applications of new technologies. They have every incentive to find such applications, but at the same time the cost of the inevitable failed experiments is not multiplied by the bureaucrat's temptation to pour good money after bad rather than admit failure.

The development of high-tech enterprises is an aspect of a business strategy which has been defined and rationalized in recent years: the search for niches. In the previous chapter, we noted that numerous small enterprises have found niches in the American economy, often in the same industries that appear to be dominated by very large enterprises.

In a broader sense, continuing organizational experiment affects not simply the individual firm, but the structure of capitalist economies as a whole. Experiments by individual firms sum up to the changing answers to such questions as what constitutes an industry or a market; the size distribution of firms that serve the market; and the functions, from furnishing the raw materials to retailing, to be performed by those firms.

And when we try to analyze some of the major systems in a national economy, such as the transportation system or the distribution of food, we find that the way these systems are organized is shaped by continuing organizational experiment by their constituent firms and their customers.

Investor-Owned Enterprises and Cooperatives

For more than a century, cooperatives have supplied an alternative to capitalist ownership of enterprises. To those who object both to capitalism and to the excesses of socialism-in-practice, as well as to those simply tired of confrontations between capital and labor, the cooperative has seemed to offer a way out. In Germany and the Scandinavian countries, before World War I, cooperatives were looked upon, even by some who thought of themselves as Marxists, as the most probable path to socialism.

If we are correct in identifying the freedom to form enterprises of all types as a basic characteristic of Western economic systems, it is of both historical and topical interest to inquire why investor-owned enterprises continue to predominate despite the ease of organizing cooperatives. Cooperatives are almost universally given government subsidies, either outright or in the form of tax preferences, and unions and pension funds have pools of capital that could be used to fund cooperatives. Why, then, has not the cooperative mode of organization been more widely used?

The probable answers differ for large and small enterprises. For large enterprises the likely explanation is that the publicly held corporation, with freely transferable and marketable shares, tends to obtain capital at lower cost, and to be more efficient in monitoring and controlling agency costs, than enterprises in which share transferability depends on status as an employee, manager, supplier, or customer. Also, a tie-in of ownership with status as a customer, supplier, or employee is not everyone's ideal of strategic flexibility and risk spreading. In small enterprises, the prevalence of investor ownership can be explained by the greater ease of forming enterprises owned by the investor-manager-promoter, as compared to obtaining participation of a group of employees, suppliers, or customers. Let us explore these points a little further.

In terms of organization theory, an enterprise or firm is, in general, an ongoing relationship among its managers, contributors of capital, employees, customers, and suppliers.[10] The relationship is fundamentally cooperative, in that all classes of participants have much to gain from cooperation with the other participants.

The gains are, however, a joint product of all classes of participants, and, like all joint products, there is no fair way to divide them. This introduces an element of conflict into the relationship. In theory, market systems resolve the conflict by giving each participant whatever is necessary to enlist participation, the amount depending on the alternatives open to the participant. The management function includes negotiating the terms of participation with investors, employees, customers, and suppliers.

A crucial factor in the organization of enterprises is that cash flow is almost never in exact balance between income from customers and outgo to the other participants. The universal practice, born of necessity, is to force a balance, agreeing that one class of participants should participate in return for the residual income remaining after the other classes have been paid their agreed compensation. This residual income may be the entire return to a participating group, such as holders of common stock, or it may be part of the return, as it is in cooperatives. By the usual definition, the ownership group is the one with the right to receive the residual income.

There is a corollary of great practical importance, since it determines how the managers of enterprises are selected. For obvious practical reasons, the right to the residual income includes also the right to select the managers. Managerial decisions critically affect the amount of residual income, and a contract by which one group participates in exchange for a promise of residual income and an adversely interested group selects the managers would be, to say the least, unlikely to obtain the voluntary adherence of the former group. This relation between the right to residual income and the right to select management has been insufficiently emphasized, no doubt because it is traditional to think of both rights under the single term ownership, without recognizing that they have appreciably different origins in the underlying bargain among the participants in the enterprise. It is worth adding that the rights to residual income and the selection of management are as inseparable in socialism as in capitalism. In the Soviet Union's version of socialism, the state has both rights. In the Yugoslavian variant, the state receives a fixed return for supplying plant and capital, and employees have both rights.

In sum, there are six forms of ownership and five potential types of cooperative, depending on whether ownership is vested in management, investors, suppliers, employees, customers, or the state.

The only distinctive trait of investor-owned cooperatives is that their shares are freely transferable, without regard to the status of the transferee as a manager, employee, customer, or supplier of the enterprise. However, cooperatives of other types could obtain capital from freely transferable bonds or other forms of fixed income indebtedness, including conceivably even a preferred stock that earned dividends payable before any distributions were made to the ownership group. Thus, while free marketability of capital shares may be expected to reduce the cost of capital, for reasons discussed in chapter 7, the return on the shares does not have to be based on residual income in order to obtain the advantages of transferability. One has to consider the more subtle point that a capital structure combining both debt (fixed-income) securities and equity (residual-income) securities will cost less than one composed of either type of security alone. Thus, transferability of shares in residual income should be of some financial advantage to capital-intensive enterprises. But investor ownership of both large and small enterprises that are not capital-intensive is also very common.

Marketable stock is also a device for controlling agency risk. Attracting and holding investors, and hence survival, depend in large part on the market performance of a corporation's stock. Although many other factors enter into its market performance, its profits and growth, past and prospective, usually influence the price of its stock enough to supply its directors and chief executive officer with an incentive to avoid unnecessary expenses and careless decisions. Directors and officers also have an incentive to seek the good opinion of securities analysts, brokers, and professional traders, whose collective judgments of the prospects of a corporation and the quality of its management are immediate determinants of its stock market performance. Any self-respecting corporate director or officer would deny that he or she needs these incentives to control agency risk, but might concede that there are others who do. Large cooperatives, such as mutual life insurance companies, savings banks, and the larger supplier and consumer cooperatives, easily fall under the control of self-perpetuating boards of trustees who are accountable to no one but themselves, and as a consequence one may expect agency costs to be less vigorously controlled than in publicly-held corporations. But again this does not explain the prevalence of investor ownership among small enterprises, whose employees or customers should be able to monitor the performance of management more effectively.

Another line of explanation seems more promising for enterprises that are not large enough to be held publicly. To the individual contemplating the organization of a new enterprise, the investor-owned firm appears simpler to organize, and it offers its organizers far greater incentives than the alternative forms. Mancur Olson's analysis of the difficulty of forming organizations when the benefits to the individual do not justify the trouble and expense of organizing applies to the promotion of cooperatives.[11] The brokerage houses that promote mutual investment funds in the expectation of large management fees and commissions are an exception with few counterparts elsewhere in the cooperative sector. By comparison, the promoter of an investor-owned enterprise can, by retaining part or all of the ownership interest, profit handsomely if the enterprise succeeds. So one might expect more investor-owned enterprises, small or large, to survive simply because far more of them are likely to be born.

Another possibility is that it may be easier to manage an enterprise for the benefit of an investor constituency than for the benefit of a constituency of one of the other possible classes of participants. Investors are the class with the fewest internal conflicts of interest. Indeed, the potential for conflict among investors seems almost negligible by comparison to the potential for conflict among employees, whose relative contributions to the joint product are hopelessly unclear and notoriously the subject of disinformation. There are advantages to employees in leaving the allocation of their compensation and promotion to an outsider with no biases in favor of any one employee, rather than placing the allocation under the influence of union and plant politics, even though that outsider may be biased against employees collectively. This preference, inarticulate though it may be, for leaving to an outside umpire the resolution of competing internal claims to whatever the enterprise is to pay employees may be one reason why employees and their unions have not pushed cooperative organization more actively.

There is also another possible reason, referred to in chapter 7. In a constantly changing world, it is not necessarily a rational investment strategy for employees to invest both their careers (their human capital) and their personal savings in the same enterprise. Advocates of employee ownership, including employers who actively promote the sale of stock to their employees, rarely emphasize the advantages of diversification of risk to employees who, like those in the steel industry, may find their jobs vanishing at the same time that their employer's earnings, and hence the value of their shares, are likewise declining. In short, if workers are to be paid enough to enable them to aspire to leave the *proletarius* for propertied status, there is a good deal to be said for their acquiring property in other forms than an interest in their employer's business. This same need for diversification encourages the founding owners of successful firms to "go public." It also helps explain why buy outs by management do not occur more frequently than they do.

The Yugoslav economy has experimented with a version of the employee cooperative in which employees elect the managers of state-owned plants. There, the evidence indicates that the employee cooperative creates a number of perverse incentives. There is an incentive to increase the income of present employees by charging high prices, which restricts output; to limit the hiring of new employees so as not to increase the number sharing in profits; to prefer capital-intensive to labor-intensive production methods, even when unemployed labor is available; and to obtain increases in capital by borrowing rather than by plowing earnings back into the enterprise. Employees nearing retirement especially tend to resist the reinvestment of earnings, since they will not receive the benefit of the reinvestment.[12]

In addition, although ownership by employees supplies a group incentive for greater productivity, the incentive to the individual is more dubious. Individual employees may calculate that a reduction of effort on their part is unlikely to be penalized by fellow employees and that the relationship between an individual's efforts and the success of the enterprise is too attenuated to matter. Peer group pressure might substitute for managerial supervision, but it too can go either way, particularly in departmentalized enterprises where the effective peer group is only a small part of the whole labor force.

In looking for explanations for the prevalence of ownership by investors, we have perhaps focused too much on its advantages and on the disadvantages of ownership by other groups. The survival of some enterprises owned by other groups is evidence that, under certain circumstances, their advantages outweigh their disadvantages. The incentives to employees who own an enterprise are well known, even if they are not beyond question. In addition, many cooperatives seem to be based on the belief that their members (consumers, employees, farmers, and so forth) were obliged to deal with economic powers capable of exacting unjust terms of trade. Thus, cooperatives are a form of self-help for those who perceive themselves as trading in markets where the adverse party has a monopolistic position. Even when this perception is mistaken or when it might be cheaper to deal with the monopoly, members of cooperatives might find the sense of assurance that they are not being oppressed worth its possible extra cost. In an economy of impersonal markets whose workings are rarely transparent, the availability of this form of self-help has substantial value. Cooperatives often seem anticapitalist, and yet, in one sense, they are quintessentially capitalist, for they enable comparatively small groups to pursue their own economic interests as they see them. It requires only a moment's reflection to appreciate how completely incompatible self-help through cooperatives would be with the goals of a planned or command economy.

Comparisons between Modes of Organization

Our principal guide in formulating an explanation of Western economic growth has been Western economic history. Since 1917, the history of socialist economies has offered the material for many comparisons that might shed further light on the sources of economic growth. Here, we touch on only two points. First, the obstacles to drawing reliable conclusions from such comparisons are formidable. Second, the socialist experience seems generally consistent with our suggestion that the West owes much to its experimental, pragmatic approach to economic organization.

Comparative economics is an enterprise made challenging by the extreme difficulty of tracing the differences in performance of different economies to their true sources. Thus there is no sure way to resolve disagreements as to which of the innumerable differences between the USSR and the U.S.A. are the most important sources of their difference in economic performance.

Comparisons between economic models of, say, a free market economy and a socialist economy are not difficult, simply because economic models are designed to facilitate human understanding. Comparisons between actual working economies are very much more difficult, because economies arise from historical processes that owe no more than a very uncertain debt to human design and that were surely not created to further ease of human understanding. Let us begin a consideration of a few of the problems in the comparison of working economies by addressing the problem of explicit deception.

1. Surface and Deep Ideologies

It has become conventional to say that the USSR, East Germany, Poland, Bulgaria, and the other Eastern Bloc countries are not Marxist. As Alexander Gerschenkron put it, "the whole history of Soviet Russia . . . is a story of actual abandonment of Marxian ideology."[13] No doubt it could be claimed, with similar force, that only Lichtenstein and perhaps Switzerland are still capitalist.

This claim that almost all countries that call themselves socialist or capitalist are guilty of misdescription reflects the fact that both those in and out of power use dual ideologies—those that actually guide their actions and those that are used as instruments of deception in waging social conflict. To quote Gerschenkron again:

> It is a peculiarity of the social sciences that the objects of our study (unlike the rock that remains mute to the geologist or mineralogist) continually make statements about themselves. This is a blessing and a curse, a source of both enlightenment and confusion. The task of the social scientist is to separate the meal of truth from the bran of deception. To a very considerable extent, the literature on ideology has been concerned precisely with this problem. At the same time, a social scientist cannot confine himself to "unmasking" an ideology as an instrument of deception. Since human action is directed by the brain, that is to say, by ideas, the scholar desirous of understanding social action must try to understand the ideas or set of ideas, in other words, the ideologies that guide the actions: the true ideologies that are operative but remain hidden behind the facade of the deceptive ones.[14]

It is, in other words, difficult but not absurd to compare two working economic systems and to make some attempt to deduce the working principles that actually guide their administrators.[15] It is also intellectually interesting to compare two theoretical systems, such as an economy of perfectly competitive markets and a socialist economy, and for many purposes it is interesting to compare a working economy to a model designed to explain it. On the other hand, a cross-comparison of a working socialist economy and a theoretical capitalist economy of perfect competition, or of a working capitalist economy and a theoretical socialist economy, is a fruitless undertaking. When an attempt is made to transform a real economy according to the model of a theoretical economy, the economy of theory acquires the operational history which will create and perhaps disclose the operative ideology beneath its surface ideology. It is not just that we cannot know what a model economy is a model of without the test of experiment. The theory of an economy is almost always its surface ideology, and we need to keep in mind Gerschenkron's point that it may be a deeply, if not necessarily intentionally, deceptive facade.

2. Differences of Meaning from Differences of Context: "Profits"

Differences in socialist and capitalist usage of the word *profit* will serve as an example both of the traps inherent in attempts to compare two different economic systems and of the difficulty of penetrating to the aspects of different modes of organization which make efficiency differences. In both systems, the term *profit* is applied to residual revenues remaining after payment of the cost of production. We pass over the differences attributable to different methods of accounting for revenues and costs. In both systems, an estimate of residual revenues is included in enterprise budgets for purposes of control and comparison to actual performance and to measure the efficiency of managers. Unwary students of the Soviet system may thus infer that it uses profit incentives in ways comparable to capitalist systems. But does it?

In the more common forms of capitalist enterprise, in which residual revenues are used to pay for contributions of capital rather than for contributions of labor or materials, the ratio of residual revenues to capital investment is the primary guide to the allocation of capital. Capital is directed where it is most urgently needed, as judged by the returns it can earn. Residual revenues (or profit) thus become the primary guide to capital allocation.

In the Soviet system, there are no similar links between residual revenues and the allocation of capital. The Soviet sources of capital are the residual revenues themselves; funds raised by taxation; and funds supplied by banks, savings deposits, and sales of bonds. But it is the difference in the part played by profits on capital that is central. In a market system, when consumers desire to purchase more of a product than is currently being produced, the initial effect is to drive up the price, thereby increasing profits and encouraging the allocation of additional capital (and additional labor) to increase output of the product. When consumers desire less of a product, the initial effect is to drive prices down and so reduce profits and encourage a shift of capital (and labor) from that product to something else.

Imperfections in the way actual markets respond to consumer preferences in allocating capital are trivial compared to the Soviet departure, for it is fundamental to the Soviet system that the allocation of capital depends on the goals and decisions of the holders of political authority, rather than on the preferences of consumers. By some ultimate calculus of the social good, the planners' judgment may be better or worse than consumers', but it is the planners' judgment to which the system is meant to give effect. This judgment is embodied in output goals. The fulfillment or overfulfillment of these goals, upon which their bonuses chiefly depend, is the primary objective of Soviet managers. The national stock of capital is allocated as necessary to achieve the centrally determined outputs. If what is desired by the planning authorities can be produced only at a loss or with little profit, that loss or low profit is what is budgeted and used for purposes of managerial control. Output is thus doubly insulated from the influence of consumers; first, by requiring the enterprise to sell its products at a fixed price, irrespective of variations in consumer demand; and, second, by determining what is to be produced, and in what quantity, irrespective of the profit resulting from its sale to consumers.

In market economies, the rate of profit on different products tends toward a common level, because the output of high-profit goods rises enough to drive prices down and the output of low-profit goods declines enough to raise prices. The Soviet system does not use any analogous system-wide profit equality as a planning criterion, because such a criterion would circumscribe the planners' discretion to determine what ought to be produced and would introduce consumer influence into the determination.

One collateral point is worth passing mention. Queuing is a major occupation of Russian consumers, basically because output is not intended to match consumers' desires, but secondarily because it is ideologically unacceptable to iron out the discrepancies between consumer and planner desires by raising the prices of goods in short supply until demand matches supply, even though the profits would go to the state. Queues are the alternative to market-clearing prices. The authorities must find queues less embarrassing than stiff prices and high profits for the state-owned enterprises that produce goods in short supply, though an outsider might find this an odd preference.

Another difference is that residual revenues in the two systems are the outcome of markedly different ranges of managerial discretion. In the USSR, as in the medieval system, the prices of purchased supplies and the rates of wages are fixed, and the prices the enterprise may charge for its output are likewise fixed. In addition, the mix of capital and labor and the layout of the plant are largely determined when the plant is built and so lie beyond the control of the plant director. Since both the volume of their output and the prices they can charge are fixed, Soviet managers can increase profits only by reducing costs. Reducing costs becomes a matter of getting more work from the work force, reducing the amount of materials used, lowering quality, or changing the product mix so as to favor the items which are cheapest to produce. Because of chronic shortages of consumer goods, the penalties for using these methods of cost reduction are less immediate and severe than they would be if consumers had a wider choice. The same methods are available to the capitalist manager, who, however, faces consumers who do have a wider choice. But the more important difference is that the capitalist manager has many other ways to increase profits, such as seeking a lower cost of inputs, raising the price of the more costly outputs, substituting cheaper inputs for more expensive inputs, making capital investments that will reduce the costs of production, changing the design of products, and changing the products that the enterprise offers for sale.

The manager in the USSR is viewed primarily as an administrator of a plan, with some marginal discretion to deal with unforeseen contingencies (such as underfulfillment of a plan by suppliers) through informal or even illegal devices. What is marginally unlawful behavior for the Soviet administrator is a primary activity of the capitalist manager. For the capitalist manager is only in part an administrator. Primarily he or she is a trader managing a continually changing set of trade-offs among inconsistent input and output possibilities and among different methods of production in an effort to maximize revenues and minimize costs, and so to maximize residual revenue—that is, profits. One of the most important trade-offs is that between capital usage and residual revenues. The capitalist manager is thus responsible not simply for maximizing residual revenues *per se*, taking capital as a given, as in the Soviet Union case, but for managing both capital usage and the generation of residual revenues so as to maximize the rate of return on capital.

There are thus striking differences in scope between the managerial actions for which Soviet profits and capitalist profits serve as an incentive—differences which make it misleading to assert that both systems use profit incentives unless one explains that they are used for much different purposes. Soviet managers have much narrower discretion than capitalist managers because restrictions on managerial discretion are necessary to give effect to the belief that how much of each product should be produced and at what price it should be made available to consumers is properly a question of political judgment, rather than market or consumer judgment. Soviet managers have a profit incentive shaped to induce them to respond to that political judgment; capitalist managers have a profit incentive which encourages them to respond to consumer judgment. The two are far from the same.

No one would contend that the Soviet system is a profit system in the sense of its capitalist counterparts. But it is often contended that it uses profit as an incentive, thus preserving whatever efficiency advantages such incentive may have. The contention loses its plausibility only slowly, as one analyzes profit by specific incentives toward specific goals.[16] This tendency of relatively simple concepts, such as residual revenues, to take on materially different connotations in the contexts of two different economic systems is a chronic obstacle to making intelligent comparisons.

3. Differences of Productivity or Differences of Goals: Surface or Deep?

There is little doubt that the Soviet system has proved less productive and efficient than the American system, when productivity and efficiency are measured by statistics of the usual sort, even with highly ingenious modifications.[17] But it does not necessarily follow that the differences are simple consequences of the fact that one system is capitalist (more or less) and the other is socialist (more or less). It is possible, for example, that the two societies are so far apart in their stages of economic development, or that they attach such different priorities to the pursuit of material well-being as compared to other goals, as to overwhelm the role of economic organization in explaining their differences of performance. To overcome this difficulty of comparison, one commentator has suggested alternative pairings between, for example, East and West Germany, Czechoslovakia and Austria, Yugoslavia and Greece.[18]

But such comparisons present a further difficulty. Westerners almost automatically assume that the goal of an economic system is to advance the economic welfare of at least a majority of the population. But this is because some such goal is almost universally propounded in surface ideologies, and, being credulous, we allow ourselves to be taken in by the surface ideology. Beyond that, we need to avoid the error of hypostasization in thinking of economic systems as having goals. It is an easy error to make, for economies often act as if they had minds of their own. Properly speaking, however, only human beings have goals; economic institutions provide a framework within which human beings pursue their goals. Institutions provide the incentives, the opportunities, and the constraints that structure the behavior of goal-seeking individuals, but they do not possess goals of their own.

It may seem a devastating comment on East German socialism that West German real wages are approximately half again as high as East German. But high real wages may be a low priority goal of government planners in East Germany. On the other hand, high wages are presumably an important goal of West German workers, and they have been able to fulfill it within the framework of West German economic institutions. Again, the Eastern bloc systems may do less well than Western systems in meeting the desires of consumers, but still be far more efficient and productive in satisfying the desires of their political power holders.

The question of the place of equality in the Soviet Union's deep ideology illustrates the difficulties of seeing into the deep goals of a society's effective power holders. The actual distribution of income in the Soviet Union is something about which tantalizingly little data are available. In a recent careful analysis, Abram Bergson found that Soviet inequalities of income are about the same as in some capitalist countries and less so than in others—that is, in much the same ballpark as inequalities in Western capitalist countries. As Bergson points out:

> International comparisons of inequality in distribution of income among consumer units are proverbially difficult to make. An attempt to compare inequality in that regard in the USSR with that in the West exemplifies that rule. Among Western countries for which Lorenz-type data at all comparable to those available for the USSR are at hand, Sweden could well be one where inequality as so represented is not greater or less than in that country. Inequality in the USSR may not be much less than that in Norway and the United Kingdom, but is no doubt less than that in the United States and France. According to especially incomplete data, inequality in the USSR could sometimes fall short of that in countries at a comparable development stage, though that need not be markedly so in the case of Japan.[19]

The point is that judging the efficiency of Soviet society by its comparative success in serving worker or consumer welfare may be like judging the efficiency of a feudal society by statistics relating to the welfare of the serfs. In all large economic systems, the power to formulate goals is distributed among a number of readily identifiable groups with varying degrees of power to fulfill their own goals or to constrain the goals of others, with the consequence that the goals being pursued within the framework of the system seldom fit any simple formula. One can try to evaluate the comparative diffusion of effective power to formulate and pursue economic goals, either by the standards of those who believe that such power should be narrowly confined within a governmental bureaucracy or by the standards of those who believe that it should be more widely distributed. One can also try to evaluate the efficiency of the system in satisfying the goals of those who have goal-making power. Finally, one can compare the degrees to which the systems are so structured that holders of economic power, in pursuing their own goals, either advance the welfare of others or are constrained from interfering with others' pursuit of their own goals. The orthodox case for capitalism, stemming from Adam Smith, stressed this third test.

These comparisons are not completely independent, because the power of a given group to form and pursue goals cannot be evaluated without considering the efficiency of the system in meeting its goal-makers' desires and the degree to which it constrains its apparent goal-makers to exercise their power with some deference to the interests of others. We also have to remember Gerschenkron's distinction between a deep ideology and a surface ideology whose office is to make the deep ideology seem respectable; the ostensible goals of holders of political and economic power are not necessarily those they use the organizational structure to fulfill.

Attempts to compare two economic systems by the moral or religious quality of their respective goals usually suffer from the twin errors of positing a single goal and then attributing it to the system, rather than to individuals. Almost always, the goal so attributed is highly simplified, and the complications arising from the multiplicity of goal-makers, the diversity of their interests, and the limitations on their power are ignored. A comparison that took account of the complications would be lengthy and undramatic, except perhaps when the emotionally provocative distinction between surface and deep goals was introduced. There is thus practical reason to prefer comparing systems by some general standard, such as rate of growth in material welfare experienced by a high proportion of their people. Such a standard embodies values of its own, more popular in the modern West than in the Soviet bloc or the feudal West. Its advantage is that it can be used to compare economies whose goal-makers have disparate priorities, such as the suppression of capitalism, the support of an armored feudal cavalry, or the making of profits, without entering into a debate over which goals are, and which are not, morally admirable.

4. Scientific Socialism and Experiment

In earlier chapters, we described a number of instances in which the Western economies were able to draw ahead of others because they were better organized to initiate change and to adapt to it. In chapter 8, for example, we outlined the remarkably successful organization of Western science, which has enabled it to employ specialization and division of labor on a large scale to produce a coherent body of knowledge, yet without the agency costs associated with hierarchical organization and control. The pursuit of industrial technology in a wide diversity of enterprises, again without acceptance of the penalties of system-wide hierarchy, proved to be a uniquely effective way to convert the achievements of pure science into advances in economic welfare. The Western system of allocation of capital, involving securities markets, a broad diffusion of power to make investment decisions, and the prospect of large rewards for successful innovation, has directed capital toward innovative projects and encouraged the breaks with the past required for economic expansion.

The West's concurrent diffusion of authority in both the organization of the scientific sphere and the organization of the economic sphere has been a point of organizational superiority over both the ancient and contemporary societies that have centralized authority over science and the economy within the political hierarchy, at least if superiority is judged by the capacity to initiate and sustain economic growth. The overall decentralization of authority in Western societies has been expressed in a freedom to experiment with new forms of economic organization and in a paucity of political restrictions on the forms of economic organization. The only process likely to produce efficient modes of organization in a real society, with all its perversities, deceptions, adaptations, and unpredictabilities, is extensive, diffuse trial, error, and retrial. That is precisely what the Western practice of decentralizing the power to form new organizations and to change old ones has made possible.

The term *scientific socialism*, therefore, seems like an attempt to borrow the credibility of science without submitting to its discipline. It is true that the Soviet Union has accumulated a large body of theory and experience about the planning and central management of a national economy, that this body of knowledge is a special professional field for highly trained experts, and that they use such familiar scientific tools as statistics, mathematics, and computers. But for a mode of organization to be properly termed scientific, something more is required. Science begins with the recognition that present beliefs and present explanations may well be unduly narrow or mistaken. Much of the work of the scientist is to formulate and to test possible supplements and alternatives. Such experiments are doubly necessary in relatively undeveloped fields, such as economic organization, whose theoretical formulations are disputed, sketchy, and often unreliable. The only mode of economic organization which could be called scientific is the one which is the product of a process that allows free rein for experiment, which has standards of judging experimental test and failure, and which abides by the results of its experiments.

In the Soviet version of socialism, a fundamental point of economic organization is not subject to experimental testing—that is, the choice of the ownership structure of the basic units of the economy—the firm or enterprise. Under conditions of free experiment, Western economies settled on a mixture of all the modes of enterprise organization that can be defined by ownership: investor, employee, manager, supplier, consumer, and government. Of these, ownership by investors became the most widely used. It is scarcely surprising that systems that deliberately reject the principal organizational solutions that have emerged under conditions of free experiment should develop organizational defects that degrade their performance. Just such a rejection of capitalist-owned or investor-owned enterprises—as well as all other modes of ownership save by the state— has been a central tenet of socialism in the USSR. Its rejection of other forms of ownership of enterprise is supported by a long line of Marxist- Leninist argument, but its comparative performance gives a measure of support to the belief that Western growth has been due in part to its experimental approach to the organization of economic activity.

Economic Growth in the Third World

An adequate treatment of the transferability of the Western pattern of economic growth to the entirely different cultural, social, and political contexts of non-Western countries would need a book of its own. We wish particularly to avoid any suggestion that the West's historical path to wealth contains any simple formula that, if used in the Third World, would produce a similar outcome.

One reason for not expecting favorable results from any simple program of imitation is that the starting conditions for growth are irretrievably different in the Third World from what they were in the West. The West began its economic rise from an economic and technological position somewhat behind Chinese and Islamic civilizations of the same period, but with no such gap as exists now between it and most Third World countries. An examination of the way the gap was created may help us understand how it might be closed, but it is most unlikely that the historical sequence of stages in Western development furnishes a model for imitation by Third World countries.

We have described a Western system of growth characterized by a separation of the political and economic spheres and by a diffusion of economic power. The Western economies developed from political systems

327

in which feudal decentralization of political power was already a fact, and some of the towns, where capitalism was to grow, had already been separated from the mainstream of feudal political organization and had developed under the political domination of their business classes. In most of today's Third World countries, by contrast, political and economic power is consolidated, and there is no easy way to undo that merger.

We have drawn a distinction between economic growth associated with an expansion of trade and economic resources and economic growth primarily attributable to innovation, and we have argued that, since the eighteenth century, Western economies have grown increasingly by innovation. Japan has also attempted to grow by innovation, but Japan came to that path as a developed country, after the Second World War. The few Third World countries which have progressed along capitalist lines have tended to find growth in much the same places Stalin planned to find it for the USSR: in increased economic resources in the form of capital, trained labor, and economically developed natural resources. It is true that most Third World countries have very substantial potential for growth along these lines before they begin to press against the limits of technological knowledge, but institutional arrangements that are unsuited to innovation are likely, sooner or later, to circumscribe further growth.

Another fundamental consideration is that the West has been remarkably willing to pay the price of growth, in the form of changing the whole structure and interpretation of Western life. True, the West has had its bitter opponents of urbanization and industrialization and the loss of innocence that goes with them, but the West has not allowed its Khomeinis to gain the upper hand. Understandably, some countries that wish to preserve their own history and culture will elect not to follow the Western economic path, for that path involves a diffusion of power and a degree of individualism which is incompatible with many modes of social life. Japan did become Westernized without entirely losing its own heritage, but one may doubt that preindustrial Japanese culture and institutions have appreciably greater vitality in modern Japan than Western preindustrial culture and institutions have in the West.

This same Western diffusion of power presupposes the existence of a merchant, entrepreneurial, or capitalist class to which can be extended the Western type of economic decision-making authority and whose members will compete in their exercise of it. There is nothing in Western history to suggest that such a class can be deliberately created, for it developed in the West out of its own internal dynamic and despite considerable political opposition. Feudal Japan had a merchant class by 1868, and the Chinese of Hong Kong, Taiwan, and Singapore have long included a class of experienced traders. Perhaps such a class can be seeded and nurtured by deliberate policy; no one really knows. The most one can suggest to a country desirous of following Western ways is to refrain from political policies obviously incompatible with the growth of a merchant class.

The view of modern Western growth that emphasizes the part played by innovation could be taken to imply that Western economies are simply not imitable, for it might well seem that no country, starting from far behind, can hope to catch up with the West's interwoven dynamics of technology, industrial production, and economic growth. There is, however, a more optimistic way of looking at the problem of imitation. Growth through technology came relatively late in the history of Western expansion. Western growth began with a stage in which trade—both overseas and domestic, but especially domestic—was its predominant source, and the obstacles to taking advantage of the opportunities for growth through trade are far less formidable than the obstacles to growth through technology. Trading economies have seldom had much difficulty in adding a manufacturing sector wherever and whenever manufacturing could pay its way. But the possibility of growth through trade depends, once again, on the development of a trading class—a development not to everyone's liking. Nevertheless, the highly successful growth performance in recent years of the so-called "Gang of Four" (South Korea, Taiwan, Hong Kong, and Singapore) is powerful evidence of the economic opportunities that lie in this direction.

One last caution. Many Third World countries face the West's old problem of large numbers of surplus agricultural workers in need of employment. A number of Third World countries have attempted to use their agricultural sectors as a source of capital for urban employment, as well as a principal source of government revenue, both by direct taxation an. by forcing farmers to sell their crops to the government at less than world market prices. Exploiting agriculture to further the growth of industry does not repeat Western history, for Western agriculture was not an important source of the capital needed for economic growth. Such a policy is likely to result in weakening the agricultural sector without corresponding gains in the urban sector. In a country whose only economic resources are agricultural, there may be no alternative to burdening the agriculture sector with the necessary costs of government and with the costs of ameliorating urban destitution, but the burden is likely to retard rather than advance economic growth.

The Western experience also indicates that proposals to borrow or expropriate funds for use as capital to provide employment should be scrutinized carefully, cautiously, and even skeptically. That the city that has been most successful in supplying employment to a flood of destitute immigrants from the countryside has been Hong Kong, which was already a financial center with sources of capital, makes it easy to conclude that Hong Kong's success was simply a matter of the availability of capital. If the Western experience is any guide, the existence of a class of small entrepreneurs who could organize efficient, labor-intensive production with very little capital had more to do with Hong Kong's success than its status as a financial center.

But if the imitation of the Western experience seems inherently difficult and costly to countries that wish to preserve their cultural and political heritage, the alternative of imitating centrally planned societies has also by now lost most of its early promise. The USSR's Five-Year plans were the prototypes of central planning. Central planning is not, strictly, a Marxist creation, for Marx had very little to say about the details of administering a socialist system. It is not even clearly Leninist, for Lenin fell back to a relatively decentralized New Economic Policy when early attempts at central control broke down. It fell to Stalin to reintroduce central planning and control, and it was Stalin, in the late 1920s, who committed the Soviet Union to central planning.

For a number of reasons, planning has great political appeal. Some of the reasons are corrupt, involving the self-interest of the political class and opportunities for self-enrichment through informal commissions on the award of construction and other contracts, tax exemptions, monopoly franchises, and numerous special privileges and dispensations available only to a political in-group.

But there are other reasons. A planned program, complete with brochures and drawings, is simple and concrete. It is very easy for a political leader to persuade himself, and hence his political followers, that he understands it. It is very easy also to exploit the xenophobic element in a population by claiming that the program avoids the enrichment of foreigners, whether multinational corporations or local Lebanese, Chinese, or Indian storekeepers. It can also be claimed that it does not enrich merchants, financiers, or others whose economic role is not widely admired, and although this claim may be factually weak, the information necessary to disprove it is not likely to be generally available. Finally, planning lends itself to the construction of a surface ideology. The several versions of Marxism-Leninism-Stalinism lie ready to hand, and others are not hard to construct.

The basic weakness of planning is that its results are usually disappointing. The disappointment is likely to be bitter, precisely because planning is so plausible in the beginning that its failure in the end seems highly blameworthy. A common consequence is that the civilian political leadership loses its dominance over the military and gives way to direct military rule. This should not happen in Leninist-Stalinist countries, where the military and political are already very closely linked, but Poland furnished an exception even to this rule.

Each failure of a planning system has its own causes. A common source of trouble is the attempt to appropriate a substantial part of a country's agricultural earnings to finance industrialization or to subsidize the urban population at the expense of the country's farmers. Almost always, the farmers respond in ways adverse to the country's economic interest. Comprehensive development plans also preempt the country's supply of foreign exchange and credit and so depress economic activity outside the plans, thereby creating unexpected sectoral crises or chronic sectoral depressions. International commodity markets are a common source of difficulty; prices have a way of going down at unplanned times, removing part of the financial underpinnings of development plans for countries that depend heavily on commodity exports. Rising prices of imports, such as oil, can be almost as troublesome. Unanticipated shortages of foreign exchange can leave the new factories and railroads barely operable for lack of spare parts, components, fuel, and raw materials. To produce adequate foreign exchange, a plan must restrict domestic consumption of consumer goods, both to provide goods for export and to avoid excessive imports. In countries where popular opinion has appreciable political consequences, there is a strong political bias against restricting domestic consumption of consumer goods, and plans are likely to reflect optimistic assumptions about the prices of exports and imports, thus making unanticipated shortages of foreign exchange one of the more dependable concomitants of planning.

The failures of planning can be attributed in part to its conception of an economic system as a lifeless machine, without the internal capacity to change, adapt, grow, renew, reproduce itself and shape its own future. Plans can lead to steel, concrete, and machinery supplied with properly trained workers, but they do not ordinarily provide for creating extensive classes of people with the capacity to engage in independent economic activities not envisioned by the plan. But a growth system is like a living organism with impulses of its own. The result of planning for growth is to produce an economy that is, if not a wholly lifeless statue of the real thing, at best a tame zoo-bred shadow of the natural animal. But economic growth depends on participation in international markets, and sustained growth of an economic animal too inflexible for life in competitive markets is not likely.

No examination of the pitfalls in central planning can match in force the fact of China's progressive abandonment of the attempt to apply central planning to its economy. The relaxation in 1984 of centralized control of Chinese industry followed an earlier relaxation of centralized control of agriculture, which had been followed by striking increases in agricultural production. Those with sufficiently long memories may compare the relaxation of control to Lenin's New Economic Policy—a reversion to market economics in the USSR in the early 1920s which markedly improved economic conditions at the time. China may find a Stalin to restore central planning; but one should not count on it, for the difference between the USSR of 1928 and the China of 1985 is that central planning was widely tried in the meantime and has lost its glow as humanity's hope for the future.

Obviously, the future of developing countries is much more problematic than it seemed in the years immediately following the end of colonial rule, before the full realization that neither the capitalist West nor the socialist East had completely mastered their own economic problems, let alone those of the rest of the world. The Third World can learn a great deal from both the capitalist and socialist experiences, but what it learns will not include a clear prescription for costless, painless economic growth. Even the discovery of oil seems to change a country's economic problems rather than to solve them. Critics of central planning have a special obligation not to try to repeat the planners' mistake by marketing an oversimplified panacea for economic growth in the Third World, no matter what the changes in the recipe.

Conclusions

We have often referred to the obvious fact that economic growth is a form of change, so that the West's path to wealth involved and required a society willing to tolerate and accept social and political change far more drastic than any previous revolution. Socially, the change went beyond urbanization, drastic enough in itself. It was accentuated by the introduction of mass education and of mass media of communication and travel that make the average city dweller of 1785 seem a bumpkin by comparison to today's city or country dweller. Politically, few revolutions have effected changes in power structures as drastic as the diffusion and realignment of political power from the absolute monarchs and their courtiers, still dominant in the Europe of 1785, to the European middle classes, and then to working classes lifted from *proletarius* status by economic growth.

Within the economic sphere, the fulfillment of aspirations to rising wealth has occurred primarily on the side of economic life which deals with change and innovation, as distinguished from the more workaday aspects of economic life in which familiar products and services are produced in familiar ways. The West has grown rich, by comparison to other economies, by allowing its economic sector the autonomy to experiment in the development of new and diverse products, methods of manufacture, modes of enterprise organization, market relations, methods of transportation and communication, and relations between capital and labor. The market institutions that developed within this context made it possible to capture high rewards for successful innovation and threatened those who failed to innovate with decline and demise.

Western economic innovation owes much to interaction between the economic and scientific spheres. Underlying the geometric growth in the output of Western economies has been a geometric growth in scientific knowledge, linked to a variety of institutions that transmute the growth in scientific knowledge into growth in material welfare. This growth of scientific knowledge has shaped, nurtured, and fueled Western economic growth. It offers a key to understanding the growth process.

The diffusion of economic power in Western societies from the center of political power in which it has resided in most societies has been indispensable to the multiplicity of technological experiments by which economies have sorted out the economically useful from the economically inapplicable scientific discoveries. This diffusion of economic power has also served to sustain a remarkably highly developed organization of basic scientific research, decentralized in a wide diversity of research institutions, comparatively free of political interference and control, and yet—or rather, therefore—producing a growing, cohesive body of knowledge about our universe.

There is no strong reason to believe that Western growth in scientific knowledge, nor the economic growth derived from it, is anywhere near the point of exhaustion. We see, in other words, nothing in the underlying sources of Western economic growth to foreclose the prospect of continued growth. This is just as well, for by absolute standards, or by comparison to the standards set by those individuals who are the wealthiest, most of the people of the West are only moderately well off economically. They have much room to grow richer. At the same time, the Western advance in material welfare has raised social and political aspirations and made it easier to think of ways to use Western wealth to create a society better in ways other than being richer. There is a danger that in thus trying to better our own society, we may pursue policies that will reduce the capacity of future generations to achieve still higher standards of material well-being, within a social and political framework more humane and compassionate than our own. To understand the sources of past growth is, we hope, in some measure to lessen the risk that we may unintentionally curtail the economic opportunities of future generations by our actions.

NOTES

1. Karl Marx, *Capital* (New York: Random House, undated) p. 836.

2. For a historical analysis built around the equilibrium between military power holders and the economic sector, see William H. McNeill, *The Pursuit of Power* (Chicago: University of Chicago Press, 1982).

3. Frederick C. Lane wrote a number of papers dealing with protection as a service whose production was capable of analysis by conventional economic tools. The quotation is from "Economic Consequences of Organized Violence," *Journal of Economic History* 18 (1958): 401–17, reprinted in *Venice and History: The Collected Papers of Frederic C. Lane.* Edited by a committee of colleagues and former students (Baltimore: Johns Hopkins University Press, 1966), pp. 412–28.

4. See Frederic C. Lane, "The Role of Governments in Economic Growth in Early Modern Times," *Journal of Economic History* 35 (March 1975): 8–17; and Douglass C. North and Robert Paul Thomas, "Discussion," ibid.: 18–19.

5. North and Thomas, "Discussion," 18.

6. See Richard Bean, "War and the Birth of the Nation State," *Journal of Economic History* 33, no. 1 (March 1973): 203–21.

7. For examples, see McNeill, "Intensified Military-Industrial Interaction, 1884–1914," chap. 8, in his *Pursuit of Power*, 262–306.

8. In "Organizational Form, Residual Claimants, and Corporate Control," *Journal of Law & Economics* 26 (June 1983): 351–66, Oliver Williamson credits the recognition of this change, and of its importance, to Alfred D. Chandler's *Strategy and Structure* (Cambridge: MIT Press, 1962). Williamson notes that although the business practice of dividing the management function in this way antedated the relevant organization theory by forty years, it is now possible to understand it in terms of W. Ross Ashby's showing "that all adaptive systems that had the capacity to respond in kind as well as degree would be characterized by double feedback. Disturbances in degree are handled in the primary feedback loop (or the operating part) within the context of extant decision rules. Disturbances in kind involve longer run adjustments in which new rules are developed in the secondary (or strategic) feedback loop." ("Organizational Form," pp. 353–54.)

9. Williamson, "Organizational Form," 362–63.

10. This discussion is based on the Barnard-Simon model of the firm, outlined for example in James G. March and Herbert A. Simon, *Organizations* (New York: John Wiley & Sons, 1958), chap. 4, pp. 84–111. See also chap. 6, above, under the heading, "Incorporation of Cooperatives and Nonprofit Enterprises."

11. Mancur Olson, *The Logic of Collective Action* (Cambridge: Harvard University Press, 1965).

12. For a fuller discussion of the Yugoslav experience and employee cooperatives, see John M. Montias, *The Structure of Economic Systems* (New Haven: Yale University Press, 1976), pp. 236–42.

13. Reply by Alexander Gerschenkron to Albert O. Hirschman's comment on Gerschenkron, "Ideology as a System Determinant," chap. 9 in *Comparison of Economic Systems*, Alexander Eckstein, ed. (Berkeley: University of California Press, 1971), p. 298. Gerschenkron goes on to say: "Professor Hirschman speaks rightly of the 'long-delayed renunciation of orthodox Marxism by the German Social-Democratic Party,' but he should have added that such a renunciation of Marxism (orthodox or unorthodox) is still missing and long overdue in the case of Soviet Bolshevism."

14. Ibid., pp. 297–98.

15. For an interesting study of this type, see Joseph S. Berliner, *Factory and Manager in the USSR* (Cambridge: Harvard University Press, 1957), especially chap. 18, "Summary and Evaluation," pp. 318–29, dealing with the use of illegal practices by factory managers that are necessary to keep the system going and are informally tolerated within some uncertain limits: (1) seeking low production quotas—the safety factor principle; (2) simulating fulfillment of the plan by manipulating product mix or quality, or by other devices; and (3) the use of the *tolkach* to obtain "all manner of scarce commodities through a combination of influence and gifts." (P. 319.)

16. For a fuller account of the profit goal in the U.S.S.R. in the middle 1950s, see ibid., chap. 5, "Profit as a Goal," pp. 57–74.

17. For two different approaches to the problem, see Robert W. Campbell, "Performance of the Soviet Economy: Productivity and Efficiency," chap. 4 in Robert W. Campbell, *Soviet Economic Power: Its Organization, Growth and Challenge* (Cambridge: Houghton Mifflin Co., 1960); and Abram Bergson, "Comparative Productivity and Efficiency in the Soviet Union and the United States," chap. 6 in Alexander Eckstein, ed., *Comparison of Economic Systems*.

18.

But it may be possible to stabilize the data for the stage of development by taking pairs of countries which were at the same stage, more or less, before one of them went socialist, and compare their performance on the Bergson scale at a later date. Such pairs may consist of East and West Germany (probably the ideal pair), Czechoslovakia and Austria, Yugoslavia and Greece, or either of these Balkan countries may be compared to Yugoslavia or Rumania (to judge the performance of Yugoslav as compared with Soviet-type socialism). It is too bad that two other good pairs—North and South Korea and North and South Vietnam—have been devastated by wars, but perhaps Burma (if that country can be regarded as socialist) and Thailand may make a pair, as may Cuba and some other Latin-American country.

(Evsey D. Domar, "On the Measurement of Comparative Efficiency," chap. 7 in Eckstein, ed., *Comparison of Economic Systems*, p. 231.)

19. Bergson, "Income Inequality under Soviet Socialism," *Journal of Economic Literature* 22 (September 1984): 1092. See also Peter Wiles, *Distribution of Income: East and West* (Amsterdam: North Holland Publishing Co., 1974).

Index

Index

Armor, 58, 76
Arrow, Kenneth, 230–31, 240 *n*29, 240 *n*30, 240 *n*31
Artisan(s): and development of manufacture, 26; inventors, 23, 28, 29, 36, 58–59, 251, 252–53, 254; in medieval towns, 50, 51; and shift to factory production, 170, 173, 175, 180, 181, 182, 183
Asceticism, "inner-worldly" vs. "otherworldly," 130
Ashby, W. Ross, 334 *n*8
Ashton, T.S., 175, 188 *n*40
Asia, 59, 70 *n*24, 71, 75, 120, 141 *n*2
Aspects of the Rise of Economic Individualism (Robertson), 142 *n*16
Aspects of the Theory of Risk Bearing (Arrow), 240 *n*29
Assembly-line, 289
Astrolabe, 84
Astronomy, 72, 148
Atack, Jeremy, 185 *n*9
Atlantic cable, 151
Australia, 17, 18
Austria, 56, 121, 323
Authority, diffusion of, 24, 29–30, 33, 326; *see also* Economic authority; Political authority
Automobile, 186 *n*12, 215, 222, 265–66, 274, 277, 282, 283, 284
Autonomy, 24–25, 33–34, 35, 145, 244, 262, 265–66, 267, 304, 308–09; *see also* Economic sphere, autonomy of
Aztecs, 17, 71

Bacon, Francis, 28, 252, 253
Baltic region, 75
Banking, 37, 100–01, 115, 132, 146, 150, 166; and corporate organization, 194, 199, 206–07, 208 *n*5, 209 *n*17, 209 *n*20
Bank of Augusta v. *Earle*, 210 *n*28
"Banks and Banking: United States" (Conant), 208 *n*5
Banks and Politics in America (Hammond), 208 *n*5
Barnard-Simon model of firm, 334 *n*10
Barter, 65
Bean, Richard, 64, 70 *n*27, 70 *n*28, 334 *n*6
Beer, J.J., 268 *n*7
Belgium, 9
Bell Laboratories, 248, 251, 274, 275
Bennett, M.K., 110 *n*3
Benston, George, 298 *n*16
Bergson, Abram, 324, 335 *n*17, 335 *n*18, 335 *n*19
Berle, Adolf A., 194, 199, 208 *n*3, 209–10 *n*22, 241 *n*32, 281
Berliner, Joseph S., 335 *n*15

Bessemer, Sir Henry, 158
Bessemer converter, 246, 250, 263
Better Times (Douai), *xii*
Beyond Economic Man (Leibenstein), 240–41 *n*32
Big Bang, discovery of residual radiation from, 258, 268 *n*9
Big Bang, The (Silk), 268 *n*9
Bills of exchange, 113, 115, 117, 121, 139
Biochemistry, 248
Biological analogy, *vii*
Birch, David, 278, 297 *n*3, 297–98 *n*6
Bismarck, 145
Blaise, Adolphe, 210 *n*26
Blast furnaces, 156–57, 186 *n*13
Bloch, Marc, 42, 44, 69 *n*8
Boorstin, Daniel, 268 *n*1
Booth, James C., 246
Boston Stock Exchange, 221
"Bottomry and respondentia bond," 118
Bourgeoisie, 50, 89, 102, 103; values, 88, 126
Branch, Ben S., 300 *n*30, 300 *n*31
Branch banks, 309
Braudel, Fernand, 39, 61, 68 *n*3, 69 *n*21, 69 *n*22, 70 *n*25, 70 *n*26, 111 *n*27, 142 *n*10, 142 *n*18, 143 *n*19, 172–73, 186 *n*13, 186 *n*17, 188 *n*37, 209 *n*18, 220
Brazil, 164
Bread, price of, 91–92
Brewing industry, 222, 239 *n*13
Brozen, Yale, 297 *n*5, 299 *n*25, 300 *n*28
Bubble Act (1720), 196, 197, 209 *n*9
Bulgaria, 318
Burdett, Sir H., 227
Burlington Railroad, 246
Business Incorporations in the United States, 1800–1843 (Evans), 209 *n*21,
Butterworth, 186 *n*20
Bythell, Duncan, 176, 188 *n*42, 188 *n*43
Byzantines, 59

Cagan, Phillip, 293
Calculation, 52–54
Calvin, John, 129–30, 132, 142 *n*14, 142 *n*18, 143 *n*19
Calvinism, 129–30, 131, 134, 143 *n*18, 166
Cambridge Economic History of Europe, The, vol. 2 (Postan and Habakkuk), 110 *n*9
Cambridge Economic History of Europe, The, vol. 4 (Rich and Wilson), 143 *n*21
Campbell, Robert W., 335 *n*17
Canada, 17
Canals, *vii*, 194–95
Cannons, 64–65, 76, 158
Capital: accumulation, 15, 16, 70 *n*26; accumulation and consumption, 165–68; ac-

Index

Commerce, *see* Trade and commerce

Commodity trading, 151

Common stock, 224, 226, 230–31

Communications, 151, 215, 263, 284

Communist Manifesto (Marx and Engels), *xii*, 73, 88, 109–10 *n*2, 110–11 *n*20

Comparative advantage, 109

"Comparative Productivity and Efficiency in the Soviet Union and the United States" (Bergson), 335 *n*17

Comparison of Economic Systems (Eckstein), 335 *n*13, 335 *n*17

Compass, 84

Competition: as a source of diversity, 270, 271–76; with few firms in market, 291, 294–95; and innovation, 22, 23, 32; and mergers, 281–86; among nation-states, and growth of trade, 136–37, 137–38; and small vs. large companies, 211

Competitive Strategy (Porter), 297 *n*1

Compulsory labor, 43, 44

Computers, 258, 263, 282, 283, 288

Conant, Charles Arthur, 208 *n*5

"Concentration and Specialization in the Lancashire Cotton Industry, 1825–50" (Taylor), 185 *n*10, 187 *n*21, 187 *n*26

Concentration, Mergers and Public Policy (Brozen), 299 *n*25

Concentration-Profits Relationship and Antitrust, The (Weiss), 300 *n*28, 300 *n*29

"Concentration vs. Market Share" (Gale and Branch), 300 *n*30, 300 *n*31

Concession, doctrine of, 196, 197

Concrete industry, 247, 268 *n*3

Confiscation, taxation as substitute for, 119–23

Conglomerates, 309, 311, 312

Consolidations, 281; *see also* Mergers

Construction industry, 247

Consumer preferences, in socialist vs. capitalist economies, 320, 321–22

Consumer response, and innovation, 258

Consumption, and capital accumulation, 165–66

Contract manufacturers, 273, 279

Contracts, 115, 139; and corporations, 197; medieval, 50, 53

Contractual problems, and exchange of labor for goods or money, 45–46

"Contribution of Small Enterprise to Growth and Employment, The" (Birch), 297 *n*3, 297–98 *n*6

Control Data, 288

Cooperatives, 202–04, 309, 313–18

Corporations, 167, 184, 298 *n*17, 298 *n*19; development of, 35, 189–208; early chartered, 190; growth of industrial, 212–41; large, 269–70, 271, 277–78, 280–83; medieval, 31; and monopoly, 289–95; group

loyalty in early, 125; value of securities, vs. value of enterprise, 228–35; *see also* Large enterprises

"Cost and Use of Water Power during Industrialization in New England and Great Britain" (Gordon), 185 *n*8

Costs: competition to achieve lower, 272–73; and market share, 291; reduction of, in USSR vs. West, 321–22; and technological innovation, 26, 32, 213, 288; *see also* Agency cost or risk

Cottage spinners, 170, 175

Cottage weavers, 170, 175, 176, 179–80, 182, 187 *n*24, 188 *n*43

"Cotton Manufacture" (Chapman), 186 *n*20, 186–87 *n*21

Cottrell, P.L., 197, 209 *n*9, 226–27, 239 *n*10, 239 *n*13, 240 *n*15, 298 *n*18

Coulborn, Rushton, 68 *n*6

Courts, *viii, ix*; development of commercial, 115–17; medieval, 47, 53, 56

Cray, 288

Credit, *viii*, 54, 113, 117, 127, 139, 140, 209 *n*20

Crete, 94

Crossbow, 63

Crusades, 42, 59, 66, 67, 99, 121

Cultural borrowing, 251–52

Cummins, Gaylord, 188 *n*43

Czechoslovakia, 323

Da Gama, Vasco, 73

Dalton, John, 245, 249, 252

Dark Ages, 20, 49, 57, 60

Davis, Lance, 221, 222, 223, 239 *n*11, 239 *n*14

Death rates, 4

Decentralization, 297; of authority, 24, 326; of economic organization, and innovation, 267; of investment decision making, 24, 30–31, 233, 234–35, 258

Decision making: decentralized, 24, 30–31, 233, 234–35, 258; and firms, 22; and innovation, 20; and markets, 23; political vs. market, and innovation, 310–11

Decline and Fall of the Roman Empire (Gibbon), 130

Decline of the West, The (Spengler), 8

Deductive science, 254

Democratic societies, 308, 309–10

Democritus, 254–55

Denmark, 134

Deposit banking, 117, 139, 166

Derry, T.K., 110 *n*13

Dickinson, H.W., 185 *n*11

Differentiation, 32, 270; as a basis of competition, 272

Disasters, and end of feudalism, 66–67, 68, 69 *n*21

Disease, 4

Index

Index

IBM, 288

Ideas, testing, 22, 257

Ideology: economic, of West, *xii;* medieval, 38; vs. organizational innovation, 34; and planning, 330; and research, 260; surface and deep, 318–19, 323, 325

"Ideology as a System Determinant" (Hirschman), 335 *n*13

Imperialism, 9–10, 12, 16–18; *see also* Colonialism

Imports, restriction of, 135–36

Incas, 17, 71

Incentives, 259–60; and diversity, 275; *see also* Rewards and penalties

Income: distribution of, in socialist vs. capitalist countries, 324; of factory workers, 175–76; inequalities, *ix,* 13–14; *see also* Equality, Inequality

"Income Inequality under Soviet Socialism" (Bergson), 335 *n*19

Independence, 153, 177

India, 11, 17, 61, 71, 193

Indo-China, 17

Industrial Concentration (Goldschmid, Mann, and Weston), 300 *n*28, 300 *n*30

Industrial Finance (Cottrell), 209 *n*11, 239 *n*10, 239 *n*13, 240 *n*15, 298 *n*18

Industrial Market Structure and Economic Performance (Scherer), 299 *n*25

"Industrial Policy" (Brozen), 297 *n*5

Industrial research laboratories, 23, 246–47, 249–51, 260–62, 266–67

Industrial Revolution, 7, 12, 15, 18, 26, 31, 35, 80, 89, 90, 100, 109, 122, 183–84; and capital accumulation, 165–68; and development of machinery, 146, 148, 150, 151; "early English," 141 *n*5; and growth of markets, 163–64, 165; and improvement of welfare, 169–70; and new enterprise formation, 277; second, 12, 36, 238; and shift to factory system, 151–52; technology of, 244; and transportation, 151

Industrial science, 28–29, 243–53, 257–62

Industrial securities, 212, 220, 221–25

Industry: antecedents of, 147–50; development of, 73–74, 78, 144–84; growth of corporations in, 211–41; "modern," 110 *n*2; science and, 23, 28–29, 243–53, 257–62; *see also* Factories; Manufacturing

Inequality, *ix,* 12, 13–14; *see also* Equality

Infant mortality, 4

Information revolution, 12

Inheritance: vs. growth, 5; and origins of capitalism, 70 *n*26, 88; right of, and pluralist aspect of feudalism, 61, 62

Innovation, 7, 20–32, 328, 333; and autonomy, 265–66; in commercial organizations, 76; and competition, 272, 273–74; and democratic politics, 309–10; and growth, 20–32,

264, 266–67; and growth of trade, 113; military, and decline of feudalism, 63–64; and monopoly, 293–94; and new enterprises, 276–79; rewards and penalties of, 259–60; and size of enterprise, 270, 271, 287–89; sources of, 262–63; system for, in West, 20–32, 243–44, 257–58

In Search of Excellence (Peters and Waterman), 297 *n*1

"Inside contracting," 236, 241 *n*36

Inside the Black Box (Rosenberg), 110 *n*19, 268 *n*10

Institutes of the Christian Religion (Calvin), 142 *n*14

Institutional synthesis, 108

Institutions, evolution of, favorable to commerce, 113–40

Insurance, 113, 115, 118–19, 139, 146, 150; analogy, 230–31

Integrated process enterprises, 309

Integrated society, transition from, to plural society, 106–08

Integration of enterprises, 157, 216–20, 273

Interdependent pricing theory, 292–93

Interest, 117, 128, 132, 142 *n*17

Interest groups, 308

Internal combustion engines, 158, 215, 216, 248, 264, 277

Interregional trade, 90–92

Intra-European trade, 75–76, 85–86, 91

"Introduction of Electric Power, The" (Du Boff), 239 *n*4, 239 *n*5

Inventions, *ix,* 28, 29, 34, 150, 151, 249–50, 251–52

Investment bankers, 224, 232

Investment(s): authority over, 234–35; opportunities, 15, 21; risks, and marketable stock, 228–31

Investor(s), 125, 198, 203, 212, 215; cooperative, 204; -owned enterprises, vs. cooperatives, 313–18

Ireland, 17

Iron and steel industry, 57, 146, 153, 156–58, 159, 163, 184, 186 *n*13, 186 *n*17, 263, 264, 282; *see also* Steel industry

Irrigation works, 43, 69 *n*11

Islamic civilization, 11, 37, 57, 58, 59, 61, 67, 71, 120, 257, 261

Italy, 9, 25, 35, 37, 51, 56, 57, 58, 63, 64, 76, 85, 98, 106, 117, 130, 135, 139–40, 141–42 *n*10, 190, 220; Northern, 76, 78

Jackson, Andrew, 209 *n*20

Jackson, Charles T., 246

James I, King of England, 122

Japan, 6, 10, 138, 180, 271, 277, 309, 324, 328; feudalism in, 60, 61, 70 *n*25, 111 *n*27

Index

Manors or manorial system *(continued)* and organization of agriculture, 57; vs. towns, 50–51

Mansfield, Lord, 53

Manufacturing, 151; emergence of unregulated, 24–25, 26; percentage of labor force employed by, 295–96; specialization, 78; sphere, autonomy of, *vii;* system, 73; use of as term by Marx, 109 *n*2; *see also* Factories; Industry

March, James G., 240 *n*32, 334 *n*10

Marconi, Guglielmo, 249, 250

Marglin, Stephen A., 160, 179, 187 *n*27, 188 *n*47

Marine insurance, 240 *n*29, 240 *n*30

Maritime commerce: and insurance, 118–19; and lawlessness, 92–96

Maritime transportation, improvements in, 80–86

Marketable securities, 225–26; and agency risk, 231–33; and cooperatives, 314–15; and investment risk, 228–31; and social risk of investment, 233–35

Marketing, 273–74, 288; integration in, 218–20

Market pricing, 72, 90–92, 95–96

Market(s), 156; colonialism and, 17–18; diversity of, 33; domestic, and population, 74–76; dominance of, 183; for firms, as factor in merger movements, 285; growth of, during Industrial Revolution, 151, 163–65; and innovation, 22, 23; as mode of organization, *x–xi,* 280; of Middle Ages, 47, 51, 52, 56; quantitative expansion of, 72, 73–76; rise of free, and freebooting, 92–96; -to- technology causation, 86–87

Market share, 240 *n*25; and profits, 291, 292, 300 *n*29, 300 *n*31, 301 *n*36

Market size: early growth of, 86–90; and rewards of innovation, 259–60

Market tests, vs. political tests of innovation, 310–11

Marx, Karl, *xii,* 9, 10–11, 15, 16, 73–74, 88–89, 102, 107, 108, 109 *n*2, 110 *n*19, 110–11 *n*20, 113 *n*37, 166, 181, 184, 236, 241 *n*34, 277, 289, 290, 299 *n*20, 303–04, 330, 334 *n*1

Marxism: Eastern bloc and, 318–19, 335 *n*13; and transition from feudalism to capitalism, 102–06

Marxists, *xii,* 14, 16, 277, 289

Mary, Queen of England, 305

Massachusetts Bay Company, 193

Mass markets, 27

Mass production, 212, 213, 216, 218–19, 222, 271, 286, 288, 289

Materials research, 248

"Mathematics and Science in China and the West" (Needham), 110 *n*18

Maxwell, James Clark, 249

Means, Gardiner C., 194, 199, 208 *n*3, 209–10 *n*22, 241 *n*32, 281

Mechanical arts, 148–49, 153, 186 *n*20, 187 *n*35, 251

Medical care, 57, 278, 283, 297 *n*5

"Medieval and Modern Commercial Enterprise" (Sombart), 141 *n*8

Medieval Trade in the Mediterranean World (Lopez and Raymond), 110 *n*10

Mediterranean, The (Braudel), 69 *n*22

Mendeleev, Dmitri, 245

Mercantilism, *xii,* 12, 44, 60, 114, 115, 134–36, 140, 143 *n*20

Mercantilism (Heckscher), 143 *n*20

Mercator chart, 84

Merchant class, 67; displacement of feudal aristocracy by, 104–06, 111 *n*27; economic power of, 98–99, 100–01, 102; emergence of, 24–25, 26, 35; in feudal China, 87–88; lack of, in Third world, 328–29; moral values of, 125–26, 131, 132, 133; rise of, 38, 70 *n*26, 72, 73, 77–78, 108–09; taxation of, 65; *see also* Mercantilism; Merchants

Merchants, 37, 50, 60; and Industrial Revolution, 184; in medieval towns, 50, 51, 52, 53; rights of, 119; rise of, 98, 109; and rural seats in England, 100–01; ships of, 81–86, 92; and taxation, 120, 121–23; and technology, 251–52; *see also* Mercantilism; Merchant class

Merchants of the Staple, 193

Merger Movements (Nelson), 298 *n*15

Mergers, 215, 223, 298 *n*14, 298 *n*15, 298 *n*16, 298 *n*17; and competition, 281–86; cyclical nature of, 285–86; role of, 270; post-depression of 1893–97, 225–28

Mergers (Steiner), 298 *n*15, 298 *n*19

Mergers and Economic Concentration (Benston), 298 *n*14, 298 *n*16

"Mergers, External Growth and Finance" (Tilly), 298 *n*17

Metallurgy, 151, 248

Metals, 246

Mexico, 17

Microcomputer, 258

Micromotives and Macrobehavior (Schelling), 240 *n*23

Microscope, 58, 72, 256

Middle classes, 6, 133; English, and factory system, 174–75

Milan, 76, 140

Military, 304–05, 306, 307, 334 *n*2; and growth of trade, 114–15; innovation, and decline of feudalism, 63–64, 67–68; land tenure and, under feudalism, 61; and steel, 158

Mill, John Stuart, 188 *n*44

Mind of the Strategist, The (Ohmae), 297 *n*1

Mining, 151, 154, 155, 157, 186 *n*19, 220

Index

Index

Index